Prologue
to
Manifest
Destiny

Prologue
to
Manifest
Destiny

Anglo-American Relations in the 1840s

Howard Jones
Donald A. Rakestraw

A Scholarly Resources Inc. Imprint
Wilmington, Delaware

Scholarly Resources Inc.
104 Greenhill Avenue
Wilmington, DE 19805-1897

Library of Congress Cataloging-in-Publication Data

Jones, Howard, 1940–
    Prologue to manifest destiny : Anglo-American relations in
the 1840s / Howard Jones, Donald A. Rakestraw.
        p.   cm.
    Includes bibliographical references and index.
    ISBN 0-8420-2488-3 (cloth : alk. paper). — ISBN 0-8420-
2498-0 (pbk. : alk. paper)
    1. United States—Foreign relations—Great Britain. 2. Great
Britain—Foreign relations—United States. 3. United States—
Territorial expansion. I. Rakestraw, Donald A. (Donald Allen),
1952–   . II. Title.
E183.8.G7J64   1997
327.41073'09'034—dc20   96-42450
                                                            CIP

⊗ The paper used in this publication meets the minimum require-
ments of the American National Standard for permanence of paper
for printed library materials, Z39.48, 1984.

3 1277 01049 9652

recycled paper

For Mary Ann and Jennie

Acknowledgments

This work represents the efforts of a number of individuals who either inspired, encouraged, supported, or labored to take it from prospectus to book. It has benefited, as have we, from the kind input of Kinley J. Brauer, Alan Downs, Scott Keller, Craig Roell, Kenneth Stevens, and James Woods, who read all or part of the manuscript and offered many useful suggestions. No one has exhibited more contagious enthusiasm or more able support than Richard M. Hopper of Scholarly Resources; his interest was apparent from the first mention of the project and remained consistent throughout. For making the tedious task of transition from manuscript to finished product not only bearable but also enjoyable, we owe lasting gratitude to Carolyn J. Travers for her guidance and to Ann M. Aydelotte for her superb editorial skills.

We also are indebted to the capable staffs of numerous libraries and archives as well as friends and colleagues on both sides of the Atlantic. In Tuscaloosa, special thanks go to the staff of the Gorgas Library, University of Alabama; and in Statesboro, to the staff of Georgia Southern University's Henderson Library and to the indispensable Peggy Smith. In Washington, the staffs of the National Archives, the Library of Congress, and the National Portrait Gallery were essential to our work. In the United Kingdom, this project drew from the expertise of the staffs of the Public Record Office, the British Library, and the Hampshire Record Office as well as from the support and encouragement of Kate Crowe at the British Foreign Office, David Willey at the Government Art Collection in London, and Eric Bird and Beryl Flitter in Oxfordshire. We would also be remiss if we did not mention our students, our constant reminder of why we chose history—Corey Andrews, Paul Grass, Brandy Berlin Scott, Carol Jackson Adams, and Jay Thompson, among others.

On a personal note, we wish to thank our families for contributions too numerous to list. To our closest friends, Mary Ann and Jennie, we express sincere appreciation for their companionship and understanding. To our daughters, Deborah and Shari, and

Charity and Emily, we acknowledge the inspiration provided by their very presence. And finally, to Timothy and Ashley (grand-children of the senior author) goes the deepest gratitude for enriching the lives of all those they touch.

If this work contains anything of value, we gladly share the credit with all those mentioned above. The inadequacies we claim as our own.

Howard Jones
Tuscaloosa, September 1996

Donald A. Rakestraw
Statesboro, September 1996

About the Authors

HOWARD JONES received his Ph.D. from Indiana University and taught at the University of Nebraska before coming to the University of Alabama in 1974. University Research Professor and Chair of the Department of History, he is the author of several books including *Union in Peril: The Crisis over British Intervention in the Civil War* (1992), a History Book Club Selection and winner of Phi Alpha Theta's Book Award for "best subsequent book"; *Mutiny on the Amistad: The Saga of a Slave Revolt and Its Impact on American Abolition, Law, and Diplomacy* (1987); *To the Webster-Ashburton Treaty: A Study in Anglo-American Relations, 1783–1843* (1977), which received the Phi Alpha Theta Book Award for "best first book" and was nominated for the Pulitzer Prize and Stuart L. Bernath Book Award; and *Quest for Security: A History of U.S. Foreign Relations* (1996). He is presently writing a study of Abraham Lincoln and slavery in the diplomacy of the Civil War.

DONALD A. RAKESTRAW received his Ph.D. from the University of Alabama and has taught at Georgia Southern University since 1988. Currently Associate Professor of U.S. Diplomatic History, he has authored a number of works including *For Honor or Destiny: The Anglo-American Crisis over the Oregon Territory* (1995); presented lectures and scholarly papers on Anglo-American relations in both the United States and the United Kingdom; and conducted seminars—"Brother Jonathan and John Bull"—at Oxford University on the history of Anglo-American relations. He is presently at work on a study of the impact of the British Foreign Office's American Ministry of Information on U.S. entry into the First World War.

Contents

Introduction

During the 1840s the United States and England resolved two crises growing out of the undefined Canadian-American border—that segment in the Northeast separating the hump of Maine from New Brunswick, and that part in the Northwest dividing Oregon from British Columbia—and cleared the way for one of the most far-reaching developments in history: a midcentury rapprochement that safeguarded each nation's honor and had ramifications reaching into the present. In 1842 the two Atlantic nations settled a host of problems with the pathbreaking Webster-Ashburton Treaty, and followed that feat with the equally important Oregon Treaty four years later. These grand achievements eased the British threat to U.S. interests in North America and thereby facilitated the Republic's expansionist efforts during the Mexican War. In a real sense, the United States might not have fulfilled its territorial ambitions in the Southwest without these two prior settlements with England. The Webster-Ashburton Treaty and the Oregon Treaty constituted the necessary prologue to manifest destiny.

Colorful, dynamic characters grace this story. On the American side the chief personalities were the robust master of rhetoric and diplomacy, Daniel Webster; the quiet and much maligned President John Tyler; the conscience-driven professor of history at Harvard, Jared Sparks; the smalltime politician and entrepreneur, Francis O. J. ("Fog") Smith; the blustering and pretentious General Winfield ("Fuss and Feathers") Scott; the wise and restrained John C. Calhoun, who called for a strategy of "masterly inactivity" regarding Oregon; the momentarily statesmanlike Secretary of State James Buchanan; the seasoned Louis McLane, who as minister to England was determined to add an Oregon settlement to his list of achievements; and the ever-suspicious and challenging James K. Polk, who was an early practitioner of brinkmanship diplomacy.

On the British side the leading luminaries were the bombastic and longtime antagonist of America, Lord Palmerston; the more staid and proper Sir Robert Peel, who as prime minister resolved to prevent another calamity like the Napoleonic Wars; Lord Aberdeen, who as foreign secretary resisted the popular clamor for war while trying to salvage national honor; the elderly and courtly Lord Ashburton, who worked closely with Webster to quiet the cries for war; and the sober British minister to Washington, Richard Pakenham, who has received unfair blame for a lost opportunity to settle the Oregon dispute.

To this day no one has integrated the Maine and Oregon settlements into a monograph that puts the resolution of these two great North American boundary questions in historical perspective. Embedded in each issue was an ambivalent Atlantic relationship tenuously held together by growing social, cultural, political, and economic ties while severely strained by mutual resentments stemming from America's consuming desire to win respect from an England reluctant to make concessions to the upstart republic. The uneasy Anglo-American relationship was further complicated by the U.S. effort to maintain its security and honor against the British in North America, who sought to contain America's self-professed manifest destiny. Both Anglo-American treaties have lived for too long in the shadows of the Mexican War and the Civil War.

The Webster-Ashburton Treaty relieved tensions on a number of issues, including the northeastern sector of the Canadian-American border, and permitted the United States to turn its attention westward. The Canadian rebellions against the British crown during the 1830s gave rise to the explosive *Caroline* and Alexander McLeod incidents, which prompted threats of war. Then, in late 1841, the South entered the gathering storm when it protested against British maritime practices during the African slave-trade and *Creole* slave-revolt controversies that likewise raised feverish demands to protect national honor. These issues came together by the early 1840s to foment a warlike crisis in America's already deeply troubled relationship with the mother country.

Despite assurances of open and honest diplomacy, the two chief negotiators—Webster and Ashburton—quickly fell into the traditional paths of Byzantine diplomacy. Backdoor meetings with secret emissaries; private exchanges of money that led to accusations of bribery at the highest levels of government; warnings of war with England trumpeted in newspaper stories underwritten by the president's secret-service fund; an intricate controversy over maps of the northeastern border that has led some historians to accuse Webster of selling out his country for personal gain; a politically and personally inspired attempt to impeach the secretary of state retroactively—all these features combined to swell the already tense undercurrents of the outwardly calm and friendly Webster-Ashburton negotiations.

Through patience, mutual trust, and a sincere desire for peace, Webster and Ashburton overcame their countries' differences and produced a historic settlement that, unfortunately, contained no resolution of the Oregon Question. In Ashburton's haste to escape the summer heat of Washington, he agreed to postpone the emerging Oregon issue to a more propitious time. He lamented to the Foreign Office, however, that the Oregon problem would soon develop into a crisis. Ashburton's prognosis proved prophetic.

Like the northeastern boundary dispute, that long-unsettled frontier controversy in the Pacific Northwest had its roots in the late eighteenth century. In 1792 an American sea captain sailed into the fabled "River of the West" and named it the Columbia after his vessel. Robert Gray's discovery, soon followed by the land explorations of Meriwether Lewis and William Clark, provided the bases of an American claim to the vast Oregon territory—that region stretching north from Spanish California to Russian Alaska and west from the Rocky Mountains to the Pacific. But, with the exception of a briefly held American trading post at Astoria, British subjects controlled the area for the next four decades. During that period any territorial arrangement between the two primary claimants remained elusive. Negotiators could do little more than postpone a solution by providing for mutual access to the territory for the subjects and citizens of both countries. This panacea seemed adequate until the 1840s. At that time, the Oregon Question rapidly escalated to the status of a full-fledged international dispute when it became an integral part of the American political scene and again shook the very foundations of the Atlantic peace.

The Oregon crisis threatened the Anglo-American rapprochement fostered by the Webster-Ashburton Treaty. The boundary problem in the Northwest intensified as a result of a number of issues: the pressure emanating from thousands of American emigrants arriving in the territory; the work of missionaries in advertising the region's attractions; the provocative antics of politically driven Washington statesmen; the competing strategic and commercial interests of the English-speaking nations; the often misunderstood and deviously vague diplomatic communiqués; and, most dangerous of all, the injection of American manifest destiny and both British and American honor into the controversy.

Only the adept maneuvering of peacemakers on both sides and the overarching importance of an expanding Atlantic interdependence could prevent the Maine and Oregon disputes from causing a third Anglo-American war. Politicians, Anglophobes, newspapers, states' rights advocates, and those more concerned about local than national interests—all worked together to raise the banner of national honor and thwart the efforts of diplomats attempting to resolve this vast array of problems. Further endangering the situation were worsening U.S. relations with Mexico: war in the Southwest likewise seemed unavoidable. Thus, failure to resolve the ongoing disputes with England could find the young republic at war with two nations at once. The history that unfolds in the following pages deserves far more attention than it has received in the past. Although it is always dangerous to speculate about what-might-have-beens, it is tempting to wonder whether the United States could have fulfilled the aims of manifest destiny and won the war with Mexico if its diplomats had been unable to resolve the twin border crises with England.

CHAPTER ONE

The "Spirit of '76" and the Search for National Honor: The Northeastern Boundary Dispute

Before the United States "can deserve the name of a wise nation," it must rid itself of its republicanism, its comically nationalistic " 'fourth of July harangues,' [and its] nonsense about 'flying eagles and never-setting stars,'. . . and the infinite superiority of the Yankee over all mankind, past, present, and to come."
—*Blackwood's Edinburgh Magazine* of London (n.d.)

As Secretary of State Daniel Webster and Special Minister Lord Ashburton gazed across the table at each other during that hot and humid June day of 1842, they may well have wondered how they were going to resolve the many entangling problems relating to the northeastern boundary. They had first tried to dispense with all the maps and detailed (and many times humdrum or outright boring) arguments pertaining to rivers, highlands, angles, and other paraphernalia that inevitably accompany boundary locations; but, alas, their best intentions had gone awry. Intrigue and backhandedness had won over honesty and straightforwardness in the negotiations, giving greater credence to that oft-cited definition of diplomacy as "lying in state."

The two diplomats had fallen victim to the same snags that had dogged their predecessors' attempts to resolve the boundary problem. The geographical descriptions in the Paris treaty of 1783 did not correspond with the contemporary maps of the region in question, and neither the treaty nor the maps matched the actual physical configuration of the land. The mutual trust between the men that had offered such high hopes at the outset of the negotiations now threatened to dissipate in the heavy, stale air that choked summertime Washington. As their discussions droned on about the rugged terrain of the distant Canadian-American boundary, both men's

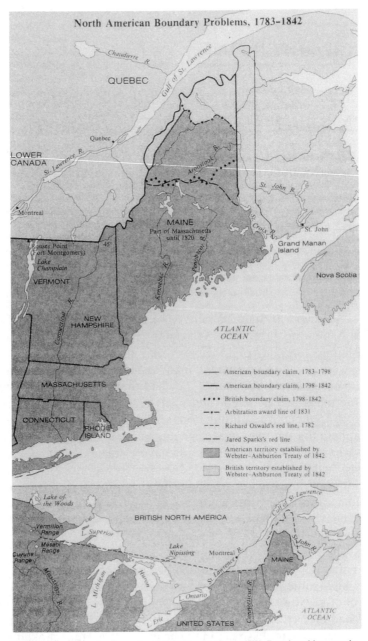

From Jones, *Quest for Security*. © 1996 by McGraw-Hill. Reprinted by permission of McGraw-Hill.

minds probably wandered over the long and uncertain history of the controversy, searching for some precise moment during which the question had been susceptible to resolution.

I

By the summer of 1842 the steadily deteriorating state of Anglo-American relations had caused war clouds to form over these border matters. The two Atlantic peoples had become almost accustomed to vicious exchanges of spoken and written abuse as they continued their uneven relationship tracing from mutual need and mutual dislike. The distrust that each side had for the other encouraged the reciprocal construction of distorted images conducive to ever-deepening hostilities. The British had had their fill of America's complaints about their refusal to grant proper respect to the Republic. *Blackwood's Edinburgh Magazine* of London derisively remarked that before the United States "can deserve the name of a wise nation," it must rid itself of its republicanism, its comically nationalistic " 'fourth of July harangues,' [its] nonsense about 'flying eagles and never-setting stars,' . . . and the infinite superiority of the Yankee over all mankind, past, present, and to come."[1]

Many conservatives in England, rigidly opposed to reform at home, denounced the American experiment in democracy as a dangerous export conducive to chaos and hence a major contributor to violence among the British rabble. *Blackwood's* criticized America's democracy as the bane of civilized order because it placed government "at the mercy of the multitude." Respected political and naval figure John Croker darkly reminded his people that the same brand of democracy had once permeated France, driving the country into a devastating revolution that led to the Napoleonic Wars.[2] Although the British fiercely denied responsibility for the heightening troubles with their Atlantic cousins, their rhythmic ridicule of the United States rang louder than did the voices of reason, encouraging the charges by Americans that their independence won in the Revolutionary War and confirmed by the War of 1812 had still failed to command the respect of the mother country.

America's long quest for strategic and commercial security still centered on alleviating the British threat in the New World. In addition to the North American boundary, Anglo-American commercial competition developed in Latin America, and arguments raged over trade with the British West Indies. If familiarity breeds contempt, then the classic illustration of this principle was Anglo-American relations before midcentury. As the British expressed open resentment toward America's democracy, its citizens bitterly rebuked an arrogant nation that claimed a monopoly on culture and exclusive control over the seas.

Economic ties between the Atlantic nations had the potential of holding them together, if only on a shaky basis because of the many issues that arose between them. By the 1840s the United States was England's best consumer, while the British relied heavily on American wheat, cotton, and other raw materials. The United States sent more than one-half of its exports to the British and received more than one-third of its imports from them in return. Indeed, it was during this period that the balance of trade began to shift in America's favor. Most striking is the realization that English merchants exported only 10 percent of their products to the United States, which amounted to only one-half of what that figure had been just fifteen years earlier.[3]

Several factors explain Britain's steadily increasing economic dependence on America. British commercial groups leaned toward free trade, which undermined the longtime allegiance to imperial preference; Parliament moved toward repeal of the Corn Laws, which would open the door to the import of other goods as well; and manufacturers turned increasingly to exports. The result was an enhanced ambivalent relationship with the United States. While economic interests pulled the Atlantic nations together, growing commercial rivalries threatened to push them apart. In this intensely competitive atmosphere, any disagreement had the potential of escalating into a conflict over national honor and security.

Only an awareness of America's resentment for Britain's alleged failure to respect the Republic can explain the serious nature of the northeastern boundary controversy. Webster and Ashburton agreed that the most perplexing and exasperating problem since the Paris peace negotiations of 1782–83 was that segment of the North American boundary winding around the hump of present-day Maine. By the time they examined the question, arguments over the boundary's location comprised thirty volumes of detailed and exhaustive evidence that, in reality, offered no solution to the matter. The roots of the controversy lay within the Treaty of Paris ending the American Revolutionary War in 1783. Its boundary provisions sounded specific: "From the North West Angle of Nova Scotia, viz. That Angle which is formed by a Line drawn due North from the Source of Saint Croix River to the Highlands along the said Highlands which divide those Rivers that empty themselves into the River St. Lawrence, from those which fall into the Atlantic Ocean, to the northwestern-most Head of the Connecticut River."[4] The source of the problem lay in the map used by the British and American negotiators in Paris. A 1775 edition of John Mitchell's Map of North America, it was flawed because the words of the treaty did not match the physical characteristics of the geographical terrain. The result was a boundary gap not only between the Atlantic Ocean and Lake Erie but also through the Great Lakes to the Lake of the Woods (in present-day Minnesota and Ontario). Most ominously, the long history of ambiguity over the northeastern boundary increasingly threatened Anglo-American relations as the two Atlantic nations became heated rivals over North America.

Due to the infusion of politics, Anglophobia, and national honor, the aftermath of the Paris negotiations constitutes a story of continued frustration over the boundary that befuddled diplomats and threatened to grow into an international conflict. Political opportunists often attacked England for both real and imagined insults to America's honor, and, in the immediate aftermath of the Revolutionary War, found such strategy especially effective in prolonging their stays in office. The Treaty of Paris of 1783 was anything but definitive, for not only did specific issues remain unresolved, but Americans also were convinced that they had not exacted a British admission that their republic deserved a place among the community of nations. Heated disputes broke out over a host of issues that included published critical remarks about the United States by British visitors, American publishers pirating British writings because of no U.S. copyright law, and American repudiation of debts to British investors following the Panic of 1837. Thus, any sort of controversy involving the British was bound to have long-lasting ramifications in North America as well as in the Atlantic. This realization became particularly evident in areas along the Canadian-American border where Americans came in direct contact with their new international neighbors to the north.

For more than a half century the Americans and the British tried to resolve the northeastern boundary question.[5] The initial problem was that no river matched the description of the St. Croix mentioned in the treaty and that Loyalists from Nova Scotia had ruffled American feelings by settling in the poorly defined area shortly after the Revolutionary War. In 1798 a joint commission established under Jay's Treaty accepted the British claim designating the Schoodic River as the one described in the treaty, rather than the

U.S.-supported Magaguadavic River located farther east. But after
the border proceeded due north, it became vague again: no one could
determine whether the terminus at the so-called highlands was
mountains or a watershed, leaving the rest of the line uncertain
west to the St. Lawrence River. Anglo-American negotiators at the
Ghent peace proceedings ending the War of 1812 followed John
Jay's example by providing for mixed commissions to deal with
the boundary above the St. Croix, along with the still unmarked
section between the Great Lakes and the Lake of the Woods. In
case of disagreement, the issues could go before a third nation acting as arbiter, whose decision would be binding. But several attempts to resolve the matter ended largely in failure, and in the
meantime Maine became a state in 1820 (separated from Massachusetts) and further complicated the situation by insisting on *all*
the land in dispute—a little more than twelve thousand square miles
of territory.[6]

At first glance the northeastern boundary controversy seemed
petty if not petulant. How could one equate national honor with
endless pine trees, countless streams, and acres upon acres of harsh
land basically unsuitable for farming and habitation? But this con-
ception was erroneous. Not only were the pine trees, the fisheries,
and much of the farmland commercially valuable, but the area itself was also important to the security of both nations. The British
objected to extending the line to the watershed between the
St. Lawrence River and the ocean (in accordance with the treaty)
because that would cost them direct commercial and military access to the Atlantic. Such a line would also place the tip of Maine
between the provinces of Quebec and New Brunswick and thereby
deprive Britain of a direct military route into the Canadian interior.
The War of 1812 demonstrated the vital nature of such a passage-
way—especially when the St. Lawrence froze over and British soldiers had to march through the area on snowshoes. The British
wanted to push the line below the St. John River, thereby gaining a
strip of land suitable for a military road to run between the
St. Lawrence and American territory and thus connect the Maritime Provinces of Nova Scotia and New Brunswick with Lower
Canada. The line sought by the Americans, however, would have
pushed their territory above the St. John River and virtually isolated the two British provinces from one another. The British insisted that their negotiators at Paris in 1782–83 would never have
agreed to a boundary that undercut their country's interests. The
Americans countered that acceptance of the British claim would

forfeit the rich soil and pine tree industry of the Aroostook Valley, alienate both Maine and Massachusetts, and dangerously enlarge the British domain in North America.

Further, the Americans wanted Rouses Point, a strategically important position located on the northwest side of Lake Champlain. A faulty survey of the 45th parallel (the team's manifest was suggestively heavy with madeira, rum, wine, and brandy) permitted the United States during the War of 1812 to construct a million-dollar defense post—Fort Montgomery—on the British side of the line running along the top of Vermont and New York. Not only was "Fort Blunder" (as critics dubbed the structure) a great embarrassment to the United States, but its ownership was critical to the nation's safety: as the War of 1812 demonstrated, Rouses Point commanded the entrance of a veritable invasion route into upper New York through Lake Champlain.[7]

In accordance with the Treaty of Ghent's provision for arbitration by "some friendly sovereign or State," the boundary issue in 1827 (after some debate over the choice of arbiter) went to King William I of the Netherlands, who agreed to examine the opposing maps and arguments and make a binding decision between the competing claims. Four years later, however, he admitted that he could not find the highlands described by the negotiators in Paris and noted numerous errors in both claimants' cases. The king had no choice but to propose a compromise: the United States to receive almost eight thousand square miles of the area in dispute, but Britain to acquire the land needed for a military road.[8]

The arbitral decision of 1831 drew a mixed reaction. The British approved the Netherlands award, although remarking that the king's responsibility had been to accept one of the two arguments, not merely split the territory between them. Maine, however, vigorously objected to any loss of territory and argued that the national government had no constitutional power to cede any part of a state without that state's consent. Such a stance, though understandable, greatly reduced the likelihood of securing Senate approval of the treaty. The president, Andrew Jackson, privately supported the king's proposal but refused to become involved in an issue that was politically unpopular in New England—particularly when his Democratic party was trying to build a base of support in that region. Jackson ultimately turned over the matter to the Senate without a recommendation, but he quietly tried to convince Maine to accept a million acres in Michigan territory (worth $1,250,000) in exchange for giving up land north of the arbitral line and hence above the St. John River. But Maine would have none of it. Politicians and Anglophobes joined forces as the state's press trumpeted the warning: "MAINE IN THE MARKET!" and "OUR FELLOW CITIZENS TRANSFERRED TO A FOREIGN POWER FOR CASH OR LAND!"[9]

In this politically charged atmosphere, suspicions became truth and blocked any chance for compromise. After lengthy debate the U.S. Senate succumbed to Maine's pressure in June 1832 and voted against the Netherlands award—albeit by the slim margin of 21 to 20. That body then followed with an equally narrow 23-to-22 vote to reopen the boundary negotiations. All hopes for a settlement vanished, however, when the government in Washington asked for navigation rights on the St. John and Britain refused to link the navigation and boundary issues. Finally, Maine's legislature thoroughly confounded the matter by announcing that no settlement between the countries would be binding without approval of a majority of the state's population.[10]

II

Tempers continued to mount in the border region over the next few years until in early 1839 the short-lived, largely bloodless, and nearly comical "Aroostook War" broke out between Maine and New Brunswick. The government in New Brunswick, under pressure from the logging industry, had extended jurisdiction over the area in dispute and granted land titles to its subjects. When Canadian lumberjacks soon moved into present-day upper Maine, they confronted American competitors who had likewise carried their business deeper into the forests. The impetus for a crisis first developed in early 1837, when the Maine legislature ordered a census of the area and New Brunswick officials responded by arresting the state's land surveyor for trespassing. Maine's citizens angrily protested, and the governor informed President Martin Van Buren, a Jacksonian Democrat, that the state expected reparations from Britain. But the ensuing demand from Washington exacted only a cool response from the Lord Melbourne ministry in London: the crown would continue to exercise jurisdiction in the area until the two nations had resolved the northeastern boundary. To establish a communication line to the area, the Maine government ordered a road cut to the upper Aroostook River, which was a southern tributary of the British-controlled St. John. Although the state had refused another

Martin Van Buren. From painting by Alonzo Chappel, in *National Portrait Gallery of Eminent Americans* (1862).

British request for land to facilitate the building of a military road, it held little bargaining power because the Aroostook Valley's economy depended on the St. John River to carry its goods through New Brunswick and into the Atlantic. Over the past fifteen years, logging companies had hauled off several hundred thousand dollars' worth of timber from the disputed area, and in January 1839 the new governor of Maine, Democrat John Fairfield, warned that the state would lose nearly $100,000 of timber in that winter alone. The legislature in Augusta appropriated $10,000 for defense of the territory.[11]

The situation quickly escalated into a crisis. The lieutenant governor of New Brunswick, Sir John Harvey, was usually tolerant but found Maine's provocative behavior beyond his endurance. Learning that nearly two hundred volunteers from Maine had entered the troubled region, he issued a proclamation sending troops of his own and directing his law officers to "adopt all necessary measures" in resisting invasion. At the head of the American contingent was Maine's land agent, Rufus McIntire, a seventy-year-old Anglophobe who was thirsting for a fight with the British intruders. His "posse," as he called his cohorts, soon arrested over a dozen "trespassers," including New Brunswick's warden of the disputed territory, James MacLauchlan. In retaliation, a group of fifty Canadians seized McIntire and two companions and clapped them in jail at Fredericton. When a Maine militia officer protested the action, he was imprisoned with McIntire.[12]

The McIntire incident became the flashpoint of the growing crisis. Both Whig and Democratic newspapers demanded revenge, while McIntire's replacement, Charles Jarvis, defiantly announced that if the British attempted to enforce their laws against him, he would "consider the approach to my station, by an armed force, as an act of hostility, which will be met by me, to the best of my ability." Expecting hostilities, Governor Fairfield asked the legislature to approve the dispatch of three hundred reinforcements to the Aroostook and sought ten thousand militia in addition to the thousand already authorized. The state, he asserted, must defend its "spirit of independence and self-respect." The lawmakers responded by unanimously voting to appropriate $800,000 for military escalation, and within a week ten thousand militiamen were en route to the Aroostook Valley. Fairfield, meanwhile, appealed for help from Governor Edward Everett of Massachusetts, and then to President Van Buren for federal troops to "cooperate with the forces of his State in repelling an invasion of our territory." If the Canadians resisted, Fairfield warned Harvey in New Brunswick, the state would retaliate.[13]

The British did not take such blustering lightly. New Brunswick's newspapers blasted Fairfield for interfering with a problem that was not his concern and accused Maine of invading British territory. The St. John *Herald* feared an American invasion of the city, but the commander of the province's militia offered assurances that his "gallant warriors" would prevent any further "encroachment." The London press did not want war with the Americans but thought it inevitable in view of their stubborn determination to promote Canadian independence and drive the British out of North America. Harvey had meanwhile secured promises of military assistance from the lieutenant governors of Lower Canada and Nova Scotia but nonetheless did everything he could to control the crisis. He ordered the seizure of illegally cut timber and assigned the proceeds from its sale to a "disputed territory fund," which would presumably compensate landowners for their losses. Over the opposition of his attorney general, Harvey freed McIntire under a "parole of honor" by which the accused agreed to appear on his trial date. Harvey hoped that if military forces replaced civil officers in the area, the entire matter might go before the higher counsels in London and Washington who preferred a peaceful resolution of the crisis. But his actions came too late.[14]

Reactions to recent events were volatile on both sides of the border. Maine's "soldiers" had already gathered in Bangor, awaiting the imminent arrival of arms, powder, wagons, and blankets. Despite the skepticism expressed by more than a few observers, the state's military preparations convinced the officer in charge of New Brunswick's militia that Maine was determined to "go the whole hog." Even while Fairfield reciprocated Harvey's conciliatory gesture by releasing MacLauchlan, the troops from Maine were chanting their intention to whip the "warriors of Waterloo."[15]

The Aroostook War promised to be a glorious event for the patriots of Maine. The Red Shirts, as they called their forces, would easily defeat the Blue Noses of New Brunswick. Every town in the state was characterized by "pomp and circumstance" in preparing for war, at least according to a letter sent by an exuberant observer to a state congressman. The people of Maine would once and for all cast off the British yoke and, to make the move even more satisfying, accomplish that noble goal with the same swords and muskets used by their grandfathers during the Revolution. Only the uniforms would be new as they drilled daily before large and boisterous crowds. At Houlton, the last stop before the Aroostook, troops attended chapel before marching off to their self-styled righteous war. According to the Reverend Caleb Bradley, warmaking was insanity. But his protests failed to stem the swelling tide. The "wicked ambition of unfeeling demagogues," he recorded in his diary, had prompted this "contemptible, disgraceful, horrible, abominable" conflict.[16]

As in all wars, only the moments before battle proved illustrious. Editors and politicians waved the flag and exalted patriotism, while songwriters and poets composed eloquent lines about bravery that revealed nothing about the harsh realities of warfare. Newspaper correspondents roamed Augusta, Bangor, and Houlton, starving for the least bit of news that they could mushroom into great stories of heroism. The Bangor *Whig* ran a column for weeks that graphically described the amazing hardships endured by the men, while the Belfast *Republican* bluntly issued the challenge of "Maine and her soil, or BLOOD!" Not to be outdone, the Augusta *Journal* ringingly proclaimed, "Let the sword be drawn and the scabbard be thrown away!" Will not the state show "a little of the spirit of '76"? The Augusta *Age* appealed to Maine to "fall back upon its original sovereignty," while the Massachusetts press attributed the coming war to the Van Buren administration's failure to settle the boundary issue. Governor Fairfield, those same newspapers declared, had the chance "to become second only to Moses and Washington" in liberating his oppressed people. To Maine's troops about to embark from Augusta, he rousingly declared that the "spirit of patriotism which lighted up the fires of the revolution, glows in the bosoms of our citizens with undiminished force." Men in Boston curled their whiskers and sported mustaches as licenses to declare the honorable word, "WAR! WAR!" The "Soldier's Song" denouncing the Redcoats appeared in countless newspapers, as did the "Maine Battle Song," rife with Anglophobia and asserting that:

> Britannia shall not rule the Maine,
> Nor shall she rule the water;
> They've sung that song full long enough,
> Much longer than they oughter.[17]

Citizens of Massachusetts became infuriated upon hearing that an American had been jailed in Canada for whistling "Yankee Doodle" and would remain there until he whistled "God Save the Queen." When Governor Everett seemed too squeamish about war, a critic called him a traitor and another quipped:

> Ye Yankee of the Bay State,
> With whom no dastards mix!
> Shall Everett dare to stifle
> The fire of seventy-six?[18]

The outburst of patriotism was not confined to the Northeast and threatened to drown out any naysayers. The legislatures of Alabama, Indiana, Kentucky, Maryland, Massachusetts, Ohio, Pennsylvania, and Virginia promised assistance. In Illinois, the brigadier general of the state militia offered military aid, while a resident of New York assured Fairfield that he could count on soldiers from every state in the country, and the Richmond *Enquirer* praised him for upholding the honor of America and the interests of Maine. To skeptics who questioned going to war with the British, Senator Reuel Williams of Maine angrily replied that his state would secure its "whole territory" even if this meant a third Anglo-American war. The Anglophobic New York *Herald* sneered at the hot winds emanating from the Montreal press and remarked that if talking won wars, the United States should surrender before the fighting began. Everyone grasped the meaning of Canadian courage: "As the little boy said to his school fellow—'You only wait till my big brother comes, and then see how I'll whip you.' "[19]

III

Despite the cries for war thundering from the Northeast, the decision for such a momentous event had to come from the national governments involved—which enhanced the role of President Van Buren. As if these border troubles were not enough, his administration still faced the massive economic problems caused by the Panic of 1837. If the Little Magician failed to find a quick remedy, these ills would undercut his chances for a second term in office. How nice it would have been to ignore these localized issues and allow time to exert its healing process. But the emotional nature of these arguments dictated that Van Buren could not take the politician's way out—that is, sit and do nothing. After all, two senators came from Maine, which provided reason enough to attempt some type of action intended to counter his political opposition. Van Buren knew that the anti-Jacksonian Democrats hated him as a wily New York politician and looked for any way possible to undermine his White House. Letting sleeping dogs lie was always the better political strategy when the times demanded a decision; but the hotheads in Maine and New Brunswick had kicked the dogs of war, and turning a blind eye would not quiet them. Van Buren had to act.

The president at first responded to the crisis in Maine with great indecision. Such an approach had actually helped to defuse another border crisis (the *Caroline*, discussed later) by allowing each side to state its position without going to war. But domestic politics, never distant from foreign policy, further complicated the situation in Maine. If Van Buren failed to help the state, Governor Fairfield pointedly warned, "God only knows what the result would be politically." War with England, Van Buren knew, was out of the question; and yet he had to find a solution that preserved his presidency while meeting what he considered to be Maine's just demands.[20]

Van Buren attempted to satisfy all sides and ended up alienating almost everyone. Before his cabinet on February 24, he blamed both Maine and New Brunswick for the border troubles. The former had not kept the provincial governor informed of its imminent military measures; the latter had no jurisdiction in the disputed territory. The president first urged Henry Fox, the British minister in Washington, to seek the withdrawal of all armed forces from the Aroostook Valley; he then assured Fairfield of national support in the event of hostilities but exhorted him to move slowly. To Congress on February 26, Van Buren publicly denied the British claim to the area and affirmed Maine's right to disperse all trespassers. In the Senate the well-known Anglophobe and later president, James Buchanan, quoted from two documents that allegedly undermined the British argument for the territory. In 1832, he noted, the State Department had declared to the British minister in Washington that neither nation should exercise jurisdiction in the disputed area until the entire matter was resolved. The following year, Buchanan added, the minister had agreed with the American position. The choice now, Buchanan bellowed, was "war or national dishonor." Then Daniel Webster, at the time senator from Massachusetts, angered the British diplomat by declaring in the midst of thunderous applause from the galleries that if the two nations did not settle the boundary question by July 4, 1839, the United States should simply occupy the territory in debate. Other influential Senate leaders entered the fray. Missouri's Thomas Hart Benton, like Buchanan a staunch Anglophobe, joined Kentucky's Henry Clay and South Carolina's John C. Calhoun in demanding White House intervention.[21]

Out of Van Buren's strategy came more uncertainty and heightened tensions as a fiery Congress threatened to seize the initiative. The Senate Foreign Relations Committee unanimously proclaimed that Britain had no exclusive rights in the area and urged the president to repel the invasion. That same day, February 28, the House Committee on Foreign Affairs resolved that Congress empower the president to halt British aggression by diplomatic or, if necessary, military means. Congress authorized him to appoint a special minister to London (a move he never carried out for political reasons) to resolve the northeastern boundary question. Then came the legislature's most telling move. By a nearly unanimous vote—all senators approving and the House concurring 201 to 6—Congress appropriated $10 million for arms and authorized the president to call for fifty thousand volunteers. The magnitude of the bill stunned Fox. The administration could not have made a "greater parade of preparation" had the British government announced an intention to return America to colonial status.[22]

Cooler heads, however, were trying to prevail over the rising tumult. On February 27, during the congressional debate, Fox and Secretary of State John Forsyth signed a memorandum intended to prevent hostilities while the two nations arranged a permanent settlement. Under this stopgap proposal, New Brunswick would not attempt to drive Maine's forces from the disputed area if the state agreed to withdraw them. Both sides would also release civil officers held in jail and thus escape the looming confrontation with some measure of respect. In the future they would cooperate in preventing trespassing. Fox realized that he had made a concession by opening the question of jurisdiction, but he thought it necessary to quiet the clamor for war. Palmerston and Van Buren immediately approved the memorandum. Senator Williams from Maine was hesitant, whereas only one of the state's newspapers, the Portland *Courier* (a Whig organ), found the terms acceptable. All others trumpeted their call for war.[23]

Van Buren decided to send General Winfield Scott to the border in an effort to prevent conflict. As a heroic figure of the War of 1812 the portly and self-righteous military career man commanded instant public attention and, for the most part, no small degree of respect. He had already conducted a similar mission of peace to the troubled Niagara border (discussed later) and emerged unscathed and with no war in the offing. Perhaps he could succeed again. Secretary of War Joel Poinsett directed Scott to depart immediately for the border and to use the Fox-Forsyth memorandum as the basis for a peaceful settlement. If the British refused to evacuate the disputed territory, Scott could call on the army to help the Maine and Massachusetts militias "enforce the determination" of the national government. As Scott prepared to leave Washington, he solemnly told Van Buren and Poinsett that if they wanted war, "I need only look on in silence"; if they wanted peace, he could assure them of nothing. Van Buren simply instructed his personal emissary to devise a peace with honor.[24]

Winfield Scott. *Courtesy Library of Congress.*

Fortunately for both nations, the local belligerents along either side of the disputed border somehow escaped serious fighting. Indeed, New Brunswick's forces were inadequately fitted for war, while their counterparts from Maine wanted only to go home. One of Harvey's officers on the troubled scene complained as late as the end of February that he still had not received arms and ammunition. In the meantime the American contingent arrived to find nearly all British subjects peacefully engaged in farming or lumbering. To keep matters that way, the militiamen constructed several blockhouses at a spot they brazenly called Fort Fairfield and laid a huge boom across the Aroostook River in a futile attempt to prevent the further passage of timber. British troops had meanwhile gathered in Madawaska on the upper St. John River, preparing for an attack that never came. The only encounter occurred in a bar in Houlton, where British and American troops had been drinking together until some hothead offered a toast to Maine. The result was a brawl in which the casualties included a few bloodied noses, one broken arm, and the incarceration of several participants. Maine's forces suffered two deaths in the war: one soldier died of measles, and a farmer at Fort Fairfield was struck by a bullet that ricocheted off a rock during a celebration. The war wound down as quickly as it had first appeared. Maine's militiamen soon returned home as heroes, exhausted and cold after six weeks in the wilderness but energetic enough to jeer at the army regulars stationed at Houlton.[25]

Scott had to find a political solution to the military crisis fomented by the politicians and the press. Accompanied by Captain Robert Anderson, who later defended Fort Sumter during the Civil War, and by Lieutenant E. D. Keyes, also to distinguish himself in that war, Scott established quarters at the governor's house in Augusta. Governor Everett of Massachusetts assured the general of militia if needed, while a state senator in Portland delivered a fiery speech that conveyed the ugly mood of New Englanders. The senator declared that he would rather see Maine "deluged in blood, and every field bleached with the bones of our citizens," than give in to the British! Scott noted in his memoirs that Americans in the area were tired of "diplomacy, parleys, and delays." They wanted him to seize control of the Aroostook Valley.[26]

Scott, however, proved to be an adept diplomat as well as soldier. He won the trust of Governor Fairfield and his council after a week-long series of three-per-day meetings while privately communicating with Lieutenant Governor Harvey in Fredericton. In weighing the views of the two sides, Scott quickly realized that his primary problem was faction-ridden Maine and not New Brunswick. Fairfield, meanwhile, covered his political bases by sending the legislature a message denouncing the Fox-Forsyth memorandum but suggesting the possibility of peace through Scott's compromise proposal. In actuality, there was no difference between it and the memorandum: Scott recommended that New Brunswick renounce its claim to exclusive jurisdiction in the disputed territory and that Maine follow this gesture of goodwill by ordering its forces home. If the situation remained charged, however, the state could leave a posse of civilians to keep order.[27]

Scott's greatest task was to win the support of the Whig minority in the Maine legislature without alienating the Democrats. Initially, the Whigs avoided the general (himself a Whig) because he seemed to have deserted the party by working with Van Buren. At a reception in the legislative hall in Augusta, soldiers and officers who had fought side by side in the War of 1812 swapped stories and revived their camaraderie; but the wall of tension remained. Scott assured them that, if necessary, he would once again join them on the battlefield, "shoulder to shoulder—breast to breast." And then, according to his memoirs, he persuaded a Whig state representative, George Evans, to invite the governor and leaders from both parties to dinner. At one end of the table sat Scott with the Whigs; at the other were Fairfield and the Democrats. Scott's efforts to win over the Whigs got nowhere until Evans whispered to them that the general "was as good a Whig as the best of them." Suddenly the political pall lifted and the two groups became one in seeking to defend the state.[28] Scott's account is doubtless apocryphal. More than likely, both political parties finally realized where their warlike challenges had taken the state and nation and had eagerly grasped the face-saving opportunity afforded by Scott to escape conflict.

With Maine now under control, Scott turned to Harvey in New Brunswick, who, the general quickly found, posed no threat to peace. The two men had fought against each other during the War of 1812 but had met and established a personal friendship in the period afterward. The maintenance of honor was essential, Scott emphasized. Toward that end, he assured Harvey that Maine would pull out of the disputed territory if New Brunswick issued a public declaration that it had no intention of forcing out the state's troops. Fairfield wanted a posse to remain in an effort to prevent further trespassing. Some of the men would locate near the boom across the Aroostook, while the remainder constructed a road from Bangor to the Fish River (in the disputed territory). Until resolution of the boundary, New Brunswick would occupy the upper St. John Valley around the Madawaska River, and Maine would retain the Aroostook Valley. In mid-March, Fairfield supported Scott's compromise with a pointed reference to the doctrine of states' rights that was aimed as much at the national government as at Britain. "The respective States of the Union," the governor declared, "are Sovereign and independent, except so far as that sovereignty has been restrained or modified by the Constitution of the United States. The General Government," he continued, "is one of limited and defined powers. The power to alienate the territory of a State, or to transfer a portion of it, or the jurisdiction and possession of it, to a foreign power, for an indefinite period or for one hour is no where, is no where granted." Maine's legislature unanimously approved Scott's compromise. New Brunswick did the same.[29]

For several reasons the month-long Aroostook War passed without serious incident. Most important, leaders in London and Washington realized that local issues had gotten out of hand and, facing greater problems elsewhere, chose peace over war. As fate would have it, Van Buren's restraint (whether sound strategy or fortunate indecision) had helped to convince the Melbourne ministry that he did not want conflict. Indeed, Fox repeatedly noted the president's peaceful intentions, and Lord John Russell assured his colleagues in Parliament that the minister's assessment was accurate. Even the saber-rattling Palmerston, who seldom overlooked an opportunity to criticize the United States, saw the wisdom in avoiding war when so much Anglo-American commerce was at stake.[30]

As the Aroostook War slipped into memory, however, the issues that had provoked it immediately resurfaced. Maine's senate unanimously called on the government in Washington to establish a joint commission with Britain intended to mark the boundary line in accordance with the Paris treaty of 1783. If unsuccessful, Maine would be the "sole judge" of the final settlement. Should the British object, the state urged the U.S. government to seize all the disputed territory. The two nations resumed their long and wearisome boundary talks, swapping projects and counterprojects for survey commissions while laboriously debating the locations of rivers, lakes, and highlands. Palmerston sent another survey commission into the disputed territory in July, hoping that such an approach might quiet the border area. Not surprisingly, the commission's report supported Britain's title to the entire area in question. By December, Governor Fairfield informed Van Buren that British forces already had violated Scott's compromise by moving into the disputed territory near Témiscouata Lake. The national government, Fairfield declared in what had become a familiar refrain, must protect the rights of Maine.[31]

The Aroostook crisis should have alerted Washington and London that if they did not negotiate a settlement of the boundary problem, the local governments might resolve it by force. But both national governments ignored the warning signs and resumed their dry discussions over the boundary location. Some members of Congress still spoke of war, but their statements were clearly driven by politics. Warden MacLauchlan repeatedly protested the jurisdictional rights claimed by Maine's posse in the disputed area, and officials in both England and Canada objected so strenuously to Harvey's alleged weak leadership that he was soon recalled to London.[32] The northeastern boundary remained a problem to only those few American and British settlers living along the still undefined border between Maine and New Brunswick.

As Webster and Ashburton pondered the seemingly unending complexities of the northeastern boundary, they realized that this problem could become the focal point of a highly volatile international situation. The steadily escalating war of words in Maine had the potential of combining with a recent and still smoldering crisis in upstate New York, where violence had threatened to erupt along the Niagara River after British military officials destroyed American property in American waters, killed an American in the melee, and blasted the government in Washington for condoning piracy. A direct result of this border trouble was the trial of a British subject for murder by local American officials determined to strike out at the hated British. Further complicating this already convoluted situation was the call for national honor and the repeated insertion of states' rights principles. Thus, while trying to extricate themselves from the horribly tangled northeastern boundary issue, Webster and Ashburton also had to deal with equally explosive feelings along still another part of the Canadian-American frontier.

CHAPTER TWO

Freedom Awakened: *"Remember the* Caroline*!"*

Surely war with England was unavoidable.
            —Correspondent, New York *Herald*, January 4, 1838

Daniel Webster and Lord Ashburton recognized that, in addition to the irritants plaguing the Maine-New Brunswick sector of the northeastern boundary, the situation along the New York part of the Canadian frontier likewise remained explosive. In late 1837 rebellions had broken out in Upper and Lower Canada against the British crown, threatening to spread all along the North American boundary and drag Americans into the conflict. What better opportunity to throw the British out of North America than to aid the Canadians' drive for freedom? Such events took on the image of another thrust for liberty and hence a continuation of the "spirit of '76." Then, in December 1837, British forces invaded American waters above Niagara Falls, commandeered the privately owned American steamboat *Caroline*—killing an American in the process—and set it afire.[1] Not since the War of 1812 were Americans so incensed. For the second time in less than three decades the United States had undergone a British invasion. And for the first time since the Battle of New Orleans, an American had been slain by a British soldier on American territory. Patriots along the Canadian border demanded war as the only means for restoring national honor. Now, five years later, bitter feelings still smoldered along the common international frontier, even as Webster and Ashburton attempted to lay to rest this and other festering problems.

I

That part of the North American boundary around upper New York had become a major troublespot on the continent by the mid-1830s. Although most Canadians remained loyal to the crown, some harbored deep resentment toward the mother country and sought greater autonomy. Such a stand attracted the support of Americans still interested in cleansing North America of Old World interference—particularly that of the British—and spreading the principles of republicanism. More than a few spoke of completing the work of the Paris negotiators of 1783 by expanding U.S. holdings northward—an early sign of manifest destiny that took the form of continental union. The *North American Review* emphasized that union would reduce the chance of hostilities toward Britain and urged Americans to work toward that end.[2]

Surely no cause could be more just than to raise the banner of liberty over another oppressed people. The stated objectives of the Canadian rebellions had indisputable merit. Popular election of all officials, greater participation in government, a fairer banking system—all these and more had adorned the lists compiled by citizens struggling to secure those basic rights guaranteed by nature. And the rebels skillfully exploited the sympathies they found south of the border. Using the American Revolution as their model, they created vigilance committees, committees of public safety, committees of correspondence, and Sons of Liberty. A chief grievance was the British Constitutional Act of 1791, which had neglected the growing demands for popular government and then, in dividing the colony into Upper and Lower Canada, maintained the barrier between the British in the west and the French in the east. The government in Upper Canada had broadened the franchise, but the executive and the legislative council (neither elected) retained the power to reject any proposal made by the elected assembly. Democratic reforms became the rallying cry of the Canadian rebels.[3]

The movement by Americans to rid the continent of British influence gathered momentum in a rash of meetings held along both sides of the frontier extending from Lake Champlain to Lake Michigan. The Panic of 1837 had left in its wake a widespread economic depression that not only encouraged an adventuresome spirit among idle Americans but also led them to believe that they would personally profit from the land vacated by the British. Recruits for the first "Patriot" army in the United States received assurances of land and money in exchange for their allegiance, and by mid-December 1837 the first so-called soldiers assembled in Buffalo, New York. This small beginning provided the seed for such rapid growth that within a month almost a thousand counted themselves as part of the fledgling army for freedom. New organizations sported well-advertised and catchy titles such as the Canadian Refugee Relief Association and the Sons of Liberty, while the Hunters' Lodges and Chasers followed the pattern of the Masons and formed secret societies complete with secret handshakes, signs, and passwords. Indeed, the Hunters installed various degrees of rank that included Snowshoes, Beavers, Master Hunters, and the ultimate honor, Patriot Hunters. Committed to clearing the British from the New World, these organizations soon dotted the vast area between Vermont and Michigan and even reached into Canada. The Hunters boasted a membership of thousands and were so sure of themselves that they elected leaders of a new Canadian republic.[4]

Most Americans opposed official governmental involvement in the Canadian rebellions, but they clearly favored a neutrality openly biased against the British crown. The Albany *Argus* supported private participation to encourage Canadian independence, increase the number of American settlements along the northeastern boundary, and achieve American navigation of the St. Lawrence River. The Washington *National Intelligencer* saw no justification for Britain's retaining Canada, particularly after Parliament had followed Lord John Russell's lead in March 1837 by coldly rejecting Lower Canada's pleas for self-government. The ensuing rebellion in that province was a godsend that the United States should promote through a friendly neutrality. There was no moral right to intervene, the *Intelligencer* declared. But no matter: Canadian independence was a certainty, just as union with the United States would naturally result from the political compatibility of the two peoples.[5]

President Martin Van Buren reacted to the border troubles with as much decision as legal, military, and political circumstances would allow. Hamstrung by his compatriots' exaltation of states' rights principles in assisting the rebels, he did all he could to prevent blatant interference with crown affairs. He invoked the Neutrality Act of 1818 to warn those Americans helping the rebellion that the U.S. government would offer them no assistance if captured by the British. But the bill allowed the president little leverage because it provided punishment after the act of interference without establishing procedures for discouraging that act. Further, anyone arrested for aiding the rebellion would find himself before a jury of his peers. Moreover, Van Buren could not call on military force; over one-half of the scant 7,130 men in uniform in December 1837 were at war with the Seminole Indians in Florida or patrolling the western frontier. Civil officials afforded no assistance;

most of them sided with the rebels and refused to enforce laws injurious to their cause. The president's political dilemma was of no small consequence, either. His Democratic party was avowedly expansionist but did not relish the prospect of war with the British. Indeed, many men in his party feared that Van Buren's loyalties to the mercurial and Anglophobic Andrew Jackson might ultimately lead to war.[6] Resolute action against Americans violating the Neutrality Act would alienate Democrats in his home state of New York; failure to act would allow his opponents to accuse him of instigating war with England. Van Buren had to maintain peace.

After the rebels in Upper Canada failed to take Toronto in early December, their leader, William Lyon Mackenzie, joined twenty-four allies in establishing a provisional government on Navy Island on the Canadian side of the Niagara River and made plans for invading the mainland at Chippewa, only a few hundred yards away. Mackenzie, a five-foot-six-inch wiry Scottish highlander, was an ardent Calvinist who came to Canada in 1820 and was elected to the provincial assembly eight years later. There, he quickly acquired a reputation for a stubborn sense of righteousness that fitted well with his piercing blue eyes, which, contemporaries swore, could peer into a man's soul. A self-proclaimed descendant of Noah, he regarded anyone who disagreed with him as dishonest and an avowed enemy. Prematurely bald because of a fever, he donned a bright red wig that he often flung at a friend or cast on the floor in moments of exuberance. In 1831 he was expelled from the assembly for libel but managed to win reelection numerous times. Three years later he became mayor of Toronto while serving in the assembly, where he led a group calling for democratic reform. When the government in London proved unresponsive to these demands, Lower Canada broke out in rebellion in November 1837, soon followed by Upper Canada. In early December, Mackenzie led a small contingent out of nearby Montgomery's Tavern in a disastrous attempt to take Toronto. After discovering neighboring Americans in Buffalo sympathetic to his cause, Mackenzie spoke excitedly before a crowd at the city's Coffee House about his plan to invade Canada. The point of departure would be Navy Island.[7]

The island was a natural fortress. Situated about three miles above Niagara Falls and slightly upstream from Chippewa in Canada and Fort Schlosser on the American side of the river, it was a veritable rock almost in midstream, densely wooded and protected by surrounding banks nearly twenty feet high. Its only building, occupied by a widow and her two daughters and son-in-law, was a tavern that harbored outlaws and became Mackenzie's headquarters. As the rebels grew in number, they increased their stock of weapons—including rifles and artillery stolen from New York's arsenals—and heightened speculation of a massive attack on Chippewa

William Lyon Mackenzie. From Guillet, *The Lives and Times of the Patriots* (1938). Reprinted by permission of the University of Toronto.

that would swell into a full-scale invasion of the mainland. Stories spread that as many as five thousand men had gathered on Navy Island, all armed and driven by intense hatred for the British and Mackenzie's promise to each man of three hundred acres and one hundred silver dollars. Although the number of recruits probably never exceeded 150, most of them were Americans, who by their presence suggested imminent U.S. intervention on a broad scale. After Mackenzie announced a program promising democratic reforms, he unveiled a flag brandishing twin stars and a new moon about to break through the clouds. Then he revealed his trump card: Colonel Rensselaer Van Rensselaer of Albany, the son of General Solomon Van Rensselaer of Revolutionary War fame, would lead the rebel force. War seemed certain, warned the lieutenant governor of Upper Canada, Sir Francis Bond Head, in a missive to Van Buren. Head sent 2,500 militiamen to Chippewa who would serve Colonel Allan MacNab, an attorney, speaker of Upper Canada's assembly, and known enemy of Mackenzie.[8]

If Philadelphia was America's Cradle of Liberty, then Navy Island became the Island of Liberty for those sons of the Canadian revolution now openly boasting of casting off the imperial yoke. The rebels fortified the island's shores and fired several cannon shots on Chippewa, damaging several buildings and killing a horse.[9]

Navy Island, Niagara River. From Nathaniel Parker Willis, *Canadian Scenery Illustrated* (1842).

Enthusiasm for the self-proclaimed righteous war grew to the point that any incident could set off an international crisis pitting the governments in Washington and London against each other in a battle over national honor and the future of North America. Such a scenario threatened to develop as a forty-five-ton American steamer, the *Caroline*, arrived on the pressure-packed scene. Owned by William Wells of Buffalo and under the command of Gilman Appleby, the small vessel chugged out of that city's harbor early on December 28, licensed to transport passengers and cargo between Buffalo and Fort Schlosser. Wells later insisted that he had entered no such agreement but had merely made his boat accessible to anyone wishing to cross the river. The truth seems to be, however, that he had chartered the vessel to the Patriots in Buffalo for $6,000 per month.[10]

As the *Caroline* made the twenty-mile journey to the Niagara area, its crew raised the American flag and, in a harbinger of what lay ahead, drew fire from the Black Rock Dam region on the Canadian shore. No one was injured as the vessel steamed on to Navy Island. On arrival the following day several passengers disembarked while the crew unloaded cargo. The *Caroline* then moved on to Fort Schlosser, where two more times that same day it transported passengers to Navy Island. The vessel brought no weapons to the island, according to Wells—although he admitted that its cargo included a six-pound cannon. This he curiously dismissed as unimportant since it belonged to a passenger. Mechanical problems forced Wells to cancel more trips that day. In the evening Appleby ordered the vessel chained to the dock at Fort Schlosser.[11]

From Chippewa, Colonel MacNab assured Head that the rebels on Navy Island had hired the *Caroline* to carry men and war matériel aimed at facilitating an attack on the mainland. Two of his men volunteered to investigate the situation firsthand: Captain Andrew Drew of the Royal Navy, and a deputy sheriff from Kingston named Alexander McLeod. The men were ill starred: Drew symbolized the crown itself, whereas McLeod had acquired a reputation as a hated Loyalist after helping to put down Mackenzie's forces at Montgomery's Tavern. During the night of December 28, Drew and McLeod rowed so close to Navy Island that they attracted musket fire from shore. Spotting the *Caroline*, they reported their findings to MacNab. The colonel saw no alternative but to destroy the intruder. A British naval vessel likewise investigating the situation had drawn cannon fire from Navy Island, and earlier that same day Chippewa had undergone musket fire from Grand Island on the American side of the river. Surely, he surmised, these events were preliminary to a major assault encouraged by the *Caroline*'s illicit activities. MacNab ordered Drew to lead the expedition.[12]

About eleven on the next night (December 29), Drew set out in command of seven boats carrying fifty-six volunteers, all answering his picturesque call for "a few fellows with cutlasses who would follow him to the Devil." On the way he revealed the mission: destroy the *Caroline*, docked at Navy Island. Paddling with great difficulty across the swift-moving Niagara as the falls thundered to their left, the men reached their destination, only to find that the *Caroline* was not there. Drew defiantly asserted to his compatriots,

Andrew Drew by H. Holmes. *Courtesy National Archives of Canada/C-025729.*

"The steamboat is our object—follow me!" He knew that the vessel must be at Fort Schlosser and directed his followers to row on across the river to the American side. Two boats had to turn back because of the rapids, leaving five boats with eight men in each to complete the mission. Stealing into the stream leading to the wharf, they soon saw the lights of the *Caroline*—moored in American waters.[13]

The hour was midnight; and if Drew hesitated to ponder the gravity of his decision, he left no evidence in support of such a claim. Inching ever closer to the *Caroline*, the British force moved within twenty yards of the steamer before its sentry discerned the approaching band of boats in the black of that night. "Boat ahoy! Who comes there?" he hailed once, twice, three times while demanding the countersign. "A friend," Drew finally replied. "Give us the countersign," the sentry demanded. "I will give you the countersign when I get on board!" By the time the sentry realized the danger, it was too late. He fired a musket shot and called for the crew, but the British were already heaving grappling hooks over the vessel's side and, led by Drew, scrambling on board, armed with cutlasses, pikes, and pistols.[14]

A fierce battle ensued as five men on the *Caroline* immediately confronted the boarding party, one of whom fired a musket into Drew's face that somehow missed. Drew used his cutlass to disable his assailant and then slashed an accomplice wielding a pistol. Kicking in the doors, the raiders burst in on the rest of the thirty-three passengers and crew below, who tried to escape up the ladders or through the portholes. But the British forced them back below. Appleby and Wells separated and hid, although both later claimed to have been in the engine room, where they saw a member of the boarding party seize one of the *Caroline*'s passengers, a stage driver from Buffalo named Amos Durfee. In the melee the British sustained several injuries, three of them taking gunshot and knife wounds. A British sailor, Shepard McCormack, was severely wounded and later claimed that three men had fought him while a number of others carried swords and pistols. Drew's force nonetheless took complete control in less than ten minutes and hustled everyone off the deck and onto the wharf. Several of those on board were drifters and never accounted for, even though only one body was found—that of Durfee's the next day on shore. His cap bore powder burns resulting from a close-range shot through the forehead that suggested an execution.[15]

Drew completed his mission by destroying the *Caroline*. After ordering the vessel set afire, he had the chain broken that held it to the dock and had it towed to the middle of the river. By the time the *Caroline* broke through a thick bed of grasslike marsh and reached its destination, flames had enveloped the wooden hull, sending the three-foot-long American flag on the stern crashing down onto the

"The Destruction of the *Caroline*" by George Tattersall. *Courtesy National Archives of Canada/C-004788.*

"The *Caroline* Descending the Great Falls" by W. R. Callington. *Courtesy National Archives of Canada/C-041076.*

deck and disappearing into the smoke and fire. Just before reaching the falls, the *Caroline* crumbled apart, its engine sinking into the water and jagged scraps of burning wood eventually hurtling over the precipice.[16]

Stories of the *Caroline*'s destruction traveled like wildfire up and down the frontier, escalating in ferocity and impact at each telling. Almost everyone in New York and neighboring Canada seemed to have seen the event firsthand, as more and more self-professed eyewitnesses breathlessly described the hordes of innocent Americans brutally victimized in the unprovoked British attack. In a statement that was probably accurate, Drew reported to MacNab that his men had killed perhaps half a dozen; but in an account that was not so accurate, a Canadian attested that in a Queenstown bar he overheard two British participants in the assault brag that they had slaughtered great numbers aboard. Appleby later told an indignant grand jury in New York that he was alive only because he had managed to escape a British soldier at the top of the stairs named Angus McLeod, who shouted, "Down, you damned Yankee!" and swung his sword, slitting the captain's vest while just missing his skin and sending him scurrying back below. Several others on the *Caroline* swore that the boarding party yelled out, "God damn them! Give them no quarter! Kill every man! Fire, fire!"[17]

If one could believe the newspapers, the attack had truly degenerated into a bloody massacre. MacNab was the "Robespierre of the age," according to the Livingston *Register* of Geneseo, New York. The "Eagle of the North" must avenge American honor on the principle of "Blood for Blood." *Niles' Register* angrily declared that the British had spared perhaps two of the more than thirty on board the *Caroline* before sending it and the remaining passengers plummeting over the falls. The *National Intelligencer* reported that a boarding party 150 strong defiantly gave three cheers for Queen Victoria before killing twenty-two defenseless passengers. Numerous New York newspapers confirmed the brazen butchery of everyone on board the vessel, an image transcribed into print and pictures by Mackenzie, who weeks afterward rekindled American ire by publishing a propaganda paper called *The Caroline Almanack*. The pamphlet denounced the "midnight assassination of the Americans at Schlosser" and displayed the boat in flames, its terrified passengers clutching the rail as the vessel veered downward over the lip of the falls. The New York *Herald*'s correspondent in Buffalo saw only one outcome: "Surely war with England was unavoidable."[18]

Out came the muskets all along the New York frontier as Americans prepared again to defend their honor against the hated British. Newspapers published military orders while story after story cajoled the angry Patriots to strike down the mother country for yet a third time. By early February 1838 the Niagara County court had issued a murder indictment against MacNab, Angus McLeod, and other participants in the dastardly deed. A poem offered a requiem for the fallen *Caroline* and its innocent victims:

> As over the shelving rocks she broke,
> And plunged in her turbulent grave,
> The slumbering genius of freedom woke,
> Baptized in Niagara's wave,
> And sounded her warning Tocsin far,
> From Atlantic's shore to the polar star.

An irate New Yorker crudely scribbled his reaction to the assault in a note to the newly appointed governor-general of Canada, Lord Durham:

> Durham!!
> how do you like to have your Steam Boat Burnt
> Drew or MacNab will git a bowie
> knife in their damd Hart when thay
> little think of such a thing
> What is the reason that navy Island was
> not taken if they was so fast for
> fighting no thay took good care to keep
> clear of that you would have had a small
> tast of New Orleans the[re] is a scrap
> brewing in Newyork with your damd steam
> ships next thing thay will be Burnt
> God Dam the Queen.[19]

Emotions continued to spiral upward. In Cleveland the customs collector reported that close to one hundred men, "comprising all the thieves, blacklegs, and scoundrels" in the city, had already joined other Patriots assembling in Detroit for an invasion of Canada. Americans seethed with anger when Loyalists in the legislature of Upper Canada commemorated the *Caroline*'s destruction by knighting MacNab and awarding swords to both him and Drew, and Lieutenant Governor Head joined the Canadian press in publicly approving the attack.[20]

War with England seemed certain. Rochester politicians inflamed large crowds with bombastic challenges to defend the country against the British. In Albany, the New York *Herald* reported a "silent, sullen, settled determination of vengeance" among "young, active, hardy, and daring men" who boasted in the streets about dining in Toronto in two weeks. Before a reported six thousand rowdy citizens in the city's park, Albany's mayor chaired a public meeting that threatened to explode in violence when hotheads led cheers of "Hurrah for the patriots!", "Three groans for MacNab!", and "Down with Sir Francis Head! Off wid his head!"[21]

The situation in Buffalo proved even more volatile. According to the *Herald*, irate New Yorkers beat drums while soldiers marched, "convulsively" grasping their muskets and wild-eyed for war. Other Patriots rolled out old cannon to protect the city from an invasion. A West Point cadet, described by onlookers as "a splendid fellow," marched a group of volunteers down to Grand Island, where they proudly planted the American flag and swore to safeguard the country. But nothing matched the spectacle surrounding the public funeral of Amos Durfee. Now a full day after the alleged slaughter at Fort Schlosser, the Patriots had gathered his remains from the battle site (where they had stayed for several hours after their discovery). On the evening of December 30, according to the *Herald*'s grisly account, his draped body was displayed in front of the Eagle Hotel, its "pale forehead, mangled by the pistol ball, and his locks matted with his blood!" His pallbearers then transported Durfee to the veranda of the city hall where they distributed coffin-shaped posters announcing the funeral. Close to three thousand people jammed the public square fronting the courthouse steps as the wake began. After an Episcopal clergyman offered a prayer for the deceased, the *Herald* proclaimed that a young attorney delivered a "speech more exciting, thrilling, and much more indignant than Mark Antony's."[22]

II

News of the *Caroline* crisis arrived in Washington in the early evening of January 4, just prior to an Executive Mansion dinner. Long after the appointed hour, the president had not yet appeared among his guests. Van Buren had called his cabinet into emergency session, while at the party General Winfield Scott, Henry Clay, nineteen Whigs, and three or four Democrats had already begun to speculate about the reason for his tardiness. Perhaps the president was writing his resignation speech, the Whigs jested to the Democrats over cocktails. Before the Democrats could counter this light-hearted remark, the short and stout Van Buren rushed in, his drawn and pale face betraying deep concern. Heading straight to Scott, who was then talking with Clay, the president somberly declared to his military chieftain, "Blood has been shed. You must go with all speed to the Niagara frontier." The secretary of war was writing instructions as they spoke.[23]

Van Buren then took several other preparatory steps. He invoked the neutrality proclamation, called up the militia, and issued a public warning that anyone who interfered with the government's attempts to maintain neutrality would be placed under arrest. But those who knew him realized that his belief in a restrained federal government would keep him from acting decisively in the new border crisis. He nonetheless gave the appearance of resolute action by asking Congress to appropriate military funds and declaring his intention to demand reparations for the *Caroline*. He also requested a stronger neutrality law. Congress immediately focused on the crisis with England.[24]

To members of Congress, British indemnification for the *Caroline* became the sole corrective for preventing war. New York Representative Millard Fillmore indignantly told his colleagues that MacNab's order to destroy the vessel had come just after his own assurances against a British invasion of America. Then Drew violated his orders and MacNab lavishly praised him. Massachusetts Representative and former president John Quincy Adams thought war a certainty. Congressmen were livid over the massacre, which Waddy Thompson of South Carolina called a "foul, wilful, deliberate, unmitigated murder." Richard Menefee of Kentucky infuriated his colleagues when, in an effort to calm them down, he claimed to see no great principles involved in the *Caroline* affair, such as the right of search and impressment of Americans. "No principle involved! Great God!" exclaimed Thompson. "No principle involved in the invasion of our territory by a hostile band of another nation, and the murder, with fiendish atrocity, of our sleeping and unoffending citizens?" In the Senate the feeling was likewise strong. Thomas Hart Benton of Missouri perhaps best expressed the sentiment of both houses when he angrily demanded full redress as the only alternative to war.[25]

The ensuing debate in Congress proved long and fiery, leaving the president without real military power until long after the crisis had passed. In response to Van Buren's recommendations, Congress appropriated $625,000 for defending the northern frontier and, at long last, approved a revised neutrality law in early March. According to the new legislation, the federal government could seize any sled, wagon, or seagoing vessel involved in hostile action. In a move that differed markedly from the Neutrality Act of 1818, government officials no longer needed warrants to commandeer any means of transportation suspected of potential military use. To enforce the act, the president could enlist the assistance of the army, navy, and state militias.[26]

The diplomats, meanwhile, had entered the fray. Throughout that tumultuous period of early 1838 the State Department exchanged many notes with the Foreign Office that permitted time to lapse and tempers to cool. Leaders in Washington and London did not want war, but they also recognized the importance of salving both sides' feelings as a necessary prelude to escaping the crisis. American honor had been the chief casualty at Fort Schlosser. Once again, Americans charged, the British government had demonstrated a calloused disregard for their status as a nation and further punctuated this calculated insult with public celebrations of victory and special homage paid to the executioners. The only way for peacemakers to deal with such rampant emotions was to allow them to run their course while the diplomats exchanged legal arguments intended to blur the issues and neutralize the flashpoints sparking war.

The central question was whether the British government had been responsible for the attack on the *Caroline*. Secretary of State John Forsyth had no doubt about the matter and expressed "extraordinary outrage" while dutifully seeking reparations for the destruction of American property and murder of American citizens. Lord Melbourne's government recognized its tenuous position in the crisis and tactfully delayed any response. British acceptance of responsibility constituted an admission to being the aggressor and thereby would belie the claims by MacNab and others that they had no intention of invading the United States. The potential problem that seemed to go unnoticed was that if British officials refused to call the assault a "public act" (committed under government orders), they made its participants automatically subject to prosecution in New York courts.[27]

More than a month after the attack the British minister in Washington, Henry Fox, finally offered a defense of his government's actions based on an allegation of piracy against the *Caroline*. Its "piratical character," he explained to Forsyth, had combined with the inability of the United States to enforce its neutrality laws to justify destruction of the vessel. The *Caroline*, as a "pirate," was therefore subject to destruction by any affected state. In February 1838 the crown's legal advisers declared that international law supported Fox's stand. In the warlike atmosphere along the frontier, they proclaimed, Fort Schlosser was not "justly entitled to the privileges of a neutral territory." British forces had acted out of "self-preservation" and were "fully justified" in regarding the *Caroline* as a belligerent vessel and destroying it wherever found.[28]

Fox did not handle the *Caroline* crisis with any degree of efficiency. Had he read his history, he could have put the United States in a highly tenuous position by referring to Andrew Jackson's punitive expedition in Florida in 1817 and accusing the White House of now denying rights to other nations that it claimed for itself. Had not Jackson (at least according to then Secretary of State John Quincy Adams) acted in self-defense in resolving the Indian problem permitted by Spanish impotence? But Fox did not push this matter. Indeed, he rarely demonstrated any exceptional talent as a diplomat while in Washington. He had received the appointment, or so it was said, because he was the only Englishman sent to America who did not complain about the heat. Gambling was his obsession, which drew the bitter comment from New York merchant Philip Hone that Fox looked more like "a little shriveled Frenchman" than an Englishman. "The sooner we get rid of him, the better . . . he sleeps all day and sits up all night; returns no visits; gives no entertainments; and does not pay his gambling debts." At one point an angry group of creditors stormed his house, demanding a date on which he would satisfy his debts. Coming to a window, he conceded that he had already made that decision. Pausing for emphasis, he contemptuously announced, "On the Day of Judgment." Fox disliked Americans and had no stomach for the fastidious diplomacy necessitated by the *Caroline* crisis. By mid-February he became so disgruntled with the American position that he informed Forsyth that any further discussion of the matter must take place in London between the American minister and the British foreign secretary, Lord Palmerston.[29]

The Van Buren administration, of course, did not agree with the British position, but it was caught in a dilemma. Forsyth insisted that the *Caroline* could not have been engaged in piracy: the owner had it registered in Buffalo as a freight and passenger vessel and it flew the American flag.[30] And yet, according to international law, America's neutrality proclamation of 1837 defined the situation in the Canadas as a war between belligerents, which meant that contraband on board a "neutral" vessel was subject to confiscation. The *Caroline* carried war matériel and volunteers for the rebel force and was no longer "neutral." With those considerations in mind, the British should have warned the American government that if the *Caroline* continued its activities along the border, they would seize the vessel and take it before a prize court; if this did not work, they could have disposed of the steamer quietly, not in a fiery burst of flames before a host of witnesses along the Niagara shore. Still, however, the British argument for destroying the vessel was not entirely without substance.

With negotiations shifting to the other side of the Atlantic, Forsyth instructed his minister in London, Andrew Stevenson of Virginia, to demand reparations. According to the secretary's directives (which rested on grossly inaccurate accounts of the incident), the British had "slaughtered" a number of nonresisting crew and passengers *after* they had surrendered the vessel. Many other Americans had disappeared, leading Forsyth to believe that they had been swept over the falls to "a watery grave in the cataract." And yet, even if the most extreme stories were unsubstantiated, Forsyth's fundamental charge remained indisputable: the British had invaded American territory and killed at least one citizen. Accordingly, Stevenson emphasized to Palmerston that one of the most revered principles in international law was the sanctity of neutral territory during war. Britain had no right to forceful entry into another "sovereign and independent state." Necessity must govern such action, Stevenson declared. And that "necessity must be imminent, and extreme," and involve "impending destruction." Since British forces were in no danger in December 1837, they had no justification for invading American territory.[31]

The British government finally recognized that it had no choice but to acknowledge the *Caroline* attack as a public act, thereby justified by the law of nations. Canadian officials had admitted that Drew followed the "Usages of War" in dispensing with the *Caroline*. Palmerston called it an act of "necessity," brought on by the "impending destruction" of British control over the frontier. In truth, the British could not evade responsibility: forces under their command had destroyed the vessel as part of an ongoing effort to suppress the rebellions against the crown; Lieutenant Governor Head of Upper Canada had voiced public approval of the act; and MacNab and Drew had received special honors from the provincial assembly. That Palmerston waited so long to reply to America's protests constituted tacit approval of the attack. Finally, almost six months after Stevenson's call for reparations, Palmerston instructed Fox on November 6, 1838, to declare formally that destruction of the *Caroline* was a public act. And yet, for perhaps the lame reason that Fox later offered—that there was never any question about the matter—the British minister did not officially inform the White House of his government's decision for two years. Perhaps he assumed that terming the *Caroline*'s activities as piracy automatically justified the destruction as self-defense and hence "public" in nature. But even this generous interpretation of Fox's conduct cannot obscure the point that his failure to deal with the crisis in a straightforward manner allowed a serious situation to become even worse.[32]

General Scott had meanwhile arrived in the troubled area. His instructions were to keep the peace by taking command of American forces along the Canadian frontier and asking the governors of New York and Vermont to contribute militia. The New York *Herald* remarked that the Van Buren administration had sent its trouble-shooter on a "fool's errand." Scott certainly recognized the dire nature of his assignment. He was expected to bring order to a poorly defined 800-mile-long frontier, enforce unenforceable neutrality laws, secure a militarily weak United States from further British invasion, and restore respect for the nation's honor—all through what he sardonically called "rhetoric and diplomacy."[33]

Scott was nonetheless equal to the task. Traveling primarily at night through areas not serviced by railroads, he and his aide and a black servant rode in a huge sleigh pulled by four horses through bitterly cold weather, each man taking turns struggling to find warmth under a stack of fur lap robes. At one point the fifty-two-year-old general caved in to exhaustion and stomach troubles and was forced to bed; but on other occasions he strutted before those Americans under his command, gaudily displaying his six-foot frame attired in an immaculate blue and gold uniform. If not the reality, then surely the symbolism of his presence drove home the point that he intended to establish stability along the border. A resident of Buffalo noted the sense of security that "this yellow-plumed, gold-laced hero" imparted to everyone. Hostile crowds turned friendly toward this brave veteran of the War of 1812 as he insisted that the United States must not interfere with British affairs. The Canadian rebellions must render their own verdict—not that of Americans. For the *Caroline*, however, the British government owed reparations and an apology. But only the federal government in Washington, he pointedly warned the staunch defenders of states' rights, should deal with the matter. Save for his sword, Scott stood unarmed before large groups of boisterous frontier Americans, theatrically thanking God for his country and then staring his listeners in the eye while offering the challenge: "I tell you, then, except it be over my body, you shall not pass this line—you shall *not* embark."[34]

Scott apparently convinced Colonel Van Rensselaer that the rebels' cause was hopeless and that his actions seriously threatened Anglo-American relations. Near Niagara Falls on the night of January 13, 1838, Scott and New York Governor William Marcy met with Van Rensselaer and hammered away at these points. The poorly supplied rebels lacked discipline, Scott emphasized. An invasion force of fewer than two hundred men could not dislodge the twenty-five hundred Loyalists at Chippewa. Indeed, at one point when Scott was not present, Marcy made clear that his only objective was to evict the rebel army from New York. According to Van Rensselaer, Marcy told him that if the force left Navy Island, "*he* knew of *no law* that could prevent my marching a body of *armed* men through the country." The governor, or so Van Rensselaer thought, had tacitly assured him against any interference with an attempt to relocate the Patriots with others who had gathered in Detroit and already launched one abortive invasion of Canada out of that city. Van Rensselaer also realized that the impending ice formations in the river would make Navy Island an untenable base by isolating it from Buffalo.[35]

It could not have been coincidental that the day after Van Rensselaer's meeting with Scott, the rebels evacuated Navy Island and relocated to American territory—at Fort Malden near Buffalo. A day later, on January 15, Marcy had Van Rensselaer arrested in Buffalo. But the rebel leader was soon out on bail and planning further military assaults on British positions in Canada. Soon afterward he jumped bail and fled to Canada where authorities captured him and put him in jail again. This time, Van Rensselaer stayed.[36]

Scott's work was still not done, however, because the Patriots had raised the possibility of a confrontation between American and British forces by securing the use of another steamer, the *Barcelona*. In an ingenious move, Scott blocked the Patriots' effort by outbidding them for the vessel and chartering it for government use. Yet the British did not know that he had eliminated this threat and prepared to destroy the *Barcelona*. Once again, Drew led the expedition, this time by stationing three armed craft in the American sector of the Niagara River and ordering fieldpieces placed on the Canadian shore. Scott protested against Drew's violation of American waters; and the next day, as the *Barcelona* trudged up the river toward an impending and deadly crossfire, the American general had his forces armed and ready at Black Rock, just across from the Canadian vessels. Tension mounted as the *Barcelona* approached the waters between the Canadian and American contingents, both glaring at each other while readying their cannon for combat. But Drew decided not to challenge Scott, and the *Barcelona* steamed unharmed between the battle lines.[37]

In perhaps the most inflammatory reminder of the *Caroline* affair, about fifty Patriots dressed in Indian attire attacked the Canadian packet vessel *Sir Robert Peel* as it refueled at Wells Island in late May of 1838. After intimidating and insulting those on board (thirty Canadian lumbermen, along with a number of passengers that included women and children), they forced everyone ashore before towing the vessel into the lake, shouting "Remember the *Caroline!*" and setting it afire. That some of the lumbermen were never seen again gave rise to stories that they had been left on board the burning ship.[38]

The *Caroline* crisis contained all the elements conducive to war, and yet the outcome was a tenuous peace. In preparing for war, the British government positioned its naval squadron at strategic locations near the United States and greatly increased the number of regulars and naval forces assigned to the North American and West Indian stations. The White House likewise took precautionary measures. Scott's intervention was a factor in easing the border troubles, although the most telling determinants were the rebels' lack of adequate supplies and capable leadership. The Hunters attempted to invade Lower Canada in early November of 1838, but the plan fell apart largely because the general leading the attack force marched behind his men. These groups attempted to invade Canada twice more in 1839, only to encounter superior British forces who hauled off captives to a penal colony below Australia and warned the remaining members of the societies to scatter to their homes.[39]

The London government also contributed to the eased sense of crisis along the frontier by sending a special mission to Canada led by Lord Durham. The report he submitted in February 1839 called for satisfying the two chief demands made by the rebels: union of the two Canadas and the establishment of popular government. The first objective was achieved by the Canada Union Act of 1840, but the second had to wait until 1848, when Lord Elgin's ministry agreed to broaden popular participation in government. The Durham Report nonetheless proved effective. It not only promised reforms that defused the Canadian rebellions, but by alleviating the border troubles it also reduced the likelihood of a third Anglo-American war.[40]

America's honor had come into serious question with the *Caroline* affair, and for that reason threatened to cause war between the Atlantic nations. Indeed, one could argue that the British invasion of American territory, their destruction of a vessel flying the American flag, and the killing of an American constituted a series of insults to national honor that at least equalled those leading to the War of 1812. Longtime animosities toward the mother country made these events all the more dangerous; rivalries over the control of North America added more trouble to an already difficult situation. Fortunately, leaders in Washington and London did everything possible to steer away from a conflict that promised mutual calamity. Politicians and the press ranted and raved about infringements on honor that justified war, but national leaders on both sides resisted the popular impulse and worked for peace. Still, however, the common meeting places of Americans and Britons along the North American border maintained explosive potential, particularly when their leaders at home once again chose the least onerous path of assigning to time the task of arranging a permanent settlement.

CHAPTER THREE

Mother Country at Bay: The Strange Case of Alexander McLeod

McLeod's Execution would produce War; war immediate and frightful in its Character.
—Lord Palmerston, February 9, 1841

Secretary of State Daniel Webster had not been directly involved in either the northeastern boundary controversy or the *Caroline* crisis, but he knew from firsthand experience in the Alexander McLeod episode that it had the potential of causing war between the Atlantic nations.[1] Not only did this unusual case resurrect all the ugly memories about the *Caroline*'s destruction, but it also revived the familiar arguments over Anglophobia, states' rights, and national honor. Almost inevitably the *Caroline* and McLeod issues had meshed, creating a crisis in 1841 that nearly resulted in a third Anglo-American war. Although the warriors and diplomats vied with one another during the early part of that stormy year, the advocates of peace had somehow managed to gain the upper hand— if only for a moment. By the time Webster and Ashburton met in Washington during the summer of 1842, the *Caroline*-McLeod issue had joined the relentless northeastern boundary dispute to create additional problems for the negotiators.

Indeed, as Webster and Ashburton opened their negotiations, the McLeod crisis was still fresh in the American memory. Less than two years before, McLeod had been arrested and charged with murder and arson during the *Caroline* assault. According to the accusation, he had killed Amos Durfee. The claim was all the more believable because McLeod had been a despised Loyalist during the Canadian rebellions and hence the avowed target of Americans along the Niagara frontier. Citizens in that area found it easy to loathe servants of the crown—particularly when those servants possessed the obstinate and brassy character so openly flaunted by

McLeod. He had already escaped one close call. In late 1837 a mob in Buffalo almost seized him while he, as secret agent, procured information about the *Caroline*'s activities.

Alexander McLeod. From Charles Lindsey, *The Life and Times of William Lyon Mackenzie* (1862).

The core of the problem was clear. Since the British government had not officially labeled the destruction of the vessel a "public act," the participants in the assault were outside the protective arm of national authorities. Consequently, McLeod and others accused of the act held the status of private citizens, subject to indictment by local officials. With President Van Buren finding it politically expedient to accept the restraints placed on the federal government by states' rights advocates, the potential for trouble increased dramatically. To the British, the arrest of McLeod sharpened every image they had of Americans as reckless and shiftless frontiersmen who showed no respect for civility or international law. To Americans, however, McLeod symbolized everything about the mother country that they abhorred: an arrogant and ruthless people who, in American territory, had destroyed a vessel flying the Stars and Stripes and murdered a defenseless citizen. National honor remained in question because of the unfinished *Caroline* business, and McLeod provided both the means for closing the books on that still inflammatory issue and the opportunity to prove the legitimacy of American nationhood once and for all.

I

Americans along the Niagara frontier had refused to allow the *Caroline* affair to fade from their consciousness. Border incidents continued sporadically from New York to Michigan, most often manned by Patriots and unemployed workers who raided towns in Upper Canada in the name of driving the British from the continent. Rowdy New York citizens participated in huge public meetings commemorating the *Caroline* and blasting the British, and elected officers of the "Republic of Canada." These emotional gatherings included regional heroes such as Captain Appleby of the ill-fated vessel, who was now dubbed the Admiral of Lake Erie. Although Canadian and American officials crushed the "republic" and the crown executed its leaders and banished their followers to Australia, this show of power did not curtail the demand for avenging the *Caroline*. Most ominously, the Niagara County court records in New York included an indictment for murder and arson against a dozen people designated as accomplices in the incident at Fort Schlosser. By the middle of 1840 several arrests had taken place, but each time the evidence was insufficient to hold the accused in jail. In the latter part of that year, however, state officials arrested

Alexander McLeod after he allegedly boasted in a tavern in Buffalo that he had killed at least one American in the assault and unsheathed his still-bloodied sword to prove it.[2]

The arrest was a travesty that would have received the ridicule it deserved had the local atmosphere not been so rife with Anglophobia. The very name McLeod had become a war cry among those frontier residents who remembered his offensive behavior during the Canadian rebellions and who now wanted to use him as a way of striking at the crown itself. In September the authorities took him to Manchester, New York, where he defiantly yelled to irate townspeople outside the jail that he had not participated in the attack but would surely not deny it if he had. Evidence was too weak to hold him, however, and he went free. But a short time later he was rearrested and taken to Niagara. Again he won release when it became clear that his brother's name, Angus, was on the warrant by mistake. By that time it seemed that everyone was out to get him. As deputy sheriff, McLeod had a well-deserved reputation for shady practices while serving writs involving money. As a result, Hezekiah Davis of New York filed suit against him for embezzlement. McLeod traveled to Buffalo to find witnesses for his defense; and on his return to Canada in November, he was arrested in Lewiston, New York, for both the civil case and the *Caroline* incident. He won dismissal on the first charge but not the second. A New York magistrate conducted a lengthy inquiry of three witnesses (including Hezekiah's brother) who swore that McLeod had bragged of his part in the *Caroline* incident, and ordered him confined to the county jail at Lockport on suspicion of murder and arson.[3]

As these local events threatened to balloon into an international crisis, British officials intervened but succeeded only in further muddling the growing controversy. The civil secretary of Upper Canada responded to McLeod's entreaties by advising the lieutenant governor, Sir George Arthur, to send a solicitor to assist McLeod in Lockport. Arthur did not need much persuasion: more than a hundred people in the Niagara district had already sent him a memorial swearing that McLeod had not taken part in the *Caroline* raid. Still, Arthur had reservations. Any form of official participation in the affair, he knew, would legitimize New York's actions; besides, he considered McLeod "a scheming kind of gentleman" who, if he *had* been present that fateful night, was the "most probable man I know to have been one of the Party." Sir Richard Jackson, head of the province's military forces, agreed with Arthur's assessment and sarcastically referred to McLeod as "that illustrious martyr." In the meantime, the provincial attorney general offered to help McLeod locate witnesses and call for bail, while two Lockport attorneys, Hiram Gardner and Alvin C. Bradley, agreed to head his defense and secure bail once set.[4]

In Washington, British Minister Fox finally admitted the obvious. He urged Secretary of State Forsyth to intervene on the basis of the "well-known" fact that the *Caroline* raid was a "publick act of persons in Her Majesty's service" and reminded him that, under international law, only the two concerned national governments could deal with the problem. Fox believed in McLeod's innocence but expressed deep concern that "border outlaws" would perjure themselves to convict him. The *Caroline*, Fox insisted, was a "hostile vessel, engaged in piratical war," thus making the British action "self-defence, rendered absolutely necessary by the circumstances of the occasion."[5]

Fox's longtime matter-of-fact approach to the crisis had exasperated and bewildered the White House. Even though both governments had initially assumed that the destruction of the *Caroline* was a public act, Palmerston had not yet responded to the first complaints from the Van Buren administration. There was no excuse for waiting this long. Palmerston was admittedly understaffed and overworked, yet he managed to keep pace with a busy schedule that included continual troubles with France and the eastern Mediterranean, numerous social affairs and parliamentary debates, and the maintenance of three mistresses. But his ill-advised delay in the *Caroline* crisis had cast a cloud of uncertainty over the case and opened the door to local officials eager to force the issue.[6]

American politicians fled from the burgeoning McLeod crisis as quickly as their rhetoric could find an honorable way out. The president, just defeated for reelection in November, reiterated his philosophical principles that precluded federal intervention in a state matter. As a lame-duck president from the troubled state of New York, Van Buren preferred that his successor, Ohio Whig William Henry Harrison, handle the McLeod issue. Fox certainly believed this to be the case. The outgoing president, cynically observed the British minister, would not "scruple or regret to bequeath a war" to his opposition. Van Buren's Democratic friends could not agree more with his politically expedient decision. Many of them were as anti-British as the most vociferous New Yorker and did not want the state to release the prisoner. Moreover, the governor of New York was William H. Seward, a Whig who detested the president and staunchly denied any federal right to intervene in state affairs.[7]

With no leadership coming from the White House, Congress went on the offensive. House members from the South praised the president's response to Fox as a "good State Rights paper" and angrily repeated their long-standing indictment of the British for invading American territory and killing an American citizen. New York's Millard Fillmore expressed hope that the jury would acquit McLeod but darkly admitted that an execution must follow a guilty verdict. A colleague from New York, Francis Granger, predicted a fair trial but solemnly agreed that a conviction necessitated the death penalty. Let the British dare to begin hostilities, he haughtily declared; if they did, the western part of New York would react as patriotically as it had during the War of 1812.[8] To the historically astute, this remark would have drawn the mockery it deserved.

In any case, more than a few Americans believed it their generation's turn to chastise the arrogant mother country again. Newspapers thought so. The Philadelphia *Public Ledger and Daily Transcript* ran an inflammatory article entitled "THE CAROLINE MURDERS," which castigated the British demand for McLeod's release as an insult. In exchange for such a concession, the British should liberate those Americans imprisoned during the Canadian rebellions and grant reparations for those executed. Any call for McLeod's unqualified freedom must meet "RESISTANCE TO THE LAST!"[9]

The British, also ignoring recent history, tartly declared their willingness to pummel Americans for a third time. To Minister Stevenson in London, Lord John Russell, the colonial secretary, warned that the execution of McLeod would inflame the British people and government. Members of the House of Lords denounced the American Congress for bringing dishonor to England. Fox was more direct: an execution meant "war of the most hateful and terrible kind, a war to avenge the shedding of innocent blood." Palmerston hotly agreed. "McLeod's Execution," he assured his emissary in Washington, "would produce War; war immediate and frightful in its Character," one of "Retaliation and of vengeance." That same day, February 9, 1841, Palmerston instructed Fox to request his papers and leave the United States should New York execute McLeod. To signal the seriousness of the situation, Fox was to call a military alert by communicating his reasons for departure to the governor-general of Canada and the naval officers commanding the Halifax and West Indian stations. "War would be the inevitable result" of an execution, Palmerston assured his brother in a private letter. Stevenson was likewise convinced. After an interview with Palmerston, the American minister wrote the president that McLeod's death meant *"immediate war!"*[10]

Palmerston's role in the rapidly developing crisis was integral, and not only because he was the foreign secretary. His slow response to the *Caroline* had permitted that issue to fester. Had he accepted official responsibility from the outset and dealt with it in the highest circles of government, the delay that he fostered would not have occurred and Americans would not have had time to conjure up images of British audacity and brutality. Instead, he withheld a formal response, which allowed local interests to prevail over national concerns and thereby foment a crisis.

In all fairness, the Van Buren administration deserves a share of the blame. When combined with Palmerston's silence, the president's hesitation to take firm action permitted local officials to exploit the situation. Van Buren had escaped the *Caroline* crisis short of war, but his reluctance to close the matter had left crucial issues unsettled that, in the event of McLeod's execution, would revive the threat of war. For a brief moment, perhaps, Van Buren's indecision in 1837–38 had suggested a wise and patient president. But now, in early 1841, his seemingly ingenious tactics were exposed as nothing more than deferral of the initiative to those whose interests were more local than national, and more emotional than rational. If he now counted on Governor Seward to issue a pardon to avert an execution, he was gambling with high stakes. Seward had already made it plain that McLeod must stand trial. And the governor was a Whig who did not care for either the president's Democratic allegiance or his personal character. Van Buren's policy of drift had contributed to a crisis over which he now had little or no control.

Leaders in London and Washington had become ensnared in a huge dilemma. Had Palmerston acted swiftly in calling the *Caroline*'s destruction a public act, he would have categorized the affair as a foreign relations matter that concerned only the two national governments involved. Had Van Buren moved quickly in calling this an international question, he could have circumvented those states' rightists and Anglophobes who thought only in terms of personal or local interests. But neither leader acted. The result was an Anglo-American crisis that adept governmental leaders and diplomats could have prevented with greater care.

Mob action in New York became a distinct possibility as McLeod sat in his cell, anxiously waiting to go free on bond. At the moment, he was in jail under a general indictment that allowed bail. Yet the county court was scheduled to meet soon and could drastically change the situation by lodging a true bill of indictment, which would cancel his eligibility for bail. A county judge had set bail at $5,000, and McLeod's attorneys hurriedly arranged his release in late January after two Lockport townsmen posted bond. But rumors had spread that he intended to flee into Canada. As McLeod prepared to leave his confines, an angry band of townspeople gathered outside, brought together by protesters who had marched through the streets, pounding drums to warn of the prisoner's impending release. McLeod briefly thought about escaping to the border but wisely dismissed the idea. The crowd had set fires outside the jail and trained two cannon on his cell window. The hour was late, and the law officers prudently decided to keep him in jail. Throughout the night the mob fired blank charges from the guns and pelted the building with rocks. The next day, the two townspeople who had posted bail withdrew their offer. Two days later, another judge raised the bail to $7,000.[11]

The conduct of the Lockport rowdies infuriated the British. Lieutenant Governor Arthur's emissary on the scene attributed the chaotic situation to democracy, which he disgustedly called a "many headed monster." Fox indignantly asked what the White House intended to do about this "manifest outrage upon law and order." Forsyth dodged this effort to place responsibility at the feet of the federal government and replied that all he and the State Department knew about the events had come from the same newspapers Fox had read. The *Times* of London ridiculed this "triumph of the mob" over law and called for "retributive justice" over the "hot-brained democracy of the northern states."[12]

In early February a Lockport grand jury announced a true bill of indictment against McLeod and thereby disallowed the right of bail. A Court of General Sessions of the Peace indicted McLeod on seventeen counts of murder and arson for his involvement in the *Caroline* affair. Governor Seward asked a member of the state's supreme court to preside over the fast-approaching trial and instructed the state's attorney general to head the prosecution. McLeod's attorneys requested a change of venue aimed at moving the trial from the western part of the state to the less volatile east.[13]

The House of Representatives now entered the growing crisis. Less than two weeks after McLeod's indictment, American lawmakers issued a virulent report first attacking the British actions in both the *Caroline* and McLeod affairs, and then broadening the assault to include remote and irrelevant concerns. The quick-tempered

Francis Pickens of South Carolina, who was chairman of the Committee on Foreign Affairs, had prepared the document and cited states' rights principles in prohibiting the White House from interfering in New York's affairs. The *Caroline*, he declared, had posed no danger to the British and was not engaged in piracy, because pirates were "freebooters, enemies of the human race" who had "no flag and no home." The British had unjustifiably invaded the United States and "cast the aegis" of their jurisdiction "over American soil." The basic problem, Pickens asserted, arose from Britain's lack of "respect for our sovereignty and independence." The two nations were not at war in 1837, he pointed out, and McLeod was therefore subject to criminal charges brought by the state of New York.[14]

The Pickens report heightened emotions. Fox called it "highly offensive," and the governor-general of Canada termed it "ridiculous." The *Times* in London angrily denounced the report as "menacing and insulting" and warned that if McLeod were executed, there would not be "three Englishmen living" who would choose peace over war. Granger sat on the committee and warned that adoption of the report constituted a virtual declaration of war on England. John Quincy Adams, former president and forever suspicious of England, nonetheless sought to excise the phrase "grasping spirit of Britain." Edward Everett agreed with his outspoken colleague from Massachusetts and argued that the report would interfere with the administration's efforts to negotiate a settlement of the problem. The only purpose of the report, Everett charged, was to embarrass the incoming president. Fillmore likewise urged Pickens to withdraw the offensive language. But hotter heads prevailed, and House members voted to publish a document that threw down the gauntlet of war before the British government.[15]

II

If anything was encouraging about the recent chain of events, it was that the locus of attention had taken a quiet turn toward the government in Washington. In March the Whigs assumed control of the White House and prepared to pursue a firmer policy than had the outgoing administration. The new president, William Henry Harrison, was the former military governor of Indiana who had defeated the Indians at Tippecanoe in 1811. Perhaps the times called for a general's leadership. The politicians and the diplomats, after

William Henry Harrison. From painting by Alonzo Chappel, in *National Portrait Gallery of Eminent Americans* (1862).

all, had proved their inability to deal with the British crisis. Harrison was new to the world of politics and diplomacy, which now seemed to be an asset rather than a liability.

Common sense suggested a way out of the present troubles, and Harrison was willing to take that path. From a general's perspective, the issues were clear. The British had violated American territorial rights in destroying the *Caroline* and killing an American, but McLeod had acted under government orders and could not be personally responsible. The British government therefore must elevate the act to an international matter by accepting responsibility and then extend an apology and make reparations to the United States. Accordingly, President Harrison directed his secretary of state, Daniel Webster, to make this position clear to the British minister in Washington. If the court in New York insisted on trying McLeod, Webster was to work toward moving judicial proceedings to the U.S. Supreme Court, where he could enter a *nolle prosequi*, or formal notice that the prosecution would drop the charges. Finally, the president intended to send U.S. Attorney General John Crittenden to Albany to inform Governor Seward, a fellow Whig, that the case must go before the Court because British avowal of the *Caroline* assault as a public act made it an international concern.[16]

Harrison's decisive action was as welcome as his choice of Webster as secretary of state. At fifty-nine years of age, the former senator from Massachusetts was in excellent health. He cut an impressive figure, standing five feet ten inches tall, with a robust chest and shoulders, a huge head with big, dark, cavernous eyes, and black bushy eyebrows and hair. Black Dan, his awestruck friends called him. Magnificent in appearance, he often accented his natural features by wearing a blue coat with brass buttons over a white shirt laced with ruffles and a wide black cravat that made his large neck look even larger. Webster was a living lie, according to a British critic of the United States: "No man on earth could be so great as he looked." Webster had won many friends during a visit to England in 1839, and he was under contract as legal adviser to the world-renowned banking firm in London, the House of Baring. Indeed, the archcritic of America, Palmerston himself, had been so impressed with Webster that he recommended that Queen Victoria relax protocol for him, "a person upon whom an act of civility would be usefully bestowed." If anyone in America could command the respect of the British, Webster was that person.[17]

This glimmer of hope was desperately needed by the spring of 1841 because Anglo-American relations had deteriorated dangerously close to war. London newspapers daily focused on the growing troubles while the usually conciliatory Sir Robert Peel, soon to become prime minister, warned a cheering House of Commons that Britain might have to defend its honor by going to war. America's minister to Paris, Lewis Cass, told Webster of reliable sources who confirmed that McLeod's execution meant war. Indeed, war preparations were already under way on both sides of the Atlantic. Secretary of War John Bell made plans to defend the east coast, while Stevenson in London took the initiative by advising Commodore Isaac Hull in Marseilles to move the American naval squadron closer to home waters. The British government also took military measures. Stevenson notified Webster of a notice at Lloyd's of London, which invited bids for transporting troops to Canada.[18]

Webster was a Whig who believed in a strong national government and, accordingly, reversed the states' rights approach followed by the Van Buren administration. He believed that Forsyth had too readily agreed with the New York government's refusal to consider the *Caroline* assault a public act. Webster accepted the British argument that international law protected McLeod from liability for any action committed under government orders. But the secretary also realized that the American judicial system did not permit him to intervene in the New York court proceedings. His only hope was to move the case to the Supreme Court on a writ of habeas corpus, which would permit the high court to determine the legality of McLeod's imprisonment and doubtless free him on the basis of its international implications.[19]

Central to the McLeod case was the role of Governor Seward. On March 12, Fox formally avowed the *Caroline* attack and demanded McLeod's release, but New York authorities refused to budge. When Crittenden tried to move the case to the Supreme Court, Seward immediately blocked that effort. The attorney general then suggested that the governor pardon McLeod *before* a trial, but Seward vehemently opposed this idea as "ignoble submission" to the British. McLeod must stand trial in New York, the governor insisted. Seward felt fairly confident of acquittal; but even if the jury returned a verdict of guilty, he was prepared to overturn an execution. Five years afterward, Seward wrote a friend that, in a private meeting during the spring of 1841, he assured Crittenden, New York secretary of state John Spencer, and one other unidentified person that if the state court convicted McLeod, he as governor would "interpose [his] Constitutional power to prevent the sentence from being executed."[20]

Webster, however, sharply disputed this story, which suggests that there was a breakdown in communication between New York and Washington. In that same year of 1846, Webster (then a senator) told Congress that as for "the intimation of the Governor of

New York" that he would use his pardoning power to prevent an execution, the "entire detail is imaginary, and altogether destitute of foundation in fact." The truth probably lies somewhere in between. Seward most assuredly never promised anyone he would grant a pardon, but he doubtless implied such action by repeatedly declaring that he could do nothing until after the trial.[21] He thought McLeod entitled to a trial and that the evidence would find him innocent. But even if the jury ruled on emotion rather than reason, he could block an execution conducive to war.

The White House did not want to risk an outbreak of violence and had already dispatched General Winfield Scott to the frontier. For a third time, the Executive Office in Washington called on him to calm border unrest by the strength of his presence and not by military force. Scott arrived in Buffalo in late March and found the region fairly quiet. He nonetheless ordered a continuing patrol of the Niagara River and, in response to Fillmore's warnings of repeated threats on McLeod's life, ordered military officers from Detroit to Lake Champlain to prepare for trouble. Scott also convinced the owner of the *Caroline*, William Wells, to drop his damage claims against McLeod and thereby "disembarrass" the case.[22] Scott then performed one more task before returning to Washington. He stopped in Rochester to serve as a pallbearer in the funeral ceremony held in honor of President Harrison, who had died of pneumonia after a single month in office.

The new president was John Tyler of Virginia, who soon became so enmeshed in bitter political controversy that he found it difficult to attend to diplomatic affairs. Harrison was the first president to die in office, which raised questions not so much about the succession as who would wield the real power in Washington. Henry Clay assumed that as speaker of the House and self-anointed king of the Whig party, he would become the power behind the presidency. Tyler, however, staunchly disagreed with Clay and with Adams; the latter had disgustedly dismissed the legal heir to the Executive Office as only "acting president" until Americans could choose another candidate. Tyler's past political experiences contributed to the confusion. He had been a longtime Jacksonian Democrat until his break with Old Hickory in the 1830s over the nullification issue in South Carolina and the later Bank War. Tyler and other states' rightists then founded the Whig party, using it as their primary means of opposing Jackson. But that party soon moved away from Tyler's principles and toward the nationalist position of Clay and most other Whigs. Placed on the presidential ticket with

Harrison in 1840 to lend sectional balance, Tyler anticipated four uneventful years as vice president, spent mostly in his home near Williamsburg. Now that he was president, he was virtually a man without a party and would doubtless become, according to former Secretary of War Joel Poinsett, the "ready tool of Mr. Clay."[23]

John Tyler. From painting by Alonzo Chappel, in *National Portrait Gallery of Eminent Americans* (1862).

Tyler nevertheless courageously vetoed Clay's national bank bill, thus sending a strong message that he intended to run the country and provoking a mass exodus from the cabinet that left only Webster—who claimed that he wanted to complete the northeastern boundary negotiations already under way.[24] The secretary of state probably had set his sights on the presidency in 1844 and thought that he had a better chance to outmaneuver Clay from inside the cabinet; if so, this did not matter to Tyler. He welcomed Webster's offer to stay and prepared to deal with the ongoing problems with England.

Tyler immediately ran into difficulty over the McLeod affair. Even though Gardner and Bradley felt confident that an alibi would win their client's acquittal, they did not follow Webster's lead in trying to remove the case to the Supreme Court. The two attorneys, he concluded with disdain, were "men of no great force." Then, in an intriguing development, Joshua Spencer, a respected politician and attorney from Utica (who also was a friend of Webster's), became the head of McLeod's defense team. It remains unclear exactly how or when Spencer made this move, except that in late March, General Scott notified Seward of the addition.[25]

Events fitted so well afterward that they appear to have been more than coincidental. Not surprisingly, Webster denied having anything to do with Spencer's official entrance into the case. Even if so, he had in fact already introduced Spencer into the case, albeit on an informal level. In a personal note dated March 11 (sixteen days before Scott's letter), Webster explained that the president was "exceedingly anxious" for McLeod's safety and emphasized "the high importance of guarding McLeod from all possible danger—consequences of the most serious nature might follow if he should become the subject of popular violence, either by his friends or his foes." On later learning that Spencer led the defense, Webster wrote him a confidential missive on April 16 offering "to carry on with you, directly, any correspondence which may be necessary" to the case. Even more suggestive, just three days after this offer, Webster sent Spencer a commission as U.S. district attorney for the northern district of New York. Thus, Spencer represented both the federal government and a British citizen against the state of New York. Webster saw no problem with this convenient arrangement.[26]

Seward's suspicions about federal interference in New York were justified. The Tyler administration's intent to involve itself in a state matter had become clear with Crittenden's arrival in Albany and subsequent attempt to move the case to Washington. Failing that effort, Seward believed, the White House now planned to manipulate the trial by gaining control over McLeod's defense counsel. The president then infuriated Seward by following Webster's advice to appoint Spencer as federal district attorney. From the governor's vantage point, this last action constituted a pivotal step in a carefully orchestrated program designed to establish federal supremacy over the state. Spencer would serve as advocate for both the national government and McLeod. Seward called for Spencer to withdraw from the case and angrily denounced him for denigrating "himself and the government with a retainer so incongruous and offensive." Webster dismissed this challenge. "Little Seward," the secretary remarked, was "a contemptible fellow—& that is the end of it." Some observers suspected (and correctly so) that the British had paid Spencer's retainer, arousing speculation that the White House had entered into some sort of secret arrangement with the government in London.[27]

Spencer's appointment as district attorney could not have been more poorly timed. The White House probably regarded the move as a means of keeping close contact with the McLeod case during the trial and then, in the event of a guilty verdict, facilitating its transfer to the Supreme Court. Moreover, questionable as it may seem, it was standard behavior during the fast and loose politics of the Jacksonian era for state and national attorneys to pursue practices that were concurrent and often heavy with conflicts of interest. But the poorly disguised attempt by the federal government to intervene in state affairs incensed Seward and reinforced suspicions that the White House and British were in collusion. In a statement that only made matters worse, Tyler blandly assured Seward of no connection between the appointment and the case. The president declared that he had not directed Spencer to serve as McLeod's counsel and denied even any knowledge that the attorney had agreed to do so until just four days prior to the State Department's sending up the commission for the new position. Still, however, Tyler did nothing to cancel the appointment. Instead, he became angry with Seward's objections and curtly informed him that the federal government had the "right to resort to all constitutional and legitimate means within its power" to meet its international responsibilities. The state of New York had licensed Spencer to practice law in its courts. Surely the state's "great and magnanimous people," Tyler snidely remarked, would not refuse counsel to even the lowliest human being.[28]

Members of the House of Representatives joined Seward in blasting the administration. John Floyd of New York presented an insulting resolution, ultimately tabled, directing the president to reveal whether he had sent his attorney general to Albany as part of some private deal to free McLeod. The congressman also demanded an explanation for Scott's mission to the area. Democrat Charles Ingersoll of Pennsylvania, a longtime political and personal enemy of Webster's, denounced the White House's actions as unconstitutional and sneered that it was miraculous that the secretary had not attempted to defend "this English pet" before the Supreme Court with the British legation on hand to guarantee justice. Webster's cowardly behavior, Ingersoll proclaimed, had taken the nation to the brink of war.[29]

Antiadministration members of the Senate also got into the political ruckus and leveled their criticisms at Webster. Perhaps such strong-willed men will always attract equally strong opposition, but Webster had not made his position any easier by remaining in the Tyler administration and inviting charges of betrayal to his party. The list of accusations grew longer. Webster should not have tried to secure McLeod's release without first winning reparations for the *Caroline*. He violated the rights of New York by sending the attorney general to the state's capital. James Buchanan of Pennsylvania upheld his well-known reputation for Anglophobia by denouncing the British and maintaining that McLeod was answerable only to New York. When the head of the Senate Foreign Relations Committee, William Cabell Rives of Virginia, came to Webster's defense, Buchanan mockingly cited the poet who once said, "Two bodies with one soul inspired." President *Harrison*, he lamented, would not have cowered before British threats. The growing chorus of anti-Webster voices grew louder as South Carolina's John C. Calhoun insisted on reparations for the *Caroline* before McLeod's release. Missouri's Thomas Hart Benton proudly declared that Andrew Jackson in 1817 had not consulted "musty volumes" of international law before executing two British subjects in Spanish Florida for stirring up the Indians against Americans. Webster's maneuverings, Benton jeered, had set up an absurd courtroom confrontation between Governor Seward's attorney general leading the prosecution and President Tyler's district attorney heading the defense.[30]

While Congress debated the case, the New York supreme court handed the Tyler administration its first defeat in the matter: Judge

Esek Cowen refused to free McLeod on a writ of habeas corpus. On May 17 the state's attorney general, Willis Hall, appeared before the court in his capacity as leader of the prosecution. Familiar arguments rang through the courtroom chambers for three days as Hall insisted on the state's right to handle the case while Spencer countered that a public act placed McLeod outside the jurisdiction of any American court. At long last, on July 12, Cowen delivered his opinion. According to international law, he explained, a war between nations—a "public" war—could not exist without the "actual concurrence of the warmaking power." He saw "nothing in the case except a body of men, without color of authority, bearing muskets and doing the deed of arson and death." It was "impossible even for diplomatic ingenuity to make a case of legitimate war." Since neither England nor the United States had declared war in 1837, the *Caroline* assault occurred in peacetime. The British had no basis for claiming self-defense because the vessel posed no threat to Canada. Destruction of the *Caroline* was unjustified, and McLeod must stand trial. Cowen did grant Spencer's request for a change of venue for the trial, moving it from the tense Niagara region to Utica.[31]

Cowen's ruling aroused the ire of many observers. Several respected jurists in the United States did not agree with his decision, and the truth is that it was more in keeping with political considerations than international law. No scholarly authority on the subject—including Hugo Grotius, Samuel Pufendorf, and Emmerich de Vattel—had ever asserted that only national governments could instigate hostilities; certainly a military commander on the scene could create a warlike situation. Webster called the decision "hollow, false, & almost dishonest, from beginning to end," and asked his longtime friend and Supreme Court Justice Joseph Story to review it. "I never saw so much mere statement with so little reasoning," Story wrote in response. The ruling avoided the crucial issues in the case by focusing on "propositions of an exceedingly questionable nature & character." But the New York *Herald* probably expressed the majority's sentiments in praising Cowen's defense of the state's judiciary while warning that Fox would demand his passport and set off events leading to war. British newspapers denounced the judge's decision, but Stevenson assured the White House that its attempt to free McLeod had won the confidence of the Melbourne ministry. Fox felt sure that the president was trying to make the most of a difficult situation but was "hopelessly embarrassed."[32]

Webster, however, had realized from the beginning that the attempt to secure a writ of habeas corpus would probably fail and had already initiated a backup plan. Even while the New York supreme court was in session, he visited New York City and advised McLeod's attorneys to prepare an appeal on a writ of error. His only recourse now was to transfer the case to the U.S. Supreme Court, where he hoped to win McLeod's freedom on a *nolle prosequi*. Fox doubted that the strategy would work, and a judge in Washington declared that the president lacked the authority to order a *nolle prosequi* in criminal cases taken before a federal court. Webster's plan, however, was never tested. McLeod preferred a trial before a New York jury to sitting in jail while the case wound through the various steps of appeal. Only an acquittal, he told Spencer, would satisfy his enemies on both sides of the border. Besides, even if the jury returned a guilty verdict, he could still appeal to the Supreme Court.[33]

Leading figures in the British government had mixed reactions to the events in New York but seemed resigned to McLeod's going on trial. Palmerston had already drawn up a contingency war plan even as he assured Fox of his "entire confidence" in the "just intentions" of the Tyler administration. The foreign secretary was nonetheless justified in seeking McLeod's release, particularly since the United States had virtually branded the assault a public act by demanding reparations for the *Caroline*. The highly respected Duke of Wellington, who was a hero of the Napoleonic Wars, thought war with the United States "probable," but others counted on commercial links holding the nations together. The governor-general of Upper Canada put his finger on the problem. Lord Sydenham assured Russell in the Colonial Office that New York would ultimately free McLeod but shrewdly observed that he had to stand trial to satisfy the American "braggadocios" who would not be happy until they had "bullied" the British government.[34]

III

In the meantime, important changes occurred in the London government during the autumn of 1841 that offered hope for an amicable settlement of the McLeod case. Sir Robert Peel succeeded Melbourne as head of the ministry in September and selected Lord Aberdeen as foreign secretary. Gone was the circuitous type of

decisionmaking that had become the trademark of the past ministry, and in came a prime minister and foreign secretary already
known for their mild-mannered and conciliatory approach to both
domestic and foreign problems. Peel was a noted advocate of expanding commercial ties with the United States, and Aberdeen was
the archetypal diplomatist—scholarly and low key in temperament,
given to compromise, and a staunch supporter of peace. Both men
had seen war firsthand and knew there was no alternative to an
honorable peace. Neither man was outspokenly anti-American—as
was Palmerston. Further, Britain had fallen out of favor with the
French because of Palmerston's aggressive diplomacy. The new
ministry thus recognized that the resolution of its problems with
the United States was a prerequisite to putting pressure on the Paris
government to settle its differences with London. "Great times
ahead!" proclaimed the usually Anglophobic New York *Herald*:
"A new Cabinet in each country!" President Tyler expressed relief
that Palmerston was gone.[35]

All these changes, of course, meant little to McLeod unless they
translated into his acquittal. While politicians, diplomats, warriors,
and publicists discussed the finer points of war and international
law, he sat by himself in the Oneida County jail in Whitesboro,
waiting for his trial to begin in Utica, only four miles away. Authorities suspected that Patriots in the area meant to cause trouble
and that the Hunters' Lodges were scheming to drag the prisoner
from his cell and unceremoniously hang him. Meanwhile, yet another incident threatened Anglo-American peace: Canadian volunteers had invaded Vermont and seized an American, James Grogan,
who had allegedly committed arson in Canada. The newspapers
whipped up old animosities and warned that McLeod's execution
might result in the same punishment for Grogan. The Peel ministry
inquired into the wisdom of awarding reparations to the United
States, and soon thereafter Grogan was freed, with compensation.
But the incident made a fair trial for McLeod even more unlikely
and, at least according to the hotheads along the border, added more
justification for war.[36]

The atmosphere surrounding the impending trial took on the
air of a city under military occupation. Someone stole two cannon
from New York's arsenals, leading Governor Seward to assign
guards outside the jail and order the militia into readiness. General
Scott stationed Brigadier General John Wool and fifty troops in an
area close to Utica. Wool then secured approval from an Oneida
County judge to deploy a volunteer artillery company of a hundred

men into town during the trial. On the local level, the sheriff swore in thirty deputies to protect McLeod, and officials in Utica established a contingent of civilians authorized to keep order. Trouble seemed likely. William Mackenzie (pardoned by President Van Buren in April 1840 from an eighteen-month prison sentence) and other Canadian rebels had arrived in Utica, creating a stir of anticipation.[37]

The Peel ministry kept an anxious eye on these events taking place thousands of miles away. Like Melbourne, the new prime minister made contingency plans for war and soon instructed Aberdeen and other officials to bolster the national defense. From London, Christopher Hughes, who was America's minister to Sweden and Norway and a longtime acquaintance of Aberdeen's, notified Webster in mid-September that the foreign secretary regarded the McLeod affair as the "gravest matter" in Anglo-American relations because it involved national honor and, for that very reason, elicited "the deepest alarm and apprehension." On October 18, Peel met with his foreign secretary and other ministers to prepare for the "*possibility* of War" with the United States. Such preparations, he informed Wellington, included the dispatch of two additional ships to Gibraltar and one each to Halifax, Nova Scotia, and Bermuda, while several frigates and steamships were readied for operations in the Plymouth area. In a note marked "Most Private," Peel warned his secretary of state for the colonies that Bermuda would be the first area attacked by the United States. With good reason, Aberdeen repeated Palmerston's directive to Fox to leave the country if New York executed McLeod.[38]

The Tyler administration meanwhile worked against great odds in taking precautionary measures against war. In the event of an execution, the president made clear that he would deny Fox's request for a passport home in an effort to buy time for London's leaders to consider the matter more carefully. Aberdeen thought this approach "unusual and extraordinary" but conceded that it demonstrated "unequivocal proof" of the president's desire for peace. Peel, perhaps swayed by Tyler's action, admitted privately that even an execution did not make war automatic and told Queen Victoria that the White House should send a special minister to London with authority to make reparations. Tyler also explained that he intended to work toward a constitutional amendment aimed at preventing similar incidents. From the frontier, however, General Scott reported heightening tensions and declared that it was "time to look to the means of taking & holding the command of these Lakes." The recent arrival of two large British steamers at Chippewa (in violation of the Rush-Bagot Agreement of 1817) suggested an imminent assault on Buffalo. At least four more American steamers were needed to control Lake Erie, Scott warned.[39]

In the meantime, the president had replaced Stevenson in London with former Massachusetts governor and representative to Congress Edward Everett, who was now professor of Greek at Harvard, editor of the *North American Review*, and a friend of Webster's. Stevenson had alienated many of his British associates with his short temper and coarse behavior. In fact, Aberdeen had hesitated to grant the minister a final audience with the queen before vacating his position. Like Aberdeen, Everett was a scholar and a gentleman who was compatible with members of British society.[40]

While the international scene remained tense, the situation in New York had become surprisingly calm. The change of venue for the trial had shifted events from the restless Niagara frontier, and the presence of American soldiers provided a stern warning to anyone looking for trouble. Indeed, the sheriff had no difficulty in maintaining order in the town, encouraging Spencer to believe that the jury would be more open to the evidence presented and that he would prove his client's innocence. Also noteworthy was the choice of the presiding judge. Seward's first selection, Judge Samuel Nelson of the state's supreme court, had taken ill and could not serve; and his replacement was Judge Philo Gridley, who Spencer knew had no special feeling for the Patriots.[41] But probably more important than quieting the area was the state's unquestioned triumph. In holding the trial, New York had withstood the pressure of two national governments while humbling the British and gaining more credibility for the doctrine of states' rights. Whatever happened to McLeod during and after the trial had become anticlimactic to the victory already claimed by Anglophobes and others in New York who sought only to embarrass the British.

Just before ten o'clock on the morning of October 4, the guards escorted McLeod into the crowded courtroom and the long-awaited trial began. Seated before the accused were Gridley and four judges of the Oneida County court, and off to the side of the room was the twelve-member jury—nine farmers, two merchants, and a doctor, several of whom were opposed to capital punishment. Behind McLeod sat a number of newspaper correspondents and spectators, all dutifully warned that any disruptive behavior guaranteed ejection from the proceedings. McLeod settled haughtily into his chair as he felt the intense gaze of those in the courtroom, most of them seeing him for the first time. Close to fifty years of age and dressed in a black suit and blue cloak, he was a little taller than average, physically fit, with striking red hair and whiskers.[42] If this Canadian deputy sheriff was the British monster that so many Anglophobes had conjured up in their wildest imaginations, then surely the image was grossly exaggerated and their lives were not at risk.

As soon as the prosecution opened its case, the chances for McLeod's release noticeably increased. The state's attorney general, Willis Hall, theatrically labeled the *Caroline* episode the "blackest in the catalogue of crimes," but he undermined his own initial dramatic effect by reading Judge Cowen's July ruling in its entirety as part of an attempt to convince the jury that the federal government had no right to intervene in a state matter. McLeod had been the one to discover the *Caroline*'s activities, Hall declared, and had then raised support for destroying the vessel. Hall spun an imaginative tale that included a graphic description of the lurid massacre of those who had resisted the British invaders, followed by an account of those survivors of the assault who had emerged from below deck "after those ruffians had left the boat, only to meet the rushing flames, and to hear the roar of Niagara." On several occasions afterward, Hall bitterly asserted, the defendant had waved his pistol and still-bloodstained sword, defiantly proclaiming that the blood had come from a "damned Yankee."[43]

Numerous witnesses paraded to the stand, attesting that McLeod had participated in the *Caroline* affair. Captain Appleby assumed that McLeod had been the felon to strike him with a sword, and a resident of Chippewa declared that he was standing ashore while the boat burned when he overheard the accused remark that people were still on board and that only the sentry had been armed. Was Appleby positive that McLeod was the assailant? asked Spencer. No, conceded Appleby: "The transaction was done in a twinkling; I did not mark the features of the man at that time; it was only a supposition of mine. I do not now say it was McLeod." To the second witness, Spencer asked how could he be sure in the dead of night that it was McLeod speaking? The witness explained that even though McLeod stood more than ten feet away and faced the opposite direction, he was recognizable by his voice and a flickering light from a window. Another witness swore that on the day of the *Caroline* assault, December 29, 1837, he saw McLeod with Captain Andrew Drew, leader of the attack, in the back room of a tavern in Chippewa. The morning after the vessel's destruction, according to the witness, McLeod boasted to a crowd that he had killed at least one Yankee. Still another witness testified that he believed it was McLeod boarding one of the craft heading for Fort Schlosser, even though he admitted that the night was black and the defendant stood more than ten feet away, in the shadows of willow trees. Then came the most dramatic testimony. A fifth witness reported that ten days after the *Caroline*'s destruction, McLeod was in a crowded bar in Niagara, Canada, when someone yelled above the noise, "Where is the man that shot Amos Durfee?" To this, McLeod shouted back, "By God, I'm the one!"; and he pulled out his pistol while drawing his sword with six inches of dried blood on the blade. "There's the blood of a damned Yankee," McLeod proudly proclaimed. "Human blood so carefully hoarded," Bradley sneered.[44]

The defense had little trouble poking holes in the prosecution's case. Spencer undermined the witnesses' credibility by showing that several of them had taken part in the rebellions against the crown and had connived to get McLeod. Some of the witnesses were members of the notorious Hunters' Lodges, one was well known for selling his testimony to anyone willing to pay (a "miserable idiot," according to Bradley), while another had earlier been charged with perjury by Judge Gridley himself. Many of the accusers admitted to hating McLeod and, when pressed, could not give the names of others present when he allegedly bragged of his part in the attack. Another weak spot in the prosecution's case was the amazing resemblance between McLeod and his brother Angus, who *had* been involved in the *Caroline* affair. The defense also noted the peculiar similarity in the wording of McLeod's alleged boast; although several heard him make the claim in different places, he always used the same words. There was more than a little truth to Bradley's bitter claim that the witnesses for the prosecution were "nothing but the collected idleness, vice, and profligacy of the border."[45]

Spencer's defense team now presented its case. Depositions from Drew and Colonel Allan MacNab, the British militia commander at Chippewa at the time of the incident, denied that McLeod had been among the volunteers. Confirmation of this claim came from a British naval officer seriously wounded in the fracas. The defense then showed that many involved in the *Caroline* attack could not remember McLeod's participation. Was not this a vital point since the prosecution had virtually called him the chief perpetrator of the assault? Then came the most wrenching moment in the trial.

Four witnesses—a retired British army colonel named John Morrison, his wife, son, and daughter—all swore that McLeod spent the night of December 29 in their home nearly four miles from Chippewa. Hall labeled Morrison's testimony worthless because of McLeod's "too successful influence" over the family. Another member of the prosecution, Seth Hawley, tried to explain that Morrison's daughter Ellen had left her husband in Buffalo and now lived in an adulterous relationship with McLeod. But Judge Gridley interrupted this line of questioning by declaring that it "had not more to do with this case than the history of the Egyptians." Instead of undermining the testimony, the prosecution had alienated the judge and probably the jury, and had inadvertently validated McLeod's alibi. If a father, a respected and retired British officer, was willing to admit publicly that his daughter shared her bed with McLeod, who in the jury could doubt this as the truth?[46]

The outcome was predictable. After eight days of testimony that droned on for ten to twelve hours per day, Gridley charged the jury (in two hours of instructions) with the responsibility of determining only the "ordinary charge of murder" and reminded its members that if they had any reasonable doubt, the accused must go free. The jury returned in less than a half hour with a verdict of not guilty. McLeod, who had not uttered a word throughout the proceedings, maintained his silence and left the courtroom.[47]

One final note remains. For safety reasons, the story was circulated that McLeod intended to book passage to England. Indeed, his name soon appeared on the passenger list for the *Arcadia* steaming out of New York City for Liverpool. It was all a ploy. Four days after the trial, a county sheriff escorted McLeod to Lake Champlain, where he boarded a steamer into Canada and later received a warm welcome in Montreal.[48]

A postmortem analysis of these courtroom events reveals several interesting aspects about the entire episode. Despite the widespread fear of violence, nothing of the sort occurred. The truth is that most Americans in the Niagara area felt satisfied that the trial of McLeod had sufficiently humbled the British. Anyone wanting to cause trouble would have confronted the military arm of the U.S. government along with the force amassed by state and local law officials. That the initial popular excitement over the trial waned so quickly furnished further evidence of the lack of local concern about what happened to McLeod himself. In fact, the reading of countless long and detailed depositions took its toll not only on the visitors but the jury as well. According to the court stenographer, the jurors became so drowsy at one point that they took on the appearance of twelve convicts sentenced to death, "broken down in mind and body."[49] Certainly this was no longer an atmosphere suggesting that war hung in the balance.

Suspicion lingered that the federal and state governments had colluded to guarantee McLeod's acquittal. The ever suspicious Fox reported a "shameful and atrocious" deal: if the jury had returned a verdict of guilty, Seward would have blocked an execution until the federal government secured British reparations for the *Caroline.* Minister Fox also declared that at least two persons had planned to testify that they had seen McLeod shoot Durfee, but that state and federal officials had kept them from the trial. By May of that year, rumors about this allegation had become so rampant that Seward had to assure the state assembly that there was no truth to the story.[50]

The evidence does not suggest any specific arrangement between New York and Washington, but it is safe to say that if the jury had found McLeod guilty, both state and federal authorities would have resisted an execution. Evidence strongly suggests that Seward, despite Webster's claims, had virtually guaranteed a pardon. Moreover, the White House could have filed a series of appeals that would have taken the case to higher courts and ultimately to the Supreme Court. There, McLeod could have won his release on a writ of habeas corpus based on Britain's assumption of responsibility for the *Caroline*'s destruction. If even that approach did not work, the government in Washington would surely have used force to halt a parody of justice that threatened to cause war with England.

Five years afterward, in 1846, Democrats in Congress accused Webster of federal interference with the trial. His longtime enemy, Charles Ingersoll, was now chairman of the House Committee on Foreign Affairs, and he had joined Democratic Senator Daniel Dickinson of New York in accusing the White House of violating the state's rights by attempting to prevent the trial and then using government funds to pay Spencer's fee of $5,000. According to the charge, Webster had warned Seward that if he did not release McLeod, New York City would be "laid in ashes" by the British. But neither Ingersoll nor Dickinson could meet Webster's challenge to present evidence for their allegations. The British, in fact, had paid Spencer's fee.[51]

A recurrence of such case seemed unlikely after December 1841, because President Tyler kept his word in pushing Congress to enact legislation authorizing the federal government to transfer cases out of state courts that affected the country's international responsibilities. In August 1842, Congress passed the Remedial Justice Act, which permitted federal judges to issue writs of habeas corpus in moving foreign relations matters from state courts. The law also recognized the validity of "public acts" by directing the release of aliens held for actions committed under orders from their government.[52]

McLeod never received adequate reparations for his lengthy ordeal. The Peel ministry agreed with his claim that the United States owed compensation, but in the interests of Anglo-American harmony it did not wish to embarrass the Tyler administration by lodging a "premature demand." Neither the White House nor the government in London pressed the matter, leading McLeod to act on his own. He filed suit against the state of New York for eleven months of false imprisonment but lost; and he later requested compensation from the government in Canada, where he found at least some support. In 1845 a committee in the Ottawa legislature called on the government in London to consider the matter, and it ultimately awarded him an annual pension of £200. McLeod did not think the amount sufficient and in late 1854 took his grievance before an Anglo-American claims commission. Its members deadlocked, and the umpire rejected the claim because "the entire matter had been ended as a subject of international discussion."[53]

The McLeod case provided enough of a war scare to drive the two Atlantic nations to the negotiating table. Fortunately, Peel and Aberdeen had replaced Melbourne and Palmerston, because the new ministry seemed determined to grant America the international respect it had long demanded. It is difficult to find any instance in history in which two nations managed to avoid war after experiencing events as explosive as the *Caroline* and McLeod affairs. National honor on both sides had undergone severe tests that found the British satisfying their pride by destroying the *Caroline* and the Americans evening the score by bringing McLeod to trial. The real issue, however, ran deeper than the actual events of 1837 to 1841. The maintenance of good Anglo-American relations depended on each nation respecting the other's honor.

McLeod's acquittal, however, had only momentarily assuaged the Atlantic nations, because the Tyler administration quickly found itself confronting an entirely different set of challenges that again raised the banner of national honor and once more caused leaders on both sides of the Atlantic to consider war. The twin issues of

CHAPTER FOUR

Honor at Sea or Slavery at Home? The African Slave Trade, Right of Search, and the Creole Mutiny

Southerners "had taken the alarm lest this concert between the United States and Great Britain for suppressing the slave-trade should turn to a concert for the abolition of slavery."
—John Quincy Adams, 1824

As Daniel Webster and Lord Ashburton pondered the recurring problems along the U.S.-Canadian border, they realized that slavery, too, had become a contentious issue within Anglo-American relations. The two countries had first focused on the matter in November 1841, when slaves mutinied on board the American brig *Creole*, which was engaged (legally) in the interstate slave trade down the Atlantic coast, and were then granted freedom after steering the vessel into the British Bahamas. As in the McLeod affair, Webster had been directly involved as secretary of state and heard the ugly talk of war. Until this time the South had demonstrated only a passing interest in the Anglo-American troubles to the far north; but as slavery became an issue both inside and outside the United States, the South became alarmed that the British would try to eliminate the institution. The crown's Emancipation Act of 1833 had abolished slavery throughout the empire, and the British had long been urging the United States to join them and other nations in suppressing the African slave trade. Was not the attempt to end this practice the first step toward destroying slavery itself? Thus did slavery have such an impact on America's foreign policy that Webster and Ashburton had to deal with it as a matter of international concern.

I

Anglo-American controversies over slavery had smoldered for years without reaching the point of crisis. Since 1808 the British government had sought the cooperation of the United States and other nations in ending the African slave trade. The Founding Fathers had decreed in 1787 that, after a twenty-year period, Congress was free to take measures to suppress the human traffic; but southern opposition based on racial considerations and the rising profitability of slavery itself had successfully defeated every meaningful move in that direction. The resulting legislation prohibited the further importation of Africans into the United States but made no serious effort to end the origins of that trade.[1]

Following the War of 1812, the British government launched a campaign intended to shut down the African slave trade that seemed to interest the United States. Article 10 of the Treaty of Ghent of 1815 permitted both nations to "use their best endeavors to accomplish" the "entire abolition" of the trade, but Americans expressed concern that stopping and boarding vessels suspected of engaging in the practice would lead to maritime abuses similar to those that had contributed to the recent war with England. At the Conference of Aix-la-Chapelle (or Aachen) in 1818, Foreign Secretary Lord Castlereagh convinced European leaders to approve mutual search in peacetime. Both he and his successor in the early 1820s, George Canning, urged the United States to join this arrangement. But Americans repeatedly declined the offer in favor of a different tactic. Congress had outlawed the African slave trade, even passing a law in 1820 that branded the business as piracy and thus a capital offense punishable by death. Enforcement of this severe measure proved so lax that it was not until the Civil War that anyone found guilty of the practice was executed.[2]

The problems were clear: international law did not bind other nations to the antislave-trade pacts negotiated by Britain, and Americans did not trust the British enough to permit them to search any suspected slave vessel flying the Stars and Stripes. Committees in the House of Representatives in 1821 and 1822 nonetheless called for a reciprocal search policy with the British, but with no success. Secretary of State John Quincy Adams, although hating the slave trade, distrusted the British and proposed an alternative: a joint cruising plan resting on the spirit of cooperation. He instructed the American minister to London, Richard Rush, to negotiate a pact whereby the British likewise defined the practice as piracy under international law and thereby made enforcement acceptable in peacetime. Rush secured the Convention of 1824 with England, which authorized mutual search of vessels suspected of engaging in the slave trade. But memories of impressment and bitter political feelings toward Adams led the Senate to exclude North American waters from the pact's jurisdiction, and the convention never went into effect because of British opposition.[3]

American resistance to a mutual search policy with the British rested on a mixture of motives, not the least of which was the South's concern about protecting slavery. To be sure, more than a few Americans feared that the right of search endangered the national honor and maritime rights so recently won by the War of 1812. Outspoken northerners such as Democratic Senator Lewis Cass of Michigan joined the South in vehemently opposing British search of American vessels as a galling reminder of impressment. Americans found it difficult to believe the British assertion that practical considerations made impressment a nonissue: desertions from the Royal Navy had sharply diminished in the aftermath of improved conditions, impressment did not exist in peacetime, and no law could halt the practice during war. And surely, one might add to the British case, the visit-and-search of a suspected slaver posed no threat to America's independence. The real issue to most southerners was British interference with slavery itself.

Abolition of slavery in the British Empire during the early 1830s made it the acknowledged leader of the world antislavery movement. By the latter part of the decade, its warships stopped vessels off the African coast that flew the American flag, which led Secretary of State John Forsyth of Georgia and the U.S. minister to London, Andrew Stevenson of Virginia (both slaveholders), to protest these actions as interference in America's rights at sea. Shortly after his appointment to the State Department in 1834, Forsyth rejected a British offer to join their government and that of France in a treaty to suppress the slave trade. Such a pact, he declared, would violate his nation's maritime rights and lead to commercial delays. But Adams in 1824 had already summed up the real concern of the South when, in speaking of the failed convention of that year, he declared that slaveowners "had taken the alarm lest this concert between the United States and Great Britain for suppressing the slave-trade should turn to a concert for the abolition of slavery."[4]

By 1840 the United States was the only important seafaring nation that had refused to join any form of treaty arrangement aimed at suppressing the slave trade. Britain meanwhile continued to work toward that objective by cooperating with several European and Latin American nations. As a consequence, its vessels patrolled great parts of the western coast of Africa and stationed blockades at the mouths of major rivers. In earlier days, before Britain signed antislave-trade conventions with France, Spain, and Portugal, their flags had safeguarded slavers. Now, with the United States refusing to participate, slave traders flew the American flag to ward off a search. Indeed, the governor of Liberia indignantly declared that "the *American* flag" was the "chief obstacle" to Britain's efforts to suppress the African slave trade: "Never was the proud banner of freedom so extensively used by those pirates upon liberty and humanity as at this season." But when the British minister in Washington had asked Adams some years before if he knew of anything more horrible than the slave trade, even he, a staunch opponent of slavery, arched his back and replied: "Yes, admitting the right of search by foreign officers of our vessels upon the seas in time of peace; for that would be making slaves of ourselves."[5] The South had acquired unusual allies in northerners such as Adams and Cass who disliked slavery but were even more concerned about Britain's violating America's honor at sea.

British attempts to eradicate the slave trade could not succeed as long as slavers claimed protection under the American flag. Whether a slave ship's origin was Brazil, Portugal, or Spain, it could fly the Stars and Stripes and even carry an American citizen as its alleged captain. A British antislave-trade cruiser could stop a suspected slaver on its voyage to Africa, but all the "captain" had to do was present his so-called American papers to prevent a search. When a slaver fraudulently flying the American flag entered African waters and loaded its human cargo, it lowered that flag and hoisted its own. The captain's reasoning was practical. If a British cruiser seized the slaver, its admiralty courts would condemn the vessel and sell it; but if an American patrol captured a loaded slaver under an American flag, the courts could prosecute the captain and crew as pirates and order their execution.[6]

Some Americans on the African slave-trade scene believed that mutual search presented the only means for halting the practice. Lieutenant John Paine, commander of the American schooner *Grampus*, patrolled the African coast and frequently saw slavers from other nations abuse his country's flag. Exasperated by the situation, he acted on his own. At Sierra Leone in March 1840, Paine signed an agreement with Commander William Tucker of the

British *Wolverine* permitting mutual search to stop the traffic. If the vessel were of American origin and engaged in the business, it fell under the jurisdiction of the American cruiser captain; if not American, the British captain took control. Before news of the agreement reached Washington, Palmerston cited the pact as justification for seizing the American vessels *Iago* and *Douglas*. In yet another instance, that involving the *Tigris*, the circuit court in Massachusetts found no basis for suspicion; reparations followed when the British commander admitted to having had no orders to stop American ships. The U.S. government, upon receiving word of this unauthorized bilateral arrangement, immediately disavowed the move.[7]

In a futile attempt to attract American support for the antislave-trade patrols, the British government tried to distinguish between a "visit" and a "search." Palmerston insisted that his naval officers had to examine a ship's papers because of the widespread illicit practice of flying the U.S. flag. Such a process, he declared, constituted only a visit; a search entailed an examination of the cargo as well. This argument did not convince Stevenson. The American minister to London saw no distinction between a visit and a search and denounced the entire claim as unacceptable. When Palmerston stepped down as foreign secretary in September 1841, his successor, Lord Aberdeen, quickly received a lengthy defense of America's opposition to mutual search that took on the appearance of a lawyer's brief. Violations of municipal law, Stevenson argued, were punishable only in the country of the law's origin; consequently, Britain had no right to enforce either treaties or domestic laws against the United States, whether by visit, search, or mere detention. Any such effort to inspect American papers during peacetime constituted "national degradation."[8]

Although Aberdeen suspected that the Virginia slaveholder feared more for slavery than for national honor, he did everything he could to ease American concerns over British intentions. The right to visit, Aberdeen argued, was essential to suppressing the slave trade. Britain's people joined him in demanding an end to the African slave trade; the only way to encourage its demise was to allow British officers to board American ships and inspect their papers and cargo—particularly in view of the extensive misuse of the U.S. flag. The new prime minister, Sir Robert Peel, sought some approach that made British actions "clearly defensible" by international law and hence a preventative to war. Toward that end,

Aberdeen proposed compensation commensurate with damage if the visit determined that the vessel was truly American.[9]

Aberdeen's idea of reparations offered the only British palliative to any wrongs that occurred. John Croker, a former first lord of the Admiralty, assured Peel that his government was correct in claiming the right of visit but admitted that reparations for injury during the process would assuage American fears. The prime minister saw no alternative. Inspection of a ship's papers did not guarantee a cargo free of slaves; but if the naval forces examined the cargo as well, the boarding became a search and therefore anathema to Americans. Thus, Peel recommended a risky approach: direct each commander to exercise utmost care in stopping suspected slavers, and produce a detailed record of every seizure. Perhaps such extended paperwork would discourage rash action leading to reparations—or so he hoped. The tedious thought invested in British efforts to keep the antislave-trade provisions alive strongly suggests that the government in London did not seek either to infringe upon American honor or to gain undue commercial advantage; its sole purpose was to stop the African slave trade.[10]

The British then engaged in an even more ambitious effort to close the traffic: they sought to establish an international organization that opposed the practice and exerted pressure on the United States to join. In late 1841, Aberdeen hosted a meeting in London that aimed at legalizing the mutual right of search in halting the business. The conference produced the Quintuple Treaty of December, which drew the signatures of Austria, Britain, France, Prussia, and Russia, and termed the slave trade piracy, punishment for which would be assigned to the country of the perpetrator's origin. Aberdeen triumphantly called it a "Holy Alliance" and invited the United States to join other Christian nations in suppressing the traffic in human beings. If the government in Washington refused, he warned, the signatory nations were prepared to visit any alleged slaver, regardless of its colors. Spokesmen in Washington protested that no government had ever claimed the right of visit in peacetime. Aberdeen disagreed. In the Gulf of Mexico, he pointed out, U.S. commanders themselves had boarded vessels, regardless of the flag flown overhead.[11]

The new minister to London, Edward Everett, proposed a way to satisfy his own antislavery sentiment while establishing American trust in British motives. He recommended that Aberdeen provide indemnification for past seizures of U.S. ships. Such a move,

Edward Everett. From painting by Alonzo Chappel, in *National Portrait Gallery of Eminent Americans* (1862).

Everett reasoned, might calm American fears, demonstrate the sincerity of Aberdeen's expressed interest in good relations with the United States, and perhaps convince the White House to sign the treaty. Aberdeen agreed to the proposal.[12]

For a fleeting moment Everett's recommendation seemed to offer a chance for success. Emphasizing Aberdeen's conciliatory approach, Everett suggested to Secretary of State Webster, who also was moderately antislavery, that the United States join the Quintuple Treaty. Might this move encourage Britain, in exchange for America's signature, to renounce impressment and restrict inspection of U.S. vessels to African waters? Such an arrangement, Everett believed, would protect the nation's honor while undermining the slave trade. But President Tyler, a slaveowner from Virginia who nonetheless disliked the traffic in Africans, expressed concern about provoking isolationists, Anglophobes, and slaveholders, and he rejected Everett's proposal. Later, when France in February 1842 decided not to ratify the treaty, Everett again pushed for U.S. participation. France's refusal to join the pact, he argued, provided the White House with an excellent opportunity to exploit Britain's troubles with the government in Paris to seek assurances against impressment. Again, however, the Tyler administration showed no interest.[13]

The search issue became an even greater focal point of Anglo-American controversy due to the efforts of Lewis Cass. Then minister to Paris, the rotund former senator from Michigan—the Michigander, as colleague Jefferson Davis of Mississippi labeled him—assumed some sort of paternal interest in relations between the Atlantic nations. Although having no authorization from Washington, he injected himself into the search question with Britain— either to satisfy his deep animosity toward that country or, as an incisive British observer believed, to attract Democratic support by using the problems with England as a "Stepping Stone to the Presidential Chair." Whatever the truth, and probably it was a mixture of Anglophobia and political self-interest, Cass's unauthorized involvement in the search controversy placed Tyler in the unenviable position of either condoning his minister's inflammatory statements or, in opposing him, leaving the impression that he did so for political reasons.[14]

Cass's public stand on the African slave-trade issue further encouraged a White House confrontation with the British over the search controversy. During the debate over the Quintuple Treaty, he anonymously published a pamphlet entitled *An Examination of the Question Now in Discussion between the American & British Governments, Concerning the Right of Search*. His identity did not remain secret for long; when asked about it, he did not deny authorship. The essay first appeared in French, published in Paris in February 1842, but it was soon reproduced in English and German and quickly won widespread circulation throughout Europe and the United States. Its message whipped up Anglophobia in both the northern and southern sections of the country.[15]

Cass's pamphlet constituted a clear challenge to Britain's supremacy at sea. The Quintuple Treaty, he warned, would further enhance the British maritime position by permitting the Royal Navy to conduct most searches. Who gave that country the right, he indignantly asked, to be the "great Prefect of police of the Ocean"? Cass did not object to a British captain's boarding a vessel that he suspected of illegally flying the American flag. But the visit, he proclaimed, constituted a *privilege* granted by the United States and not a *right* asserted by Britain. Whether or not an injury ensued in the search process, the London government must make reparations—thereby acknowledging its infringement of American rights at sea. The United States, Cass stressed, could not admit to an absolute British right to search its vessels; such admission condoned violations of the nation's maritime honor and legitimized the principle behind impressment.[16]

The Tyler administration recognized the domestic political ramifications of Cass's pamphlet and reacted to it with considerable uncertainty. Cass assured Webster that the pamphlet had drawn great support from European leaders and thereby undermined French interest in the treaty. The president soon publicly approved Cass's actions, and Webster lauded the "respectable" work done by his minister in Paris. But after the initial praise, the secretary of state upbraided Cass for interfering in Anglo-American relations. Indeed, correspondence between the men turned so bitter that when the administration failed to win British renunciation of the right of search, Cass angrily resigned his position in Paris and openly rebuked the White House for the failure.[17]

Everett in London had meanwhile become incensed over Cass's interference in Anglo-American affairs. Such uninvited involvement, he warned Webster, hindered the ongoing negotiations between the nations. Cass had put the White House in an untenable position. If France rejected the treaty, the United States would receive the blame; if France signed the pact over the protests of the American minister, U.S. prestige would sustain a serious blow. Everett believed that Cass's motives were purely political. While a member of President Jackson's cabinet, Cass had expressed no opposition to the Anglo-French treaties of the early 1830s that approved the right of search. It was wrong, Everett charged, to "electioneer" on questions of peace and war with Britain.[18]

Cass deservedly claimed credit for France's ultimate refusal to sign the Quintuple Treaty. Foreign Minister François P. G. Guizot

Lewis Cass. From painting by Alonzo Chappel, in *National Portrait Gallery of Eminent Americans* (1862).

and the Chamber of Deputies had decided—even before Cass's pamphlet appeared—to reject the treaty. Members of the Chamber had long been upset with the Melbourne ministry in London for drawing the treaty without consulting the government in Paris. Aberdeen's unilateral efforts to promote the pact further incensed the French. They also opposed Britain's efforts to suppress the African slave trade—especially when Royal Navy officers expected to search French vessels. Even more important, Britain's recent successes over the French in the Near East revived their longtime animosity and led Aberdeen to reshape his nation's foreign policy toward improving relations with both the French and the Americans. As part of this effort, Aberdeen sought to placate the United States and thereby pressure the French into becoming more amenable to British wishes. Guizot had acted out of his own country's interests, but he was shrewd enough to allow Cass to think that he had been instrumental in the French decision to oppose the treaty. France distrusted Britain and was not averse to using Aberdeen's own strategy of trying to play off one country against the other.[19]

The African slave-trade issue angered many Americans, and yet it never reached a crisis stage. For one reason, many Americans felt little concern about slavery and did not see how the commerce in slaves related to them. Another consideration is that, despite the excitement, British antislave-trade patrols actually stopped only a small number of vessels flying the American flag. And even on those rare occasions, news of their occurrence did not reach the United States until weeks afterward. In addition, antislavery groups did not want to encourage the slave trade by resisting the British claim to search. Further, abolitionists in the United States had aroused little support for their cause and could not attract much interest in something so distant as the African slave trade. As for those Americans engaged in the illicit practice, they could lodge no protests against the British; to do so would be an admission of piracy, punishable by death. Thus, the arguments over the African slave trade continually irritated Anglo-American relations but did not produce a serious breach.[20]

II

Although Anglo-American controversies over slavery continued throughout this sensitive period, no single event had yet brought focus to this provocative issue. This situation changed dramatically in late 1841, when slaves mutinied on board the *Creole*, as it passed south along the Atlantic coast in the legitimate pursuit of the domestic slave trade. After British officers in the Bahamas freed the mutineers, the African slave-trade issue and the *Creole* slave revolt became entangled with each other, provoking heated demands from both North and South that the British either respect national honor or risk a confrontation over slavery itself.[21]

The eruption of slavery as an issue in Anglo-American relations must have surprised most contemporary observers. Before 1841 the South had expressed little interest in the border crises in the North. Cotton had provided the basis for close economic ties with Britain—so much so that the South had developed a special relationship with the mother country that was seemingly capable of surviving almost any strain. But southerners had not forgotten British infringements on American honor that provoked the War of 1812. Particularly galling had been the practice of impressment— defined by the British as the right to capture deserters from the Royal Navy but denounced by Americans as kidnapping. Americans before 1812 had upheld freedom of the seas as essential to national honor and, failing to win this admission, went to war. Suddenly now, in late 1841, the British had apparently returned to their old imperial ways of dictating the world's maritime lanes, even to the point of expunging the African slave trade as a poorly masked first step toward abolishing the institution of slavery.

It is difficult to determine the sincerity of the South's defense of maritime honor, so closely was it tied to the security of slavery. But by the end of the 1830s that section of the country had come under heavy attack for slavery and had therefore developed an elaborate defense of that institution which rested on several sources, including the Bible and squelching any incendiary talk about the subject. During the early part of that decade, South Carolina had threatened to nullify a high tariff law passed by Congress as an act of oppression by the North. It is clear now, however, that the state's major concern was to block a precedent establishing federal supremacy over the states that might eventually grow into an outright attack on slavery.[22] If slaves realized that mutinies and other rebellions ultimately led to a freedom sanctified by Britain, the impetus to black insurrection could endanger the entire South.

Even though the *Creole* mutiny and ensuing events had enormous impact on domestic politics and the sanctity of slavery, they more importantly raised questions of national honor that defined the entire scope of relations between the Atlantic countries. As if a preview of the torrid events that eventually catapulted the Republic into civil war, the *Creole* case aroused all those arguments pertaining to slavery that thundered across the American political landscape in the tumultuous 1850s. Most important for this study, the *Creole* slave revolt raised cries among southerners and other Americans for a third war with England that might, at long last, ensure British respect.

The details of the *Creole* mutiny comprise a fascinating story that could stand on its own as pure adventure. The vessel had departed Hampton Roads, Virginia, for New Orleans in October 1841. Manned by a crew of ten, it carried a cargo of tobacco, eight black servants, 135 slaves (one-third of them female), and seven white passengers—the captain's wife and two children (daughter and niece), along with four men in charge of the slaves, one of whom was the nephew of Thomas McCargo, who owned twenty-six of the slaves aboard. For almost eleven days the brig wound its way down the Atlantic coast until, during the evening hours of November 7, it dropped anchor to prepare for docking at nearby Abaco Island in the Bahamas the following morning. Around 9:30 that night, one of the slaves on deck, Elijah Morris, informed the first mate, Zephaniah Gifford, that a male slave was in the hold with the females—a violation of regulations that required a whipping. After Gifford called William Merritt, the white overseer, the two men went to the main hatchway, where Merritt remained while Gifford fetched a lamp and matches. They then lifted the heavy grate, allowing Merritt to enter the dark hold and light the lantern.

After a brief search, he found Madison Washington, the muscular twenty-two-year-old head cook of the slaves who had earlier escaped into Canada and was only recently recaptured in Virginia after returning for his wife. "You are the last person I should expect to find here, and that would disobey the orders of the ship," declared Merritt with surprise. "Yes, sir, it is me," Washington replied as he suddenly broke toward the ladder. Merritt tried to grab him by the leg as he climbed toward the hatch, but with the lamp in one hand he lost his grip and Washington made it up the ladder. On reaching the deck, he shoved Gifford, nearly knocking him into the hold. At that point another slave fired a pistol, its ball grazing the back of Gifford's head as he fell. Regaining his feet, Gifford stumbled toward the cabin to warn the others of the mutiny. As if the shot were a signal, Washington called out to other slaves on deck: "Come on, my boys, we have commenced; we must go through with it!" To the slaves in the hold below, he yelled, "Come up, every damned one of you; if you don't and lend a hand, I will kill you all and throw you overboard!"[23]

Merritt had meanwhile heard the ruckus and, after blowing out the light, headed up the ladder where he emerged onto the faintly lit deck to encounter two blacks. One grabbed him as the other swung a piece of wood at Merritt that barely missed and hit the other black, knocking him to the floor. "Kill him, by God," yelled one of them as Merritt escaped into the cabin and through the corridor to join Gifford in alerting the others. "There's a mutiny on deck," Gifford panted to Captain Robert Ensor, still lying half asleep on the cabin floor. "I am shot." Second mate Lucius Stevens came out of his stateroom to see a large number of blacks near the cabin door, hovering around the skylights above the quarterdeck and armed with a pistol, knives, and handspikes. "Kill them!", one exclaimed. "When they come up, kill the damn Captain. Kill the damn sons of bitches!"[24]

Only eighteen responded to Washington's cry, but the timing of the revolt proved opportune. Most of the crew and all the passengers were asleep when it began, suggesting a well-fashioned plan. Further, the outbreak of such violence on domestic slave vessels had been so rare that those in charge had taken few precautionary measures. Consequently, the nineteen mutineers—led by Washington, Morris, Ben Johnstone (or Blacksmith), and Doctor Ruffin— had easily armed themselves with every kind of weapon available on the ship and now stood menacingly at the cabin door, waiting for the whites to come out.[25]

John Hewell, who was on board as representative of the slave-trading firm of McCargo and Son, joined the captain in a frantic search for a gun. Hewell found a musket in Stevens's stateroom and, waving it at four blacks who had descended into the corridor, fiercely warned them to move back. When they retreated up the ladder, he likewise proceeded to the deck where he immediately got into a scuffle with them and others. Whipping the barrel toward them, he pulled the trigger. To his shock, the gun was not loaded. Realizing that the click had discharged only powder, several blacks closed in on Hewell, tearing the musket away and threatening to kill him. At that point he grabbed a handspike, which in the dark appeared to be another gun, and momentarily drove back his attackers.[26]

In the meantime, Ensor had brandished his bowie knife and joined Hewell in the standoff. The blacks charged the two men, stabbing the captain several times and knocking Hewell to the deck. As Ensor managed to climb toward the maintop, Johnstone retrieved Ensor's knife and thrust it repeatedly into Hewell's chest. Bleeding profusely, Hewell cried out, "I am stabbed and believe I am dying," and staggered back down into the cabin, where he collapsed in a berth and died shortly afterward.[27]

The mutineers meanwhile went after the other whites. "Kill every white person on board," one black yelled; "don't spare one!" Another shouted, "The captain, the mate, and Hewell are all dead, and now we'll have that long, tall son-of-a-bitch the second mate." As a group of blacks gathered at the door of the cabin, three others searched the starboard staterooms for Stevens. They found instead the captain's wife huddled with the two children, trembling in a corner of the tiny room. "We will not hurt you," Morris assured Mrs. Ensor as she begged for mercy. "But the damned Captain and mate we will have, by God. Merritt shan't live. Merritt shan't live, by God." Another black agreed: "We want the second mate, when the brig will then be ours." Not long afterward, they found Stevens. Four blacks burst into the room, one carrying a gun, which he thrust into Stevens's chest and prepared to fire. But Stevens shoved the muzzle aside, sending the ball into one of the blacks at the door and crumpling him to his knees. In the confusion, Stevens slipped by his assailants and ran up to the deck, narrowly escaping a blow from a knife and wildly looking for a place to hide.[28]

By 1 A.M. the situation had calmed as Washington and the other mutineers secured control of the *Creole*. After taking what they wanted from the provisions below, they dragged Hewell's body (which someone had almost decapitated) onto the deck and threw it into the sea. The group then confined the captain's wife, the two children, Merritt (found hiding under a mattress), and the cabin servants in the afterhold. Around 4:30 that morning, Morris and four others discovered Stevens high on the yardarm. "Come down, you damn son-of-a-bitch. Receive your message. That is the very one we want." Stevens complied—slowly—as they continued shouting threats and calling him names. On touching the foretop, Stevens asked why they wanted to kill him. "Damn you," Morris shot back, "come down and receive your message!" When Stevens finally reached the deck, he promised that if they spared his life, he would take them to any English port in three days. "We will give you three days," came the bitter reply; "if you don't, we will throw you overboard, if not before."[29]

Washington and his cohorts had commandeered the *Creole* with few casualties, largely because the passengers and crew put up little resistance and Washington and Morris restrained their followers from killing all the whites on board. Indeed, only Hewell was killed. Ensor, although severely wounded, had somehow joined Gifford and two crew members in escaping to the maintop. Ensor soon passed out from the heavy loss of blood, but Gifford secured him to the rigging. With daylight now illuminating the vessel, the mutineers spotted Gifford in the maintop and ordered him to come down or be shot. He complied. Eight hours later, crew members lowered Ensor in a sling and put him in captivity with the passengers. Two of the crew sustained serious wounds, as did one of the blacks.[30]

As the *Creole* tossed uneasily in the rhythmic pitch of the ocean, Washington joined the other three leaders of the mutiny in an animated discussion about where to sail the vessel. They had agreed to spare Merritt's life if he navigated the *Creole* into a port of their choice. Washington at first had wanted to go to Liberia, but Merritt convinced him that the vessel had inadequate provisions for such a long journey. Washington's comrades then demanded that they turn toward the British islands. Johnstone had heard that the American schooner *Hermosa* had shipwrecked a year earlier at Abaco and that British wreckers had taken the slaves from the *Hermosa* to Nassau, New Providence, where the authorities set them free. His sources were reliable: ninety slaves on the *Creole* belonged to Robert Lumpkin, who had owned several of the slaves on the *Hermosa*. Washington and his three comrades decided on Nassau. Gathered around a table laden with apples, bread, brandy, wine, and whisky, they carefully watched Merritt plot the ship's passage on the chart.[31]

Around eight o'clock on the morning of November 9, the *Creole* reached the lighthouse at Nassau. At that point, Washington ordered all weapons thrown overboard just before entering the harbor, purposely removing all visible threats and putting him and his followers at the mercy of the British officials. As the *Creole* approached the dock, the quarantine officer came alongside. Washington permitted Gifford to go ashore and inform the American consul, John Bacon, of the mutiny. Bacon immediately had the wounded men removed and asked the colonial governor, Francis Cockburn, to send a guard to the vessel to prevent the blacks from escaping into the islands. Several of them, Bacon declared, were guilty of murder and it was necessary to identify them and bring them to trial.[32]

Bacon was not pleased with the British reaction to his requests. Cockburn at first expressed doubt that he had the authority to take any action, but close to noon he finally dispatched twenty-two black soldiers under the command of a white officer to board the *Creole* and keep order. In the meantime the Council of Nassau hurriedly convened and soon emerged to announce that the islands' municipal courts lacked jurisdiction because the alleged mutiny and murder had occurred on the high seas. The Council would launch an inquiry into the matter that same day—before the soldiers brought the accused ashore—but emphasized that after such investigation, those blacks who did not participate in the revolt would go free in accordance with the Emancipation Act of 1833. A full report of the affair would be sent to the British minister in Washington.[33]

Violence threatened, however, when black islanders learned that not all the blacks aboard the *Creole* would go free. The attorney general of Nassau, George Anderson, had boarded the vessel on that first day, anxiously watching several boats lingering nearby that were manned by unruly-looking islanders bearing clubs and other weapons. The first few craft had appeared by noon, and by 1:30 that afternoon the number had grown to nearly fifty. Bacon heard that the islanders intended to free all the blacks on the *Creole* once the soldiers withdrew. Indeed, Stevens claimed that the islanders were swinging their clubs in a "threatening manner" and using "insulting language" to intimidate the crew. Bacon urged Cockburn to take preventive action, but the governor blandly assured him that British subjects would not "act so improperly." If they moved to do so, Cockburn promised, "I shall be quite ready to use every authorized means to prevent it." Anderson warned those in the boats not to interfere with the legal proceedings. They assured him that they intended only to provide transportation ashore for anyone on the *Creole* who needed assistance. At Anderson's request, the islanders tossed overboard more than a dozen clubs that they were carrying.[34]

That same day, Bacon got a further portent of what lay ahead when he appeared before a second meeting of the governor and Council to appeal for cooperation in dealing with the growing problem. Would British authorities, he asked, hold the *Creole*'s blacks in custody until an American war vessel arrived from Indian Key in Florida, nearly four hundred miles away? Cockburn refused. Bacon then sought approval for the American ships still at Nassau to escort the *Creole* and its passengers and crew to New Orleans. This appeal Cockburn likewise denied. Finally, Bacon requested that the governor send the nineteen black mutineers to the United States to stand trial. Again, Cockburn refused. Bacon left the meeting and directed Gifford back to the *Creole* to protest any efforts made by Anderson's party to free the blacks on board. The governor, Bacon knew, had already labeled the *Creole*'s blacks as "passengers." Moreover, black soldiers on the island openly assured the females on the *Creole* that they were free. And soon afterward, two Episcopal clergymen came aboard, apparently giving directions to the blacks as the females began putting on their bonnets in preparation to leave. The white commander of the black company told the mutineers that "they were fools not to have killed all hands when they had a chance, when they would all have been free without further trouble."[35]

Tension persisted as Bacon decided to take matters into his own hands. The British inquiry, conducted by two magistrates and a clerk, had stretched over three days (one day's delay caused by the captain's illness) before leading to the identification of the nineteen mutineers. Bacon realized that if any of the blacks won freedom, the precedent of such a move would constitute a veritable invitation to others to mutiny, and he therefore conspired with a group of Americans in the islands to seize control of the *Creole* and leave Nassau. According to the plan, Captain William Woodside of an American barque then in port, the *Louisa*, would command four sailors of the American brig *Congress* in taking over the *Creole* and sailing it to Indian Key. Just before dawn on November 12 the small band of men rowed to the *Creole*, their three muskets, three cutlasses, and two horse pistols hidden in an American flag folded at the bottom of their boat. While en route, however, a black islander in a boat nearby spotted them and, after carefully observing their actions, alerted the British officer in charge of the *Creole*. By the time the five Americans reached the *Creole*, they saw standing before them on the bow twenty-three British soldiers, armed with muskets and fixed bayonets. "Keep off," the commander warned, "or I will fire into you." Woodside withdrew.[36]

Later that same morning, British authorities released those blacks who had not participated in the revolt but retained the nineteen mutineers in custody until directives came from London pertaining to a trial. Anderson boarded the vessel and explained that all the blacks had been held there until witnesses identified the mutineers. That task completed, Anderson turned to those not involved in the revolt and announced: "My friends," you are "free and at liberty to go on shore and wherever you please." Amid the excitement, Gifford and Woodside told Anderson that only the nineteen mutineers could go ashore. The attorney general quickly pulled Woodside and Gifford aside and warned them that if they put up any opposition, the islanders would surely kill them and anyone else who resisted.[37]

There was no way to halt the subsequent course of events. Anderson left the *Creole* where, in short order, British officials on board gave a prearranged signal, and with a shout the black islanders rowed alongside. As the British soldiers stood on deck, over one hundred blacks who had not participated in the revolt silently walked in a lengthy procession past Gifford, Woodside, and the ship's crew, and climbed into the small boats waiting to carry them ashore and to freedom. Booming cheers greeted them as they hit the beach, where hundreds of joyous islanders accompanied them to the superintendent of police to register their names. In the meantime, British officials took the nineteen mutineers into custody. The liberated blacks were free to go anywhere in the islands, although five had hidden in the hold of the *Creole* and chose to return to the United States. One schooner left for Jamaica on November 18 carrying fifty blacks, a large portion of whom were from the *Creole*. Another vessel sailed for the same destination on December 4, transporting about the same number.[38]

Despite the protests lodged by the American consul in Nassau, the truth is that there was no alternative to the great bulk of the *Creole*'s blacks going free. The islands were a British possession, which meant that British municipal law reigned. Although the accused murderers remained in custody, most of the blacks had won their freedom through a successful revolt, and to place them in custody at this point was tantamount to returning them to slavery. The islanders would not have allowed this to happen. Gifford had noted that as he walked the streets of Nassau, both blacks and whites bitterly remarked, "There goes one of the damned pirates and slavers." Consequently, the British attorney general invoked the Emancipation Act, which recognized the blacks' freedom because they were on British soil. On a practical level, no step short of violence could have denied them their right to live free in the islands. The *Creole*'s crew and captain were powerless, and the black islanders outnumbered the whites at Nassau by about four to one. For these and other reasons, even the nineteen mutineers might go free. But that decision had to come from London.[39]

III

The *Creole*'s belated arrival in New Orleans on December 2 caused an angry uproar that was not confined to the South. The New Orleans *Commercial Bulletin* proclaimed that the city had been "thrown into a flame" by the "inhuman" actions of the British. Surely the time had come to settle the question of "whether British authority can strip American citizens of their property without their consent." Many southerners were already sensitive about this interference with American maritime matters and now demanded reparations for the liberated slaves. Bitter denunciations of the British came from newspapers in New Orleans, Nashville, Washington, and Jackson, Mississippi, while the legislatures of Louisiana, Mississippi, and Virginia passed resolutions demanding compensation. The entire South, according to the Baltimore *Sun* and Charleston *Courier*, condemned Britain. But the fury did not emanate from that region alone. In the Senate, Thomas Hart Benton of Missouri blasted the British for condoning mutiny and murder; Henry Clay of Kentucky predicted more problems for the nation's coastal trade; and John C. Calhoun of South Carolina reminded Americans that national honor and property rights were in jeopardy. If the British could interfere with domestic slavers passing through Atlantic coastal waters, Calhoun solemnly warned, they could do the same with vessels carrying cotton.[40]

As fate would have it, the Supreme Court had recently handed down a decision in a case that, on the surface, seemed similar to that of the *Creole* and thereby provided a legal basis for the South's protests. In 1839 the Spanish slaver *Amistad* had been transporting fifty-three blacks (captured in Africa) from Havana to another Cuban port, when Joseph Cinqué led a mutiny that resulted in the deaths of the captain and crew. Then, in a remarkable odyssey, the Gulf Stream carried the *Amistad* from the Caribbean to Long Island, where federal authorities seized the vessel and all survivors aboard for salvage. But abolitionists heard of the incident and brought it to court, where they sought to expose the evils of the slave trade and win the blacks' freedom on the basis of their natural right of self-defense as "kidnapped Africans." The Spanish minister in Washington appealed to treaties between his government and the United States—Pinckney's Treaty of 1795 and the Adams-Onís Treaty of 1819—which called for the restoration of property taken from their owners for reasons beyond their control. President Martin Van Buren, trying to avoid a divisive issue such as slavery on the eve of his reelection bid, prepared to comply with Spain's demand. But the Supreme Court agreed with the abolitionists and in March 1841 (with former president and now Massachusetts congressman John Quincy Adams leading the defense) freed the captives on the basis of Spain's outlawry of the African slave trade in 1820. Southerners noted that there had been no reparations for the *Amistad* blacks because their captors had been illegally engaged in the African slave trade; by reverse logic, they now argued that there should be reparations for the *Creole*'s blacks because they had belonged to citizens of a nation recognizing the legality of slavery and the domestic slave trade.[41]

Even more relevant, some southerners drew comparisons between the *Creole* case and other similar episodes involving the Bahamas. Three American vessels, the *Comet*, the *Encomium*, and the *Enterprise*, had also been forced into the British islands by circumstances beyond their control (bad weather), and in all three instances the colonial governor had freed the slaves on board. Less than a year before the *Creole* affair, the *Formosa* had been bound for Louisiana from Virginia, when it wrecked near Nassau and British authorities freed all thirty-eight slaves aboard. In that case, the Louisiana Insurance Company of New Orleans reimbursed the owners for their property loss and then sought reimbursement from the government in Washington. A brief debate in the Senate led to an outpouring of anger from Alexander Barrow of Louisiana, who proclaimed that if the White House would not defend southern rights at sea, the South should destroy Nassau.[42]

The *Creole* affair proved especially noteworthy in this list of incidents involving charges of British interference in the domestic slave trade. For the first time, mutiny and loss of life had occurred. The British government granted indemnification for the *Comet* and *Encomium* because the act of liberation had taken place before the Emancipation Act of 1833, but it refused to do the same for the *Enterprise* because that incident had come afterward. The British had likewise offered no restitution for the *Formosa* incident, and the prognosis for the *Creole* seemed just as hopeless.[43]

Southerners were not totally convincing in their complaints of British infringements on national honor; more than a few contemporaries believed this stand a transparent attempt to protect slavery. Several newspapers, including the Richmond *Enquirer*,

Baltimore *Sun,* and *National Intelligencer,* had earlier praised Stevenson's efforts to defend the country's honor by criticizing British search tactics in suppressing the African slave trade. The antislavery Portsmouth *Journal* of New Hampshire, however, did not believe the argument. Stevenson's sole objective, the paper argued with disgust, had been to preempt an assault on slavery by undermining the effort to suppress the African slave trade. The Mobile *Register & Journal* of Alabama and the Baltimore *Sun* did not hide their real concern: British interference with the coastal trade would encourage slave uprisings by assuring freedom in neighboring British possessions. The New Orleans *Picayune* initially complained about violations of national honor but finally asserted that the British were enticing the South's slaves to engage in mutiny and murder to win freedom. Northern abolitionist newspapers indignantly warned southerners not to exploit appeals to national honor in a backhanded effort to protect slavery. The Boston *Liberator* defiantly dared the White House to go to war with Britain over the "hellish slave trade," and the *Spy* of Worcester, Massachusetts, declared that surely the North would not go to war to "DEFEND OUR AMERICAN SLAVE TRADE."[44]

The *Creole* revolt provided an excellent opportunity for abolitionists to highlight the evils of slavery. During early 1842, at the height of the *Creole* excitement, abolitionists from the United States and Britain, including Theodore Weld, Joshua Leavitt of the *Emancipator,* and Lord Morpeth of the British and Foreign Anti-Slavery Society, gathered in Washington to work with John Quincy Adams and other antislavery legislators in drawing up petitions denouncing slavery. James G. Birney, who had been the Liberty party's candidate for the presidency in 1840 (and would be again in 1844), authored an article in the New York *American* that supported freedom for the *Creole*'s blacks. The highly acclaimed New England writer and editor of the *Pennsylvania Freeman,* John Greenleaf Whittier, wrote the chairman of the British and Foreign Anti-Slavery Society in London, happily describing the furor in the South caused by the *Creole* affair. To the same group, the corresponding secretary of the American and Foreign Anti-Slavery Society expressed approval of the British government's actions. That same American Society then assured the Peel ministry in London that to grant compensation for the freed blacks would make the British government the guarantor of the American interstate slave trade. Abolitionist Lewis Tappan of New York, who had led the way in securing legal counsel for the Africans of the *Amistad,* warned of trouble if either the American or British government indemnified the owners of the *Creole*'s slaves.[45]

The House of Representatives soon became the focal point of the growing furor over the *Creole* and slavery. Abolitionist Joshua Giddings of Ohio presented Weld's resolutions asserting that a state had exclusive jurisdiction only over slaves within its boundaries, and that on the high seas the Constitution did not require the federal government to seek redress for liberated slaves. The most explosive resolution declared that "the persons on board the ship, in resuming their natural rights of personal liberty, violated no law of the United States, incurred no legal penalty, and are justly liable to no punishment." House members blasted Giddings for justifying mutiny and murder, and the next day they censured him by a vote of 125 to 69. The following day he resigned his seat, but his antislavery supporters defiantly returned him to the House by an overwhelming margin in a special election held in April. In the meantime, the abolitionists took advantage of the *Creole* revolt to launch another attack on the "gag rule," which prohibited antislavery discussions in the House. Southern lawmakers ultimately decided against countering this barrage with resolutions of their own, probably because such a strategy would expose the entire question of slavery to debate and undermine the gag rule itself. The Baltimore *Sun* warned that approval of these antislavery resolutions was tantamount to putting a knife in the hands of every slave and inviting him to commit murder.[46]

The *Creole* affair caused enormous problems for both the American and British governments. President Tyler could find no legal ground for demanding the return of the nineteen mutineers as fugitives: the only Anglo-American extradition provision (part of Jay's Treaty) had expired in 1807. Fox informed Aberdeen that in 1838 federal authorities in the United States had prevented the state of New York from surrendering two British citizens charged with murder. Two years later, the British minister noted, the Supreme Court ruled in *Holmes* v. *Jennison* that the federal government should not return a murderer who had escaped from Canada. At first glance, it seemed that restoration of the freed blacks was out of the question. And yet, both the United States and Britain realized that when an issue threatened peace between them, international law condoned the surrender of fugitives, regardless of the lack of a treaty of extradition. But there were complicating factors. Fox knew that to surrender the *Creole*'s blacks ensured death or imprisonment for those who had participated in the revolt, and a return to slavery for all the others. No British government could survive if it gave in to the South's demands.[47]

The Tyler administration's only recourse was to appeal for the blacks' return on the principle of comity—which encouraged a nation to help a foreign vessel that had entered its port for reasons beyond its control. British authorities in Nassau, Webster wrote Everett in London, had not adhered to the understandings of hospitality; the government in London owed reparations for the freed slaves. The *Creole* had been legally engaged in the domestic slave trade and carried a cargo of slaves that the U.S. Constitution recognized as property. After the mutineers had forced the vessel into the Bahamas, British officials should have done everything possible to permit it and everyone aboard to resume their voyage to New Orleans. According to Palmerston's own argument made in 1837 (pertaining to the *Comet*, *Encomium*, and *Enterprise* cases), Webster explained, compensation was in order when officials interfered with the slaves of another country, even if that action occurred in British territory. British municipal law (the Emancipation Act) did not apply to anyone who entered British territory because of "disaster and distress."[48]

Even while Webster explained the White House position on the *Creole* affair to Everett, the Peel ministry solicited an opinion from the crown's law officers. Lord Stanley in the Colonial Office had already approved Cockburn's conduct in the initial stages of the problem and now sought legal guidance on what should happen to the blacks accused of mutiny and murder. The law officers found no basis under either international law or British municipal law for charging the *Creole*'s blacks with piracy: the blacks had no intention of plundering the vessel or of seizing it for their own use, except to sail it to some port where they might secure their freedom. The case, therefore, could not come before the Court of Commissioners in the Bahamas or any other British court. Subjects of the United States led the revolt, and it occurred on an American vessel; consequently, only American courts had jurisdiction. As for Consul Bacon's protest against the liberation of those blacks who did not participate in the rebellion, the law officers pointed out that the blacks had arrived as free people in free British territory and had every legal right to continue that freedom.[49]

The White House could not have been surprised by the British ruling on the *Creole*'s blacks involved in the revolt, but it must have been stunned by the decision pertaining to the nineteen accused of murder and mutiny. The crown's advisers declared that the acts did not take place on a British vessel and could not come before a British tribunal. The blacks committed their alleged crime as American subjects on an American ship and against American citizens. The matter belonged exclusively to American courts. And yet, the law officers noted, there was no treaty between the United States and Britain that required extradition, and international law contained no rule to this effect. Indeed, no power existed anywhere to bring the blacks to trial. They must go free because of the lack of either treaty provision or municipal law sanctioning extradition.[50]

Abolitionists and nonabolitionists alike in Parliament approved the law officers' decision. Abolitionist Lord Henry Brougham conferred with members of the British and Foreign Anti-Slavery Society before arguing in the House of Lords that even if a treaty authorized extradition of criminals, a municipal law to that effect would still be necessary to carry out that treaty. Fellow abolitionist Lord Thomas Denman referred to Sir Edward Coke's claim that nations were sanctuaries for those seeking safety and that Justice Joseph Story of the U.S. Supreme Court had, in a recent edition of his *Conflict of Laws* (1841), cited Coke as the authority. Lord Campbell, who also opposed slavery, noted that Henry Wheaton, then American minister in Berlin and a distinguished lawyer and publicist, argued in his book on international law that extradition of fugitives existed only by special agreement. The *Creole*'s slaves, Campbell insisted, became free upon arrival in British territory. The United States had no right to indemnification.[51]

The Peel ministry had thus attracted widespread support for its refusal to surrender any of the *Creole*'s blacks. In addition to the approval of Parliament and the *Times* of London, both the Hibernian Anti-Slavery Society in Dublin and the British and Foreign Anti-Slavery Society stood behind the ministry. Aberdeen assured a very receptive House of Lords that the ministry would neither bring the mutineers to trial nor return the others to the U.S. government. To Everett, the foreign secretary justified the decision by pointing out that the revolt had taken place outside of British waters and that the lack of an extradition agreement precluded island authorities from turning over the mutineers to the United States. If the charge had been piracy, British colonial courts could have taken the case. Indeed, the British government had informed the U.S. consul in Nassau that if he wanted to accuse the nineteen blacks of piracy, its local tribunals were available for a trial. The consul,

Aberdeen noted, showed no interest in the proposal. Soon thereafter, on April 16, 1842, the chief justice of Nassau declared the nineteen prisoners free.[52]

The Tyler administration recognized its weak legal position and never demanded the surrender of the mutineers. Everett vainly called for reparations on the basis of the Nassau officials' refusal to bring the mutineers to justice and assist the vessel in completing its voyage. But he, like those on the Nassau scene, attributed the outcome to the intimidation resulting from the large number of black islanders nearby. Thus did the slaves' overseer on the *Creole* give "seeming consent" to their liberation. And yet, Everett argued, the British were inconsistent in promoting the unconditional freedom of American slaves when they had only instituted conditional emancipation (with compensation) within their own confines. Everett's protest did not alter the ministry's decision to free all the *Creole*'s slaves.[53]

Before the *Creole* mutiny, southerners had shown little concern over the numerous issues blocking good Anglo-American relations. Neither the northeastern boundary dispute nor the *Caroline* and McLeod crises directly affected the South, and good commercial ties with the British further promoted a fairly sound economic interdependency. But the African slave-trade issue and the *Creole* revolt suddenly exposed the common interests that the South had with the rest of the nation in protesting British policies. Although the issue of slavery seemed far removed from the border disputes in the North, both sectional matters rested on one central concern and for that reason held great potential for trouble: they raised the question of national honor and, like the intangibles that helped bring on the War of 1812, could do the same in 1842 if the diplomats failed at the negotiating table.

CHAPTER FIVE

Machiavellian Prelude to Negotiations: Toward the National Interest

The Ashburton mission will "disarm us of those suspicions and jealousies of the Mother Country which we inherited from our Fathers, & which have constituted hitherto, &, I suppose, will always continue to constitute, the greatest source of danger to the peace of the two Countries."
—Robert C. Winthrop, April 23, 1842

As in all diplomatic negotiations, the appearance is considerably different from the reality. In this regard, the talks between Daniel Webster and Lord Ashburton were not unique. On the surface, the two men seemed like old friends who had decided to settle a family squabble by engaging in open and honest discussions. The first part of the preceding observation was correct; the second was not. As wily and capable diplomats, both men realized that the national interest and not personal friendships must provide the guideline for each country's actions. Webster and Ashburton worked toward the satisfaction of national honor and did so through Machiavellian means. Webster, however, proved more adept at this time-tested craft than did his counterpart.

I

The Canadian-American boundary continued to be the most vexing problem between the Atlantic nations. Nearly six decades after the establishment of American independence, the final delineation of the northern boundary remained elusive. Difficulties along the Maine-New Brunswick border persisted throughout this period, while farther west Americans had become increasingly concerned about the Oregon boundary. For Webster and Ashburton, however, recent events in the Northeast necessitated a focus on that region.

The most obvious solution to the northeastern boundary problem was a compromise, but this simple-sounding approach ran counter to the recurring issues of Anglophobia, states' rights, domestic politics, combative newspaper stories, and national honor. Numerous letters among New Brunswick officials indicate that they wanted only peace in the area. The major obstacle was Maine, whose people did not trust either the London or the Washington government. But even those Americans not directly involved in the boundary issue demanded British respect for the Republic. A British writer in the *Edinburgh Review* of London understood the concern of Americans about winning an admission to their legitimacy as a nation. Although he denied that the United States was "undervalued in England," he admitted that "there is a nation by whom America is anxious to be esteemed—or, to speak more correctly, to be admired and feared—and that is England." This obsession, according to the writer, had caused America to think that by adopting a "bold, or even a threatening tone towards England, she will obtain our respect." This was not the case. England, he declared, disliked America's "swagger or . . . bully" and feared its expansionist aims in Canada.[1]

General Winfield Scott's compromise arrangement of March 1839 had only temporarily alleviated the problem by assigning the Madawaska settlements to Britain and the Aroostook Valley to the United States. Almost predictably, a dispute developed over the boundary between these areas. British Minister Henry Fox repeatedly recommended arbitration of the matter but received no favorable response from Washington.[2] On the local level, Loyalists from both countries resided in this region and had much at stake. From a broader viewpoint, however, the British government was concerned about America's northward growth and sought to protect Canada by constructing a military road linking the Maritime Provinces with Quebec. The St. John River offered a natural boundary, but it wound through Madawaska and, if accepted, would place British settlers on the American side. A compromise with equivalents provided the most logical solution, but neither Maine nor New Brunswick would consider the idea because it entailed the concession of something each antagonist thought it rightfully owned.

The events that had led to the Aroostook War of 1839 seemed about to occur again in late 1840, when Madawaska became the flashpoint of Anglo-American trouble. About one hundred Americans and a few French Canadians, protected by the posse from Maine (see Chapter 1), had gathered near the mouth of the Fish River (north of the Aroostook River) to cast their votes for president of the United States. New Brunswick's warden of this disputed area complained that these actions violated British jursidiction. When the provincial justice of the peace arrived on the scene to object to the assembly, however, a group of spirited Americans roughly escorted him and a fellow officer out of the meeting and told them not to return. The government in London angrily declared that its dominion included the areas in dispute and warned against further "encroachments"; Maine defiantly countered that its jurisdiction encompassed that entire region and protested against any British claim to it. Contemporaries must have experienced a sense of déjà vu as the Anglophobic New York *Herald* dramatically recounted riotous activities along the border and the government in Washington warned the British to withdraw their troops.[3]

As in the Aroostook War, the local problems that developed in 1840 threatened to cause a crisis between Britain and the United States. The new governor of Maine, Edward Kent, warned New Brunswick to remove its troops before he called on the federal government to intervene. In London, Colonial Secretary Lord John Russell refused to comply with Maine's demand and, to demonstrate his government's resolve, approved the dispatch of additional soldiers to Madawaska. Foreign Secretary Palmerston blasted the "cunning" Yankees for deriding British conciliation as timidity and cynically remarked that the United States relied "very much upon bully." Maine's legislature likewise rejected any thought of retreat. It prepared resolutions urging the governor to evict the British intruders and asked the government in Washington for help in doing so. Members of Parliament denounced Maine's actions as a virtual declaration of war and urged the ministry in London to station naval vessels outside American harbors and troops along the disputed border. By the end of March 1841 the states of Alabama, Indiana, and Maryland promised assistance to Maine and called on the White House to force British soldiers from American soil.[4]

Such was the tinderbox along the border when Webster assumed the position of secretary of state in the spring of 1841. He had quickly become preoccupied with the McLeod crisis in New York but somehow had to attend to the emotional events in the Northeast as well. Questions of national honor linked the two matters in a commotion threatening to produce serious consequences. But they also meshed on issues of Anglophobia, states' rights, and domestic politics. Any suggestion of monetary compensation for territorial concessions constituted an insult to the Patriots in Maine who vehemently opposed any attempt to "barter her birthright" for money. The British likewise rejected any financial settlement as an admission of Maine's right to the territory in question. By summer the people of Maine complained that the British had made their state a veritable thoroughfare for their troops and warned of war. The British, however, could not evacuate the area without implicitly conceding all of Madawaska to Maine. Many British subjects, according to a Catholic priest on the scene, preferred war to union with the United States.[5]

Both Webster and President Tyler realized that to resolve this renewed border crisis peacefully (as with the McLeod case), it was necessary to wrest the issue from local and state hands and place it on the national level, where the two governments could broker a compromise. With that objective in mind, the president proposed to the British minister that, in the interests of peace, federal troops replace Maine's posse at the mouth of the Fish River. British forces, he suggested, should remain only along the north bank of the St. John River. Webster tried to soften the impact of such a withdrawal by recommending that the British coordinate the deployment of troops opposite the fort with the federal replacement of the posse at Fort Fairfield as a gesture of moral support to their people in Madawaska. The British government rejected the arrangement and jealously guarded its alleged right to locate troops on both sides of the river.[6]

Matters might have drifted into another full-scale crisis had not the White House received unexpected support from a relatively obscure figure from Maine—Francis O. J. Smith (known appropriately as "Fog"), who was an attorney, newspaper publisher, and former congressman and state senator. Smith's personal fortunes had been capricious in both business and politics, but by the time he contacted Webster about the boundary issue he had financial interests in the commerce and railroads of Portland and was also part owner of the Augusta *Age*, the Augusta *Patriot*, and the Portland *Eastern Argus*. Smith had everything to gain from a peaceful settlement of the boundary problem.[7]

During the spring of 1841, Smith contacted Webster and proposed a series of steps intended to promote a boundary agreement. The White House, Smith declared, should orchestrate a newspaper campaign in the Northeast aimed at convincing the people of that region that war could result if they did not consent to a boundary compromise. The idea was not new to Smith. In late 1837 he had tried to convince President Van Buren to send a secret agent to Maine and New Brunswick to devise terms acceptable to both sides. But the president preferred to deal directly with the British government. Van Buren's mistake, Smith told Webster, was to negotiate "at the wrong end of the dispute." Maine and New Brunswick were the problem, not Washington and London. Maine would accept a compromise, Smith argued, only if its political leaders and newspaper editors realized that the alternative was war.[8]

Webster appreciated the wisdom of Smith's proposal. Such a newspaper campaign, the secretary knew, would cost far less than either continued negotiations or war. Webster first won the support of the president and then approved Smith's request to head the program. Expenses plus a payment of $3,500 per year would be acceptable remuneration, Smith declared. If successful, he expected a "liberal commission" on whatever financial exchanges took place during the negotiations with Britain. Webster and Tyler agreed to terms. The president advanced Smith $500 from a special source—the Executive Office's secret-service fund, authorized by Congress in 1810 as an annual appropriation of $30,000 "for the contingent expenses of intercourse between the United States and foreign nations." What made the fund "secret" was the provision allowing the president to block the public disclosure of certain expenditures though maintaining a private record of such transactions through certificates or vouchers. The newspaper campaign lasted ten months and required an expenditure of over $12,000 from the fund.[9]

With the financial matters cleared, Webster and Smith proceeded with the plan. The secretary drew up terms for a boundary compromise that Smith arranged to have published in the Portland *Christian Mirror*, a politically neutral religious journal having wide circulation in New England. Other newspapers in the region, they believed, would reprint the articles. Three editorials appeared in the *Mirror* on November 18 and December 2, 1841, and on February 3, 1842, all signed by "Agricola" and entitled "NORTHEASTERN BOUNDARY—WHY NOT SETTLE IT?" and all asserting that the choice was narrowed to compromise or war. Maine's people should petition their legislature in Augusta to seek the following terms: the state's title to the disputed territory; Britain's acquisition of the land necessary for a military road into the Canadian interior; free navigation by Americans of the St. John River for fifty years; federal compensation to Maine for past defense of the disputed territory; and British indemnity to Maine (and Massachusetts, which also had property concerns affected by any boundary settlement, in accordance with their act of separation of 1819) for relinquishing part of the land in question. The objective was a compromise boundary in exchange for equivalents.[10]

Webster was confident that the program would work. In addition to the newspaper articles, he had memorials circulated throughout Maine that urged legislative action. By mid-December, Webster believed that the state would approve the principle of compromise. As he had hoped, other newspapers, including some outside Maine, reprinted the articles. The Portland *Eastern Argus*, which was the most influential Democratic paper in Maine and the only one with a sizable circulation outside the state, switched from opposition to enthusiastic support. The articles also appeared in newspapers as far away as the Chicago *American*, the *Democratic Free Press* and the *Constitutional Democrat* of Detroit, and the Little Rock *Arkansas Times and Advocate*. Even the Richmond *Enquirer*, spokesman of southern Democrats and no admirer of Webster and the Whig party, quoted the *Eastern Argus* in calling for a settlement with Britain.[11]

Then, in late 1841, Webster learned that the Peel ministry had taken a pivotal step toward the maintenance of peace. It appointed the highly respected and influential Alexander Baring, Lord Ashburton, as special minister to Washington to resolve all problems with the United States. The appointment had come at the behest of many people in Britain who called for a peaceful resolution of these issues. London's *Quarterly Review* argued for "a large and liberal spirit of conciliation and equity as well as of strict justice." The *Foreign Quarterly Review* urged a settlement and downplayed the issue by insisting that "the American question is not one of the greatest difficulties with which the [British] cabinet has to contend in its foreign policy." Peel and his foreign secretary, Lord Aberdeen, realized that the welfare of their own country rested largely on its relations with France and the United States. To pressure France into a less combative attitude, they sought to improve relations with America. Such a special task required a special emissary.[12]

Ashburton's close ties with the United States made him an ideal choice. While a young man of twenty, he had purchased over a million acres in Maine (then part of Massachusetts) from William Bingham, Federalist senator from Philadelphia, and Henry Knox, former secretary of war. (None of the land, it is important to note, was in the disputed territory of the 1840s.) Shortly afterward, Baring met Bingham's sixteen-year-old daughter Anne Louisa and soon married her. Five years later, in 1803, Baring Brothers helped finance the Louisiana Purchase. From 1806 until he became Lord

Ashburton in 1835, he served in the House of Commons where, in the tumultuous period before the War of 1812, he appeared to be a defender of American interests by fighting against British commercial restrictions on the United States—albeit out of concern for his own country's economy. At present the Baring firm was engaged in resolving America's state-debts problems with British investors. Indeed, Webster had served as legal adviser for the banking house since 1831 and continued in that position during the controversy over state bonds after the Panic of 1837. Further, Ashburton had struck up a friendship with Webster when they met in England in 1839.[13]

The Peel ministry had other considerations in selecting Ashburton as special emissary. As the retired head of the powerful banking firm of Baring Brothers and Company, he held a fortune of £3 million and had nothing personal to gain from a boundary settlement. From 1810 to his retirement in 1832 he led the banking house to such financial heights that Lord Byron, in one of the cantos of *Don Juan*, asked in 1823:

> Who hold the balance of the world? Who reign
> O'er Congress, whether royalist or liberal?

Rothschild and Baring, he replied. A respected member of the Conservative party, Baring served as president of the Board of Trade in Peel's abbreviated ministry of 1834–35 and received an invitation, which he declined, to join the new cabinet in 1841. The Peel ministry realized that it could not work through its minister in Washington: Fox had become immensely unpopular because of his outspoken disdain for America. The announcement of a special mission was admittedly dangerous—failure through regular diplomatic channels was easier to keep quiet—but the benefits derived from winning credibility in the United States far outweighed the risk. Had not the United States set such a precedent by sending John Jay as special envoy to England in the 1790s?[14]

In December 1841, Ashburton accepted the position with "fear & trembling," but he soon wrote Webster that good Anglo-American relations were vital to the "moral improvement and the progressive civilization of the world." The sixty-seven-year-old financial magnate sorrowfully noted that absence from his family would be "painful," but he would undergo such personal sacrifice for a month. On Christmas Eve, Aberdeen told Queen Victoria of the decision, and she immediately approved. Shortly afterward, Aberdeen informed Edward Everett of the special mission and called

it a gesture of goodwill that aimed at resolving all differences between the Atlantic nations—even the right of search, which Aberdeen considered the most explosive issue. The American minister
expressed surprise but delight and continued cultivating his warm
relationship with the foreign secretary that would complement the
oncoming negotiations in Washington. In a personal note to Webster,
Lady Ashburton commented that Englishmen considered her husband "most zealous" in the cause of America. "If you don't like
him," she asserted, "we can send you nothing better."[15]

On the last day of 1841 the *Times* of London announced the
Ashburton mission to the United States and, for the most part, drew
a favorable response from both sides of the Atlantic. The London
Morning Chronicle noted that commercial groups praised the move
and that confidence had risen in state stocks. The *Times* welcomed
the news as a sincere effort by the Peel ministry to keep the peace,
and the London *Examiner* lauded the Americans for seeking harmonious relations. The Halifax *Novascotian* agreed with these comments. Some observers, however, expressed skepticism. The *Foreign
Quarterly Review* warned that Americans were "not reasonable,
wherever their pride is involved," whereas others were concerned
because of Ashburton's well-known "vacillation and irresolution"
combined with his age and lengthy absence from public affairs. In
the United States the reaction was similar. Robert C. Winthrop of
Massachusetts, a Whig representative and friend of Webster's,
thought that Ashburton's impeccable character would "disarm us
of those suspicions and jealousies of the Mother Country which we
inherited from our Fathers, & which have constituted hitherto, &, I
suppose, will always continue to constitute, the greatest source of
danger to the peace of the two Countries." Two Democratic papers,
doubtless for political reasons, did not share this enthusiasm. The
Richmond *Enquirer* warned that Ashburton would seek only what
was good for his country, and the Washington *Globe* sourly observed that Webster had recently accepted an unusual fee of £1,000
from the Baring firm for a "sort of professional opinion." The Boston *Courier* and Nashville *Union* were dubious about successful
negotiations, and Governor John Davis of Massachusetts warned
Webster that Britain intended to carve out large sectors of Maine in
an effort "to enlarge her powers" at the expense of the United States.
America's hatred for the British, wrote Senator Willie Mangum of
North Carolina to a friend, left a "strong proclivity" for war.[16]

These American concerns soon faded in the excitement over
the realization that the Peel ministry had shown enough respect for

the United States to send a special mission. Diarist Philip Hone expressed the widespread feelings of Americans when he called Ashburton's appointment "an unusual piece of condescension" by the nation's "haughty" mother country. President Tyler thought the mission a critical move toward the maintenance of peace, as did Albert Gallatin, veteran of Anglo-American boundary talks and longtime friend of Ashburton.[17] For the first time since the brief euphoria following the War of 1812, Americans believed that the British were ready to accept the Republic into the family of nations.

II

A considerable amount of groundwork remained for both sides before the negotiations could begin. While the Peel ministry drafted final instructions for Ashburton, the Tyler administration prepared to receive the illustrious envoy. Goodwill abounded so openly in both countries that contemporaries automatically assumed that the negotiations in Washington would reflect this openness and, for one of the few times in history, lead to a sensible solution that rested on simple, honest discussion—or so it seemed to the uninitiated observers of diplomacy.

Despite the Peel ministry's sincere desire for peace, it would certainly enter no pact that threatened British interests. The prime objective was to secure enough land along the Canadian-American boundary to permit the construction of a military road that facilitated the defense of British North America by connecting Montreal with the Atlantic seaboard. Ashburton was to seek the best line possible, but he was not to accept anything less than the boundary suggested by the king of the Netherlands in 1831. This concession was dangerous, complained the Duke of Wellington, who spoke from long military experience and now, as a member of Peel's cabinet, warned that the award line of 1831 was strategically suspect because it came too close to the St. Lawrence River. The British must push the American frontier farther south—well below the St. John River. Aberdeen realized that Wellington's proposal could abort the negotiations, but the foreign secretary's priority was a military road. Toward that goal, he even authorized his emissary to concede Rouses Point at the top of Lake Champlain, which more than a few British considered crucial to the defense of Montreal. Such a concession, Aberdeen believed, would signal Washington that the British had no designs on invading the United States. Acquisition of land for a military road would balance off the advantages gained by American ownership of Rouses Point. Besides, Aberdeen reasoned, that key strategic area sat in the midst of Americans living in New York and Vermont. In a striking move toward an accommodation with the United States, Aberdeen authorized Ashburton to concede part of the Madawaska settlements along with navigation rights on the St. John River.[18]

A smaller though less controversial sector of the Canadian boundary likewise remained unresolved: the northwestern piece of the border stretching from Lake Huron through Lake Superior to the Lake of the Woods. On two occasions—in the King-Hawkesbury Convention of 1803 (which failed in the Senate) and the Treaty of Ghent in 1815—the two nations attempted to settle ownership of this territory. Even now, Aberdeen did not consider the area of "paramount importance" and would give the United States what it wanted with little sacrifice by the crown. The British could maintain control of the fur trade by holding on to the upper lakes region, and their new military road would thwart any American move northward. In exchange for some suitable equivalent from Oregon or elsewhere along the northern border, Ashburton could even give up St. George's Island (Sugar Island), which was located in the St. Mary's River between Lakes Huron and Superior.[19]

In mid-February 1842, even before Aberdeen had completed all the instructions, Ashburton boarded the *Warspite*, an ominously named frigate of fifty-four guns and crew of five hundred that was bound for the United States. His hurried departure had come for several reasons. He and Aberdeen feared that a further delay might find the treaty caught within a political fight in the fall congressional elections. Whig control of the Senate, they knew, was critical; Anglophobes in the Democratic party would undo any pact signed with Britain. Further, the ministry in London wanted Ashburton on his way before Parliament assembled; any debate over the appointment would delay the mission. Already, however, events were not going as planned: Ashburton's wife had become ill and remained behind.[20]

While these developments proceeded in England, a more intriguing series of events unfolded in the United States that Ashburton later called the "battle of the maps." How prophetic he was in observing that it "may remain a vexed question to puzzle future historians"! As fate would have it, several maps surfaced that raised questions about which one most accurately portrayed the boundary

line agreed upon by the Anglo-American negotiators in Paris in
1783. By using more than one map in Paris that all contained boundary markings, the peace commissioners inadvertently bequeathed a
terrible tangle. It was therefore crucial to determine whether the
lines were mere proposals or actual and final boundaries. In short,
the credibility of a map rested on its authenticity as an artifact used
in the Paris talks and its validity as a final agreement. If a map
failed to meet both of these conditions, its inscriptions could not be
conclusive.[21]

Interestingly enough, the map controversy had its origins in
the research of a historian. The newspaper campaign in New England was barely under way when Webster received a private letter
from his friend Jared Sparks, who was McLean Professor of History at Harvard, biographer of George Washington, and author and
editor of numerous other works. Sparks had recently returned to
Cambridge, Massachusetts, following a research trip to France,
where he had worked in the Paris archives of the French Foreign
Office. While sifting through documents on the Revolutionary War,
he discovered a letter of December 6, 1782, from Benjamin Franklin,
chief negotiator in the Paris peace talks, to the French foreign minister, the Comte de Vergennes. In the missive, Franklin wrote that
on a map he had drawn "a strong red line" marking the Canadian-
American boundary established in the preliminary peace negotiations in Paris. Much to Sparks's chagrin, the map was not with the
letter. But he knew that the French maintained a well-indexed and
catalogued collection of such items and, quickly locating the keeper
of the archives, began an extensive search through more than 60,000
maps and charts relating to American affairs.[22]

With surprisingly little effort, Sparks unearthed a map of North
America that contained a red-ink boundary along the northern part
of the United States which he believed to be the one described in
Franklin's letter. Excited by his discovery, Sparks neglected to examine the trademark of the cartographer to determine whether this
map had been in the hands of the peace negotiators at Paris in 1782–
83. This haste proved to be a monumental mistake: the "red-line
map" held by Sparks was one by French cartographer Jean-Baptiste
Bourguignon d'Anville of 1746, whereas Franklin and all the other
negotiators in Paris had used a French edition of a map by English
cartographer John Mitchell and furnished by the British representatives. Sparks's only concern was that the map he found supported
British claims to the disputed territory. Indeed, upon close examination, the map revealed a boundary running considerably below

the St. John River and thereby granting more land to Britain than the crown had ever claimed. The United States had no right to any of the disputed territory—including the Aroostook Valley.[23] Stunned by the dire implications of his discovery, Sparks faced a true moral dilemma. As a historian, was he bound to expose the map for posterity's sake and undermine his country's claims to the territory in dispute? Or, as an American, should he bury the evidence and allow the negotiations to determine some sort of compromise that awarded the United States far more than it rightfully deserved?

Sparks wrestled with this problem as he left the archives for his apartment that evening. By the time he arrived at his lodgings he had concluded—for reasons that doubtless grew out of the touchy situation in which he found himself—that there was "no positive proof" that this was Franklin's map. In this observation he was correct—but for probably all the wrong reasons. With that decision made, however, he now followed with a predictable move: from memory and notes he reconstructed the boundary in black onto a nineteenth-century map of Maine in his possession. Sparks then packaged the map, planning on his return to Washington to forward it to Webster.[24] Thus, Sparks cleared his conscience by deciding to share his finding with the proper authorities, and yet he must have known that passing on this information to the secretary of state was tantamount to burying it. Webster was a veteran attorney and now head of the State Department who realized that neither lawyer nor diplomat was bound to reveal evidence damaging to his client.

Sparks's submission was not the revelation he believed it to be. More than three years earlier, Webster had received another map containing a red-line boundary "too much like this." In 1838 the British consul in New York had the chance to purchase a Mitchell map of 1775 that had belonged to Revolutionary War leader Baron Friedrich von Steuben and that had red lines matching those on Sparks's map. The consul had doubted the map's authenticity because there was no way to determine who had drawn the boundary or how Steuben had acquired the map. Later that same year, however, Webster bought the Steuben map from the baron's heir for $200 and, probably to put pressure on Maine to compromise on the boundary, sold it for the same price to Charles Daveis, an agent of the Maine government who was then in Washington working with the state's congressional delegation to locate the Paris treaty line of 1783.[25]

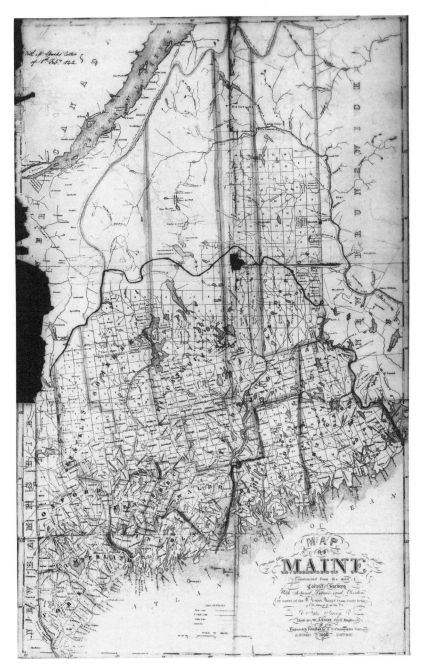

Jared Sparks's map of Maine. *Courtesy National Archives.*

The trail of maps then took a sharp turn eastward when, in May 1842, more than a month after Ashburton's arrival in Washington, Everett in London became curious about whether the British had concealed maps from the United States. He had asked Aberdeen about the wisdom of searching the British archives for the map used in Paris during the negotiations of 1783, and the foreign secretary seemed evasive. Aberdeen admitted to hearing that the archives contained an old map, but Everett came away from the meeting convinced that it was not the Mitchell map used in the Paris talks by the British negotiators, Richard Oswald and Henry Strachey. Everett remained certain, however, that another map was somewhere within the Foreign Office.[26]

Although Everett did not know it at the time, the map referred to by Aberdeen was later found in the State Paper Office (the present-day Public Record Office) in June 1842. It was a Mitchell map of 1755 and traced the British claim with a red line. The Foreign Office immediately informed the cabinet of the discovery, and it assigned three cartographers the task of authenticating the map. A close acquaintance of several members of the Peel ministry, Charles Greville, recorded in his diary that British officials were confident that the map had been used in Paris. Yet it seems likely that Aberdeen doubted the feasibility of using it to validate British claims; his correspondence with Ashburton contains nothing about the matter.[27]

Everett strongly suspected that the map used by Oswald in the Paris negotiations was in the British archives and that it supported the American claim to the disputed territory. Indeed, Everett's suspicions have caused some historians to deduce that both he and Sparks thought as early as 1838 that the papers of the Earl of Lansdowne (previously Lord Shelburne, prime minister in 1782) contained materials proving the American claims. This charge seems unlikely. Sparks later assured Everett that there was no evidence of this sort in the Lansdowne papers; further, Everett's reasoning probably rested on something other than any alleged item in the collection. He told Webster in mid-June 1842 that the Paris negotiators had used Mitchell maps from London; that the Americans had sent their copy home whereas the British had not; and that British officials had recently been scrutinizing everyone, including Sparks, who worked in the State Paper Office. For about a month, Everett added, four clerks had been culling through Revolutionary War documents. But Webster had made a decision even before receiving this note. Confident that a boundary settlement was within reach and that further map revelations would have an adverse effect, he instructed Everett to *"forbear to press the search after maps in England or elsewhere."*[28]

Regardless of the unreliability of both the Sparks and Steuben maps, they supported the British claims, and for that reason Webster intended to conceal them until the negotiations were over. Their release would force the London government to demand all territory in dispute, and the outcome would be war—particularly because of Maine's rigid opposition to giving up any of the land. Sparks's revelation had created a potential problem that Webster had to avoid. In truth, the red line on Sparks's map (dated 1746) was probably the southern edge of France's claims against Britain before the French and Indian War. In any case, it is difficult to believe that a shrewd diplomat such as Franklin would have conceded so much land to the British. Webster was justified in hiding the maps.[29]

While the map issue simmered, Webster took an unconventional step: he invited Maine and Massachusetts to send representatives to the negotiations in Washington. Given the sensitive nature of federal and state relations, this was a wise move. Further, he realized that Senate approval of any treaty with Britain greatly depended on whether these two states condoned the proposed settlement. In a private letter to Reuel Williams, Democratic senator from Maine and archcritic of the White House, Webster emphasized the importance of a boundary compromise with compensation and, at the president's suggestion, made an important request: Would the state consider sending delegates to the talks with Ashburton? Williams seemed amenable to the proposal but stipulated certain conditions: Maine might consider equivalents in exchange for granting land to Britain for a military road, but only after the British withdrew their troops from the disputed area. Williams and others in the state did not believe that the British would accept a compromise. Until Her Majesty's Government publicly declared its willingness to do so, Maine's legislature refused to consider Webster's proposal.[30]

Webster made inquiries among Maine's legislators to determine whether they were open to a compromise. He sent two men to Augusta: Peleg Sprague, a federal district judge in Boston and former senator from Maine who had tempered his original demands on the boundary; and Albert Smith, a former federal marshal and now lame-duck congressman from the state. They discovered that both Whigs and Democrats privately preferred a peaceful resolution of the issue but were afraid to take a public stand because of the political consequences. Leaders in Maine seemed prepared to give up land north of the St. John River—to accommodate Britain's desired military road—in exchange for navigation rights on the river and a reciprocal concession in land. They were also willing to send a commission to the negotiations in Washington but were concerned that the step would be politically calamitous. For their mission to Maine, Sprague received $250, though reporting an expense of only $30, while Smith received $600 for his ninety days, which included trips to Augusta, Boston, and Portland. All compensation came from the president's secret-service fund.[31]

The Sprague-Smith mission offered Webster more than a faint glimmer of hope. In view of the favorable impact of the newspaper campaign, it seemed likely that Maine would support the idea of a boundary compromise with reciprocity as the guiding principle in the Washington negotiations. The key to success, Webster believed, was to have representatives from Maine present at the table. In that regard, he agreed with Francis Smith, who had earlier emphasized that Maine posed the real problem. Since that state's attitude was pivotal to the success of the Ashburton talks, Webster felt justified in drawing from the president's secret-service fund. Some historians have nonetheless criticized the secretary of state for using this fund illegally or improperly, and they have insisted that the newspaper campaign was a mere program in propaganda that used unwarranted scare tactics to achieve a White House goal.[32] And yet, Maine's actions had direct impact on Anglo-American relations, which fitted the provisions of the law establishing the secret-service fund—"for the contingent expenses of intercourse between the United States and foreign nations."

In fact, there were no deceptions or distortions contained in the newspaper articles, which are the usual trademarks of propaganda. As a practical-minded diplomat, Webster knew that he had to deal with a number of variables that affected the coming talks in Washington. Anglophobia, states' rights, domestic politics, and national honor had combined to pose formidable obstacles to an international settlement. By writing editorials calling for a boundary compromise with equivalents, by inviting Maine and Massachusetts to send delegates to Washington, by concealing dubious maps that could only cause further trouble, and by financing much of the above with money earmarked for issues affecting foreign relations, Webster laid the groundwork for the best opportunity since 1783 to delineate the northeastern border of the United States.

III

Early on the morning of April 4, Lord Ashburton, weary from a long and arduous voyage across the stormy Atlantic, arrived in the United States. Ill winds had blown the *Warspite* off course from New York and into the waters of Annapolis, where he received a ceremonious welcome by Maryland state officials. The emissary's entourage was impressive: three secretaries (including his son-in-law from the Foreign Office, Humphrey Mildmay), five servants, a carriage with three horses, and a large amount of baggage. Webster had prepared lodgings near his own residence in Washington, a huge and grandly furnished dwelling on Lafayette Square (the present-day parish house of St. John's Episcopal Church), which Ashburton leased for $1,000 per month. After traveling to Washington, he met briefly with President Tyler and delivered a short speech before presenting his credentials. With these formalities concluded, Ashburton joined Webster for a tour of the city that included the Capitol, Senate, and Library of Congress.[33]

Most Americans were confident of success in the negotiations now that Ashburton had arrived, while others preferred to withhold judgment. The normally Anglophobic New York *Herald* conceded that the emissary was "republican" in demeanor and appearance. Nearly six feet tall, stooped in walk, pale in color, and heavyset, he had dark eyes, thick eyebrows, and thinning white hair. But he was graced with an "active step," a "quick eye," and a plainness in manner that suggested a capacity to understand Americans. Even the staunch critic of Britain, Senator Thomas Hart Benton of Missouri, admired Ashburton. *Niles' Register* predicted a treaty that satisfied all antagonists. Not everyone agreed with this optimistic view. In the House, Joshua Lowell of Maine solemnly warned that Ashburton had come with olive branch in one hand and sword in the other, emblematic of the choice awaiting the United States. Even the name of the ship—the *Warspite*—was portentous. In actuality, Lowell was campaigning for more money to facilitate the defense of the border, but he expressed an attitude common to more than a few Americans: Ashburton must first win the trust of Maine before he had a chance of securing a treaty.[34]

After Ashburton offered assurances of his willingness to compromise on the boundary, Webster informed him of the necessity of having Maine and Massachusetts take part in the negotiations. Ashburton expressed grave reservations about such an unusual procedure. America's democratic institutions, he believed, were most notable for the chaos they created. The Maine legislature, he confided to Aberdeen, was a "wild and uncertain Body." In any case, the Senate would not allow the state to participate in drawing a treaty. Was not such a procedure unconstitutional? Could a delegation from Maine agree on anything? Tyler and Webster, Ashburton thought, wanted a peaceful settlement but were restricted by their frenetic political system. Indeed, the government in Washington acted under the influence of a "lower description" of people than in any other part of the world. And yet, somehow a "strange Confused state of Government moves on." Clumsy though it was, this "Mass of ungovernable and unmanageable anarchy" could unite in war and demonstrate tremendous power. It was wise to "humour the wild Beast."[35] And so Ashburton gave his reluctant consent to Webster's proposal.

Webster acted before Ashburton had a chance to change his mind. The secretary warned Governor Fairfield of Maine and Governor Davis of Massachusetts that it was in their best interests to send commissioners to Washington as quickly as possible. Fairfield's Democratic party was deeply divided, however, and many leaders urged him to call a special session of the legislature to emphasize the necessity of joining the negotiations before the two chief diplomats settled on boundary terms without Maine's input. Such a dramatic approach, Fairfield's advisers believed, might also undercut the popular clamor against compromise. Indeed, the Portland *Advertiser* carried an article (written by Francis Smith) praising Webster's invitation. At long last, the date for a special session was set—May 18. In the meantime, Webster learned that the governor of Massachusetts had received authorization, with his council's advice, to appoint a commission. Davis was a politician and thus found it necessary to posture first by blasting Britain publicly as a thief and warning it to stop "bullying" the United States; but then he privately assured Webster that the state would agree to a boundary settlement with suitable equivalents.[36] Once Maine agreed to send commissioners to Washington, Massachusetts would do the same.

Webster now took the final step toward securing Maine's participation. He used the red-line maps to persuade the state's leaders that further delay might cost them far more in territory than any form of compromise settlement. In preparation for this objective, Webster covertly traveled to Boston to apprise Governor Davis of the Sparks map supporting the British claim to the entire area in dispute. While there, the secretary drew $300 from the president's secret-service fund to buy back the Steuben map from Charles Daveis, who had recently converted to the principle of compromise and had brought the map to Boston for Webster. Now, in mid-May, just days before the opening of the special legislative session in Maine, Webster sent Jared Sparks to Augusta to show Fairfield the Sparks and Steuben maps. Webster hoped that the governor might convince political leaders to accept the principle of compromise before they lost the entire area. Governor Fairfield agreed that the time had come to resolve the boundary dispute.[37]

Some writers have questioned the ethics of Webster's using the Sparks map in such a manner, but surely he was justified in doing so.[38] He doubtless knew that both it and the Steuben maps were at the very least of questionable validity, and yet this was not the critical issue. Publication of these maps at some indeterminate time in the future would harden British demands for the disputed territory, no matter how dubious the maps were. Maine would have to decide whether to give up the entire area or urge the government in Washington to go to war on the state's behalf. The Atlantic nations were closer to a boundary settlement than ever before; Maine's failure to attend the negotiations would assure the absence of Massachusetts and hence abort the highly promising talks about to begin. Further delay would provide more time for more maps to appear that favored the British claim. Use of the maps, regardless of their spurious character, constituted a legitimate warning based on the very real possibility of war.

Those unaware of Webster's private machinations must have been surprised at the rapidity with which the Maine legislature approved the commission idea. On the day that the legislature convened, May 18, Fairfield recommended the appointment of commissioners, and a joint committee unanimously approved. Indeed, the legislature approved the principle of compromise without imposing any restrictions on the commissioners' actions in the negotiations. Webster had been concerned that the imposition of conditions would reduce Ashburton's latitude to accept or reject terms and thereby leave little flexibility in the talks. But Peleg Sprague proved correct in assuring Webster that even though a few of Maine's legislators urged a referendum on the question of giving directives to the commissioners, their proposal would not pass. The legislature emphasized, however, that it would not accept money from Britain because such a step implied the sale of land and hence an insult to the state's honor. In exchange for giving up any of the land in dispute, Maine wanted free navigation of the St. John River and federal reimbursement for the costs of defending the territory in the past.[39]

Webster's adept use of the Sparks and Steuben maps proved decisive in softening Maine's disposition toward the negotiations. On May 26 the legislature voted 177 to 11 in the house and 29 to 0 in the senate to send four commissioners to Washington. The only restriction on their behavior was a directive to accept no compromise without unanimous consent. As commissioners, the most notable were Democrat William Pitt Preble, erstwhile and often irascible leader of the opposition to the Netherlands award of 1831, and former Whig governor Edward Kent. The other two selected were Democrat Edward Kavanagh and Whig John Otis. Predictably, Massachusetts followed suit. In that same month, Governor Davis appointed a three-member delegation composed of Charles Allen, Abbott Lawrence, and John Mills—all Whigs.[40]

Webster requested that both delegations appear in Washington no later than June 12. Maine's delegation arrived on that date and notified Webster of its readiness to begin work. The next day the Massachusetts group arrived. Later that same day Webster met with both delegations in the State Department and was delighted to see that even Preble seemed amenable to compromise. And yet, a settlement was by no means assured: Ashburton had already been in the United States for a month longer than the one month he had allowed for the mission, and the two diplomats had still not begun any meaningful talks on the boundary. But Webster felt confident about dealing with a trusted friend, especially now that the two chief obstacles—Maine and Massachusetts—were committed to the principle of compromise. For the first time since 1783 the outcome of the long-standing border disputes depended on peacekeepers in Washington and London.[41]

Unknown to Webster, however, the problems so endemic to international negotiations had already begun to develop—with the initial complication coming out of London. While Ashburton was en route to the United States, Aberdeen had conferred with Wellington and other military figures for advice on a boundary that assured the security of British North America, and the result was a stiffening of directives that took away much of the flexibility previously given to Ashburton. Rather than accept the Netherlands award as the minimal objective, Ashburton was to call for more land between the upper St. John and St. Lawrence rivers, thereby running the boundary along the St. John from its source in a northeasterly direction to its junction with the St. Francis. Britain would acquire a land buffer that made it easier to protect the new military road between Halifax and Quebec. Ashburton's son-in-law and companion in Washington, Humphrey Mildmay, reacted with alarm. Such demand for land above the St. John would wreck the negotiations, he wrote Aberdeen. But the Peel ministry remained insistent on the revised instructions and directed its special minister to allow only moderate concessions in the lower St. John Valley.[42]

Then a second and equally stealthy problem arose—the offer of cash in the negotiations. Aberdeen did not grasp the negative implications that such a financial transaction would have on Maine's sense of honor, and he cavalierly remarked that if it did not accept equivalents in the form of territory, the British government "would be disposed to indemnify" the state with a "pecuniary compensation." Such payment, he penned in a private note to Ashburton, need not be excessive in view of the poor financial condition of America. Although leaders in London were not aware of Maine's rigid opposition to accepting money from Britain, Peel showed some insight in warning Ashburton to exercise discretion with the subject. The prime minister did not take into consideration the negative impact that an exchange of money would have on Maine's honor, as its legislators had emphasized; rather, he feared that such an approach might hurt British interests. Maine, Peel declared, might refuse to sell and interpret the financial offer as a British admission to the state's sovereignty over the disputed territory.[43]

Once the issue of money became fair game for official disclosure, it opened a veritable Pandora's box of possibilities. In a private letter to Ashburton, New Brunswick's lieutenant governor, Sir William Colebrooke, insisted that Maine would accept money in the negotiations, despite its self-righteous "bluster" about refusing to sell American land. But Colebrooke warned that any financial proposal must come from Maine. A friend of President Tyler's, James Hamilton, told him of having recently attended a dinner party in London at which Aberdeen "plainly intimated" that Britain would pay up to $500,000 to secure land for a military road. When Hamilton remarked that New Englanders were "pretty sharp at a bargain," Aberdeen craftily replied, "Where there is a will there is a way." When Ashburton asked Aberdeen about the exchange, the foreign secretary denied any mention of money in the conversation but noted that a modest sum would be acceptable to Parliament as long as the offer originated with the Tyler administration and the result was an improvement on the Netherlands award. Hamilton's story, according to Ashburton, had "set Governor Davis [of Massachusetts] dreaming about money"—so much so that he probably "promoted the same Golden visions" throughout his own state and Maine as well.[44]

Whatever the truth of the story, Ashburton had gotten approval to dispense money in the negotiations and immediately informed Webster. The secretary of state was surprisingly reluctant to approve such an approach. Not only would Maine object, he declared, but also many other Americans would denounce a British payment as a real estate purchase of American land. As for Davis's lofty expectations on the amount, Webster dismissed them as absurd. Ashburton meanwhile lightheartedly assured London that he would defend the Exchequer from the avaricious Americans. The important point was that the money issue was now inextricably linked to the boundary issue and hence a vital part of the negotiations despite the predictable complaints from Maine.[45]

One final complication entered the scene even before the negotiations began. In an effort to reach a settlement satisfactory to New Brunswick, Ashburton acted on his own in writing Lieutenant Governor Colebrooke for advice. Without first consulting either Peel or Aberdeen, he made the ill-advised and highly secretive decision to ask Colebrooke to send someone knowledgeable about the boundary to Washington. In response to Ashburton's letter, Colebrooke sent a three-member secret delegation composed of James MacLauchlan, the warden of the disputed territory; a private secretary from the lieutenant governor's office; and the speaker of the New Brunswick assembly, a wealthy businessman who owned land in the town of St. John and along the river. In addition to their private meeting with Ashburton in Washington, another person conferred with the emissary as well: Sir John Caldwell, who had discussed the boundary problems with Maine legislators during the Aroostook crisis of 1839 and owned one of the largest sawmills in the area.[46]

Webster was probably aware of these men's presence in Washington, but he could not have known that it was their territorial demands that nearly wrecked the discussions. Ashburton learned that in exchange for an "equitable adjustment," New Brunswick would permit Maine to have free use of the St. John River; but the British province staunchly refused to give up any of the Madawaska settlements. Such a concession, the three-man delegation warned, would alienate the British settlers in the region and effectively close communications between Nova Scotia and the Canadian interior. Above all, they declared, no Americans could be in the St. John

Valley.[47] Ashburton's well-meaning but highly unorthodox approach to diplomacy had exposed the obvious: local interests in the disputed territory had always been much more extreme than those advanced by either national government. Aberdeen had authorized his emissary to compromise on the Madawaska settlements; New Brunswick demanded them all. Not only did Ashburton have to resolve the boundary problems between the United States and Britain, but he also must first settle those between his home government and that of New Brunswick.

Despite the Machiavellian tactics used by the major participants in the swiftly approaching negotiations, the outward appearance continued to be that of two dignitaries prepared to discuss Anglo-American difficulties in an open, honest, and harmonious manner. The reality was far different. Diplomats on both sides had, almost as a matter of course, taken the Byzantine paths of diplomacy: intrigue, scheming, and secret maneuverings, all justified in the name of national honor—or, more broadly, the national interest. Whether right or wrong in their methods, Webster and Ashburton had finally put the northeastern boundary question into the hands of the two national governments involved. And that was a good sign.

CHAPTER SIX

Epilogue to the American Revolution: The Webster-Ashburton Treaty and National Honor

Blessed are the peacemakers.
—President John Tyler, August 1842

At last, on June 18, Daniel Webster and Lord Ashburton began their negotiations. Their first decision suggested the tenor of the talks: the conversations would be informal and general, purposely ignoring diplomatic protocol in favor of open, honest, and friendly discussions. After all, Ashburton observed, he was dealing with a person of "Penetration" who did not have to resort to the "tools of ordinary diplomacy." To encourage straightforward negotiations, Ashburton had also decided against having any direct communications with the seven state commissioners; they must express their interests only through Webster. Moreover, the two diplomats did not want minutes kept of their meetings; such an approach would promote candor. After reaching agreements, they would submit their written exchanges regarding those agreements to President Tyler for his approval before their release to the public.[1]

The atmosphere of congeniality and friendship spread beyond the meeting room. Each dignitary hosted lavish dinner parties and other social events heralding the imminent settlement of all differences between the Atlantic nations. Ashburton supplemented his fine foods with rare wines and exquisite desserts prepared by a French chef, while Webster graced his table with American specialties that included oysters, Maine salmon, Virginia terrapin, Maryland crabs, and Chesapeake duck. Webster buoyantly wrote an acquaintance in Parliament that there had never been "a pair of more friendly negotiators" to "put their heads together." They would "smooth away all frowns and scowls" from skeptics on both sides of the ocean and replace them with the "most gracious smiles."[2] High-sounding and laudable objectives, certainly—but such procedures guaranteed more problems for historians investigating this complex story.

I

Despite these good intentions, the old and familiar patterns of diplomacy once again crept onto the scene as the two chief negotiators reverted to secrecy and private arrangements. Neither man was very experienced in international affairs and had already resorted to unorthodox methods that introduced new meaning to the so-called art of diplomacy. Both men had engaged in clandestine activities that further complicated an already complicated situation. Ashburton had initially assured Webster that the British position rested on flexibility, and yet his covert and unauthorized inquiry into New Brunswick's sentiments soon produced a negative impact. It put enormous pressure on him to go beyond Lord Aberdeen's instructions and demand all of Madawaska, an area populated by British subjects and situated above Grand Falls and along both sides of the upper St. John River.

Thus, when Webster and Ashburton focused on the northeastern boundary, they quickly became mired down in the same detailed arguments over rivers, valleys, angles, and parallels that had frustrated all previous attempts at a settlement. The British emissary found himself caught between his directives from home, which permitted him to sacrifice Madawaska in the interests of compromise, and the stipulations from New Brunswick, which approved no compromise. Consequently, Ashburton first appealed for all of the area by pointing out that British subjects south of the St. John River would never be happy under American rule. Madawaska, he explained, had come into existence through the efforts of French settlers from Acadia and had always been under either French or British governance. Its residents had recently petitioned the queen to oppose any incorporation by the United States. Not only was it a matter of honor, Ashburton emphasized, but it was also integral to national security. American hegemony over the south bank of the St. John would jeopardize London's chief objective of securing an all-season military link between the Canadian hinterland and the Atlantic.[3]

Daniel Webster. *Courtesy Library of Congress.*

The only solution, Ashburton noted, lay in British control of the entire Madawaska Valley; a split would unjustifiably award the Americans the southern part, which was considerably richer in farms and timberland than that in the north. In exchange for U.S. recognition of British rights to the river valley, he would permit Maine free navigation of the St. John for transporting produce into New

Brunswick (which benefited Britain as much as the United States). Ashburton also would concede the fertile lands at the head of the Connecticut River and a piece of territory along the British side of the 45th parallel, which included the American fort at Rouses Point. This was no small concession; by it, the United States would gain a strategically important slice of land already populated by Americans. His only goal, he emphasized to Webster, was to placate the residents of all areas concerned.[4]

There was little chance that Aberdeen would support New Brunswick's demand for all of Madawaska. More important than these local concerns were the interests of the British Empire. The foreign secretary's central goal was to acquire sufficient land for an all-weather military road. He could never have held out for more than the Netherlands award (which he had already stipulated as the minimum boundary requirement), nor could he have supported a plea for even more land than that demanded by his military advisers. Aberdeen did not welcome the "ugly appearance" of Americans living within sight of Quebec, regardless of whether that territory between the upper St. John and St. Lawrence rivers was a "mere swamp." But in protecting Quebec, he never contemplated pushing the Americans out of Madawaska. To secure the minimum land necessary for a military road, he authorized Ashburton to grant Maine navigation rights on the St. John. Aberdeen certainly thought that an American settlement of the boundary question would lead to better British relations with France; he also feared that failure of the Ashburton mission could ultimately lead to hostilities with the United States. It was wiser to erect a longer military road around the hump of Maine and through a slimmer belt of land between New Brunswick and Quebec than to risk war by refusing to compromise on the disputed territory.[5]

Ashburton (still without Aberdeen's knowledge) proved so persistent, however, in his demands for Madawaska that by the end of June, Webster's lofty expectations of an early boundary settlement had disappeared. Acrimony had set in not only between the two chief diplomats but also between Washington and the state commissioners, and between the Maine and Massachusetts commissioners themselves. Webster was not aware of New Brunswick's demands, but he sensed that something was wrong: Ashburton seemed under a severe strain, probably due to the poor health of his wife combined with the sweltering heat of Washington and stiffened directives from the Foreign Office. In any case, by mid-July the emissary seemed interested only in returning home. Webster, too, felt frustrated by the sour turn of events and even convinced Ashburton to meet with the state commissioners. Nothing good came of the discussion, however, and Ashburton expressed his mounting disgust in a note to Aberdeen: "My real difficulty is with Webster who yields & promises everything, but when it comes to execution is so weak & timid and irresolute that he is frightened by everybody and at last does nothing."[6]

As the negotiations careened toward failure, Webster asked Tyler to talk with the minister. Although the president's wife was sickly and near death, he took time from his personal tribulations to cajole Ashburton into continuing the negotiations. Surely the British lord would not have crossed the Atlantic to undertake such an arduous mission, Tyler told him in a personal conversation, unless he really wanted to resolve all problems between the English-speaking peoples. If "you cannot settle them," the president concluded, "what man in England can?" Ashburton responded to the flattery as hoped: "Well! Well! Mr. President, we must try again."[7]

Despite the brief flair of optimism, the negotiations continued to bog down in detail and rigid demands by both sides. In response to Ashburton's appeal for all of Madawaska, Maine sternly maintained its initial position of refusing to accept any line south of the St. John River. The state admitted to the reasonable nature of Britain's call for a stretch of land between Halifax and Quebec for a military road, but it insisted that Ashburton's inflated territorial demand was excessive and unfair—particularly when the exalted British emissary offered nothing comparable in return. Navigation rights on the St. John constituted no meaningful concession: the British would profit as much as the Americans from the increased commerce passing down the river. If he continued in this demand, the state commissioners warned Webster, they would return home. Had they known that Ashburton intended to take a stand for all of the disputed territory, they would not have come to Washington in the first place. The only settlement agreeable to Maine (and Massachusetts) was a boundary at the St. John along with free use of the river.[8]

Ashburton unjustly blamed everyone but himself for the stalled negotiations. He had led Webster to believe that the only British guideline was compromise, and the secretary of state had acted accordingly in maneuvering Maine with the newspaper campaign and red-line maps and then inviting both New England states to the Washington talks. But Ashburton, and understandably so, considered it improper for a special emissary to talk with state representatives. And yet, he secretly pursued the same tactics with New Brunswick. Then, instead of opening his own private overtures with an emphasis on compromise (as Webster did), Ashburton made the huge mistake of asking what New Brunswick wanted. The answer was predictable: all of the disputed territory. Not recognizing the dangerous implications of his own ill-advised actions, he castigated others. He condemned Webster's weakness in the face of Maine's obstreperous behavior. Ashburton then focused on the oppressive heat of summertime Washington and declared that his only goal was to "move out of this oven." Finally, he admonished Aberdeen in a letter: "You, My Dear Lord, have not contributed much to get me out of it." American domestic politics, the emissary's favorite object of scorn, also drew his criticism as deteriorating Mexican affairs demanded U.S. attention and President Tyler became preoccupied with his bitter battle against Henry Clay's bank bill. No boundary settlement seemed possible, Ashburton lamented—even if he gave up Madawaska.[9]

To Webster, Ashburton privately wrote a sarcastic note that revealed how his good nature and high expectations had evaporated in the stifling heat of Washington:

> I must throw myself on your compassion to contrive somehow or other to get me released.—
>
> I contrive to crawl about in this heat by day & to live my nights in a sleepless fever. In short I shall positively not outlive this affair if it is to be much prolonged. I had hoped that these Gentlemen from the North East would be Equally averse to this roasting. Could you not press them to come to the point and say whether we can or can not agree? I do not see why I should be kept waiting while Maine & Massachusetts settle their accounts with the General Government. . . .
>
> Pray save me from these profound politicians for my nerves will not stand so much cunning wisdom.[10]

Ashburton's ire soon focused on the most influential member of the Maine commission, William Pitt Preble, who had emerged as the "very obstinate" leader of the obstructionists. The emissary's undisguised rancor toward Preble created an unfortunate situation, because Webster had realized from the start that his primary task was to convince the Maine commissioner that the state could not have all the territory in question. Preble had bitterly fought against the Netherlands award of 1831 and certainly would reject any British demand exceeding that decision. What an achievement to win over Preble to the principle of compromise! But Ashburton's demand for all of Madawaska had revived Preble's demand for the entire area in dispute and ensured a major confrontation with the British emissary. Preble angrily urged his colleagues to leave Wash-

Alexander Baring, Lord Ashburton. *Courtesy Library of Congress.*

ington and warn the state's people that the imperious British intended to expand below the St. John River.[11] Ashburton had brought on this highly intensified situation, and yet he pointed an accusing finger at Preble before laying the ultimate blame at Webster's feet for inviting state commissioners to a meeting between nations.

Ashburton's discomfiture was not eased by Aberdeen's clumsy attempt to seek outside assistance in the struggling negotiations. The foreign secretary realized that the British consul in Boston, Thomas Grattan, was familiar with the boundary controversy and with many of the persons involved; indeed, the Maine commissioners had invited him to accompany them to Washington. Grattan assured Aberdeen that the vote of the state representatives had to be unanimous and warned that Ashburton must somehow satisfy them. In a move that clearly angered Ashburton, Aberdeen recommended that Grattan talk with Preble about a possible compromise line. Such a suggestion demonstrates again that Ashburton had not informed the Foreign Office of the private talks with New Brunswick. It also put the emissary in an awkward position. He had already stated his demand for all of Madawaska and now would have to retreat due to the intrusion of a lowly consul from Boston. Nonetheless, Ashburton put up a convincing front of cooperation—to the point that Grattan later declared that he had followed the emissary's "repeated urgent request" to bring harmony to the talks. But in the end, at least according to Grattan's version, he himself had been responsible for convincing Preble to remain in Washington.[12]

Maine's commissioners were uplifted by the poorly concealed enmity between Ashburton and Grattan. No matter how well Ashburton played the role of conciliator, they knew that he had demanded more than what Grattan found acceptable. The consul had meanwhile become frustrated with Preble and told Aberdeen that the commissioner's lodgings were littered with maps, reports, and other detailed documents relating to the boundary, all confirming his rigid determination to exploit any loophole to Maine's advantage. Throughout Grattan's intercession, Ashburton maintained a cordial demeanor, but he privately expressed dislike for the consul's aggressive behavior, relished his defeat, and yearned to celebrate his return to Boston.[13]

Like Ashburton, Grattan attributed the failing negotiations to considerations other than the obvious cause of competing local interests. Maine had agreed to a compromise that would take its territory to the St. John River; Ashburton had insisted on every bit of the land in dispute—the entire St. John Valley—and thus revived bitter memories about British imperialism, obstinate behavior, and utter lack of respect for America. Ashburton's unauthorized contact with New Brunswick had forced him to violate his instructions from London along with his own initial assurance of compromise. In other times, his actions would have led to his recall. But his position was not in danger because he had not informed Aberdeen of the source of the problem, and, in any case, the foreign secretary realized that the special mission must work. No other diplomatic approach remained. As the negotiations continued to fail, Ashburton should not have been surprised that Preble wrote an informal memorandum containing "some rather coarse insinuations" about British motives.[14]

II

With the negotiations at a standstill, it was almost inevitable that issues of money and self-interest entered the scene—particularly because of Webster's rapacious pecuniary appetite and insatiable personal ambitions. For years historians have debated whether the secretary of state privately accepted money from Ashburton in exchange for a boundary settlement favorable to England. According to the accusation, Webster's foremost objective in the negotiations was to win favor in England and thereby facilitate his bid for replacing Everett as minister. Thus, the story goes that Webster gave up Maine's legitimate claim to the territory in question, choosing to sacrifice the state's interests for those of his own and thereby discrediting himself in the process. The bribery charges rest on Webster's deployment of the Sparks and Steuben maps supporting the British claim to all the disputed area, his alleged obsession with the London post, and, most important, a private note dated August 9, 1842, from Ashburton to Aberdeen.[15]

It is easy to counter the arguments regarding the maps and the alleged desire for the ministerial post in London. As shown earlier, both the Sparks and Steuben maps were invalid, and no one has presented conclusive evidence that Webster sold out his country in an effort to win the Peel ministry's support for his diplomatic appointment to England. In the first place, no amount of popularity in England could assure him a foreign post that required Senate approval. Second, and even more noteworthy, he and Everett exchanged a number of private letters showing that by the late summer of 1842 the secretary maintained his close friendship with Everett (who even offered to resign) and did not seek his place in London. Granted, Webster entertained thoughts of heading a special mission to deal with the growing Oregon Question, but only because of the importance of the matter and the realization that the appointment would be of limited duration. Given his longtime interest in the presidency, it seems unlikely that he would accept a position outside the country that would cost him daily personal contact with supporters at home.[16]

Even if one dismissed all the above as inconclusive, several questions remain that undermine the charges against Webster. Would he have given up the American claim to the disputed territory, particularly since it lay in his native New England? How could he expect the Senate to condone such a clear sacrifice of U.S. territory? If an inquiry took place, how could he keep Maine from revealing the maps and accusing him of making a nefarious deal?

The argument relating to the letter of August 9, 1842, from Ashburton to Aberdeen is equally faulty. In it the British minister raised the subject of money and, in doing so, stirred up provocative questions about whether Webster was guilty of misconduct. "The money I wrote about," Ashburton explained, "went to compensate Sparkes [*sic*] & to send him, on my first arrival, to the Governors of Maine & Massachusetts. My informant thinks that without this stimulant Maine would never have yielded." After then discussing a number of other items in this lengthy letter, Ashburton returned to the topic of money: "I have drawn on you a bill for £2,998.1 [about $14,500] . . . for the purpose mentioned in my former private letter and you will find this put into proper form. I am not likely to want any thing more." Only Webster, according to his detractors, could have shared information of this nature with Ashburton. This letter, according to their argument, proves that Ashburton used British funds to fill the secretary's pockets and thus lay the basis for a favorable boundary settlement. In return, Webster could build a following in England that facilitated his long-desired appointment to the post in London.[17]

Following the trail of money is always an intriguing quest, and it was no less so in this instance. In the confidential postscript of a private note to Aberdeen of June 14, 1842 (the "former private letter" mentioned above), Ashburton expressed his suspicions that Webster had uncovered some shadowy piece of evidence supporting the British boundary claim—clearly the Sparks and Steuben maps, although not yet realized by Ashburton—and had used it in some manner with the state commissioners. The timing of this letter could not have been coincidental. Just the day before, Webster showed at least the Sparks map to the Maine delegates. Ashburton's anonymous source of information was high-level in position or influence and hence reliable. Aberdeen certainly thought so. On July 2 he hastily replied that he had passed on the June 14 letter to Peel "under injunctions of the strictest secrecy."[18]

These tantalizing statements made the search for the monetary Grail even more engrossing. The confidential postscript, it became clear, would supply a critical piece to the puzzle that has long eluded those historians writing about the Webster-Ashburton negotiations. Unfortunately, a search for the letter in both the Peel and Aberdeen papers in London yielded nothing. This omission proved especially exasperating because in Aberdeen's letter of July 2 he alluded to a pivotal event:

> But this incident [whatever was discussed in the missing postscript] has, I confess, quite taken me by surprise, and opens a new view of measures which perhaps may be followed up with advantage, should there yet be time for you to do so. In order to insure success, you need not be afraid of employing the same means to a greater extent in any quarter where it may be necessary. In what you have done you have been perfectly right; and indeed I look upon the proposal made to you from such a quarter, as the most certain indication we could receive of a determination to bring the negotiation to a happy issue. In any further transactions of the same kind, I have only to desire that it may be made the means of leading to success, as the condition of having recourse to it. If you can command success you need not hesitate.[19]

However undeniable Webster's voracious appetite for money, no justification exists for claiming, as some writers have done, that he was Ashburton's informant.[20] Nowhere in the letter does Webster's name appear. Indeed, the only certainty is that the British minister paid an unnamed confidant some or all of £2,998.1 for information of an unspecified nature. More important, it is highly unlikely that Webster would have shown the Sparks and Steuben maps to both the Maine commissioners and Ashburton. The maps supported the British claim, and it would have been consistent with the secretary's newspaper campaign and the dispatch of Sparks to Maine in February to unveil them to the commissioners as part of the administration's ongoing effort to secure a compromise. For that same reason it made no sense to show the same maps to Ashburton; it would have hardened his demands for Madawaska and perhaps even expanded them southward. Further, Ashburton does not even mention whether the information he sought was a map. His private letter to Aberdeen of June 14 suggests that he had not seen any information to this point: "I have some reason to suspect that Webster has discovered some evidence, known at present to nobody, but favorable to our claim, and that he is using it with the Commissioners. I have some clue to this fact and hope to get at it."

If Ashburton had learned of the maps supporting the entire British claim, he could not have given in without betraying his own people. Evidence establishes that Webster showed the red-line maps to him, but only after he had agreed to a boundary compromise— on August 9 at the signing ceremony. That same day, Ashburton wrote Aberdeen with a clear sense of relief: "I should certainly, if I had known the secret earlier, have made my stand on the upper St. Johns & probably at the Madawaska settlements."[21] Such a demand would have aborted the negotiations, because Maine felt entitled to at least the southern half of the disputed territory and would have resisted anything less. Webster's longtime experience with the boundary controversy surely made him recognize that sharing the maps with Ashburton would have crushed all hopes for a boundary settlement.

Other considerations likewise show that Webster did not receive money from Ashburton during the negotiations. From February through December of 1842 the secretary was frantically trying to borrow from other sources. Some writers have argued that Ashburton's remark, "the money I wrote about," referred to British funds that passed through Webster's hands before financing Sparks's mission to Augusta. Thus, Ashburton again broached the subject of money at the end of the letter when he talked of the £2,998.1. But this argument is a flawed one. After his initial reference to money, he turned to various other matters affecting the negotiations before returning to the subject in the concluding section that addressed the £2,998.1 drawn from Aberdeen. The two references were not to the same British source. Ashburton had likely learned from his informant that the money underwriting Sparks's mission to Augusta had come from the White House—perhaps even from the president's secret-service fund. The second reference was to the amount transferred from British sources to the unnamed informant. When Aberdeen instructed his emissary to use the "same means" where prudent, he referred to the money paid by Ashburton to his informant.[22]

There is yet another compelling point. It is doubtful that an adept businessman such as Ashburton (the former head of Baring Brothers) would have approved the allotment of that much money for a task already completed and much more unlikely that he paid so dearly for evidence that he did not see until late July or early August—nearly six months after the Sparks mission. Ashburton wrote Aberdeen on August 9: "Since I communicated to you the very extraordinary information about the Boundary, I have seen Sparkes's [*sic*] letter and the map to which he refers." Explaining that he had only been shown the map that very day by Webster, Ashburton continued: "If I had known it before I agreed to sign [in late July] I should have asked your orders, notwithstanding the manner of my becoming acquainted with it. At the same time the communication was strictly confidential and then communicated because I had agreed to sign."[23]

Ashburton then noted the nonexistent parameters of this so-called secret. This "very extraordinary information," he wrote Aberdeen, was known to the president, his cabinet, the governors of Maine and Massachusetts, the seven state commissioners, and six senators, including William Cabell Rives, chairman of the Foreign Relations Committee and an ardent defender of the Tyler administration.[24] Surely, Webster would not have leaked what Ashburton called so "singular a Secret" to at least twenty-one people. Moreover, it is impossible to tell how many others besides Maine's boundary agent, Charles Daveis, knew about the Steuben map that he sold back to Webster in May 1842. Instead of accusing Webster of treasonous activity, one should realize that over twenty others shared the same information—along with anyone else to whom they themselves might have confided. So singular a secret this was, as Ashburton aptly termed it.

Ashburton's suspicions did have one paradoxical effect: they help to explain both why he held out so long for all of Madawaska and why he finally accepted the principle of compromise. For some time he had believed that Webster possessed some type of information supporting the British claim to the disputed territory and wanted to maintain his call for all of Madawaska until that information became known. Not until at least mid-July did Ashburton realize that Maine would never accept the line he advocated; and, despite the high hopes that there was evidence substantiating the British argument, the fact remained that he had not seen that evidence. If the negotiations ended in failure because of his demand for more than what his instructions stipulated as the minimum—the Netherlands award line—he would have fed all the fears that Americans had of Britain's imperialist ambitions and thereby earned the wrath of many English-speaking people on both sides of the Atlantic.

Ashburton had to relent because the risk of holding out was too great. He might have begun to fear that his informant was wrong—that there never was information favoring the British claim. Certainly, Maine and Massachusetts showed no signs of capitulation, nor did Webster. All American spokesmen insisted on the St. John River and vehemently rejected Ashburton's argument for all of Madawaska. And even if a map (or maps) existed that justified his demand for the entire territory in dispute, he doubtless realized that Maine would not surrender the Aroostook for the same reason that he could not give up Madawaska: the first area had American inhabitants who did not want to become British, whereas the second area had British inhabitants who did not want to become American. The only feasible solution was what Aberdeen, Webster, and the Maine and Massachusetts commissioners had urged at the outset of the negotiations—compromise.[25]

A critical observation follows. It actually made no difference whether Webster revealed his red-line maps to Ashburton during the negotiations. The latter could have argued for the British claim, but Maine (and Webster) would have denied the validity of the maps and, in any case, would have refused to give up an area occupied by Americans. Moreover, Ashburton would have been on shaky ground in demanding the entire territory in question since he himself had made the argument for all of Madawaska because it was occupied by British subjects. To continue the demand for land inhabited by Americans would have insulted and infuriated Maine—a dangerous policy that, Ashburton well knew, had caused violent disagreements with Americans over national honor and helped bring on the War of 1812. He finally realized that, despite the possible existence of evidence supporting the entire British claim, he had to retreat from demanding all of Madawaska because another Anglo-American war was too high a price for several hundred miles of pinewood and farmland—hence the compelling need for compromise.

The subterfuge that characterized the negotiations had remained hidden from the public eye. In mid-July, when Webster and Ashburton reached a compromise agreement on the boundary and then resolved most of the other problems, observers attributed the seemingly amicable settlement to the patience, the goodwill, and the personal relationship between the peacemakers. On the most crucial issue, the northeastern boundary, Webster explained that he had acted in accordance with the wishes of the state commissioners, Congress, and public opinion in securing the St. John River as the border. Experience, he asserted, demonstrated that rivers and mountains were better national boundaries than arbitrary lines on land. Ashburton meanwhile compromised after becoming convinced that Maine would not surrender southern Madawaska and that the Senate and others outside New England considered his demands extreme.[26] With a common sense of relief, they hurried to finish work on the boundary settlement so they could turn to the other issues.

Webster immediately sought to convince the state commissioners that the boundary proposal was just. In a note to Maine's delegation, he explained that the recommended line would give the United States 7,015 square miles of land, whereas Britain would receive 5,012. He admitted that the Netherlands award had apportioned more land to the United States—7,908 square miles of territory to only 4,119 to the British—but he emphasized that the additional 893 square miles going to Britain were unsuitable for farming or settlement. Americans would receive all the good land south of the St. Francis River and west of the St. John, meaning that even though their share amounted to only seven-twelfths of the land in dispute, it made up four-fifths of the land's assessed value. In addition, Maine could send its timber down the St. John toll free. Further, the United States retained control over Rouses Point, which benefited both the nation as a whole and the regional states in particular; that strategic position was essential to defending Lake Champlain and repelling any invasion from the north. If the commissioners accepted the boundary proposal, Webster noted, the government in Washington (not the British) would pay Maine and Massachusetts $125,000 each and reimburse Maine for the past costs of repeated surveys and maintenance of the civil posse in the disputed territory.[27]

A little more than a week after receiving the note, both state commissions notified Webster of their acceptance of the boundary compromise. The Massachusetts delegation asked that use of the St. John include the passage of grain as well as timber and that the government in Washington raise each state's compensation to $150,000. Washington consented; and when Webster and Ashburton agreed to the changes, the delegation unanimously supported the settlement. Two days later, after first releasing a gratuitous statement praising their own "forbearance and patience" in the face of "unfounded pretensions, and unwarrantable delays, and irritating encroachments," the Maine representatives wrote Webster of their approval. They also enclosed a memorandum urging New

Brunswick to pay the United States the amount of the "disputed territory fund" (fines levied by the province for illegally cut timber in the area), to be divided equally between Maine and Massachusetts. Ashburton accepted this provision as part of the treaty. With no small degree of satisfaction, he sat with pen in one hand and fan in the other to write Aberdeen a few days later that the representatives of Maine had been most difficult to deal with and that when Preble reluctantly yielded, he "went off to his wilds in Maine as sulky as a Bear."[28]

The sense of relief that accompanied the final delineation of the northeastern boundary made the other part of the still-undefined international border—the northwestern sector from Lake Superior to the Lake of the Woods—seem almost inconsequential. Surveyors had considered it a barren and mountainous area, complete with countless rapids and streams. But it was a haven for fur traders and fishermen, which made the location of the boundary important—particularly to the fur trade—because the Pigeon River linked Montreal with the Canadian heartland. Further, St. George's Island in the St. Mary's River held almost twenty-six thousand acres of rich soil and provided a good source of revenue from the sugar and syrup derived from maple trees. Farther west and moving toward the Lake of the Woods, the terrain changed markedly to include lush river valleys, plentiful timber, and rich land suitable for cultivation.[29]

The British placed small emphasis on this part of the boundary. They already felt safe in this area because of their control of the upper lakes region and had therefore focused on completing their security belt by winning a favorable boundary around Maine. Ashburton quickly forfeited any claim to St. George's Island and recommended that the line follow the Pigeon River and the Grand Portage to Rainy Lake. His only stipulation (which Webster accepted) was that both countries could use all waters in the adjoining area. Ashburton realized that British fur traders wanted a route farther north, but he believed that use of the Grand Portage balanced off this loss. The United States thus received a tract of land about sixty-five hundred square miles in size.[30]

Not until the last quarter of the nineteenth century did the great value of this northwestern territory become known. Americans at this time discovered that the land in present-day Minnesota included the rich Vermilion iron deposits and a segment of the Mesabi Range. Rumors had long held that the region contained minerals, but no proof of their existence had appeared by the time of the Webster-Ashburton negotiations. In his message accompanying the treaty sent to the Senate, President Tyler declared that the United States had acquired territory "considered valuable as a mineral region." But he, of course, cited no authority for this statement and might have been purposely exalting the area as part of the overall effort to promote acceptance of the treaty. Ten years after the pact went into effect, traces of iron ore were detected in the Mesabi and Vermilion regions. But it was not until 1875 that the great wealth of the Vermilion Range became clear and yet another fifteen years before the Mesabi holdings became visible.[31]

In an interesting twist, both nations gained important military advantages that promoted a balance of power on the North American continent. The retention by the United States of Rouses Point, according to Secretary of War John Spencer, was more valuable militarily than all the area conceded above the St. John River. Webster, in fact, told the Senate some time later that the acquisition of this strategic spot outweighed anything gained by the British in the negotiations. Their control of Rouses Point, he emphasized, would have afforded them an invasion route into the United States. On the other side of the ledger, the British had received enough land for constructing a military road connecting the Bay of Fundy with Quebec. Indeed, the arbitral award of 1831 would have placed the American border within thirty miles of Quebec and the St. Lawrence River; the Webster-Ashburton Treaty pushed back the line fifty miles. The arrangement created a still-thinly populated buffer zone below British North America of five thousand square miles of dense pine forest wrapped around the top of Maine. Most important from London's point of view, the treaty settlement promoted an Anglo-American rapprochement that had the potential dividend of improved relations with France.[32]

Webster was probably correct in boasting afterward that the "grand stroke" in resolving the boundary was his use of the red-line maps to convince Maine and Massachusetts of the necessity for compromise.[33] The situation had not changed in Maine. The same reckless brand of political leadership prevailed; the Anglophobes still worked with the outspoken and often irresponsible press and local interests to stir up controversy at every opportunity. No new breed of Americans had emerged with enough foresight to realize that an Anglo-American understanding benefited everyone. Webster had cleverly moved Maine's states' rightists toward a

compromise by orchestrating a newspaper campaign aimed at showing that the only alternative was war. He then followed this tactic
with an invitation to Maine and Massachusetts to participate in the
boundary settlement.

Webster had meanwhile kept the pressure on Ashburton to yield
on his demand for all the territory in dispute. Both sides had defensible claims to the area in question. Sixty years of controversy provided graphic proof that neither side would ever succeed in
convincing the other to surrender the entire area. The land yielded
to Britain was of little or no value to the United States; and yet, it
was of strategic importance in providing enough room for a military road capable of affording protection for British North America.
Thus, Webster acted wisely in withholding the maps once the negotiations were under way.

Webster's diplomacy stands above reproach if one correctly
understands the central task of a diplomatist: to protect the national
interest by any means available, including compromise. He had
outmaneuvered Ashburton in the talks and then waited patiently
for him to retreat from his extreme demands in the interest of maintaining peace. Webster knew that the British government wanted a
military road and that Ashburton dared not risk a war over a few
hundred miles of rough terrain that exceeded the land already conceded for that road. He understandably kept the maps secret until
Ashburton agreed to terms. It would be unfair to criticize Webster
for failing to secure all the area in dispute. Compromise is the es-
sence of diplomacy.[34]

III

Resolution of the boundary question proved crucial to the settlement of other issues between the Atlantic nations.[35] The remaining
problems had already come under general discussion—the African
slave trade, right of search, impressment, the *Creole* case and extradition, the *Caroline* and McLeod affairs, and Oregon—but the
two diplomats had focused on these matters only long enough to
realize that they, like the boundary, raised serious questions about
national honor. Ashburton at first saw no problem in completing
the task—until he realized the intensity of Anglophobia and how
deeply rooted slavery was in southern thinking. At one point in the
early discussions with Webster, they faced the possibility of slavery combining with national honor to wreck all the negotiations.

The most entangling problem that remained after the boundary was the African slave trade, because it was related to the issues of search, impressment, the *Creole*, and slavery. Each matter by itself constituted a serious problem; together, they threatened to become insurmountable. The War of 1812 had ended less than thirty years before, and many adult Americans of the 1840s bitterly recalled the issues that had driven the Madison administration into war against Britain. In the years following the Treaty of Ghent, the British had refused to renounce the rights of search and impressment while insisting that they stood at the vanguard of civilization in seeking to destroy the African slave trade. To Americans in general, the British remained reluctant to accept them into the community of nations; to southerners in particular, British interference in their maritime activities—particularly the domestic slave trade and the *Creole* mutiny—signaled the first major step in a cleverly designed campaign to end slavery. President Tyler grasped the importance of first resolving the impressment issue: British renunciation of the practice would add "luster" to the negotiations and prove pivotal to good relations.[36]

Once again, Lewis Cass's unauthorized interference in impressment exacerbated the problems of the Atlantic nations. His pamphlet denouncing the British right of search had heated up matters in early 1842; and now, in a further effort to destroy the African slave trade without violating America's rights at sea, he had a proposal: assign an American to each British cruiser off the coast of Africa. On sighting a suspicious vessel flying the Stars and Stripes, the American would lead the search and, if necessary, order the capture of the ship. Such a program, Cass insisted, would avert any problems regarding impressment and search while guaranteeing a more effective attack on the African slave trade.[37]

Here was a foolish idea that deserved no serious attention; and yet, Ashburton, anxious to resolve this matter in any way possible, thought it worth consideration. The Royal Navy, he knew, would oppose having Americans assigned to its ships, but the idea might become palatable by attaching the following conditions: the American on board must be a civilian; he could take action only when the slaver flew the American flag; and the British would retain the right to determine the nationality of suspicious ships. On hearing of Ashburton's proposal through Aberdeen, Peel flatly rejected it. The inspector on board would be an "Intruder" whose very presence would arouse animosity. No British captain could maintain authority on his ship if his orders were subject to an American's scrutiny.[38]

Cass's intervention brought focus to the impressment issue and now made it the key to resolving the search question and matters related to slavery. From the American perspective, both impressment and search violated freedom of the seas. These matters became especially serious to southerners who feared that if British sailors could board alleged American slave ships to suppress the African slave trade, the government in London might expand its activities to attack slavery. Again, the entire question of maritime rights made strange bedfellows. Many Americans, not even concerned about slavery, criticized British search practices as a poorly disguised effort to gain supremacy at sea. Webster told Ashburton that London's attempt to enforce its municipal laws on the high seas constituted a violation of international law. The British doctrine underlying the claim to impressment—the "perpetual & indissoluble allegiance of the subject"—was wrong. Britons, like subjects in other countries, had the right to renounce their loyalties and become naturalized American citizens. Since the close of the War of 1812, Webster argued, the Royal Navy had shown no inclination to impress seamen; for this and other reasons, relations between the English-speaking nations had improved. There was no better time to renounce impressment than now, during the negotiations in Washington.[39]

Ashburton, however, could not take such action. He realized that impressment had helped bring on the War of 1812, and he detested the practice now as much as he had then. It was, he told Aberdeen, "the most serious cause of animosity and ill will." Perhaps, he observed, there was a way to steer around the issue. If Britain went to war and Washington declared neutrality, the crown should renounce impressment on the condition that the U.S. government bar British subjects from its merchant marine until they had lived in the United States for five years. Why not surrender an unenforceable right? But Aberdeen feared that in the present time of troubles with France, any move suggesting the imminent disavowal of impressment would invite desertions from the navy and jeopardize national security. Sometime later, in conversation with Everett, Aberdeen explained that his people were as sensitive about desertions as Americans were about search. Privately, however, the foreign secretary assured Everett that British sailors would never again impress Americans, but he could not say this publicly. There was a huge difference between not exercising a right that his government possessed and officially renouncing it. The distinction involved British honor.[40]

As in the stormy days before the War of 1812, the two Atlantic nations had adopted irreconcilable positions over matters affecting national honor; and so, in the interests of Anglo-American harmony, Webster and Ashburton wisely decided against attempting to reach any formal settlement on impressment. Instead, they followed Everett's recommendation to record their opposing positions on paper and attach these documents to the treaty package without incorporating them into the pact itself. Thus, the final exchanges between the United States and Britain over impressment took place in the quiet chambers of the negotiations and not in the public arena. Webster dutifully composed a long diplomatic note summarizing his country's grievances against impressment, and Ashburton reciprocated with an essay defending the British position. If such an exchange of notes ended the discussion on impressment and nudged the nations toward better relations, he would support it. Aberdeen concurred, and the matter was closed.[41]

While the impressment issue moved toward a silent resolution, Webster took the lead in trying to resolve the African slave-trade controversy. Borrowing from John Quincy Adams's abortive suggestion of the early 1820s, Webster proposed a joint cruising scheme by which the two Atlantic nations would avoid the pitfalls of mutual search by stationing pairs of cruisers along the African coast which relied on cooperation to combat the slave trade. In January 1839 the commissioners at Sierra Leone had presented a similar idea to Palmerston; but when the British minister in Washington passed the proposal to the State Department, it took no action. Webster's suggestion was also much like the short-lived Paine-Tucker agreement of March 1840, except that it had authorized mutual search. And he might also have been acting in response to the urging of President Tyler, who wrote his son years afterward that the joint cruising arrangement had become part of the treaty "upon my own suggestion." Whatever the source, Webster's proposal maintained the country's traditional opposition to European entanglements by standing clear of the Quintuple Treaty negotiated by Britain the previous December, calling for the establishment of a joint squadron for a specified period, and refusing to authorize mutual search. The United States, he declared, found it "more manly and elevated" to enforce its own laws rather than depend on others.[42]

Ashburton responded favorably to the idea and easily won Aberdeen's support. Use of a joint squadron, they knew, would sidestep the search issue, double the effort to end the slave trade while sharing the costs, and enhance effectiveness by subjecting suspected slavers flying the American flag to inspection by American cruisers. The joint squadron arrangement, Ashburton declared, would be the "very best fruit" of the mission.[43] The "African squadron clause" in the treaty, however, proved more impressive in theory than in practice. Article 8 required each nation to maintain a naval force of at least eighty guns along the West African coast. Each squadron would enforce only its own government's laws, although they could cooperate with each other when necessary. The results were predictable: the United States did not meet its obligations under the agreement. The biggest reason was the lack of support in Congress—much of it due to southern influence. Less than five years after the treaty went into effect, the United States seldom kept eighty guns in African waters. While the British and French (who, though not party to the Quintuple Treaty, agreed in 1845 to assign a fleet to the West African coast to help end the slave trade) maintained at least twenty-five vessels, the United States rarely had more than five—and many of these were inadequately supplied and generally too slow to apprehend the sleek, fast-moving slavers.

This dire situation, in part, was attributable to the small number of vessels in the U.S. Navy; but it was also due to southern pressure to relax enforcement of Article 8. From 1843 until the outbreak of the Civil War in 1861 the Navy Department altered the squadron's original objective of suppressing the African slave trade to protecting other types of commerce along the West African coast. During this long period, six of the nine secretaries of the navy were from the South and two others openly sympathized with its interests. In 1853 southern congressmen led the way in reducing the annual appropriation for the program from $20,000 to $8,000. The following year they tried—and failed—to abrogate the entire treaty article and to replace the death penalty with life imprisonment. Effective action against the African slave trade did not begin until 1863, the year of the Emancipation Proclamation.[44]

The *Creole* affair also presented major problems, particularly after Aberdeen decided in early 1842 to free the ship's nineteen mutineers. The Tyler administration repeatedly called for reparations, but Ashburton explained that his people so enthusiastically approved Peel's antislavery policy that it could not grant compensation. Webster privately believed that the British position was sound and never demanded the slaves' return as fugitives. His friend on the Supreme Court, Justice Joseph Story, had advised him that in the absence of an extradition treaty, the administration could appeal for the mutineers' return only on the basis of comity or hospitality. In addition, Story noted, international law provided that persons committing offenses on the high seas were subject to trial only in the municipal courts of the country to which the vessel belonged. But Tyler strongly disagreed with Story's opinion. Indeed, Ashburton feared that the president had become so "sore and testy" about the matter that he might hold back on a convention to halt the African slave trade until fellow southerners found satisfaction concerning the *Creole*. The issue of slavery, Ashburton gloomily observed, threatened to undermine the entire treaty.[45]

By the end of July, Ashburton was so disgusted with the *Creole* affair that he acted on his own in arranging a settlement satisfactory to Webster. Without authorization from London, the emissary promised Webster (in a note later attached to the treaty) that directives would go to Nassau officials to observe hospitality and enforce municipal law in a way intended to avoid "officious interference" (unauthorized or unofficial) with American ships "driven by accident or by violence" into British ports. He also proposed linking an extradition agreement with the informal *Creole* settlement. The result was Article 10 of the treaty, which provided for the extradition of individuals accused of seven nonpolitical crimes: "murder, or assault with intent to commit murder, or Piracy, or arson, or robbery, or Forgery, or the utterance of forged paper." Webster had attempted to include mutiny and revolt on the list of crimes, but Ashburton recognized the implications for slaves attempting to win their freedom and refused to accept the change. Tyler had misgivings about including an extradition agreement and acceded to it only with great reluctance. British officials, he feared, might refuse to surrender a slave who had killed his master and escaped. Might not a British court call this self-defense?[46]

The *Creole* matter lingered until 1853, when an Anglo-American claims commission awarded $110,330 to owners of the liberated slaves, thereby vindicating the position of both the South and the White House in the controversy. Slavery was an act of inhumanity, according to the umpire, but nonetheless legal under international law. The *Creole* had been engaged in a lawful voyage when "unavoidable necessity" forced it into Nassau, where its captain had a right to expect shelter from the officials of a friendly power. The British Emancipation Act had no bearing on the case, because municipal law did not authorize the forceful boarding of the vessel of another country. The authorities in Nassau had violated international law, meaning that the government in London must compensate owners of the *Creole*'s slaves.[47]

As for the *Caroline* and McLeod affairs, the two diplomats satisfied both nations' sense of honor by exchanging notes expressing mutual regrets over the troubles caused, which each country liberally interpreted as an apology. Webster emphasized that destruction of the *Caroline* had violated the "Sovereignty and the dignity of the United States" and therefore raised questions about America's "self-respect, the consciousness of independence and national equality." Under the principle of what became known as the "*Caroline* doctrine" in international law, a nation had the right of self-defense in the face of imminent danger. To avert a confrontation, Ashburton skillfully composed a response containing a "degree of apology" with a "decided justification" of the act. Although admitting that Palmerston should have issued an apology immediately after the assault, Ashburton for two days resisted Webster's appeals before finally agreeing to use the word "apology" in the note. He could grant no compensation, however; the *Caroline* had been engaged in illegal activities. Webster nonetheless termed this an apology and, in return, expressed regret for Alexander McLeod's long ordeal. When Congress in late August enacted a law establishing federal jurisdiction over cases similar to McLeod's, the *Caroline* issue at last was resolved.[48]

One final matter came before the two diplomats for discussion—Oregon—but they decided to postpone it. Although Oregon was not a pressing issue by the summer of 1842, the enormous region offered great agricultural, commercial, and strategic potential and was coming under rapid settlement. The Peel ministry thought that since the two nations wanted to smooth all their differences, they might deal with Oregon as well. But Aberdeen's hastily written instructions stipulated a boundary that awarded Britain three-fourths of the territory and denied the United States a harbor in the strait above the Columbia River. The ministry would permit joint navigation of the river, but under no conditions would it approve a boundary along the 49th parallel from the Rocky Mountains to the Pacific.[49]

The negotiators' first discussion of Oregon demonstrated the impossibility of a settlement. The British government had reverted to its brisk and cavalier treatment of American interests, dredging up bitter memories of the mother country's imperialist ambitions. In what became known as the "tripartite plan," Webster "intimated" that Ashburton's boundary terms might be acceptable if his government persuaded Mexico to transfer San Francisco and its harbor to the United States. But Ashburton could not commit his country to such a proposition. He soon opted to defer the matter rather than have it interfere with progress on the other issues. The Oregon Question, he concluded, must "sleep for the present."[50]

Webster and Ashburton had not resolved all the issues between the Atlantic nations, but they had dispensed with most of them while establishing a higher degree of mutual respect for each other's interests. Most important to the improved relationship, Britain had openly treated the United States as an equal nation. The result was a treaty that affirmed American honor and promoted a better Anglo-American understanding. At a huge dinner party later held in Ashburton's honor, President Tyler stood and turned toward the British emissary and Webster while offering the toast: "Blessed are the peacemakers."[51]

The story should have ended here, but it did not. As in most great international settlements, there were domestic political repercussions on both sides of the ocean that, in this instance, threatened ratification of the Webster-Ashburton Treaty. During a time of bitter warfare between the Tylers and the Clays, and between the Peels and the Palmerstons, it was predictable that a pact involving so many long-standing disputes was subject to attack. Anglophobe Thomas Hart Benton used the Senate chamber and the Washington *Globe* to blast the treaty, whereas America's chief critic, Lord Palmerston, relied on Parliament and the London *Morning Chronicle* to do the same. Both antagonists denounced the arrangement as a betrayal of national honor, which, in a bitter twist of irony, actually underlined the success of the two diplomats in devising a true compromise. In Parliament the "battle of the maps" thundered to a final conclusion, whereas in the United States the rancor became so intense that, four years after the negotiations, Democrats in Congress accused Webster (then in the Senate) of illegal use of the president's secret-service fund and sought to impeach him retroactively. Such charges lingered for generations, encouraging a few historians to believe that, in negotiating the treaty, Webster had betrayed his own country.

Despite the bombast led by Benton and fellow Anglophobe James Buchanan of Pennsylvania, the Senate soon overwhelmingly approved the treaty; but ratification was far more difficult to achieve in Britain. However contrived Palmerston's opposition was, it presented a sensitive problem for the Peel ministry. Shortly after news of the treaty reached London in the autumn of 1842, the *Times* ran a series of letters, signed by "Tenax" and probably written by Palmerston, which opposed the treaty and set the tone for further criticisms found in the *Morning Chronicle, Morning Herald, Evening Star,* and *Punch.* But nothing could match the virulence streaming through the unsigned articles found in the *Morning Chronicle.* The treaty, according to the stories, was a "wretchedly bad arrangement," a "needless, gratuitous, and imbecile surrender" that endangered British North America by shifting the balance of power on the continent in America's favor. The pact was a "pitiful exhibition of imbecility" that resulted in "Lord Ashburton's capitulation."[52]

At this point one could simply dismiss the above as sheer political rhetoric, fully predictable within the context of midnineteenth-century style; but in January 1843 news of the Sparks map reached the British public and threatened to add substance to Palmerston's charges as Parliament prepared to convene the following month. As Palmerston now berated the ministry for giving away territory rightfully belonging to Britain, Peel made a revelation in Parliament that fired the final shot at his archenemy: another red-line map recently uncovered in London that supported the American claim to all the area in dispute. Owned by Richard Oswald, one of the British negotiators in Paris during the peace talks of 1782–83, it was a Mitchell map (the type used in Paris) and appeared to be valid as well as authentic because it carried an endorsement apparently in the handwriting of King George III himself and had these words written four times around the edges—"Boundary as described by Mr. Oswald." Especially stunning was the ministry's further revelation that Palmerston had seen the map while foreign secretary in 1839 and had ordered it hidden in the Foreign Office. It was indeed satisfying to the Peel ministry that Palmerston had denounced Webster's duplicity and Ashburton's stupidity and now found himself vulnerable to both charges.[53]

How coincidental it was that the Peel ministry unearthed the Oswald map at such a propitious time! Or was it mere coincidence? The supreme irony in this battle over the maps is that Ashburton himself—the chief target of Palmerston's verbal abuse—had found the Oswald map after returning to England. In his capacity as trustee of the British Museum, he had secured entry to search for other maps supporting the ministry and found the warrant authorizing the transfer of the Oswald map to the Foreign Office in April 1839. Its revelation and the accompanying news that Palmerston had concealed the evidence supporting the American claim affirmed the wisdom of compromise and instantly deflated opposition to the treaty. The following quip from the *Times* must have caused even Palmerston's allies to hold back a grin: "Our contemporary [editor of the *Chronicle*] is, no doubt, wise in loading his guns heavily, but before he applies the match, he would be wiser if he would take care that Lord PALMERSTON is not standing before the muzzle."[54]

The story of the maps still remains incomplete. Which of the maps contained the final boundary markings outlined in the Paris treaty? The answer is that none of them did. All red-line maps contained only proposed boundaries, not lines agreed to as final by the Paris diplomats. Oswald had joined John Jay (who also had a red-line Mitchell map, discovered in 1843) and Benjamin Franklin in seeking to defer the northeastern boundary to settlement by a joint commission after the war, which meant that their red lines could only have been suggestions. Franklin himself wrote that his line was drawn during the preliminary peace talks. The negotiators' intent to establish a postwar commission, though defeated, strongly implies their realization that the terms of any border described in the treaty would be difficult, if not impossible, to execute. Ashburton thought so. To Aberdeen in early 1843 he admitted that "although Franklin's map seems quite conclusive as to the instructions of the Negotiators, it would not be Easy to maintain in argument that those intentions were Executed by the Words of the Treaty [of 1783]." Shortly afterward, Webster wrote Everett that none of the maps "shows a line, clearly purporting to be a line, drawn for the purpose of shewing [*sic*] on the map, a boundary which had been agreed on." In other words, the Franklin, Oswald, and Jay maps were all authentic—used in Paris—but none of them was valid—accepted as final. The only solution was that set forth by Webster and Ashburton: compromise.[55]

In 1846 the ugly accusations relating to Webster and the treaty arose again, when his old personal and political enemy, Democrat Charles Ingersoll of Pennsylvania, took the offensive. After first failing to prove federal obstruction of justice in the McLeod trial, he turned to the treaty negotiations themselves. In the House of Representatives, Ingersoll called for an investigation of Webster based on three charges: unlawful use of the president's secret-service fund, improper allocation of the money to "corrupt party presses," and embezzlement of more than $2,000 from the State Department. Since Webster was no longer secretary of state, Ingersoll sought an unprecedented retroactive impeachment, the only such action in America's history. Conviction of misconduct while secretary of state, Ingersoll declared, would remove Webster from his present position of senator and bar him from ever holding public office again. But the bizarre effort ended in failure. After lengthy testimonies by former President Tyler, Francis O. J. Smith, and Edward Stubbs, the disbursing clerk of the State Department, the House committee voted 4 to 1 to exonerate Webster on all charges. The president had authorized Webster to draw from the secret-service fund; there was nothing corrupt about the newspaper campaign in New England; and all State Department accounts were in balance when Webster left office.[56]

"FAIR ROSAMOND; OR, THE ASHBURTON TREATY." *Punch* (London), July–December 1842.

Webster and Ashburton have only recently received well-deserved recognition for negotiating a treaty that relieved their two nations of a host of grievances conducive to war and set the path toward a monumental midcentury Anglo-American rapprochement.[57] Both diplomats accepted the harsh attacks on their treaty because they recognized that this was the expected outcome of compromise and that even more important than winning a war is keeping the peace, with national honor intact. The Webster-Ashburton Treaty temporarily reduced the danger of a third Anglo-American conflict while encouraging the chances of better Anglo-French relations.

The threat of war was real to contemporaries on both sides of the Atlantic. Anglophobes, newspapers, politicians, states' rightists, and local interests—all combined in the United States to whip up emotions for a conflict that they intended to fight in the name of national honor. British recognition of American independence, they complained, had come in name only. On the British side of the Atlantic, the Peel ministry adhered to the warnings of military advisers in drawing secret contingency war plans. Both nations had grave interests at stake. Webster and Ashburton had confronted their governments' central dilemma of having to find space in North America for two peoples so similar in international objectives that they became natural, bitter rivals. The two diplomats succeeded in establishing a peace in the Northeast that permitted America's attention to turn west—to Oregon, in particular, where another Anglo-American crisis over North America was silently building as part of the coming fury over westward expansion that Americans soon called "manifest destiny."

CHAPTER SEVEN

A New and Even More Troublesome Boundary Dispute: Northwest to Oregon

> Oregon was before us in its future glory, and we grasped the prospect of its coming as the impulse of our scheme. We needed no speeches, no reports, to awaken us. Oregon invited us.
> —*Oregonian*, April 1839

Lord Ashburton was understandably pleased as he returned home with his treaty in 1842. He had left New York with cheers of celebration ringing in his ears and arrived in England to the sound of cannon salutes both on ship and on shore. He realized that his feeling of triumph was premature, however, because his negotiations were incomplete. Despite his resolution of the sensitive northeastern boundary dispute, he had been unable to achieve the same success with that seemingly less urgent boundary problem in the Northwest. In fact, Ashburton noted before his escape from the Washington heat that a new and even more troublesome dispute was likely to develop in the near future. He was correct. Over the next four years rowdy, free-spirited Americans converged on the territory while equally unruly and outspoken statesmen on both sides of the Atlantic transformed the distant territory into the flashpoint of another war-threatening crisis.

I

Like the northeastern boundary, that in the Northwest had a long and complicated history. When the Americans won their independence from Great Britain in 1783, the vast and largely unknown area west of the Mississippi River was of little immediate concern. Louisiana was seemingly in the firm grasp of Europeans and presented a substantial barrier to American movement toward the Pacific. Surely the people of the newly founded United States would be content to occupy themselves with the frontiers east of the great river. In the last decade of the eighteenth century, however, subtle signs indicated that this restraint would not hold for long. While the British pursued their practice of expanding into unsettled and often unclaimed parts of North America, Americans interested in the Pacific trade joined Britain and others in approaching the Oregon Territory from the sea.[1]

In 1792 the paths of American and British seamen crossed in the waters of the Pacific Northwest. Veteran British Captain George Vancouver and Boston's Robert Gray had been skirting the same stretch of coastline and observed "river-colored water" at approximately 46°10'. Vancouver dismissed the phenomenon, his judgment perhaps skewed by the negative reports of earlier expeditions that had labeled landmarks in that vicinity Cape Disappointment and Deception Bay. He chose instead to continue northward to Nootka Sound to complete the primary directive of his mission—the fulfillment of the terms of an agreement made between London and Madrid two years earlier. Precipitated by the Spanish takeover of a British trading post at Nootka, the Nootka Sound Convention of 1790 had both reduced tension in Anglo-Spanish relations and acknowledged a British presence in the region. Meanwhile, Gray, after meeting with Vancouver's lieutenants, returned to the area to investigate the source of the river-colored water. Much to the dismay of Vancouver and to the ultimate consternation of British diplomats, Gray found that the source was none other than the fabled "Oregon," or river of the west—that mythologized artery said to hold the key to the American hinterland. As the Bostonian christened the impressive waterway "Columbia" after his vessel, he must have conjured up images of the legendary Northwest Passage and its potential for Pacific trade.[2]

Vancouver certainly appreciated the significance of Gray's discovery and retreated southward at the first opportunity in an attempt to limit the damage of his oversight. But he was too late. Gray's discovery had established the first U.S. claim to the Columbia River Country and to the most significant river penetrating the North American continent from the northern Pacific. Vancouver was nonetheless unwilling to concede the strategic territory to the United States and dispatched an expedition to explore the reaches of the Columbia for a distance of approximately one hundred miles. He thus added the exploration of the river to an impressive list of

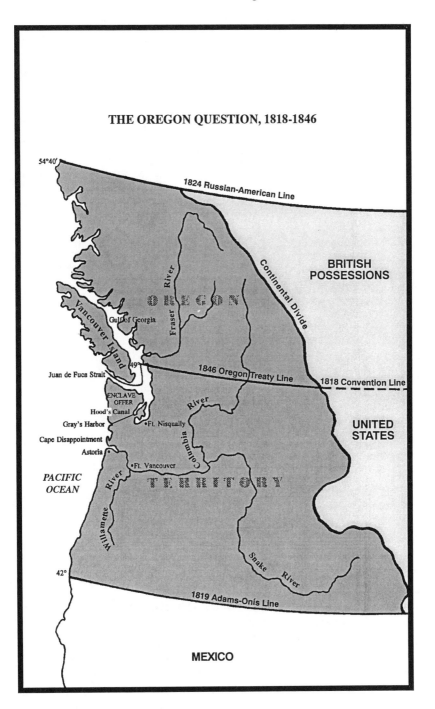

THE OREGON QUESTION, 1818-1846

claims—Puget Sound, the Gulf of Georgia, and Port Discovery, among others—made for the crown during this voyage. These laudable efforts, however, did not undercut the importance of Gray's accomplishment. The Anglo-American contest for the territory had begun.[3]

Almost immediately the two nations began to press their interests in the area. Following close on Vancouver's efforts, Alexander Mackenzie crossed North America for the Canadian North West Company and followed the Tacoutche Tesse (Fraser River) almost to the Pacific. The company hoped to link the fur trade of the Northwest to a trading system that encompassed all Canada and ultimately attached North America to the lucrative Asian markets. At the turn of the century the company's operatives began the construction of outposts that eventually touched the upper reaches of the Columbia. Likewise, the United States shored up its position in the area. In 1803 the European buffer to overland westward expansion vanished with President Thomas Jefferson's adroit purchase of Louisiana. The following year he dispatched Meriwether Lewis and William Clark to examine the extent of the new American domain. Their famous expedition not only explored the territory west of the Mississippi but also mapped out much of the area from the Rockies to the mouth of the Columbia. On the heels of Lewis and Clark, American traders helped to clear a path from Missouri up the Snake River Valley and into Oregon.[4]

This competition between the United States and Great Britain prompted Mackenzie to call on London to oppose U.S. movement into the territory. But it was the British who seemed most aggressive during the early years of the century. David Thompson, Duncan McGillivray, and Simon Fraser worked incessantly to establish posts in the name of the crown. Within a few years, traders under Thompson's tutelage secured control of both sides of the 49th parallel in two distinct trading areas, the Fraser River basin and the Columbia River basin. Between these two areas emerged a no-man's-land that became the subject of diplomatic exchanges in 1807.[5]

American plenipotentiaries James Monroe and William Pinkney met that year with British commissioners Lords Holland and Auckland to discuss the possibility of constructing a line separating Rupert's Land and Louisiana. Although their negotiations did not produce a treaty acceptable to Jefferson, the diplomats did suggest that, based on a reading of the Treaty of Utrecht of 1713, the boundary between the two nations should follow the 49th parallel west from the Lake of the Woods "as far as the respective territories of the two parties extend in that quarter." Thus, from an early date, the 49th parallel surfaced as the probable boundary across an undetermined extent of territory west of the Old Northwest.[6]

Meanwhile, the U.S. claim to this area received a substantial boost as Americans sought to occupy the Oregon Territory on their own. German-born entrepreneur John Jacob Astor maneuvered for about three years to secure for his Pacific Fur Company a post near the mouth of the Columbia River. Astor, like Mackenzie for Britain, hoped to incorporate such a post into an American commercial empire. With this in mind, he established Astoria on the Columbia River in the spring of 1811 and mounted his first trading expedition in the area before the end of summer. Although trade was certainly Astor's central motive, on the broader stage of national design the mere presence of an American post was of immense importance. By planting its citizens at the mouth of the Columbia, the United States added occupation to discovery in substantiating its claim to the territory. But before Americans had time to appreciate the post's significance, they lost it to the British during the War of 1812.[7]

At the onset of war, the crown moved to secure the Pacific Northwest by seizing control of the mouth of the Columbia. But while HMS *Raccoon* made its way to the territory, the Astorians accepted the seemingly inevitable and offered to sell the post to the North West Company for $50,000. By the time the *Raccoon* arrived in December the transaction was complete and the post already in the hands of British subjects. Nevertheless, Captain William Black of the *Raccoon* proceeded with his instructions and staged a ceremony officially transferring the post to the crown and renaming it Fort George. This act, he determined, made the post "doubly British" and left no doubt about its possession. Ironically, far from securing the post for Great Britain, Black's formal act of transfer opened a loophole through which the United States could reclaim Astoria after the war.[8]

Recognition of this loophole prompted the debut of the Oregon Country in American diplomacy in March 1814. Secretary of State James Monroe informed the peace legation at Ghent that the United States had lost a post on the Columbia River to the British as a result of the war. The U.S. representatives should demand its restoration and indicate to the British that the United States not only refused to acknowledge any claim to American territory south of the northern boundary but, in fact, also rejected any British claim to territory on the Pacific coast. The significance of this communication was clear. The State Department considered the Oregon Country within U.S. boundaries, making American claims to the territory exclusive.[9]

Although Astoria was not mentioned by name at Ghent, the implication for the British-American border could not have been missed. To see that it was not, Monroe explained in July to the British chargé in Washington, Anthony Baker, that his government planned to reclaim Astoria under the terms of the Treaty of Ghent. Article 1 of that document stated that "all territory, places, and possessions, whatsoever, taken by either party from the other during the War, or which may be taken after the signing of this Treaty, . . . shall be restored without delay." Baker, however, was in no position to appease Monroe and asserted that a decision of this nature required instructions from the Foreign Office. Besides, he did not believe that any Americans were in the area to accept restitution. If Baker knew anything about the Oregon situation, he must have cringed at the realization that the unnecessary ceremony staged by Captain Black had technically placed Astoria within the purview of Article 1. Had the post simply changed hands as a result of a legitimate sale, America would have had little or no grounds for its position.[10]

The point was temporarily moot since the United States had limited capacity to restore the post "without delay." Caught up with Spain over the Floridas, the Barbary Coast pirates in the Mediterranean, and a navy that was inadequate for promoting the nation's expanding aspirations, Washington could do little more than postpone restoration schemes from calendar to calendar. Over the next two years President James Madison considered various diplomatic missions, only to see them sacrificed to more pressing needs. In 1816, Astor approached Secretary of the Treasury Albert Gallatin with a plan to resume trade on the Columbia River. But he would only pursue it, he stated, under cover of the American flag. When this was not forthcoming, he dropped his plan. Not until fall of 1817 was the United States able to make good on the promise to restore Astoria. In that year Captain James Biddle's sloop-of-war *Ontario* acted under orders in conveying the State Department's John B. Prevost to Astoria to reinstate U.S. authority.[11]

Although Monroe failed to inform Charles Bagot, the British minister in Washington, of the *Ontario*'s mission, Simon M'Gillivray of the North West Company made certain that he knew. Consequently, an extremely agitated Bagot expressed his concern to

Secretary of State John Quincy Adams. Bagot apparently feared that the mission would renew American interest in the area and threaten that of Britain and the North West Company. Adams offered little solace when he noted that the United States was merely implementing the terms of Ghent. Besides, the secretary sharply stated, an area so remote to Britain was not worth a fight with the United States.[12]

The interview with Adams angered Bagot, prompting him to call on his government to take preemptive action. Fort George, Bagot charged, should be warned of the approach of the *Ontario*, and the Royal Navy should dispatch a warship to secure the post. But the introspective foreign secretary, Lord Castlereagh, was not eager to confront the United States and dismissed these provocative recommendations. With his government shaky and European peace tenuous, he tacitly accepted Adams's opinion that the territory was not worth a quarrel.[13] Meanwhile in the territory, the twin British actions that had transferred the post were doubly reversed. Biddle and Prevost arrived separately and each staged a restoration ceremony. Prevost replaced the Union Jack with the Star and Stripes in October and departed. The North West Company, seeing no Americans remaining to contest its position, simply resumed de facto control of the territory and continued to exploit Oregon in the name of the crown.[14]

The astute Castlereagh was not as concerned about the actual occupants at Fort George as he was about the impact that the transfer would have on the future status of the territory. With this in mind, he instructed both the Admiralty and Bagot to issue disclaimers before completing the transfer. The United States, he warned, should not take the British concession to mean a forfeiture of claims to the territory. Rather, he stressed, the transfer applied only to a single post. Unfortunately, Castlereagh's caution came to naught. Neither Bagot in Washington nor the British agents in Oregon communicated his reservation. The omission would allow the United States in future negotiations to proceed from the assumption that any territory open to compromise lay north of Astoria and the Columbia River. The first of those negotiations began in the summer of 1818.[15]

As the flags were switched over Fort George, the diplomats made ready to meet in London. In late August 1818, American plenipotentiaries Richard Rush and Albert Gallatin faced British commissioners Frederick Robinson and Henry Goulburn to discuss several outstanding issues that had troubled the two nations since

Ghent. One of the most difficult issues, and one that the two Americans would become uncomfortably familiar with over the next few years, concerned the western boundary between British North America and the United States. Since the early days of the Republic this line had been vague and problematic. Now that the British were resigned to the permanence of the American republic, that line needed clarification. Rush and Gallatin took the initiative and, although admitting that the U.S. claim to the territory west of the Rockies was not exclusive, contended that it was as credible as that of the British. It would be reasonable, they asserted, to follow the so-called Utrecht line of 49 degrees all the way west from the Lake of the Woods at the edge of the Old Northwest to the Pacific Ocean. Understanding the importance of the waterways in the Northwest, the Americans further proposed that all rivers remain open to both countries from their intersection with 49 degrees to the sea.[16]

The British were not willing to divide the unsettled territory west of the Rockies but were prepared to cordon off a section of the territory between 45 degrees and 49 degrees for the mutual use of both nations. Rush and Gallatin, however, correctly believed that this would amount to an unnecessary U.S. concession and countered with a proposal to open the entire Oregon Territory to both parties for a period of ten years.[17] Under this plan, the line dividing British North America and the United States would extend from the Lake of the Woods to the Rockies. Territory west of the mountains would remain open to the citizens and subjects of both nations for a ten-year period. But Gallatin was not about to forfeit an opportunity to achieve a final resolution and made one last proposition before the conference ended. He unofficially intimated that his government might permit the line west of the mountains to deviate far enough to the south to allow the British to control the entire Gulf of Georgia. This measure would give them the deepwater ports that they required but leave the Columbia to the United States.[18]

The British apparently assumed that this intimation meant an invitation to resume bargaining and countered Gallatin's suggestion with a proposed line running along the 49th parallel to its intersection with the Columbia. From that point the boundary would follow the river's channel to the sea. This idea was no more acceptable than the earlier British proposal. The four negotiators, therefore, defaulted to the open-access proposal for the territory west of the Rockies and were satisfied to have at least resolved the border from the Lake of the Woods to the mountains.[19]

At the time of the London conference, the contest for the Oregon Territory still involved four nations—the United States, Great Britain, Russia, and, to a lesser degree, Spain. Over the next several years expansion-minded John Quincy Adams worked to narrow the contest to two competitors. In the year following the 1818 conference, he met with Spanish minister Luis de Onís to sort out the status of the Floridas. The secretary of state subtly broadened the discussions to include the unsettled boundary extending across the Southwest and thereby transformed the treaty into one that advanced America's boundary from Texas to the Pacific. This move provided the country with a recognized claim to frontage on the Pacific and added the principle of territorial contiguity to the U.S. argument for Oregon. Within five years, Adams, under the auspices of his noncolonization concept contained in the so-called Monroe Doctrine, had convinced the czar to concede claims to the territory south of Russian Alaska. After the British had negotiated a similar arrangement with Russia, the Oregon Territory became an exclusive Anglo-American contest.[20]

Over these five years, America's appetite for preserving territory for republican virtue had increased. As Spain retreated from the hemisphere, a vision emerged of expanding American nationalism and territory that would block further intrusions by a corrupt and monarchical Europe. Outspoken Senator Thomas Hart Benton of Missouri provided a loud voice in support of that vision as he attacked every sign of concession to Europeans. The stubborn and persistent congressman John Floyd, whose fascination with the Oregon Territory derived from friends among the Astorians and explorer William Clark, introduced Oregon into the congressional debate. In late 1820, Floyd formed a committee to study the potential of the territory and reported early the next year that the United States had much to gain from asserting control over it. The committee lauded advantages ranging from the Atlantic-Pacific trade to the addition of abundant resources to sustain the growing nation. Many exponents of U.S. influence over the territory were so-called limitationists who had in mind a sister republic based on the American model, such as that contemplated by Jefferson earlier in the century and advocated by Benton in 1825. Nonetheless, the zealous rhetoric that rose from the halls of Congress was so provocative that it elicited a bitter reaction from the British.[21]

The British minister in Washington, Stratford Canning, hurried over to the State Department to demand an explanation of American intentions for the territory. A rather comical exchange ensued in which Secretary Adams insisted that the United States did not accept without question British claims to the territory or, for that matter, any territory.

> "Have you any claim," said I [Adams], "to the mouth of the Columbia River?"
> "Why, do you not know," replied he [Canning], "that we have a claim?"
> "I do not know," said I, "what you claim nor what you do not claim. You claim India; you claim Africa; you claim—"
> "Perhaps," said he, "a piece of the moon."
> "No," said I, "I have not heard that you claim exclusively any part of the moon; but there is not a spot on this habitable globe that I could affirm you do not claim; and there is none which you may not claim with as much color of right as you can have to the Columbia River or its mouth."
> "And how far would you consider," said he, "this exclusion of right to extend?"
> "To all the shores of the South Sea," said I. "We know of no right that you have there."
> "Suppose," said he, "Great Britain should undertake to make a settlement there; would you object to it?"
> "I have no doubt we should," said I.[22]

As it happened, London was not nearly as concerned as Canning over the implications of the Floyd bill. The British cabinet simply determined that the projected American action did nothing that violated the 1818 arrangement. Canning was told to let the matter rest.[23]

II

Letting it rest was not easy, for while Adams fenced with Canning, American lawmakers increased their noise over the Oregon Territory. The navy was under orders to look into the cost and potential of establishing a military position at the mouth of the Columbia. Floyd and others were now joined by New Englanders such as William Sturgis of Boston, who contended that the deep harbors of the Juan de Fuca Strait and Puget Sound were essential for America's Pacific trade. Floyd in December 1822 exalted the glorious rewards that Americans would gain from Oregon. Linking it to the Missouri and Mississippi, he proclaimed, would "open a mine of wealth . . . surpassing hope of avarice itself."[24]

As Floyd lauded the potential of the territory, colleagues lined up against him in a vain attempt to halt the move west. Drawing on the recent reports of the Stephen Long expedition, some dismissed the region on both sides of the Rockies as a barren desert incapable of supporting an agricultural society such as that of the United States. Others took the higher ground in arguing that the development of so remote a territory was inconsistent with the principles of the Republic and might result in its submission to a contemptible colonialism. These arguments, though eloquently stated, fell on unsympathetic ears that, in the wake of the nationalism produced by the War of 1812, preferred the more romantic call of continental expansion.[25]

Adams, John C. Calhoun of South Carolina, and others rejected the idealized notion that the territory was destined to become an independent republic generated from a cell of the United States placed at the mouth of the Columbia. Theirs was a more pragmatic approach. Whereas Benton, Floyd, and like-minded men seemed content with the limitationist approach that would yield a newly populated area linked to America by republican principles, blood, and heritage, Adams's supporters preferred the view of a territory preserved for the physical expansion of the United States. Although the limitationists and expansionists had different ideas of the ultimate fate of the Pacific Northwest, they agreed on one point: it would not be a European territory.[26]

The charged atmosphere generated by these lawmakers made it evident that the diplomats could not ignore Washington's interest in the Oregon Territory. In late 1824, Floyd escalated the situation by pushing a bill through the House that instructed the president to establish a military post to secure Oregon. Floyd's bill did not sit well with the American minister in London, who had already become anxious about the impact of such activities on an already difficult negotiation. Rush, who as a young and less experienced diplomat had been overshadowed by the veteran Gallatin in 1818, was now in London shouldering considerable responsibility for U.S. relations with Europe. Adams had directed Rush not only to settle the Oregon boundary issue but also to articulate the secretary's noncolonization principle. In this bold statement, Adams had contended that the United States rejected the "application of colonial principles of exclusion" or the claim of possession by Europeans "upon any part of the Northwest Coast of America." Rush was to solicit the London government's de facto acceptance of this policy by securing a delineation of each nation's settlements in the area. When this exchange took place, the Russians were still claimants to the territory and had, in fact, stiffened Adams's determination to deter European encroachment in the northern Pacific. Therefore, a division of the territory would involve three nations. Under the American plan, the United States would restrict settlement to south of the 51st parallel, Russia would do likewise above the 55th parallel, and Britain would be free to enter the territory lying between the two. Rush thought this a reasonable offer because the United States had secured Spanish claims between the 42d and 60th parallels by the Adams-Onís Treaty of 1819.[27]

A flabbergasted George Canning, who had taken over at the Foreign Office after the tragic suicide of the friendlier Castlereagh, responded to the American offer in typical Yankeephobic fashion. Flat on his back suffering from gout, the foreign secretary began his reply to Rush with an indignant, "Do I read Mr. Rush aright?" Canning could not believe the U.S. presumption to draw the line between British and Russian claims. He demanded to know whether Washington meant "to travel north to get between us and Russia" and if the Americans intended "to stipulate against Great Britain, in favor of Russia, or reserve to themselves whatever Russia may not want?"[28] By the time Canning got the full picture of what became known as the Monroe Doctrine, it had broadened into an even bolder policy statement that made Rush's prospects of resolving the Oregon dispute slim at best. In December, President Monroe pronounced all the Americas off limits to Europe and established the United States as the guarantor of Latin America. Canning had hoped for British participation in any guarantee of the future security of that region and was furious with Monroe's unilateral declaration. Rush's ensuing discussion with the British commissioners in the spring of 1824 consequently amounted to little more than going through the motions.

The British not surprisingly dismissed Rush's offer to partition the American and British areas at 51 degrees because it totally neglected their rights acquired by both use and occupancy. The Rush proposal did, however, evoke a counterproposal. The British commissioners suggested a boundary drawn west from the Rockies along the 49th parallel to its intersection with McGillivray's River (the northernmost branch of the Columbia) and then along the channel of the river to the sea. Behind these lines all future settlement would be confined.[29] Rush continued the bargaining by dropping back to the by-now customary 49th parallel. Following the anticipated rejection, the American minister reiterated Adams's noncolonization policy. Since unoccupied territory was off limits to Europeans, he intimated, the United States held exclusive rights to all territory associated with the Columbia and its streams and tributaries. The British, he patronizingly held, should be satisfied: America's 49-degree concession was more than reasonable.[30]

Again, the British saw the suggestion as not only unreasonable but also outrageous. Their negotiators indignantly declared that their people would not hesitate to colonize any available part of America. They concluded this round of talks with an official offer of 49 degrees to the northernmost Columbia branch but added a suggestion that the channel of the river remain perpetually free to both nations and that the two nations approve a period of ten years for relocation of present settlements to the appropriate sides of the newly drawn boundary. The futile negotiations ended with this proposal still on the table awaiting a reply from Rush.[31]

By the mid-1820s the powerful Hudson's Bay Company, having absorbed the North West Company by royal mandate in 1821, had persuaded the London government of the need to preserve the Columbia River for Britain. After brief talk of conceding the area due to diminishing returns from the fur trade, George Simpson, a young and energetic Scotsman, took over management of the territory and started a reorganization of the company's efforts in that region. Simpson placed the dynamic John McLoughlin—Great White Eagle to the local Indians—over a reconstituted Columbia Department. As one of McLoughlin's first duties, he changed the name of Fort George to Fort Vancouver and relocated it on the north bank of the Columbia just above its junction with the south-flowing Willamette River.[32]

With this new commitment to the Columbia came renewed pressure on the London government to hold all territory associated with and including that river. Simpson had the company's London governor propose a partition line to Canning. It first followed the Continental Divide from the 49th parallel to 46°20' where Lewis and Clark had crossed the mountains, then traced the Snake River to the Columbia, and finally tracked the course of that river to the sea. In late 1825, Simpson met with Undersecretary of State Henry Addington in London and convinced him that the Columbia was absolutely essential for the successful exploitation of the Pacific Northwest. This pressure from the Hudson's Bay Company, combined with the continued banter of American politicos, prompted Canning to invite another series of negotiations. Ironically, had it not been for these pressures, Lord Liverpool's government might have considered Rush's offer of 49 degrees. Liverpool and the so-called Little Englanders, who debated the costs of maintaining a far-flung empire, would have found a settlement at 49 degrees a fair price for reduced tension with the United States and the commercial benefits likely to accrue. The blustering of Americans, however, had allowed Canning to tap the pride of empire in convincing British subjects to stand their ground on Oregon.[33]

Had Gallatin discerned Canning's motives in 1826, he would have been far from optimistic when assigned the task of negotiating with Britain. The talks in London were to deal with several problems between the Atlantic nations, not the least of which was the Northwest boundary. There was little chance that Gallatin would succeed in this task. His instructions contained the same boundary that the British had rejected in 1824. Adams, now president, probably assumed that since Canning had invited the conference, he was ready to compromise. Such, it quickly became clear, was not the case. Canning refused to yield to the upstart republic in the face of the inflammatory rhetoric spewing across the Atlantic. Further, he had become convinced that the Columbia River would serve as the great hub of Pacific trade with China. Since the United States was the prime competitor for that trade, it would be foolish to sacrifice that critical advantage to American commerce.[34]

Late in 1826 the talks began as Gallatin sat opposite William Huskisson and the same Henry Addington who had been indoctrinated by Simpson the previous year to seek the Columbia River. The British referred Gallatin to the unanswered proposal of 1824 that Rush had left on the table. It seemed as though the talks would end abruptly when Gallatin rejected that offer and immediately proposed the already proven inadmissible 49-degree line. Gallatin may have placed false hopes in the added concession of navigation to all waterways south of 49 degrees since the commissioners at least passed it along to Canning for advice.[35]

While awaiting a response from the British cabinet, the two sides vainly set about to convince one another of their superior claims. Gallatin produced a list of foundational items to support the U.S. position that became all too familiar to British diplomats over the course of the controversy: Gray's discovery, Lewis and Clark's exploration, the establishment of Astoria, and the principle of contiguity derived from the Spanish line to the Pacific contained in the Adams-Onís Treaty of 1819. Huskisson and Addington denounced most of these items as weak, if not outright groundless. The Spanish, they declared, had relinquished their claim at Nootka in 1790 and had nothing in Oregon to transfer to the United States in 1819. Further, the British had not only explored but also occupied the territory. The crown's rights, they adamantly contended, were solid to Oregon from the Columbia northward. This apparently rigid position actually contained a subtle admission. It conceded that the territory south of the river fell outside the purview of British claims. This important admission in effect narrowed the contested territory to that lying north and west of the Columbia and south of 49 degrees.[36]

During Gallatin's discussions in 1826–27 it also became evident that both sides required access to the deep harbors at and above 49 degrees. The British rejected the 49-degree line because it sacrificed both the harbors of the Gulf of Georgia and the southern end of Vancouver Island. Recognizing that the Americans had precisely the same argument against forfeiting the territory north of the Columbia, Huskisson and Addington sought a compromise on the deep-water ports. Perhaps, contemplated the two commissioners, Britain could design a boundary that released to the United States all territory south of the Columbia but with an additional enclave of territory on the Juan de Fuca Strait. This move, they thought, should pacify the United States without sacrificing British interests; the territory would be divided but with both nations retaining access to the Columbia and the deep harbors on the strait.

Huskisson and Addington, with a certain reserved optimism, approached Gallatin with a suggestion that would yield the Olympic Peninsula to the United States. To sweeten the deal, they added shared control of Admiralty Inlet. But even reserved optimism attached to this intimation was ill founded. Gallatin knew that Washington would not consider an enclave isolated within a region controlled by Britain an equitable swap for the lion's share of the territory. This enclave, true enough, would give the United States the mandatory ports, but those ports constituted little more than an island station on the Pacific coast. In fact, Gallatin probably recalled the intransigent counsel that he had received from Secretary of State Henry Clay before he departed Washington. In attempting to draw more negotiating latitude from Clay, Gallatin had stated that an agent of Astor described the territory north and west of the Columbia as worthless. Clay had responded sarcastically that, if this was indeed the case, then the British should give it up. Although Gallatin did not consider the enclave offer viable, it left considerable diplomatic residue. The enclave offer breached the British claim to the contested territory and indicated that even the rigid Canning was willing to yield territory north of the Columbia.[37]

The diplomatic impasse soon convinced both sides that a partition in 1827 was not possible. They therefore set about renewing the soon-to-expire 1818 arrangement for open access. The British wanted to renew it long enough to allow their people to solidify their holdings and block the projected American military posts. Gallatin flanked their attempt by arguing that the 1818 agreement dealt with commerce and neither prohibited military posts nor provisional governments unless they affected that commerce. Having reserved America's rights to outposts and institutions in the territory, Gallatin turned to a renewal of the 1818 convention. The time factor, the negotiators addressed simply by agreeing that open access would continue until either party issued a twelve-month notice of its intent to abrogate the arrangement. With acceptance of the 1827 agreement, Gallatin's efforts succeeded only in consigning the Anglo-American contest to future negotiations.[38]

Unfortunately, the diplomats did not get back to the Oregon controversy until settlers and agents from both nations had converged on the area and created the potential for a disastrous confrontation. After Gallatin's mission, he ironically predicted that the British would eventually let the territory slip quietly out of their hands to be inhabited and organized by Americans who would make good Jefferson's forecast of establishing an independent state. Gallatin certainly missed the mark. The British continued to exploit the area while U.S. citizens moved into the territory accompanied by the assurance that they were not leaving the States.[39]

During the years immediately following the 1827 convention, it appeared that the British would be free to exploit the territory. They controlled the harbors, the Columbia River, and the only permanent settlements in the area. And, apart from the occasional American ship that ventured into the Columbia River, the Hudson's Bay Company maintained Britain's uncontested authority over Oregon. To secure control, the company had systematically trapped down the Snake River and the area south and east of the Columbia. This attempt to create a buffer to dissuade American encroachment was short-lived. Americans slowly awakened to the attractions of the territory. Individuals such as Boston schoolteacher Hall J. Kelley and Missouri fur trader Joshua Pilcher recognized the potential of the territory and were convinced that, with a little encouragement, the tenacious Americans would find their way there.[40]

Reports of corridors breaching the mountain barrier and the overall accessibility of the territory overland joined with America's mission spirit to provide that encouragement. Even the most adventurous immigrants needed some guarantee that they would not be turned back by the formidable obstacle that Benton referred to as the "fabled god, Terminus," which formed the divide between the United States and a new western republic. By 1830, Terminus was toppled by reports of wagons winding their way through South Pass. In that year a wagon train made the trek from St. Louis to the Wind River-Popo Agie junction near South Pass and reported to Washington that the "ease and safety with which it was done, prove the facility of communicating over land with the Pacific."[41]

No stimulus was more important to the early movement of Americans into the territory than the call of the Christian mission. Those caught up in the religious fervor of the 1830s were captivated by an account of a legation of Nez Percé Indians who came to St. Louis in search of Christianity. "My people," the Indian spokesman reportedly pleaded, "will die in darkness" with "no White Man's Book to make the way plain." How could decent and dedicated Christian workers like Jason and Daniel Lee resist such an emotional plea? By the spring of 1834 the Lees were on their way to the Oregon Country, initiating a wave of missionaries who, over the next few years, came seeking souls but found alluring land in the fertile Willamette Valley. In 1836 the famous Marcus Whitman party journeyed to the territory. The Lees, the Whitmans, and other missionaries were, as it turned out, more important to the ultimate ownership of the territory than to the afterlife of those who called them. While they continued to work with the local tribes, the broader significance of their presence in Oregon arose from the distinctive nature of their settlement. They did not come to the territory for immediate commercial gain or advantage but rather to establish themselves as long-term U.S residents.[42]

At the same time that the missionaries moved toward Oregon, Andrew Jackson's presidential administration instructed a purser in the U.S. Navy, William Slacum, to file a report on the territory. Secretary of State John Forsyth wanted Slacum to determine to which nation the occupants of the territory claimed allegiance. Slacum filed a report in 1837 that could only be described as troubling. The British, he declared, operated from their substantial headquarters at Fort Vancouver in exercising almost exclusive control of the territory by trapping as far south as 40 degrees. Within their domain they had trained the Indians to accept them as the absolute masters of the region and, he stated in alarm, had taken to arming the Indians, a fearful prospect in the American pioneer experience. Yet the greatest danger to U.S. interests, he reported, came from the Hudson's Bay Company, which practically held the Americans in the area hostage to its monopoly on essential supplies. Perhaps the most critical part of Slacum's report concerned a possible partition of the territory. Obviously the best way to secure the Americans in the area was to see that it became U.S. soil. Slacum contended that since both the Columbia and Puget Sound were important to the nation's interests, a boundary at the 49th parallel was an absolute minimum.[43]

III

By the time Jackson's successor, Martin Van Buren, delivered Slacum's report to Congress, variables outside the territory reflected the developing U.S. interest in the region. In that same year of 1837 financial panic swept the nation, beginning a period of insecurity that made land beyond the Rockies attractive and joined with a sense of mission to promote a steadily increasing stream of Americans into the territory. But how would struggling Americans learn of the territory? As fate would have it, along with the economic stress in the United States came a growing body of literature that lauded Oregon as an "Eden" on the Pacific. The literature ranged from books such as Washington Irving's *Astoria* to newspapers such as the Alton, Illinois, *Telegraph* that described the territory as "the future of the power which shall rule the Pacific . . . the theatre on which mankind is to act a part not yet performed in the drama of life and government," a region whose "far-spreading seas and mighty rivers are to teem with the commerce of the empire, and whose boundless prairies and verdant vales are to feel the footsteps of civilized millions."[44]

These footsteps were at first hesitant, awaiting assurance from the federal government that the American flag would follow. Prospective settlers did not have to wait long for that assurance. It arose from the floor of the Senate, championed by zealots such as the junior senator from Missouri, Lewis Linn, and his congressional colleague, Massachusetts Representative Caleb Cushing. Beginning in 1838, Linn dispensed an almost steady flow of memorials and legislation that called for the military occupation of the Columbia River and abrogation of the existing agreement with Britain. Although Cushing was not as extreme in his views, he promoted the commercial advantages of the territory, generated thousands of pages of propaganda stubbornly advocating its retention to 54°40', and affirmed the need for law and order there. Meanwhile, Linn contended, the territory should come within the jurisdiction of U.S. laws and, to promote that objective, free land should be offered to American citizens. In a passionate appeal for the United States to assert control over the territory in 1841, the senator promised that American settlers "would be numbered with the dead" before Britain would compromise on Oregon.[45]

Although these pronouncements from Congress had little impact on either legislation or Britain's position in the territory, they were not missed by the struggling Americans east of the Missouri. Sinking deeper and deeper into the nation's economic woes of the late 1830s and early 1840s, these farmers and mechanics grasped at the opportunity for fertile land in the Columbia and Willamette valleys. The combination of promised "American" land, a tightening economy, vanishing markets, constricting currency, and the propaganda of the missionaries regarding the wonders of the territory spurred many to join the so-called Great Reinforcement that made its way west in 1840. Most important, these new settlers came to Oregon for the soil and not the soul and had every intention of staying. Even the missionaries, Simpson admitted in 1841, were directing "their attention more to temporal than spiritual affairs."[46]

Even though the Americans remained south of the Columbia River, the British in the area recognized the challenge that these permanent residents presented to Her Majesty's claim. The Hudson's Bay Company's longtime control of the territory seemed threatened by this new influx of Americans. Despite British efforts to expand the company's enterprises to include the Puget Sound Agricultural Company and the Cowlitz Farms, they continued to emphasize the commercial exploitation of the territory. And besides, if British subjects were interested in colonization, they found a more attractive outlet for that interest in Australia and New Zealand. The company thus inspired only as much settlement in the Pacific Northwest as was needed to secure its commercial enterprise. The British government, especially after the eruption of rebellions in Canada during the late 1830s, had to question the expediency of holding remote colonies, particularly those that benefited so narrow a group.[47]

The perception nonetheless prevailed that the two peoples were aggressively targeting the same territory for colonization. Thomas Farnham, leader of a group of Americans to the territory in 1840, wrote the State Department that the queen had given a huge tract of land to the Hudson's Bay Company and that the company was parceling it out to loyal servants of the crown. Even though the British adamantly denied the report, it was evident that both peoples in the territory were becoming increasingly anxious at the prospect of losing it. Simpson cautioned London about the approach of Farnham's contingent. There was, Simpson wrote, a substantial group of "men of desperate character and fortune" on their way. They came with the attitude that "we [British] are intruders, without a shadow of right to be there." Among the settlers "few will be scrupulous as to the mode or means of asserting their imaginary rights."[48]

Simpson was correct in his estimation but wrong in the belief that the rights were imaginary. As a contagious "Oregon fever" infected citizens across the nation and drew them toward the territory, they carried with them rights that they considered to be grounded in the reality of an aggressively expansive nation. Anyone who doubted this assertion need only pick up one of many American newspapers to read the pronouncements of statesmen in Washington or the reports of the "Oregon meetings" in the Midwest. Whatever the source, many Americans were convinced that Oregon belonged to the United States and that national honor and providential design demanded that they have it.

How much of Oregon, however, would it take to accommodate the American desire for territory and the maintenance of national honor? Could such exalted goals be achieved south of the Columbia? If there had been any thought of this question prior to 1842, it was put to rest that year by the mission of Lt. Charles Wilkes. Sent by Van Buren in 1838 to explore the Pacific coast, Wilkes reported in the early 1840s that the sandbar across the mouth of the Columbia River made it too treacherous to satisfy the strategic and commercial needs of the United States. Therefore, Wilkes asserted, the nation could not relinquish title to any territory that forfeited the Juan de Fuca Strait. With railroad linkage to the Pacific becoming less of a fantasy, and with the Columbia River eliminated as the optimum terminus for future rail transport, the harbors on the Strait appeared more critical than ever to U.S. trade in the Pacific. But there was one small matter with which to dispense before the United States could secure those harbors—the British.[49]

The mere assertion of an American desire for the harbors meant little as long as the British clung to the Columbia River. Despite his acceptance of Wilkes's assessment of the Columbia and a pending decision to relocate company headquarters to Vancouver Island, Simpson wrote London that it was imperative that the crown retain the Columbia in any territorial partition. As it happened, his admonition went to a receptive desk at the Foreign Office—that of the same Addington who, at Simpson's hands, had become a devotee of the Columbia River years before. More important, Addington now held a pivotal position. Due to the resignation of longtime Foreign Office undersecretary John Backhouse, the post had gone to retired diplomat Addington at the beginning of 1842, just in time to affect the preparation of the Oregon instructions for the Ashburton mission.[50]

As a result, those instructions were conspicuously similar to the position that Simpson had enunciated in the 1820s and stood by in the 1840s—the Columbia River as boundary. This stance was unfortunate. The recent assessment of the Columbia actually confirmed what Addington had acknowledged in the 1820s: the United States considered the issue of the ports north of the river as nonnegotiable. Had Addington approached the instructions from this starting point, Ashburton's Oregon directives would have had more potential for success. The undersecretary seemed to have forgotten his enclave offer of the 1826–27 negotiations. He thus allowed Ashburton to join Webster in Washington with instructions that actually offered less than that previously offered and rejected in the last set of talks. This poor strategy doomed the Oregon segment of the negotiations and completely ignored the altered circumstances of almost two decades. If an offer of the Columbia as boundary had been rejected in the 1820s when there were no American citizens in Oregon and the significance of the deep harbors was not fully appreciated, what hope would such an offer have in the 1840s when a steady stream of "desperate characters" from the United States flowed into the territory and the harbors on the Strait had been confirmed as indispensable?[51]

Daniel Webster, not surprisingly, wasted little time before rejecting Ashburton's offer. The secretary of state, however, attempted to redeem the Oregon discussion with a novel counter: the "tripartite" plan. Under this creative proposal, the United States would accept the oft-rejected Columbia River boundary in return for the California port of San Francisco. Ashburton readily supported this plan since it required nothing of Britain but the promise to respect the transfer of San Francisco by Mexico to the United States. "We shall," he wrote Aberdeen, "probably get our boundary with the understanding I mention, but without waiting for our Treaty the conclusion of their arrangements with Mexico."[52]

The British minister's confidence in this scheme revealed his own lack of understanding of the circumstances touching the

Pacific coast. First, given the current piqued attitude of Mexico City toward Washington, there was little reason to expect that Mexico would willingly forfeit any territory to the United States, much less the port of San Francisco. Second, Ashburton, in his communication with Aberdeen, expressed the erroneous belief that there were "few if any" American settlers in Oregon. Simpson had communicated to London before the Ashburton mission that approximately five hundred Americans were in the territory; and, at the very moment of Ashburton's despatch, one of the largest groups ever to move west was reportedly preparing to depart Missouri for the Pacific coast. Not only was the American population substantial and growing, but an official of the U.S. government, Dr. Elijah White, had been assigned to the territory. And third, the British minister opined that the Indians earlier relocated west of the Mississippi now presented a barrier that would discourage the western movement of American citizens and that the hostile tribes in the territory would delay, if not prevent, the establishment of permanent settlements. Again, Ashburton was wrong. It was clear from the steady movement westward that Americans did not find the relocated tribes a barrier. In fact, setting aside an earlier belief that the Indians would gradually—and to their benefit—become immersed in white civilization, Americans now accepted that the inferior peoples of the hinterland had and would yield to a Providence-sanctioned expansion of the United States. An observant Ashburton should have noted that this attitude gave license under the banner of republican virtue for advancing Americans to sweep aside anyone in their path.[53]

It is not easy to explain why Ashburton was so ill prepared for the Oregon negotiations. Perhaps the urgency of the other issues prompting his mission had obscured Oregon. Or maybe he believed that the agenda for the 1842 negotiations was too ambitious; if something needed sacrificing, the remote Oregon Question seemed the best candidate. Had he been better informed on the matter, he would have realized that the same potential for a local eruption existed in the Northwest that had recently caused the Anglo-American crisis in the Northeast. But he was not informed. In fact, Addington had withheld information from the British diplomat and drafted his instructions on Oregon so narrowly that Ashburton was left with precious little detail or latitude. He supplied Ashburton with minutes from the Rush negotiation, the 1825 Simpson proposal, Addington's own 1820s defense of Britain's claim, and a sketch of the history of the conflict. Notably absent was the enclave offer.

It is possible that Addington intentionally concealed the enclave offer, knowing that it had weakened the British bargaining position. He had appreciated at the time the potential problem that it presented for future negotiations and, consequently, had requested that the rejected offer be stricken from the official record. Although he would later disingenuously argue that he had merely forgotten it, there is little doubt that in 1842 he was still trying to preserve the British claim to territory north of the Columbia River. The omission of this information from Ashburton's instructions was significant. Had he known that the Yankeephobic Canning had been willing to concede harbors north of the Columbia to the United States, he surely would have challenged Addington's hastily prepared instructions. But Addington's performance does not exonerate Ashburton completely. Details of the last Oregon negotiations were not dependent solely on Addington's memory. Congress had ordered the record of the conference made public in 1828.[54]

That public record, of course, was also available to Webster, who, like his British friend, failed to use it to prepare adequately for the Oregon discussion. Had Webster done his homework, he would have known that Ashburton's offer was a retreat from the last British offer and hence did not warrant a counteroffer such as the curious tripartite intimation. Also like Ashburton, Webster ignored the current circumstances of the Oregon Territory. He overlooked the presence of several hundred Americans there with more on the way; he did not consider the emergence of a provisional government by Americans in Oregon; he dismissed the persistent cries of his congressional colleagues for government-sponsored occupation of the region; and he did not fully appreciate news from the U.S. consul in Honolulu, Peter Brinsmade, of the importance of the Pacific Northwest harbors. The region, Brinsmade declared, "for its facilities for ship building and the lumber trade" will be "to the Pacific Coast of vastly greater importance than that of Maine to the Atlantic Coast."[55]

In short, Webster devoted his attention to securing as much of Maine as possible and did not recognize that the Oregon Territory was equally important and potentially as volatile as the Northeast. In July, after the country had become stirred up by the broadcast of Wilkes's report and the British minister had determined that an Oregon resolution would not be forthcoming, Ashburton cynically wrote about Webster: "I have attached too much importance to his concessions [tripartite plan] which I thought worth something, but which he is wholly unable to realize."[56] But to chastise the American and British negotiators of 1842 is perhaps unfair. Their accomplishments were significant and they did, in fact, resolve or pacify a number of urgent matters, not the least of which was the Northeast boundary dispute. The achievement had been taxing, and the two diplomats were exhausted and understandably sought a respite from their labor.

One cannot help but feel sympathetic toward the elderly Ashburton, who pleaded with both his American colleague and the Foreign Office to be delivered from the Washington heat and politicians. To escape, however, meant leaving the Oregon dispute unresolved. Before his departure from Washington he had finally, though belatedly, realized the danger in such a delay. A "new and troublesome Boundary question," he confessed, "may grow up on that distant shore at no remote period." He was correct. Even as Ashburton retreated from the discomfort of the tidewater climate, hundreds of Americans were gazing westward and plotting their own escape from the oppression of a strained economy. Oregon fever was spreading; there would indeed be a "troublesome Boundary question." The American settlers and their advocates in Washington would see to it.[57]

CHAPTER EIGHT

Rising Temperature:
Feed a Cold, Starve a Fever

It is better to defend the first inch of territory than the last. . . . Let
us have no red lines upon the map of Oregon.
                                        —Lewis Cass, July 4, 1843

Despite the inability of Webster and Ashburton to settle the Oregon boundary issue, a certain optimism remained within the Peel government in London that the Atlantic nations would soon resolve this problem. Aberdeen attempted to nurture this optimism, but it gradually fell victim to charges of capitulation, heightened rhetoric by Washington's lawmakers, and a potent American device called "masterly inactivity." The Whig voice of Palmerston wailed against the compromise on the northeastern boundary— blasted as the "Ashburton capitulation"—and argued that there was little room for compromise with an administration bent on ejecting all the British from North America. Although only the most bombastic of congressional politicos took this extremist position, there was ample evidence that the United States wanted as much of the continent as Providence permitted. As wagons rolled westward in ever-increasing numbers, Oregon was the cause that fitted perfectly with this desire and became the bellwether for an emotional vision for a transcontinental republic. Thus, while Aberdeen attempted to talk, American statesmen either stalled or lashed out with dangerously aggressive proposals, and American families set their faces toward Oregon and their feet upon the Oregon Trail.

I

The determination of Americans to push aside any barrier, diplomatic or natural, became increasingly apparent in the aftermath of the Webster-Ashburton negotiations. The White-Hastings wagon train of 1842 doubled the existing American population in Oregon and delivered news from Washington that Missouri Senator Lewis Linn hoped to provide 640 acres to every white male settler in the territory. In November of that same year zealous citizens met in Illinois to demand government action designed to promote settlement. If more sanguine types thought that this meant either a shared territory or a compromised boundary, they needed only to note the declarations of these Illinois citizens. There would be no surrender, they defiantly decreed, of "any part of that territory lying between Russian and Mexican boundaries, to any nation, for any consideration whatever."[1]

Ironically, Aberdeen would have been among the last to willfully contest this assertion. In fact, he would have gladly released the territory for almost "any consideration" short of a challenge to national honor. It became evident over the following years that the foreign secretary found little to gain and much to lose from an argument with America over the remote Pacific wilderness called Oregon. He instructed his minister in Washington, Henry Fox, to find a solution to the controversy, and at the same time he informed the U.S. minister in London, Edward Everett, of his interest in resolving the Oregon problem "on a basis of equitable compromise." Unfortunately, Aberdeen still believed that such an arrangement might involve Webster's San Francisco intimation. When Aberdeen alluded to the tripartite plan in a conversation with Everett, the American minister was a bit confused about how such a transaction would progress and what part London would take in the process. Aberdeen had not locked his sights on the San Francisco plan, however, but merely used it to reopen the subject.[2]

With this opening, Aberdeen hoped to initiate talks with Everett that might bear fruit in the friendly environment recently created by the Ashburton mission. The foreign secretary realized that those conditions were fragile and fleeting. When the next Congress convened in Washington, it would likely take up where the other had left off on the Oregon debate—with "ill-considered declarations" that would not bode well for an amicable settlement. Unfortunately, Aberdeen's hopes would be dashed and his fears realized as miscues and indecision between Washington and London prevented the resumption of the Oregon talks. Webster, whom Fox believed had designs on heading a mission to London, alleged that the Oregon issue was too complicated for allocation to his friend Everett. Although Fox later confused both Aberdeen and Everett with an errant message that the Tyler administration had reconsidered and

was prepared to proceed with a London negotiation, the president
had simply conveyed a token statement of his willingness to settle
the issue.[3]

Fox soon determined that President Tyler was more willing to
talk of settlement than to actually negotiate and that, indeed, the
new Congress intended to renew its Oregon agitation. The
president's December message to Congress pretentiously referred
to Oregon as the "Territory of the United States" and asserted that
his administration would "urge" the British to settle the boundary
issue. Fox irately wrote Aberdeen that the Americans were trying
to place responsibility for delay at the feet of the British. This, Fox
contended, was a disingenuous and deceptive account. In truth, the
London government had been ready and willing to take up the issue and thus required no "urging."[4]

In Congress the new debate resulted from yet another Oregon
bill from Senator Linn. This aggressive proposal called for a line
of forts extending from the Missouri and Arkansas rivers to the
mouth of the Columbia, generous land grants to white males age
eighteen or older, and the extension of U.S. laws from the 42d parallel to Russian America. Lawmakers from all sections of the country
weighed into the discussion, placing Oregon within the context of
U.S. economic recovery, the growing Pacific trade, and the expanding relationship of British industry to American cotton.[5]

It is small wonder that Aberdeen called Everett to the Foreign
Office after news arrived from Fox in early January 1843 of Tyler's
address and the Linn bill. Everett must have been extremely frustrated. He had just communicated to Webster Aberdeen's positive
reception to a November suggestion regarding the Oregon boundary that came from the secretary of state. Drawing from the proposal of a member of the Wilkes expedition, Webster had offered
to discuss a line running from the Juan de Fuca Strait southward
until it intersected the Columbia River just below Fort Vancouver.
The line would then turn eastward and follow the Columbia to the
49th parallel. This arrangement would satisfy both nations' demands
for access to essential waterways. "I do not think," Aberdeen had
responded to Everett, "we should have any difficulty in settling it."
But then came word of the latest public outburst from America.
How could Aberdeen seek compromise in the face of such inflammatory rhetoric? He was in the midst of a politically delicate effort
to develop entente with the French. It would be too much for him
to simultaneously invite his political opponents to charge the ministry with exposing national honor to the boorish Americans.

Ashburton cautioned the foreign secretary that these Americans were capable of pushing the issue if they perceived weakness and that they might have misread the recent treaty over Maine as an indication of British readiness to concede. If Britain considered a compromise boundary along the lines sketched by Everett, the aged diplomat cautioned, "we run a risk, in the present state of parties, of making the concession without obtaining our Treaty." All this excitement amounted to one thing to Aberdeen: the opportunity to exploit the amity of the Ashburton mission was lost. As he had feared, the American statesmen had engaged in another campaign of provocative bluster.[6]

The Senate at that moment was generating, as if according to script, a steady barrage of Yankee bravado. If the United States failed to implement the rights asserted in his bill, Linn declared, the nation would face their forfeiture. Why? Because the Hudson's Bay Company, Linn crowed, would do for Britain in Oregon what other powerful trading companies had done for the crown in India—possess it. The federal government, he argued, should at least equalize the contest by meeting British influence with American initiatives. Congress should award free land to those who were willing to take up roots and move to the Pacific. Most of the proponents of U.S. action remained relatively controlled and statesmanlike. But, as expected, some went off into emotional and —considering the rising hackles of British honor—dangerous flights of fancy. Senator Thomas Hart Benton of Missouri began his soliloquy calmly enough but concluded with exactly the kind of rhetoric that Aberdeen had feared. The British, he howled, "have crossed the 49th degree, come down upon the Columbia, taken possession of it from the head to the mouth, fortified it and colonized it." They have taken complete control of the fur trade, "driven all our traders across the mountains, [and] killed more than a thousand of them. . . . Peace is our policy. War is the policy of England, and war with us is now her favorite policy. Let it come rather than dishonor!"[7]

As the debate escalated in intensity, opponents lined up to either challenge or, at least, calm the agitation. Some argued that the 1827 convention required the United States to issue the twelve-month notice of abrogation before pursuing Linn's suggestions. Others trumpeted the time-worn argument that the western lands constituted an American desert and, as South Carolina's George McDuffie chided, were not worth a "pinch of snuff." McDuffie's South Carolina colleague produced the most brilliant argument for the opposition—do nothing. In what would become known as "mas-

John C. Calhoun. From painting by Alonzo Chappel, in *National Portrait Gallery of Eminent Americans* (1862).

terly inactivity," Senator John C. Calhoun argued that destiny would guarantee America's eventual absorption of its natural domain without any assistance from Washington legislators. "Time," he coolly concluded, "is acting for us, and, if we shall have the wisdom to trust its operation, it will assert and maintain our right with resist-less force, without costing a cent of money, or a drop of blood."⁸

Much to the surprise of Fox and Aberdeen, the Linn bill passed the Senate. Fox had received assurances from influential senators that it would not, and he had communicated as much to his chief in London. As it happened, a despatch arrived from Aberdeen on the day of the vote instructing Fox, on the doubtful chance that the bill passed, to remind the secretary of state of the 1827 convention's commitment to guard against "all hazard of misunderstanding." In unusually strong language for Aberdeen, he warned that the British would respond "as they might think fit for the assertion and maintenance" of their nation's claims.⁹ Fox's anxiety eased considerably when the bill went to committee in the House of Representatives, where it remained for the rest of the congressional session. "No further trouble," a relieved Fox wrote the home office, "need be apprehended from legislative enactment, upon the subject of the Oregon Territory, until the next session of Congress." By then, he stated optimistically, the dispute may "have been placed in a train of amicable adjustment between the two Governments."¹⁰

Fortunately, that train had not been completely derailed. Aberdeen remained receptive to a reasonable solution. Webster continued to promote a plan that involved San Francisco, but he should have realized that the headstrong capture of Monterey by the American maverick Commodore Thomas ap Catesby Jones in October 1842 had closed the door on any deal with Mexico. And besides, Britain had decided not to participate in any such transaction. Nevertheless, Everett and Aberdeen had a very promising discussion in February during which the foreign secretary pointed to a map in emphasizing the "small extent" of the territory actually contested and displayed some of his resilient optimism to Everett. There should be no problem, Aberdeen stated, "in coming to an amicable & reasonable settlement." While his country "could not go on giving up every thing," he continued, the Peel government "had no wish or feeling but for an honorable settlement."¹¹

While Everett and Aberdeen gazed at their map in London (an activity that, in the aftermath of the Ashburton mission, was best done in private), a new wave of Pacific-bound settlers set their wagon wheels in the deepening ruts of the Oregon Trail. These were not the small contingents of previous years but were great wagon trains drawing ever-growing numbers of families who had to do little more than show up ready to go. A common newspaper advertisement read: "If interested in joining the 1843 Oregon Train, come equipped with wagon and animals to Sapling Grove during the month of March." Letters, memorials, and meetings continually encouraged Americans to move to the territory. Oregon, a letter from Iowa stated, is the "pioneer's land of promise. Hundreds are already prepared to start thither with the spring, while hundreds of others are anxiously awaiting the action of congress in reference to that country, as the signal for their departure." Firsthand reports from the territory helped to raise the temperature by supplying flattering accounts of Oregon, painting it "to their neighbors in the brightest colors; these have told it to others; the Oregon fever has broke out, and is now raging like any other contagion."[12]

In February a meeting in Illinois called for the government to resist British encroachment in the territory and preserve its tremendous commercial potential for the United States. This call was echoed in the spring by a group from Ohio, who added that each new wagon train made the path more convenient "until a journey to the Columbia will be considered, in a few years, an undertaking of no great magnitude, except as to time and distance." In the early summer two hundred wagons left Missouri to inaugurate the "Great Migration." The first installment added over eight hundred Americans to the territory with hundreds more gathering for the trip in the summer. Spurred by the promise of the Linn bill, along with the rains, floods, and disease in the heartland, they moved west—and in large numbers. Over one hundred Democrats from six states met in Cincinnati in July and called for the occupation of the territory "by the arms and laws of the Republic" as far northward as 54°40'. Their call for blocking the British "intrusion" in the Pacific Northwest resonated with the rhetoric of Michigan Democrat Lewis Cass's Fourth of July speech. England, he warned, was set on "encircling the globe with her stations wherever she can best accomplish her scheme of aggrandizement."[13]

Meanwhile, London seemed oblivious to this feverish activity. At the very moment of the Great Migration, a London journal confidently stated that no matter how "the political questions between England and America, as to the ownership of Oregon may be decided, Oregon will never be colonized overland from the United States." As much in the dark as Ashburton had been the previous year, the journal continued that the "world must assume a new face, before the American wagons make plain the road to the Columbia as they have done to the Ohio" and that "the future owners of Oregon would come from Europe." The British, it seemed, had been lulled into a certain complacency by the Hudson's Bay Company's years of dominating the area. The company, however, was under no such delusion. It had become well aware of its precarious position on the Columbia created by the unchecked migration of Americans. A company official wrote Simpson in October that Calhoun's masterly inactivity had produced its "effect, and there can be no doubt of the final success of the plan, if the country remains open a few years longer."[14]

The British finally awakened to the possibility of a real contest over Oregon in 1843. Pursuit of the Linn bill, Palmerston menacingly warned in March, was equivalent to a declaration of war. He believed that the ballyhoo emanating from Congress was symptomatic of a generally agitated mood and stood ready to defend British honor against the recalcitrant Americans. And although Peel assured him that the Linn bill would not clear the desk of the president and that the matter was in the diplomatic track, Palmerston's suspicions joined with a growing interest by the British journals to persuade their people that their national honor was threatened. *Fraser's Magazine* of London proclaimed that the government should remove the American nuisance in Oregon by war if necessary. We are the ones, challenged the author, "that have the possession, the forts, the armed men, and the determination to keep what we have got."[15]

While the Oregon virus caused the temperature to rise on both sides of the Atlantic, Aberdeen still sought an opening in which to pursue the "diplomatic track." If that meant conducting the negotiations in Washington, he wrote Fox, the president should receive word of British willingness to do so. Aberdeen had resigned himself to the fact that Tyler's suspicious nature would not permit the Whig appointee and Anglophilic Everett to treat the controversy in London. He therefore offered the significant compromise of once again agreeing to deliberations in Washington. And Aberdeen would go one step farther toward accommodating the Tyler administration. He would replace the unpopular Fox with a minister plenipotentiary who, coming from his post in Mexico City, would not be hamstrung by an established reputation in the Capitol: the Anglo-Irish career diplomat, Richard Pakenham.[16]

Tyler, however, had also decided to compromise. Despite his reservations about Everett, a number of factors had combined to convince the president that he should now seek a resolution of the Oregon problem. In May the provocative seizure of Hawaii by British Admiral Lord George Paulet had apparently affected Tyler's Oregon position. Paulet's unauthorized adventure had resulted in

Richard Pakenham. *Courtesy Government Art Collection, London.*

the cession of the island kingdom to Queen Victoria by the Hawaiian king and the admiral's bold pronouncement that the Pacific pearl belonged to the empire. Although the British quickly censured Paulet's action and preempted a likely international protest, a rattled Tyler wrote Hugh Legaré that the United States "should lose no time in opening a negotiation" on the Oregon dispute. The constant clamor of influential Americans such as Caleb Cushing, chairman of the House Foreign Relations Committee, *Madisonian* editor John Jones, and James Gordon Bennett of the New York *Herald* had helped to convince Tyler of the importance of Oregon in Anglo-American commercial competition in the Pacific. The president's belief that the country's economy depended on the nurturing of world markets to absorb surplus goods naturally connected him to the vision of an expanding Pacific trade. This realization became evident in his administration's persistent attempts to shore up the U.S. position in Hawaii, China, and Japan. Tyler instructed Everett to proceed with negotiations in London.[17]

II

At long last, a compromise became a real possibility. Everett and Aberdeen had talked about Oregon throughout 1843, and each believed that they could come to terms on a reasonable partition of the territory. When Everett had informed Aberdeen of Canning's enclave offer, the foreign secretary's hand was freed to compromise with little risk to British honor. After all, he would only be deferring to a previous British offer. Likewise, hope for an arrangement arrived in the form of Everett's instructions to treat the matter in London. He was to offer a boundary at the 49th parallel with Britain receiving navigation rights on the Columbia. And, acknowledging the importance that the British attached to Vancouver Island, Everett suggested the possibility of bending the boundary through the Juan de Fuca Strait to preserve all of the island to the crown. If both sides now desired a settlement, this move should have provided a good foundation. Unfortunately, however, Aberdeen had determined to leave the matter with Pakenham, who was en route to his post in Washington.[18]

Not coincidentally, Pakenham carried instructions to repeat the offer of the 1820s with the inclusion of the Olympic Peninsula enclave; this failing, the British minister could propose American access to ports below 49 degrees, arbitration, or an extension of the existing arrangement. Reminiscent of Henry Addington's thinking decades earlier, Aberdeen told Pakenham that if the offer was rejected, the crown would not be bound to it in future negotiations. This statement was rather naive considering what had recently transpired as a consequence of Addington's offer to Albert Gallatin. Aberdeen acknowledged that it would indeed be difficult to retreat from the offer once made and, as if in subconscious admission to the difficulty, he held the United States to previous offers that had relinquished claims to the territory north of the 49th parallel. The foreign secretary provided Pakenham with a proposal that allowed him to hold out the additional concession of U.S. access to harbors on either Vancouver Island or the mainland south of 49 degrees, or to yield free use of all ports on the Juan de Fuca Strait and below the 49th parallel. If the United States rejected all attempts to partition the territory, Pakenham should propose either arbitration or the formal extension of the open-access agreement. Aberdeen cautioned that Washington should not view any of these British overtures as a sign that Her Majesty's Government was willing to sacrifice the rights of its subjects. These rights, the foreign secretary asserted, were just, and his country would defend them.[19]

On its surface the foreign secretary's directives appeared to be straightforward and clear: offer proposal B at the failure of proposal A, then proposal C. But Aberdeen did not leave the issue to the formal instructions. Between the end of 1843, when Pakenham received them, and the time he was to open negotiations in Washington early the following year, Aberdeen wrote Pakenham to draw an American offer to divide the territory at the 49th parallel, with joint navigation of the Columbia, and all of Vancouver Island left to the British side of the line—in other words, the terms that Everett had been prepared to offer in London.

This communiqué from Aberdeen must have struck Pakenham as curious since the sober Scot confessed that he had not approached the cabinet about such a compromise. The British minister had considerable latitude to assess the feasibility of such an arrangement. "I trust entirely," Aberdeen told him, "to the judgement and discretion with which you will carry them into effect in case of necessity." If such an arrangement seemed possible, Pakenham should communicate as much to the Foreign Office so that it could issue new instructions to him in Washington. This "if" would prove extremely hazardous. Whereas a Lord Ashburton might have boldly seized the latitude intimated and taken any offer resembling that sketched out by Aberdeen in his private letter as feasible, a less self-possessed career diplomat would scrutinize any offer against the details of his formal instructions and, perhaps, the informal letter. If the offer did not align precisely, would he assume the risk of presenting it to London without so much as an attempt to have it adjusted? Three weeks removed from the advice of his chief, he would not. His decision on this issue, as it turned out, held dangerous implications for Anglo-American relations.[20]

Between the time of Pakenham's departure from London and his arrival in Washington the atmosphere had turned far less favorable for negotiation. Tyler's December message to Congress again lit the flame under the Oregon dispute by claiming that the entire territory from Mexican California to Alaska was within the proper domain of the United States. Citizens who moved to the territory, he declared, should fall under the protection and laws of the federal government. Tyler's words typified those arising from the House and Senate chambers. Although death had silenced the voice of Lewis Linn, his colleagues in Congress continued the refrain for the Oregon Country. Another Missourian, David Atchison, heralded U.S. claims to Oregon as far north as 54°40'. Beginning in December and continuing into the new year of 1844, Atchison and his supporters proposed legislation that encouraged permanent settlement and recommended abrogation of the open-access agreement.[21]

Fox watched this recent activity and became ever more exasperated. He was especially indignant over President Tyler's persistent depiction of Britain as the dawdler responsible for the prolonged controversy. The British minister could not imagine how Tyler could "reconcile to the principles of honesty and fair dealing these repeated and wilful inaccuracies in the mode of narrating the progress of an important negotiation." When the president responded to a congressional request for all correspondence associated with the Oregon issue by stating that it had already been made available, an incredulous Fox erupted. None of his exchanges with Webster that illustrated Britain's readiness to negotiate had been included. And yet, before the end of January, Fox observed that cooler heads had calmed Congress into delaying action on Oregon until it became clear what course the negotiation in Washington would take. In other words, give Pakenham a chance.[22]

Pakenham's chance would come, but it followed a frustrating and tedious process that edged forward under the watchful eye of an all-Oregon western coterie in Congress and an equally expansionist-minded cadre of Texas annexationists. His official contact with Washington started with what might have been an omen of the dark future of the Oregon negotiation. He had anticipated working with Secretary of State Abel Upshur, who, though preoccupied with Texas since his appointment in 1843, had shown an interest in resolving the Oregon problem. But on February 28, just before Pakenham was to take up the issue with him, Upshur was killed in an unfortunate accident on board the USS *Princeton* when its bow gun, ironically named "Peacemaker," blew up during an exposition voyage.[23]

The congressional debate meanwhile centered on a Democratic push for an immediate settlement and a Whig desire to leave the issue with the executive rather than produce provocative legislation that might lead to a needless confrontation with the British. Senator William Archer warned in mid-March that abrogation of the open-access arrangement would interrupt the diplomatic process and bring on another war with the British.[24]

The single-minded British minister was intent on sowing his tenure in Washington with promising seed. In March, Pakenham reported the defeat of the abrogation bill and expressed his belief, based on assurances from influential lawmakers, that all such legislation would likely meet the same fate. Even if a definite settlement of the boundary eluded the two parties, he confidently asserted, "there will be no quarrel—no scandal—to alarm the publick in England or otherwise seriously to embarrass Her Majesty's Government." He early developed the opinion that the United States feared a rupture with Britain and that the "mischievous declarations in Congress" were merely the result of electioneering intended for the domestic audience, not the British. Pakenham's determination to put forward the best foot, however, had clouded his vision because many Americans believed that the British appetite for cotton made it more likely that *they* would fear a rupture. The anticipated annexation of Texas magnified the power of American cotton by presenting the United States with a virtual monopoly over the critical commodity. There was no incentive to hurry: this advantage would do nothing but increase over time. Upshur's replacement certainly understood this; after all, he was the author of masterly inactivity.[25]

Calhoun, that sometimes wild-eyed and always intense senior statesman from South Carolina, had become head of the State Department after the death of Upshur. But Calhoun was so caught up with the southern campaign for Texas and his conviction that the British were scheming to block annexation that he stalled Pakenham's efforts to discuss Oregon until late summer. Pakenham realized that Calhoun had his eyes fixed on Texas; and, knowing that London preferred an independent Texas Republic, he too watched developments on that issue closely.[26]

In April, while awaiting Calhoun's preparations for the Oregon talks, Pakenham heard more than enough about Texas. For over a year the Tyler administration had ingested exaggerated reports of British intrigue in Texas. Tyler's agent in London, Duff Green, had convinced the president, Upshur, Calhoun, and others that the British were intent on forcing the preservation of an independent Texas that would abolish slavery and ensure Britain's commercial position in the hemisphere. Reflecting the administration's acceptance of this notion, the *Madisonian* asserted in early summer that should the British pursue "a design to possess Mexico or Texas, or to intervene in any manner with the slaves of the Southern States," that pursuit would "rouse the whole American People to arms like one vast nest of hornets. The great Western States, at the call of 'Captain Tyler,' would pour their noble sons down the Mississippi Valley by MILLIONS." Calhoun, in broader terms that left no doubt of his sentiments, wrote that no other "nation, in ancient, or modern time, ever pursued dominion and commercial monopoly more perseveringly & vehemently" than Britain.[27]

It is small wonder that Pakenham, who read that the president's most laudable trait was that he was the "enemy of England," became quickly suspicious of Tyler and frustrated with his secretary of state. Calhoun, as he had before he hesitatingly accepted Tyler's appointment, relentlessly portrayed British abolitionism and commercial avarice as justification for the U.S. annexation of Texas. The South Carolinian further argued that British plotting in that young republic presented a major impediment to a successful annexation treaty. Pennsylvania's Charles Ingersoll, chairman of the House Foreign Affairs Committee, accused Pakenham of having at the heart of his mission a scheme to derail America's acquisition of Texas. The Oregon dispute, he contended, was mere camouflage. Although it was true that the British and the French contemplated a joint move to preserve Mexican integrity and Texas independence (driven as much by concern for faltering Anglo-French entente as for the preservation of Texas),[28] there was no evidence that Pakenham had come to Washington as a covert agent of such a scheme. In fact, when he discussed the subject with Calhoun, the British minister offered assurances that his government had no desire to intervene in Texas, and he openly intimated the possibility of a trilateral promise by the United States, France, and Britain to safeguard the Texas Republic. To the latter suggestion, the wary southerner predictably expressed no interest and cynically responded, Pakenham wrote, "with a smile."[29]

Calhoun's cockiness contributed to the unraveling of his Texas treaty. In replying to Aberdeen's pacific assurances in a note to Pakenham, Calhoun singled out the British admission that they preferred the abolition of slavery and seized on that issue as a challenge to the South. In the note, Calhoun admonished the minister of the importance of slavery to the "peace, safety, and prosperity" of the southern states. When the note appeared along with the Texas correspondence requested by Congress, the attachment of the controversial "peculiar institution" to the treaty doomed it to failure. In this atmosphere a beleaguered Pakenham determined that as long as Texas was on the table, he could do little else but wait for Calhoun to initiate Oregon talks. The Texas experience also intensified the British minister's skepticism about the prospects for a successful resolution of the Oregon dispute—if and when the question was finally addressed. "The American government," he declared in frustration, "may be influenced by some sinister motive which I have not been able to penetrate."[30]

If motives in Washington were difficult to penetrate, those of U.S. citizens interested in the Pacific Northwest were crystal clear— to establish a piece of America in the Oregon Territory. The yield of the Great Migration, almost nine hundred settlers from the heartland, arrived in the Willamette Valley in autumn 1843 and found a provisional government already in place that claimed jurisdiction from the farms south of the Columbia River and northward to Russian America. The new and headstrong midwesterners constituted a majority of the settlers and soon modified that government by instituting a local tax system, compliance with which they tied to protection of the law.[31]

This action constituted a severe blow to the Hudson's Bay Company's nearly exclusive control over the area for over two decades and led John McLoughlin to intervene. He feared that the claim of jurisdiction all the way to Alaska by an American-led government would inspire irresponsible rhetoric in Washington and London among those intent on making Oregon an impediment to good Anglo-American relations and hence a threat to company holdings. Since no Americans at the time resided north of the river, he proposed that the new government confine its authority to south of the river. The Americans agreed to this concession, but it was short-lived. Another twelve hundred settlers joined the community before the end of the year, causing the government to revoke the agreement. Restriction of its authority to south of the Columbia amounted to tacit acceptance of British claims to the rest of the territory. The government therefore decreed that its territory reached as far north as 54°40'. A month later, McLoughlin, at the behest of Governor Simpson, relocated company headquarters to Fort Victoria on Vancouver Island.[32]

Company officials had become apprehensive with good reason. Already, American settlers had encroached on company land and nearly provoked confrontation. The larger the American community grew, the bolder its residents became and the less dependent they were on the Hudson's Bay Company. The days were past when a wily McLoughlin could extend a Christian hand to weary pioneers and maneuver them to areas south of the Columbia, planting them harmlessly in the Willamette Valley. Now those pioneers, no longer so weary, seized the land and determined to hold it until an administration in Washington acted on their behalf.[33]

The settlers who arrived late in the year brought with them assurances that just such an administration was bound for the White House. In May the Democrats had met in Baltimore with plans to launch former President Martin Van Buren into a campaign to retake the presidency from the foundering Whigs and their estranged chief executive, now derisively called His Accidency. Van Buren, however, unwittingly doomed his candidacy by broadcasting in the Washington *Globe* the month before the convention his opposition to the immediate annexation of Texas. His would-be Whig opponent Henry Clay likewise failed to recognize the popular mood for expansionism and repeated Van Buren's error by announcing his opposition to Texas's annexation in a letter that was published in the *National Intelligencer* on the same day as Van Buren's. But unlike Clay, who won his party's nomination by acclamation despite his April letter, Van Buren ran headlong into expansionist Democrats who engineered the selection process in a manner intended to undercut the Little Magician. Ballot after ballot failed to produce a party standard-bearer. With each vote Van Buren's support dwindled and that for expansionist Michigan Democrat Lewis Cass swelled.

A split in the party seemed likely. But pro-Texas delegates maneuvered the votes in favor of a dark horse from Tennessee—the lean, solemn, and meticulous Jacksonian James K. Polk, former governor and congressman. On the ninth ballot Polk was selected, the expansionists got their champion, and the party constructed a bold platform calling for the "reannexation of Texas" and the "reoccupation of Oregon." The Texas plank, party leaders assumed, would please the slaveholding southerners who had longed for its annexation at least since the Lone Star Republic's separation from Mexico in the 1830s and would appease those who continued to carp about the alleged forfeiture of the territory by John Quincy Adams to Luis de Onís in 1819. The Oregon plank would not only

James K. Polk. From painting by Alonzo Chappel, in *National Portrait Gallery of Eminent Americans* (1862).

satisfy westerners but also mollify northern voters who believed that the Pacific harbors were essential to the future expansion of U.S. commerce and that Oregon's acquisition would ease abolitionist anxiety by providing a nonslave balance to Texas.[34]

The expansionist vision that had been apparent since the early days of the Republic was on its way to becoming a national obsession in 1845, when it took on the label of "manifest destiny." According to its tenets, the United States was destined to extend its model republic from the Atlantic to the Pacific and to open that land to accommodate a freedom-loving population. By the 1840s that drive had drawn together a number of different forces from all parts of the nation. New Englanders were determined that Washington preserve the harbors of the Pacific Northwest for their Pacific trade. And despite the belief by some that an independent Oregon might serve their commercial purposes, most supported the possession of the territory under the exclusive jurisdiction of U.S. law. Many southerners interested in Texas saw the promise of Oregon as a means of appeasing northerners and expediting the annexation of the Lone Star Republic. Most southerners, however, were not prepared to provoke Britain over Oregon while the prospects of masterly inactivity remained hopeful.

This was not the case for midwesterners, however. Americans from the heartland were determined to secure every inch of real estate between the Mississippi Valley and the Pacific Ocean. If "you suppose that the West will yield one acre—ay, one inch—of our northwestern territory, as long as there is a man left to defend it," asserted Indiana's Andrew Kennedy, "then, sir, you or I have mistaken the character of that western people." When elements of the North and South aligned with the West and captured the imagination of the press, there was little chance of casting off the spell of manifest destiny. The genie had escaped the bottle. The Democrats astutely recognized it in 1844 and, buoyed by nearly 100 percent support from the Irish and aided by the defection of Whigs to the Liberty party (factors that combined to serve up the critical New York electors), seized power under the banner of westward expansion.[35]

III

Meanwhile, across the Atlantic, Everett was not content to let the matter pass quietly to Washington and continued to discuss a possible Oregon compromise with Aberdeen. The foreign secretary, Everett observed, understood that the chief obstacle to compromise lay in the extreme positions historically argued by both sides. It would be difficult for either nation to retreat from its longtime position without exposing the delicate question of national honor to exploitation by domestic opponents. Thus, in Aberdeen's view, the ticklish part of the Oregon dispute was not whether to compromise, but how to do so without losing face. Everett did not miss the importance of Aberdeen's admission and moved quickly to test this opportunity. Perhaps, Everett declared, the British would be satisfied to divide the territory at the 49th parallel if they could retain all of Vancouver Island and if they could present such an offer as an American sacrifice of the greater share of the territory. Everett believed that the U.S. argument for the entire region up to 54°40' might allow Aberdeen to disguise a compromise as a diplomatic victory. Understanding that he had to guard sensitivities at home, Everett cautioned Tyler to take care in how loudly he argued for the extreme position. It is possible, Everett warned, "to state our right up to 54°40' so strongly, as to put ourselves in the wrong in receding from it."[36]

While statesmen debated, diplomats fretted, settlers settled, and heads of state guarded national honor, both nations conspicuously flexed their maritime muscles. When, in 1844, French colonial designs in North Africa and the Pacific threatened Aberdeen's Anglo-French entente, the challenge encouraged Peel to heed the admonition of pro-navy ministers to strengthen the fleet. The 1845 budget received a substantial increase for the Royal Navy to build new bases, shore up existing ones, refurbish the fleet, and construct new ships. These expenditures were not directed exclusively at the French, however. The belligerent tones issuing from the United States convinced the Peel government that anything less than the increases proposed for the defense budget would be imprudent. But words were not all that moved Peel. If there was any single source of British anxiety over American naval capability, it originated on the Great Lakes. In April, word came to Lord Stanley that a recent buildup, including steamers, would give the United States an advantage on the Lakes. Canadian officials, though not expecting hostilities, thought that the Admiralty should meet the American buildup to "prevent our being overpowered if war should ever occur."[37]

Pakenham argued that the buildup violated the Rush-Bagot Agreement of 1817 and approached Calhoun to lodge a protest. But while Pakenham presented his case, he was well aware that his country, following the border turmoil of the last decade, likewise had violated the 1817 agreement. As Pakenham and Calhoun discussed the Great Lakes and the British minister warned that his government would respond in kind to American persistence in that region, the warship HMS *Modeste* put in at the mouth of the Columbia for the singular purpose of demonstrating British resolve. The Peel government had directed the Admiralty, since early in the decade, to "show the flag" on the Pacific coast as a reminder to the Americans there that Britain intended to protect its rights in the territory.[38]

In early June the Texas annexation bill had gone down to defeat because of a number of factors: political animosity toward Tyler, support for Henry Clay, rejection of land speculation, dismissal of the exaggerated British threat, and, most decisively, opposition to slavery and resistance to war with Mexico. War had been very much on the minds of those who heard the emotional rhetoric coming from Washington—and not only with Mexico but with Great Britain over Oregon as well. Even before Calhoun took the cabinet post, Whig Senator Samuel Phelps of Vermont had urged him to rescue Americans "from indiscretion and folly and from a war engendered in national pride." Pakenham feared that Tyler was so distraught over the failure of his Texas project that the despondent president would hazard war to salvage his political future. If Tyler believed, wrote Pakenham, "that, by bringing about a war with England, on the Oregon question, or by any other maneuver equally desperate and condemnable, he could add to his prospects of success, he would resort to it at a moment's notice."[39]

Pakenham struggled to bring Calhoun to the table to discuss Oregon, but the secretary was committed to masterly inactivity and continued to stall. Surely, Pakenham thought, when the Texas issue was set aside, Calhoun would agree to discuss Oregon. Since Calhoun had accepted the State Department appointment strictly to address the Texas and Oregon questions, Pakenham's assumption was logical. But from the moment Calhoun took the position, he had frustrated the British minister with a plethora of excuses ranging from fatigue to a desire to study the complicated issue before taking up the negotiation. Perhaps now, with the Texas bill defeated and having had ample time to prepare, Calhoun would open the talks. But he stunned Pakenham in July by announcing that he no longer considered Oregon urgent. To this statement, a flustered Pakenham replied that he would add this exchange to the record in an effort to remove any question about Britain's willingness to negotiate.[40]

Pakenham's subtle dig at Calhoun probably had less effect on the secretary than did a much-needed respite from the rigorous Texas campaign. After a break, Calhoun finally yielded to Pakenham's persistence and agreed to take up the Oregon problem. In late August the two diplomats opened a series of six conferences beginning with a review of the status of the dispute and a request by Calhoun to hear "any fresh proposal" that Pakenham had been instructed to offer. At the second meeting Pakenham formally offered a partition of the Oregon Territory along a line that followed from the existing boundary east of the Rockies along 49 degrees to McGillivray's River. The line would proceed down the channel of that river until it met the primary trunk of the Columbia; from there it would follow the Columbia to the Pacific Ocean. Reflecting the impact of Everett's discussions with Aberdeen, Pakenham added an enclave offer to the partition proposal that encompassed a detached area on the coast from Bulfinch's Harbor to Hood's Canal. The crown would also, Pakenham conceded, grant free access to any ports that the United States desired in the area between the Columbia and the 49th parallel. If Calhoun had anticipated "fresh" to mean "original," he was probably disappointed. This offer was little more than a return to the enclave offer of the 1820s. Not surprisingly, Calhoun declined it, with the argument that it would yield American access to most of a region to which the United States had clear title and to a territory whose population now had a contiguous relationship to the rest of the nation.[41]

When the two diplomats met about a week later, Pakenham challenged Calhoun's assertion of America's clear title to the territory. The only novel point raised by Calhoun was that of contiguity. All of his other points merely revisited past contentions such as the purchase of Louisiana, the exploratory efforts of Lewis and Clark, the settlement at Astoria, and the acquisition of Spanish rights in 1819. Pakenham dismissed each of these in turn, arguing that there could be no basis for Pacific frontage found in the Louisiana Purchase. To so contend, he caustically conveyed to Aberdeen, was "so very far-fetched, not to say absurd, as scarcely to require serious notice." The Spanish, Pakenham informed Calhoun, had compromised their exclusive claims to the region in the Nootka Convention of 1790. Further, the British had actively explored the region before and after the Lewis and Clark expedition. And although Britain returned Astoria to the United States after the War of 1812, the move did not, as Calhoun claimed, substantiate a right to the entire territory. At best, Astoria only gave Washington a claim to the post itself, and even that claim was abated by the fact that no Americans had actually returned to occupy the area. Pakenham concluded that the only hope of resolving the dispute fairly was to partition the territory along the line that he had recommended. This move would leave to each side "almost acre for acre half of the territory."[42]

The British minister suspected that Calhoun, like any good haggler, would call for more at the beginning to achieve more at the end. Calhoun confirmed this belief for Pakenham in the fifth session when, after elaborating on the significance of the Adams-Onís negotiations of 1819, he tried to expand the scope of the discussion to north of the 49th parallel. But Pakenham informed Calhoun during the last session that he could not discuss any territory outside of that delineated by previous offers. Thus, the British minister clearly identified the actual area in contention for all future negotiations as that triangle lying north and west of the Columbia and south of the 49th parallel. In fact, Pakenham in October would propose to Whitehall that it issue a formal statement conceding the area south of the Columbia in return for U.S. forfeiture of claims north of the 49th parallel. Although the proposal was not pursued, Aberdeen found it worthy of discussion.[43]

As Aberdeen monitored the futile exchange between Calhoun and Pakenham, he became resigned to its likely failure. The foreign secretary did not believe, he wrote Pakenham in early November, that Calhoun would accept a settlement "which we could safely and honourably adopt." The expansionist frenzy of the election year had created an atmosphere that was not conducive to compromise. Aberdeen understood this political reality and told Pakenham to suggest arbitration of the issue. If this, too, failed—and Aberdeen had every reason to believe that it would—Pakenham should propose a renewal of the existing open-access agreement for a period of ten years.[44]

While Aberdeen's despatch traversed the Atlantic in a routine mail packet, something far from routine occurred in the United States: a dark horse won the presidency. When Polk emerged triumphant in his campaign of 1844, he declared the victory a mandate for territorial expansion. Suddenly, Calhoun's and Pakenham's inability to strike a deal on Oregon loomed dangerously large. Calhoun remained content in his belief that delay worked to America's advantage and exhibited only token concern to his British associate. Pakenham, however, was distressed as he watched the people reject Clay's moderate position and select the expansionist platform of Polk that asserted the claim to Oregon as "clear and unquestionable." The British minister had been hearing since summer such exclamations as that aired by Robert J. Walker. "Great Britain," the influential Democrat stressed, "openly claims our territory, and proposes to plant her flag upon our soil, on the coast of the Pacific." If Clay won the presidency, Walker warned, Britain would "obtain all she desires of Texas and Oregon."[45]

In December the lame-duck president delivered his annual address to an equally lame-duck Congress and touched off another round of debates similar to that of the previous year when he called for a new push for Texas and Oregon. Pakenham had anticipated an extreme pronouncement from the deflated Tyler, whose coterie had been unable to rally support for an extension of his administration. Indeed, Pakenham was relieved that the address was not even more provocative. Although the president called for support of emigration, the extension of U.S. law, and construction of military posts along the route to the territory, Pakenham admitted that none of these suggestions violated the existing arrangement. Tyler reported that while negotiations on the Oregon Question were pending, the United States should implement his recommendations to ensure the protection of the settlers and to provide its citizens with the same foundation in the territory as that of the British. Congress should understand, Tyler insisted, that any acceptable resolution of the dispute would have to be "compatible with the public honor."[46]

Before the end of the month both houses of Congress introduced legislation that acknowledged Tyler's recommendations. The lawmakers called for a territorial government for the entire region, the construction of military forts on the Oregon Trail, and the distribution of land to Oregon-bound Americans. Alexander Duncan of Ohio championed a House bill to establish such a government on December 16. Within a week, Atchison resumed his efforts with a Senate bill that also called for a territorial government. The entire territory, the junior Missouri senator declared, should not only come under U.S. jurisdiction but also should be parceled out in land grants to American citizens whose passage to the territory would be facilitated by the construction of forts along the way. Conspicuously absent from these proposals was any consideration of the current open-access arrangement with Britain. Would the United States give the required twelve-month notice or arrogantly move to absorb the territory without reference to British claims?[47]

Pakenham certainly was interested in the answer to this question since the "pending" negotiations were in fact nearly paralyzed. The minister hurried to Calhoun's office to express concern about the new agitation swelling around the Oregon issue. Pakenham hoped to ascertain its likely reception and had held back his arbitration proposal until after the president's address. He also wanted to determine whether enough American statesmen would temper their expansionist zeal or restrain their expansionist colleagues to induce a reluctant government to accept arbitration.[48]

The British minister weighed his instructions against the transitional government to anticipate their prospects for success. For the time being he believed that the Senate Foreign Relations Committee would support a moderate position. The new Congress would alter this, however, with the addition to the committee of a number of all-Oregon members. But even as it stood in December, Pakenham placed little hope in a renewal of the open-access agreement. Arbitration remained the best option.

From the end of December 1844 until mid-January 1845, Pakenham continued to probe the political atmosphere for the probable fate of an arbitration proposal. He was particularly watchful of the Atchison bill which was designed, he conjectured, to attach Oregon "completely and exclusively to the jurisdiction of the United States." Although Calhoun and others reassured him, Pakenham remained fretful, noting that the "temper of the Senate" had become unpredictable and was moved by an impassioned public. He finally concluded from observation and conversation that the Americans would probably reject arbitration since they believed "that England may, in the long-run, be teazed and worried into a compromise more advantageous to this country than could be obtained by the decision of an impartial arbiter." Just before a discouraged Pakenham made the vain arbitration offer, he reported that the House would probably pass its Oregon bill but that the Senate, preoccupied again with Texas, would not. But, the British minister sarcastically noted to Aberdeen, you "must not be surprised at any thing that may happen in the present state and temper of Parties" in the United States. Over the next two weeks he and Calhoun went through the motions of proposing and declining arbitration. The president, Calhoun told his British associate, preferred a resumption of direct talks to involving an arbiter. At this juncture, Pakenham questioned the sincerity of Calhoun's excuse but had no recourse. He seemed to take solace in having the record of his offer demonstrate his sincerity to his American friends.[49]

In early February, Pakenham's projection proved correct. The House bill passed by a resounding vote of 140 to 59. He did not, however, anticipate the sense of urgency that the bill produced by its inclusion of an amendment to serve notice of abrogation of the

1827 agreement. Calhoun, who continued to prefer delay, was as distressed as Pakenham and called the British minister to his home to initiate damage control. Although Calhoun offered to have Tyler assure Congress that direct negotiations were under way, the urgency passed when the Senate, as predicted, closed its session without acting on Oregon. Despite fervent efforts by western senators to force Oregon to the floor for a vote, the lawmakers were content to pass a Texas annexation resolution and leave the Oregon issue alone. This decision antagonized some of the western members of the expansionist coalition who had assumed that their southern colleagues would hold out with them for the northern territory.[50]

While Congress debated, Everett conducted informal talks with Aberdeen. During these conversations the foreign secretary shared the details of his arbitration instructions to Pakenham. Contrary to the attitude of most American spokesmen, Everett believed that the suggestion had potential. Under Aberdeen's plan the arbiter would determine whether the U.S. claims to the territory were exclusive. If not, what constituted a reasonable partition line? Everett wrote Calhoun that the plan had merit because it started from a scrutiny not of the extent of British claims but of the exclusive nature of America's. If the arbiter found Washington's claims to be sound, the United States would receive its desired territory. But if the arbiter ruled against those exclusive claims, the United States was no worse off since the arbiter would then propose a partition based on equal consideration of the claims of both nations. Although Everett would later become skeptical of arbitration, in early 1844 he believed that such a partition might stand at 49 degrees and, further, that Aberdeen would favor such a line.[51]

Recent congressional action, however, met a negative response from the foreign secretary. Aggravated by the implication of sovereignty contained in the abrogation amendment to the House bill, Aberdeen warned Everett with uncharacteristically hostile language that Britain would deploy forces into the area "adequate to maintain her present position." Even the most tolerant and pacific of leaders, he confessed to Everett, could be pushed too far. Aberdeen was clearly approaching that point. If the United States terminated the existing arrangement in an effort to seize the disputed territory, then "War was inevitable."[52]

Everett knew that hostile talk from the Peel government should not be taken lightly. Aberdeen had been dueling for some time with cabinet colleagues who insisted that Britain increase its preparedness not only in Europe but also in the Oregon Territory. The House bill and the overall temper of the American people only excited Lord Wellington and his militant associates that much more. Aberdeen indicated that he was softening under their pressure when he submitted to Peel's proposal to send the Pacific squadron's flagship to Oregon in the event of passage of the Senate bill. He did not, however, approve the recommendations to increase preparations at home. This step, Aberdeen believed, would only arouse the British public.

There was indeed a growing sense that the temperature between the nations was rising. Fellow diplomats told Everett that they feared that the tension between the Americans and British had become uncomfortably high. The French thought that war over the Oregon dispute was very likely; even an uninformed observer would have viewed the ongoing increase in the Royal Navy as a sign of that likelihood. But Everett knew better—the naval buildup drew from budgetary decisions that predated the recent agitation over Oregon. Nevertheless, the *Times*, a paper that expressed the government's sentiments, warned that "in the present temper of American Citizens, we suspect that silent but resolute determination to put our positions there [Oregon] in a state of defence and to send a sufficient squadron to that Coast, is the wisest answer to these measures of the House of Representatives."[53]

If the discourse of Washington politicos during Tyler's tenure had truly raised British hackles, real danger lay ahead. The mantle of command would soon pass from the embattled Tyler to James K. Polk, a stern and vigorous Tennessean mentored by the hot-tempered Andrew Jackson. The new president would come to the White House with his sights set on more than the disputed territory north of the Columbia—he would come to champion manifest destiny. With an expansionist leading the crusade, the fever would produce a steadily rising temperature. And nothing expressed this fever more than the popular call for all Oregon that surrounded the new administration: Ohio Senator William Allen issued the challenge of "Fifty-four Forty or Fight!" If Young Hickory had his way, there indeed would be "no red lines upon the map of Oregon."[54]

CHAPTER NINE

Only at the Cannon's Mouth: Young Hickory Takes Charge

All the power in the world cannot prevent this country [United States] occupying Oregon in time. . . . 'Tis a mania with the people, and the mob is furious.

—William Irving, July 30, 1845

On a rainy spring day in 1845 a stouthearted crowd listened intently to the inaugural address of their eleventh president, James K. Polk. The relatively obscure Tennessean had endured Whig jeers of "Who is James K. Polk?" throughout the campaign year. Now they knew, and soon everyone would understand the new president's steely determination to make his promised single term in office yield maximum results. Polk was a veteran of state and national politics, having served as governor of Tennessee and U.S. congressman. Indeed, he was a highly effective Speaker of the House from 1835 to 1839. As was the case with many of his political peers, the promise of Jacksonian Democracy captured his imagination, and Polk latched on to Old Hickory's long and powerful coattails. With this political tutelage, he was almost genetically an expansionist. It therefore had been less of a stretch than some had argued when the Democrats selected him as their presidential hopeful in 1844. Polk believed that his narrow victory over Whig Henry Clay had come on the rising tide of a passionate American design to seize the remainder of the North American continent. Newspapermen and legislators had turned that long-held dream into a crusade with Polk at its head.

When President Polk addressed the crowd on that wet March day, he affirmed his leadership in the expansionist drive by targeting the dispute with Britain over the Oregon Territory. Tyler's resolution scheme for Texas had cleared Congress just before Polk's inauguration, although it would remain for Polk to sort out the problematic details of annexation and the dangerous implications for U.S.-Mexican relations. He therefore focused on the Oregon Country by reiterating the Democratic party's claim that U.S. title to the region was "clear and unquestionable." The crowd cheered. Americans were already convinced that Oregon belonged to the United States, but British subjects both at the address and elsewhere were not. They were determined to argue their title and hold back American expansion in the territory. The tenacious Polk thus began his administration with two struggles. He had to balance tension with Mexico over Texas and potential conflict with Britain over Oregon. The maintenance of that balance could spell the difference between peace and war.

During the first ten months of his administration, Polk revealed a reckless propensity toward the latter. Lacking diplomatic ability or an understanding of the nuances of foreign relations, the new president antagonized both Britain and Mexico. Although his secretary of state, James Buchanan, tried to temper Polk's approach, the chief executive was a meticulous micromanager who intended to direct his own policy. Besides, it early became apparent that the hard-working Tennessean offered only a skeptical ear to the advice of his secretary of state; on one occasion, Polk referred to the indecisive and opportunistic Buchanan as an "old maid." By the time he again formally addressed the nation the following December, Polk had turned the Oregon dispute into a new crisis in Anglo-American relations.[1]

I

The inauguration afforded Polk the first opportunity to express his position on the Oregon dispute, and he was determined to take it. Many wondered if the successful annexation of Texas would appease the expansionists and permit the new administration to start out with a measure of restraint. They were probably correct; the euphoria over Texas likely would have obscured any criticism of a token mention of the Oregon Question. But Polk saw it differently. His campaign had stood on a platform calling for the "reannexation of Texas" and the "reoccupation of Oregon." Tyler had seen to the first; Polk felt both an obligation and a desire to achieve the second. The only real question concerned the tenor of his remarks. When he drafted his speech, Polk considered drawing a stern line against the British by leveling the dormant noncolonization principle at them and their Oregon endeavors. But in part due to the urging of John C. Calhoun, the president-elect dropped the notion from his finished copy. In fact, he was relatively subdued in his Oregon statement. Although he declared America's title above challenge and called for settlers to help secure it, he did not specify the degree of north latitude to which that title extended. The absence of this point, Richard Pakenham must have thought, suggested at least a ray of hope.[2] On the day following the inaugural festivities, Pakenham sent Lord Aberdeen a guardedly optimistic despatch concerning Oregon. The Senate, the British minister "happily" reported, had adjourned without rendering a decision on the Oregon Question. This positive result, he stated, had occurred in the face of a dogged attempt by William Allen to force the issue.[3]

Throughout March, Pakenham continued to spin bad news into good. On the face of it, Polk's cabinet appointments should have made the British minister nervous. Although reminding his chief that both Buchanan and the treasury secretary, Robert John Walker, were known for their anti-British sentiments, he excused their past pronouncements as political rhetoric. The new secretary of state had in recent conversation offered his personal assurance that the late bluster from the Senate should not preclude the pursuit of amicable relations. In fact, Buchanan wanted to have his own record of hostile comments more or less dismissed. This piece of news must have made a considerable impression on Pakenham who, though friendly with the Pennsylvania senator, had heard him call for an American Oregon that extended all the way to 54°40'. Further, as Pakenham broached the notion of arbitration to Buchanan, he must have remembered that the latter, while a member of the Senate Foreign Relations Committee, had asked why Britain objected to arbitration as an amicable approach to settlement.[4]

Pakenham reported that in Buchanan's new capacity as secretary of state, he vowed to approach the Oregon Question with "the principle of giving and taking." This declaration probably meant, the British minister conjectured, a proposed partition line along 49 degrees to the Juan de Fuca Strait and thence around Vancouver Island to the sea. Britain, he concluded, would gain the entire island and unhindered navigation of the Columbia River. Given the present mood of Americans, Pakenham knew that he could not propose such a partition, but he thought that Buchanan might do so. If not, Pakenham confidently told Aberdeen, another friend in the Senate, William Archer, had assured him that the Polk administration would choose arbitration over war with Britain.[5]

James Buchanan. From painting by Alonzo Chappel, in *National Portrait Gallery of Emi-nent Americans* (1862).

While observers in Washington scrutinized the agenda of the new administration, Aberdeen fretted over the winter's congressional agitation concerning Oregon. As Polk delivered his inaugural address, Aberdeen posted a despatch to Washington. After making the comforting projection that the Senate probably would reject the House proposal to move toward termination of the 1827 convention, he directed Pakenham to stress to the secretary of state the importance of arbitration. The foreign secretary also directed the Admiralty to have Her Majesty's vessels routinely visit the Oregon region. To make the display of force more imposing, the flagship and person of Rear Admiral Sir George F. Seymour, commander of the Pacific fleet, should join the demonstration. While taking care not to alarm the American settlers, the Royal Navy should, Aberdeen continued, impress upon them the crown's determination to guard British rights and subjects. A few days later, the Foreign Office, apparently in response to an Admiralty message indicating that Seymour's ship the *Collingwood* was without its captain, renewed its directive to have Seymour himself participate in the exhibition. This level of anxiety over Oregon suggested that any hope by Pakenham that his chief would react calmly to Polk's inaugural message was in vain.[6]

The tenor of Polk's address drew an immediate and piqued reaction in London. The *Times* was shocked that the United States would risk war with the British while it was so close to hostilities with Mexico over Texas. Aberdeen, obviously troubled by Polk's comments, wrote Pakenham that if Washington rejected arbitration and failed to present a reasonable alternative, London would assume an end to negotiations and to the 1827 convention as well. War between the two nations would probably result from a "local collision" in the territory. Meanwhile, Pakenham should withhold a proposal to extend the open-access arrangement since, in Aberdeen's estimation, the United States would take advantage of any delay to shore up its position "in active preparation for future hostility." Great Britain, the foreign secretary asserted, must "be prepared for any contingency. Our naval force in the Pacific is amply sufficient to maintain our supremacy in that sea." Aberdeen punctuated this remark with news of Seymour's instructions to move to the Oregon coast as quickly as possible. The British minister should be firm with the Americans, Aberdeen admonished, and make clear that Her Majesty's Government would not bend to "force or menace."[7]

Edward Everett was disturbed by the volatile mood exhibited by both the British press and government. Nothing short of war, the *Times* threatened, would wrestle Oregon from the crown. While he consoled Washington that the press exaggerated the disposition of the government, he admitted that the loyal opposition was determined, "by the bitterest taunts, to goad the government into

extreme measures." Although Everett had faith in the calming influence of statesmen such as Whig economist Nassau Senior who
wrote a conciliatory piece in the *Examiner*, he nevertheless sensed
a generally hostile public attitude over Oregon. The British mind,
Everett wrote Buchanan, "is more seriously and deeply impressed
with the critical state of affairs, than it has been for many years." In
the House of Lords, Aberdeen affirmed his determination to preserve national honor, "a substantial property that we can never ne-
glect." In a cynical jab at Polk, he pronounced British claims to
Oregon as "clear and unquestionable" and promised to maintain
those rights. While the foreign secretary's remarks met enthusiastic cheers in one house of Parliament, his chief gave essentially the
same message to the other house. "If our rights shall be invaded,"
Prime Minister Peel adamantly declared in the Commons, "we are
resolved—and we are prepared—to maintain them."[8]

The Peel government was indeed prepared to maintain the British position in Oregon. Aberdeen had recently solicited military
information from the Colonial Office and proposed the deployment
of a covert reconnaissance mission out of Canada into the territory.
This mission would be jointly coordinated by the governor-general
of Canada and George Simpson of the Hudson's Bay Company.
Simpson had transmitted a lengthy letter to London calling for military preparations to secure British rights in the territory. The crown,
he proposed, should send forces to the Red River that included a
rifle company manned by local Indians and "half-breeds" under
British commanders. But perhaps most significant, Simpson called
for two British warships with a detachment of marines and two
steamers to protect the mouth of the Columbia and the Oregon coast.
Also, he suggested the erection of a substantial battery at Cape
Disappointment because it overlooked the Columbia and thus commanded movement in and out of the river. This suggestion probably came as no surprise to Peel, who had just approved a naval
buildup that Everett believed reflected the strain over Oregon.
Simpson wanted part of that navy to guarantee the company's interests in the territory and to secure the Columbia. Despite the
changes in the region over the intervening decades, he stood by his
argument of the 1820s. If the territory was to be divided, the line
should trace the 49th parallel only as far westward as the Rocky
Mountains. From that point it should follow the Columbia to the
Pacific.[9]

While Aberdeen made defiant gestures and directed Pakenham
to "use strong language," he also prepared less than clear instruc-

tions for renewed negotiations with the American government. If Buchanan reopened the Oregon discussion, Pakenham could, at his own discretion, offer the United States free access to all ports south of the 49th parallel. Should the secretary of state again reject the British proposal, Pakenham was to revert to arbitration. But "beyond this degree of compromise," the foreign secretary sternly contended, "Her Majesty's Government could not consent to go."[10]

After drawing this rigid line, however, Aberdeen immediately confused Pakenham with a private letter that suggested a more flexible position. If, he speculated, Buchanan offered to partition Oregon at the 49th parallel but left to the crown all of Vancouver Island and access to the Juan de Fuca Strait, "I should not regard his proposal as perfectly inadmissible." Perhaps the offer could develop into some workable compromise, "although I do not think it at all likely, & of course you will give no encouragement to the notion." Aberdeen further told Pakenham that he might forward such an offer to London for consideration. Pakenham must have been perplexed by the disparity between the rigidity of the formal directive and the flexibility of the private letter. Could he reconcile the two? If so, how much discretion could he exercise? He did not, after all, hold the special ministerial status of Lord Ashburton. These questions and the divergent messages from Aberdeen would loom large by the end of the summer. Pakenham was three weeks removed from any clarification by his government and would indeed be his own counsel.[11]

Curiously, on its surface, Aberdeen's private letter was not reconcilable with his formal instructions to Pakenham. Rather than relying on his official instructions, the foreign secretary had subtly opened the way, or so he thought, to compromise. Aberdeen, unlike Polk who seemed oblivious to counterpurposes, weighed the impact of an Anglo-American conflict on the broader interests of his nation. The Peel government was dedicated to domestic reform and had recently added free trade to its agenda. With the Democratic party's commitment to reducing U.S. tariffs, British free traders hoped to produce mutually propitious trade adjustments. Neither Peel nor Aberdeen believed that the Oregon Territory was worth jeopardizing the potential rewards anticipated from such adjustments.

Aberdeen also feared that his frail entente with France might not survive an Anglo-American conflict over Oregon. Indeed, such a scenario might resuscitate the dormant Franco-American alliance against Britain. Although it was widely known that the French were sympathetic to the U.S. position on Oregon, the sentiment was not universally held. Many Frenchmen wanted to advance entente and, as Everett reported, supported British claims in the territory. Nevertheless, old war-horses like Wellington continued to cast an anxious gaze across the English Channel and pressed for strengthened coastal defenses against the new steam-powered potential of the

"WHO'S AFRAID? OR, THE OREGON QUESTION." *Punch* (London), April 5, 1845.

French. Any move by Aberdeen over Oregon thus took place with a watchful eye toward France.

And, of course, there were eyes on Aberdeen as well. The foreign secretary had to gauge his actions against Palmerston's charge of appeasement. That dauntless nemesis of the Peel government, Everett reported in April, had renewed his criticism of the so-called Ashburton capitulation and placed Aberdeen on notice that any show of conciliation toward the United States would confirm his weakness. Thus, Aberdeen drafted his communiqués to Pakenham in the context of a need to balance several factors—the preservation of peace with the United States, the reparation of the foundering entente with France, the maintenance of British honor, and a defense of the Peel government against the barbs of the Whig opposition.[12]

Meanwhile, Britain's miffed response to Polk's inaugural comments had traversed the Atlantic and had, in turn, worked up Yankee ire. The American public, Pakenham noted, was accustomed to hostile pronouncements from its own statesmen but was stunned at the angry rhetoric coming from the more restrained British. Maybe, he speculated, the English refusal to yield quietly would produce a sobering effect by creating a "more wholesome state of publick feeling." Ironically, at the moment of Pakenham's observation, Aberdeen assured Everett that Americans should not overreact to British ship movements or to the remarks of British lawmakers because they were no more than essential political responses to Polk's comments. To convey the grim effect of his countrymen's reaction, Pakenham forwarded some of the more temperate American newspaper reports to the Foreign Office. However, he did not include any samples from western papers. Unlike the more mollifying northeastern and southern papers, the western press would gladly exchange words (and blows, if necessary) with the British over Oregon. Shortly after Pakenham's despatch, the *Illinois State Register* stated that "nothing would please the people of the entire West half so well as a war with England," and it contended that Peel and Parliament had already been provocative enough to warrant a declaration of war by Congress. The article concluded, "We are all for War! War!"[13]

Heated rhetoric from both sides of the Atlantic made resolution of the dispute all the more difficult. Despite the lack of enthusiasm for confrontation over Oregon among the eastern United States, the verbal volleys from both American and British sources raised the stakes to include something dear to every citizen and subject—national honor. On the American side the tall, angular, and rigid Polk was an obstinate southerner to whom honor was an almost tangible commodity. For U.S. honor to undergo challenge by anyone was unacceptable; to be challenged by the detested British was downright intolerable. Polk had been reared in the Anglophobic tradition of his mentor and wore his monicker Young Hickory deservedly. Andrew Jackson had bequeathed to Polk an attitude toward the British that bore scars from the famous boot-polishing incident during the American Revolution and that had been reinforced by all subsequent diplomatic encounters, beginning with George Canning and ending with Lord Palmerston. It was no surprise that the aging Jackson advised President Polk to maintain a firm position when dealing with London.[14]

Polk ignored the changed temper of the Foreign Office that occurred when the more sanguine Aberdeen replaced the eruptive Palmerston, and he remained steadfastly determined to follow Jackson's advice. Aberdeen had proved, in his handling of the disputes of the early 1840s, to be far more flexible than his predecessor, but Polk continued to measure British policy against the more familiar Palmerston. This approach was unfortunate because there was adequate indication that Aberdeen was amenable to compromise. Even during the storm of protest following Polk's address, some still observed in Aberdeen a desire to compromise. About the time of Jackson's letter, British and American commercial interests noted that Aberdeen remained open to a partition at the 49th parallel. This information quickly found its way through Navy Secretary George Bancroft to Polk, but to little effect.[15]

The spirit of compromise struggled against more than the intractable Polk. Peel, likewise, had assumed a posture that allowed little room for concession. In February he reacted to the recent activity in the House of Representatives and Calhoun's rejection of arbitration by complaining to Aberdeen that "compromise and concession" had been made "ten times more difficult," because the sensitive "point of Honour" had been "brought into the foreground." The Peel government, Everett reported several weeks later, felt bound by popular opinion to press for arbitration as the only viable and honorable approach to a settlement. Peel, apparently losing hope that direct negotiation could produce an acceptable compromise, publicly predicted a break with the United States. A "bold stance" and the sensitive image of national honor made a dangerous mix that greatly inhibited negotiations and precluded even Aberdeen from easily reaching a settlement.[16]

When Pakenham finally persuaded Buchanan to take up the Oregon issue in early May, he asked the secretary what his government planned to do about the only remaining problem "persisting between the two countries." Buchanan's response, however, amounted to little more than the transmission of Polk's rejection of arbitration. Pakenham wished to force the issue and asked if the United States was "prepared to resort to war, in preference to arbitration." This thinly disguised threat nudged Buchanan to admit that the United States should put forward a proposal. He did not do so, however, and stated that the administration preferred to have Everett's replacement named and in place before reopening the negotiations. Pakenham suspected that Buchanan wanted to clear away the Mexican trouble first so that Washington could risk a dispute with London.[17]

It was no surprise to Pakenham that Polk intended to replace Everett, but he probably cringed to hear that the president's first choice was the author of masterly inactivity, John C. Calhoun. The British minister might have breathed a sigh of relief when Calhoun declined. The former secretary of state would take the post only if guaranteed substantial latitude on issues involving commerce and fugitive slaves as well as the Oregon Question. After two of the South Carolinian's lieutenants also declined, Polk settled on a choice that should have been encouraging to Pakenham and distressing to fellow Democrats. The former secretary of state and minister to Great Britain, Louis McLane of Baltimore, accepted the appointment. He had established cordial relations with the British in an earlier mission and opposed the extremist position of 54°40'.

It did not go unnoticed that McLane, as president of the Baltimore & Ohio Railroad, had a fiscal interest in maintaining Anglo-American peace. The company counted among its patrons suppliers whose goods traveled B&O rail lines toward British consumption. Closing these markets would present a notable loss to the company. McLane also had an affinity for British society that he had developed while negotiating a reciprocity treaty for President Jackson in the 1820s. Coincidentally, on that mission he had established warm relations with British leaders, including the Scottish peer, Lord Aberdeen. All indications had boded ill for compromise, but the selection of McLane went far to revive hope for an amicable settlement.[18] At the same time, however, Polk's choice must have raised the eyebrows of western Democrats who viewed the move as a first sign of the president's vacillation on his "All Oregon" campaign pledge. Their suspicions were justified. As Polk dispatched McLane to London, he prepared a compromise offer intended to partition the territory.[19]

In mid-July, Buchanan resumed official negotiations with Pakenham by presenting the first U.S. offer since Albert Gallatin's of the 1820s. He prefaced his proposal with an elaborate history of

Louis McLane. *Courtesy Library of Congress.*

the dispute and a detailed defense of America's exclusive claims to
the entire territory. Its rights, Buchanan asserted, were grounded in
the essentials of discovery, exploration, possession, and treaty.
Pakenham must have nodded patronizingly at the first three only to
turn incredulous when the secretary contended that Spain had ceded
its territorial rights to the United States in the Adams-Onís Treaty
of 1819. Buchanan, anticipating the British position, argued that
the crown's conflict with Spain in 1796 had nullified any similar
claim that Pakenham might draw from the Nootka Convention of
1790. Despite the overwhelming strength of the U.S. position in
the territory, the Polk administration had determined to propose a
compromise boundary. The only reason for acquiescing, Buchanan
conceded, was out of deference to previous offers by earlier ad-
ministrations. In this rather arrogant fashion he proposed a line at

49 degrees from the Rocky Mountains to the Pacific along with free ports for Britain on the southern end of Vancouver Island.[20]

Meanwhile, the secretary of state issued instructions to McLane to prepare him for his role in the dispute. Reiterating the historical foundation of American claims, Buchanan informed the new minister of the obligatory offer of a partition at 49 degrees. As if to put a bold face on compromise, the secretary added the bombastic decree that "war before dishonor is a maxim deeply engraven upon the hearts of the American people; and this maxim ever shall regulate" the president's "conduct towards foreign nations." But a war not preceded by a reasonable attempt at compromise would be difficult to justify before world opinion. The proposal thus would accomplish one of two ends: either the British would accept and thereby settle the dispute with part of the territory sacrificed to the preservation of peace and to the satisfaction of prior commitment, or the British would reject the offer and free Polk to pursue the all-Oregon crusade.[21]

It must have concerned McLane that Buchanan so cavalierly had suggested war as the possible consequence of rejection. But it must have stunned him when the secretary indicated that he saw virtually no prospect for the offer's success. In fact, Buchanan confessed that the lack of any concession on the Columbia River probably made the proposal a nonstarter. Perhaps, he added with strained hope, the ports on Vancouver would provide "a refuge for British pride" within which the Peel government could salvage honor. Buchanan then permitted McLane to add to the "refuge" the cession of the southern tip of Vancouver Island. After all, this area meant little to the United States but was "of considerable value to Great Britain." Under no circumstances, however, was McLane to let Aberdeen assume a British position south of 49 degrees.[22]

McLane departed Washington with mixed emotions about his mission. Could he persuade Aberdeen to accept what the British had consistently rejected in every previous Oregon negotiation? There was little doubt that this would be his task. The timing of his appointment made it a certainty. Apparently, Polk hoped to coordinate McLane's replacement of Everett with the transmission of the offer through Pakenham to London. McLane could even offer the addition of Vancouver Island. It is evident that the Polk administration anticipated London's participation; in other words, Pakenham would send the proposal to the Foreign Office for advice. Otherwise, Buchanan would have intimated the possible cession of Vancouver Island and access to the Juan de Fuca Strait to keep

Pakenham talking and to verify America's willingness to "give and take." That the administration made the offer without such a hint suggests that Polk expected McLane to have the opportunity to influence Aberdeen with the additional concessions. If so, either the timing was off, or Pakenham's reaction was totally unexpected. The failure to allude to possible concessions and, most important, the omission of any mention of the Columbia provoked Pakenham to decline the offer outright. London would not have the opportunity to participate; and McLane, at least for the moment, would have no role to play.[23]

The British minister promptly responded to Buchanan's proposal by countering each of America's claims to the territory. First, Pakenham declared, the secretary's assumption that Britain's claims rested on the Nootka convention was false. It had established title to the territory by way of discovery, exploration, and settlement. In fact, Spain had no place in the negotiation over Oregon. It was obvious from Madrid's silence that it did not claim the territory and had had none to transfer to the United States in the Adams-Onís Treaty. Britain's claim being superior to that of the United States, Pakenham saw no reason to consider the partition proposal. He testily concluded that the secretary should "offer some further proposal" that was "more consistent with fairness and equity and with the reasonable expectations of the British Government."[24]

Pakenham did not realize how provocative his rejection might appear to the Polk administration. Either he was insensitive to the volatile nature of the president, or he was so frustrated that his year-and-a-half investment had yielded such an unreasonable offer that he felt his indignant reply justified. Where, he mused, was the promised "give and take"? The offer, he reported to Aberdeen, was "totally altogether" unacceptable. Perhaps an absolute rejection would wheedle a more rational offer that would initiate a typical back-and-forth negotiation toward compromise. Meanwhile, Pakenham informed his chief, the Foreign Office should not expect any progress until the new U.S. minister had reported back to Washington.[25]

II

As negotiations started their painfully slow process on the two sides of the Atlantic, relations among the occupants of Oregon along the Pacific were becoming equally tense. Chief Factor John

McLoughlin believed that Americans in the area had become impatient with their uncertain status and would probably move to establish an independent Oregon if the boundary remained undecided for much longer. McLoughlin had worked to relieve the "hostile feelings" of Americans toward their British neighbors. But as he had reported the previous March, the task became futile in the face of the inflammatory rhetoric drifting in from Washington. Boisterous politicos in the Capitol reported outrageous stories such as the one asserting that the Hudson's Bay Company had resurrected the hated British practice of inciting the local Indian tribes against the settlers. By the end of summer, a well-defined "national hostility" was evident in Oregon. Although the company's employees were admittedly good folks, an American settler declared, "I cannot like them, and moreover do not like those who like them."[26]

Perhaps the only thing that prevented this dislike from erupting into a full-blown conflict was the establishment of a territorial government. McLoughlin joined the Americans in this effort to preempt violent exchanges between the nationalities that might escalate into an Anglo-American war. There was good reason for this fear. The so-called Williamson incident of February had already occurred in which an American settler had challenged the claims of the company by squatting on Hudson's Bay's land. The arrival of three thousand more American settlers in the area at the end of summer significantly multiplied the potential for such incidents. The western papers described a trail of ever-increasing traffic, with the settlers packing a copy of the *Emigrant's Guide to Oregon and California* and full confidence that a resolution of the boundary would end in their favor. Only the diplomats in Washington and London could determine whether their confidence was misplaced.[27]

Meanwhile, the new American minister in London settled into his post and attempted to read the British mood on the Oregon Question. Since Aberdeen was away from the Foreign Office, McLane had to discern this mood through unofficial channels. Encouraged to learn of Aberdeen's proclivity for compromise, McLane had hopes that this tendency would open the door to a settlement that would make his stay in London both pleasant and productive. But Aberdeen, he was cautioned, had to move slowly out of deference to the powerful Hudson's Bay Company. Perhaps under calmer circumstances it would not have been necessary, but there was a distinct anti-American mood evident in the British press. The London print intimated that the United States was weak and could be coerced into surrendering its interests. But if this indeed was the predominant British attitude, it was soon dispelled. The Polk administration, Attorney General John Y. Mason wrote McLane, would not only stand its ground but also had elected to withdraw the July compromise offer. This news was distressing for the American minister, who wondered what this meant for his mission. He was suddenly in jeopardy of becoming "a minister with no role to play." Negotiations had broken down before he had any opportunity to contribute.[28]

McLane's counterpart in Washington was also in danger of impotence and perhaps worse: Pakenham would see squandered a substantial investment of time and effort. When Polk learned of the British rejection, he indignantly directed Buchanan to withdraw the offer. At an August 26 meeting of the cabinet, the secretary of state attempted to calm the president. The administration, he counseled, should accompany its withdrawal with an invitation for a British proposal. When Polk argued that the British were perfectly capable of extending an offer without an invitation, Buchanan cautioned that the abrupt withdrawal without some gesture designed to keep the talks alive would provoke a war that the American people would not countenance. Besides, he continued, the United States must move carefully as long as the problem with Mexico persisted. But there was no coaxing Polk. He seemed confident that the onus of war in the wake of the rude British rejection rested on the crown. The American people, Polk confidently asserted, would be "prompt and ready to sustain the government in the course" he elected to follow. We should therefore "do our duty towards both Mexico and Great Britain and firmly maintain our rights, and leave the rest to God and country." An incredulous Buchanan doubted that God would sanction a war waged for the northern half of Oregon. The secretary's remonstrance was futile, however. Polk had made up his mind, and Buchanan's pleading or carping would not change it. Could it be that the projected scenario discussed earlier with McLane was about to engage? Some knowledgeable people feared so. Curiously, Calhoun, who ordinarily advocated delay, warned Buchanan that the issue left undone could lead to war with Britain and the ultimate loss of Oregon.[29]

When Buchanan delivered the president's response to Pakenham's rejection, he rehashed his defense of America's position and refuted Pakenham's ploy to undercut the impact on U.S. rights of the Adams-Onís Treaty. The British, he proclaimed, had no business intruding in any transaction between Washington and Madrid. The aim of Buchanan's riposte, however, had little to do with whether Britain or the United States could better interpret a fine point of the history of the dispute. The president had made a good-faith attempt at compromise—one he did not have to make but nevertheless did as a matter of honor and responsibility. And how did the British receive this effort to remove the sole obstacle to "a long career of mutual friendship and beneficial commerce between the two nations"? It was declined, Buchanan lamented, "without even a reference" to the Foreign Office. The Polk administration not only refused to submit a "more reasonable" offer but also withdrew the offer already made.[30]

Pakenham was stunned by the abrupt end to the long-awaited negotiations. Surely the Polk administration had not assumed that he would or could accept the July proposal! The president, Pakenham determined, did not have the inclination or the political latitude to proffer a legitimate settlement. Rather, he was forced to act "with timid reserve to party views." The Oregon dispute was as far from resolution as ever with the American position so "far-fetched" as to defy consideration. The problem, Pakenham confessed to Aberdeen, would continue in its pernicious state until a crisis forced the U.S. government to comply with the opinion of the civilized world and rational Americans and accept arbitration.[31]

A crisis was in the making, and Pakenham had unwittingly provoked it. Although he was not as responsible for the impasse and subsequent tension as many have supposed, the British minister had contributed to a dangerous breach in the diplomatic process. His primary error did not lie so much in an alleged violation of the will of his government or even in his unilateral decision to reject the July offer. It is understandable that he deemed the American offer so far short of Aberdeen's minimum that it did not merit transmission to London. What is surprising, however, is that the minister did not use the concessions provided by Aberdeen to extend a counter to the American offer. If for no other purpose, it would have kept the negotiations alive long enough for McLane to ascertain Aberdeen's willingness to settle for partition at 49 degrees. By failing to extend an offer and hence aborting the negotiations, Pakenham ruffled the precise Polk, who assumed that the London government supported the rejection. The British, Polk thought, had led him to believe that they sought a settlement and then embarrassed him with a flat rebuff of his offer. The short-tempered Jacksonian was furious.[32]

Meanwhile, McLane worked in London to sort out his unhappy predicament. Obviously upset at the unexpected turn of events in

Washington, he expressed both disappointment and concern to Buchanan. McLane feared that a rejection of the American offer would not, as some predicted, align world opinion with the United States in a resulting Anglo-American altercation. Calhoun, the American minister advised, had not adequately eliminated arbitration as a viable remedy for the dispute. London would thus appear completely reasonable to present it as an amicable method of resolution. Since Polk had withdrawn the offer, McLane fretted, the liability for the impasse rested at America's feet. If the United States must come to blows with Great Britain, he pontificated, "let us fight in earnest, and let the world see that we fight in a good and just cause." McLane was at a loss to determine the mind and direction of Polk on the issue and asked for clarification. It was small comfort to find that Buchanan claimed to be as much in the dark as McLane about Polk's intent. Did Polk, McLane inquired, still retain the basic position communicated to him before he left for London? The president, Buchanan blandly responded, would submit any acceptable offer to the Senate for consideration. The problem, however, was in determining what Polk deemed acceptable. Even if a proposal went to the Senate, Buchanan doubted that it would win approval.[33]

In late September, Aberdeen called McLane to his home to determine what, if anything, they could do from their end to salvage the situation. Pakenham, the foreign secretary lamented, had erred in rejecting the Polk offer out of hand and should have sent it to the Foreign Office for advice. McLane must have uttered an incredulous sigh when Aberdeen declared that Polk's proposal could have provided a basis for settlement. Certainly, McLane conjured up images of the glory that had so needlessly slipped out of his grasp because of the tactless (implicit in Aberdeen's opinion) actions of the British minister in Washington. But what could the two parties do to redeem the situation? The London government, Aberdeen confessed, found itself in an awkward position. Polk could well go beyond the withdrawal and terminate all means toward settlement. But if Aberdeen could glean some indication of Polk's likely response to a British offer, the Foreign Office might yet find a settlement. The only alternative, Aberdeen reiterated, was arbitration. McLane was at a loss to offer any assurance of Polk's reaction. But "in the present state of public sentiment," he found it difficult to repeat the recently rejected offer.

The anti-British sentiment involved more than the Oregon Question. The American public, McLane asserted, was convinced that

Britain and France had interfered in the Texas annexation plans and was angry with the verbal barbs of the British press. In defense of his president, McLane contended that the political climate left Polk no alternative but to withdraw the offer in the face of Pakenham's curt rejection. Unfortunately, there was little they could do in London to restart the negotiation process. Since the impasse had developed in Washington, Aberdeen conceded, Buchanan and Pakenham must find a way to resume the talks. Meanwhile, the Peel government would convey to Pakenham its regret over the manner in which he had handled the July exchange.[34]

This last promise Aberdeen kept almost immediately. In early October he informed Pakenham of Whitehall's disappointment over the recent Oregon developments. Although he admitted that the American offer was unacceptable and inconsistent with the instructions under which Pakenham worked, he chastised the minister for failing to seek the advice of the Foreign Office. Aberdeen ignored his own directive for Pakenham to rely on his own judgment and told him that he should have allowed the Foreign Office to handle the July offer as it thought proper. In drafting this reproach, Aberdeen exposed some of his own indecision that had contributed to the problem. He began with the statement that he had "no intention whatever to blame" Pakenham, "but . . ."[35]

While Aberdeen attempted to control the damage resulting from the July rejection, Buchanan tried to rein in Polk's rancor. McLane's despatch came before the cabinet and provoked a discussion that confirmed the president's obdurate position. Still fuming over the rejection, Polk asserted that he would not initiate any Oregon deliberations; if they were to resume, the British must first submit a formal proposal. Such a demand, Buchanan cautioned, would likely cause a confrontation. But an unflinching Polk declared that he not only opposed renewing the talks but also would dismiss as unacceptable any British submission resembling his own of July. In fact, the president added, he had not wanted to compromise from the start and now felt relieved of any obligation to do so. Buchanan was unwilling to walk away from the meeting empty-handed and asked if he could at least assure Pakenham that a British offer would go before the Senate for consideration. Once again, Polk stood firm. In his forthcoming annual message to Congress, he declared, he would exhibit a "bold and strong stand" rooted in the noncolonization pronouncement of the Monroe administration. To McLane, Polk repeated that the British were free to make an offer, but that he was not optimistic about the reception by either the American people or the Senate of an offer even approximating the one rejected by Pakenham the previous summer.[36]

In late October, Pakenham tried desperately to redeem himself by undoing the recent exchanges and putting the best possible spin on his actions. First, he argued, there was "more apparent than real" difference between what Aberdeen said he should have done and what he actually did. Since Buchanan had informed him that transmission of the proposal to the Foreign Office would have legitimized the offer, there was no way for him to send it. It was "contrary to Diplomatik practice," he continued, to send such a signal when the offer was so far short of the minimum established by his official instructions. Besides, Pakenham explained, Buchanan could not have been sincere about a settlement or he would have put forth a more reasonable offer that ensured McLane's participation from London. The abrupt termination of the negotiations, however, guaranteed that there would be no time for the new minister to have an effect.

It had not been the secretary of state who took the hard line. He had been willing to pass a confidential proposal before the president for advance opinion, but Polk refused. Pakenham tried to turn back the clock by requesting that Buchanan retract the withdrawal. After all, the shrewd diplomat argued, he had not technically rejected the July offer but had merely communicated his inability to accept it. This subtle distinction, however, did not impress the American secretary. Likewise, Pakenham failed in his ploy to get an advance indication from Polk to the probable reception of a British offer. The president, at an October 28 cabinet meeting, once again frustrated Buchanan's efforts to moderate the U.S. position and renewed his stubborn contention that no British offer was acceptable. If Pakenham wished to submit one, Polk asserted, he should do so formally and take his chances. This the dubious minister was unwilling to do.[37] Having failed to reverse the damage of the summer, Pakenham despondently pleaded for his recall. "For God's sake," he begged Aberdeen, "remove me from this country, in which nothing but pain and mortification can henceforth attend my course." But Aberdeen, perhaps recognizing his contribution to the confusion, ignored Pakenham's plea and softened his subsequent communiqués to mollify the morose minister.[38]

Aberdeen found this scenario intensely frustrating since the squabble was over a territory in which he had little or no interest. According to his brother, Captain John Gordon, who had cruised the northern Pacific coast, the territory was "not worth five straws."

British subjects in North America similarly believed the territory not worth a fight. "People here," wrote an observer from New London, "are decidedly of the opinion that Oregon belongs to the United States" and that the ordinarily individualistic Americans seemed ready to unify for war in defense of their territorial rights. It would be unwise, he concluded, to wage war over an area destined to become American. Britain, Aberdeen believed, had already lost the region that was significant to the crown—Texas. An independent republic on the Gulf between Mexico and the United States would have slowed U.S. expansion, offered Britain an alternate cotton source, and opened valuable markets for its goods. But Texas had now come formally under U.S. control and would shortly be annexed officially as the twenty-eighth state. Why, he wondered, was he now asked to risk confrontation over Oregon when he had not done so over Texas?[39]

Few defenders of British retention of Oregon outside of the Hudson's Bay Company could make a case on practical grounds. But, alas, the question of honor overshadowed logic and good sense. Aberdeen and McLane thought that they could settle the dispute on its merits in a matter of hours (Aberdeen on one occasion claimed it could be resolved in less than one hour). In fact, Aberdeen had initiated a propaganda campaign to persuade the British people that the territory was not worth a squabble with the United States. In the autumn, the British papers, concerned with the more tangible issue of commerce, announced that a commercial treaty with the United States would be an equitable exchange for Oregon. And yet, out of deference to public sensitivities over honor on both sides of the Atlantic, forces for compromise in each camp had to move slowly and cautiously.[40]

While Aberdeen worked to downplay the importance of Oregon to the Empire, an opposite campaign was under way on the other side of the Atlantic as Americans devoted increased attention to the territory. Manifest destiny was recruiting thousands and thereby solidifying a long-standing commitment to a continental republic. If there had been any doubt that a divine hand had sanctioned such a vision, Texas's acquisition went far to remove it. Restless Americans gazed westward, where they saw an Oregon ready for settlement, and toward Washington, where a Democratic administration promised to make the territory part of a United States that extended from the Atlantic to the Pacific. The territory would soon be populated by five thousand Americans—a number outpacing that of British occupants by a better than 5-to-1 margin. Citizens met in various locales to announce support for U.S. occupation while the American press fired a steady barrage of pro-Oregon copy. New York publisher John L. O'Sullivan, who had coined the term "manifest destiny" earlier in 1845, used his *Morning News* and *Democratic Review* to herald the glories of expansion and to call upon U.S. statesmen to reassert the Monroe Doctrine to make it so. Other New York papers that added to the growing chorus for expansion included James Gordon Bennett's *Herald* and Moses Beach's *Sun*. Newspapers known to reflect the views of members of the administration included Boston's *Bay State Democrat*, which carried the opinion of Navy Secretary Bancroft, and Thomas Ritchie's *Union*, which broadcast the views of the president. The so-called Young America movement likewise adopted the issue. "Young America," Theophilus Fisk's *United States Journal* (Washington) proclaimed, "stands in strength" with "its right foot upon the northern verge of Oregon, and its left upon the Atlantic crag, and waving the stars and stripes in the face of the once proud Mistress of the Ocean, bids her, if she dare, 'Cry havoc, and let slip the dogs of war.' "[41]

Although the importance of commerce precluded many of the northeastern papers from pressing expansion to its dangerous all-Oregon extreme, they did exhibit an appreciation of the commercial value attached to the harbors of the disputed territory —particularly following Caleb Cushing's opening of five new Chinese ports to U.S. trade the year before. The support for Oregon in the Northeast, however, revealed a common constraint on the application of manifest destiny to the Pacific Northwest. The desire for peace and hence the maintenance of trade with Britain put the commercial states at odds with the all-Oregon zealots. As long as hope remained that the diplomats could secure both peace and the critical harbors of Oregon with a partition at 49 degrees, northeasterners would be content to revise America's destiny to south of that line.[42]

While war remained an option, it is small wonder that the United States and Britain took special notice of any move by the other that resembled preparation for such a contingency. British activities included the appropriation of funds to Simpson to shore up defenses in the territory and the routine movement of Her Majesty's ships in and out of Oregon waters by Rear Admiral Sir George Seymour. British subjects in the territory, Seymour reported in the autumn, were assured by his presence that their rights and person were under the crown's protection. Among the ships appearing off the Pacific Northwest was the one from which Aberdeen's brother reported, HMS *America*. This activity did not go unnoticed by McLane in London. In fact, he reported a notable military buildup by the Peel government. Although McLane confessed that the British could have directed the buildup at either the United States or France, the rising tension with the former made it of particular concern. From the North American perspective, reports of British movement on the Great Lakes further emphasized the serious state of Anglo-American relations.[43]

The British decision to fortify the Great Lakes reflected London's concern over Washington's military moves. Canadian Governor-General Lord Metcalfe warned that should a war ensue over Oregon, the United States would attempt to force Britain from Canada as well. U.S. Army Colonel Stephen Kearny, Pakenham reported in early August, was leading a regiment of dragoons toward Oregon. They would not, he continued, move into the territory but would merely stand ready if needed. The news affected even the usually pacific Aberdeen. "We ought to make all necessary preparations," he admitted to Peel, "both on the Lakes and on our whole frontier where necessary, without delay. There is real danger in that Quarter, whether it may arise from Oregon or not." Although Pakenham later modified his report on the regiment to say that it was no more than a reconnaissance mission to the Columbia, he attached to the same despatch a challenge from a Missouri paper that declared, in reference to the Kearny mission, that "our Yankee troops can march to Oregon or Santa Fe" if required. About a month later Simpson noted for the Hudson's Bay officers in London that U.S. cavalry had appeared along the Red River. They were probably in the vicinity, he conjectured, to see that local Indian tribes aligned with Washington in the event of an Anglo-American war. Perhaps the most unnerving news was the departure of the USS *Congress* for Oregon. The ship was under the command of Captain Robert Stockton, whom Pakenham described as a man of a "mischievous and dangerous" reputation. Stockton, the minister feared, would "push matters to extremity should any difficulty or emergency arise."[44]

III

For the remainder of the year both Pakenham and McLane attempted to work through conflicting signals and discern the intent of each other's government. Pakenham observed in November that the American press, although busy with the subject of Oregon, opposed "any violent course of proceeding with reference" to the territory and that Daniel Webster spoke publicly for compromise. Buchanan, the British minister reported, had "talked rather mysteriously" about a plan of settlement regarding Oregon and displayed confidence that the dispute was "now more likely to be settled than 6 months ago." In fact, Buchanan seemed satisfied with the rejection of the July offer since it might not have cleared the Senate. But the secretary dropped obscure hints that Pakenham was at a loss to divine. "What all this means," the skeptical minister wondered, "I do not presume to conjecture." With that disclaimer, he immediately proceeded to do so: "Can it be that the American government have conceived the idea of combining the settlement of the Oregon Question with some arrangement for obtaining California?" Buchanan's conciliatory tone was significant, Pakenham concluded, but one should also remember that the secretary "is a man whose civility I think sometimes gets the better of His sincerity, so that absolute confidence ought not be placed in such pacifick assurances coming from His mouth."[45]

Indeed, as Polk made evident at the next cabinet meeting, he had no mysterious plan for a peaceful settlement. Perhaps Buchanan placed unwarranted confidence in his own ability to sway the president. If so, he was relieved of that notion when Polk held defiantly to his hard line and flatly rejected Buchanan's assertion that neither Congress nor the American people would fight for the territory north of 49 degrees. Pakenham also derived a false impression of the state of the dispute from Aberdeen, who seemed to reinforce Buchanan's belief that a settlement was near. Had Pakenham and McLane compared notes, they would have scratched their heads in mutual bewilderment.[46]

McLane, following a meeting with Aberdeen at about the same time, came away with the understanding that the British would offer arbitration as an ultimatum. Perhaps Aberdeen's mixed signals were in part the result of the unauthorized input of Whigs such as Everett who had assured him that the United States would, when pressed, accept a compromise as long as it aligned with the 49th parallel. Whatever the source, this belief was short-lived. Before the end of the year, Aberdeen told Pakenham that arbitration might be the only way to avoid a "rupture upon a point which, however its importance may be magnified by national pride or popular passion on both sides is, in reality, but of comparatively small publick value." Aberdeen concluded the despatch with a warning that Her Majesty's Government would have "no choice but to maintain unimpaired those rights which they believe Great Britain to possess."[47]

Polk likewise prepared to display his adamant stance to the American people in the form of his annual message to Congress. Throughout the autumn of 1845 he had contemplated the best approach to the Oregon Question. In late October he consulted Senator Thomas Hart Benton on the possibility of issuing the twelve-month notice to abrogate the 1827 arrangement. Benton not only concurred with this idea but also insisted that the federal government extend its jurisdiction over the Americans in the territory, that it send three regiments of cavalry to safeguard the passage of emigrants to Oregon, and that it apply its Indian policy to the territory. Polk, however, could not gain Benton's support for invoking the noncolonization principle to thwart British ambitions in the region. This move, Polk believed, would counter an apparent European interest in establishing a balance of power in North America. The president hoped to discourage such a scheme by canonizing Monroe's principle as a formal doctrine in American foreign policy. Benton opposed applying the doctrine to the whole of Oregon since the British claim to the Fraser River Valley was as justified as the U.S. claim to the Columbia. The doctrine, the senator believed, should apply only to California. This suggestion later drew the approval of Buchanan and Bancroft, although the secretary of state still considered Polk's comments on Oregon too harsh. But the president remained opposed to moderation. In his December message to Congress he would challenge the British to hold their territory.[48]

On December 2 the president delivered his message and, as expected, pressed the Oregon issue and the nation's unique position in North America. Congress, he declared, should serve notice to Britain of the U.S. intent to abrogate the 1827 open-access arrangement. Having prefaced his remarks with an assertion of America's claim to the entire territory, he directed the members to extend the laws and protection of the United States over the American settlers in Oregon. Further, Congress should provide land grants to "patriotic pioneers" leading the way to the territory. This would be the year of decision for Oregon, at the end of which "the national rights [there] must either be abandoned or firmly maintained." Polk then boldly broadened his message to embrace, in its first public appearance since its debut in 1823, Monroe's doctrine guarding U.S. interests in the hemisphere. Polk asserted America's opposition to any designs by Europeans on creating a "balance of power" in North America to "check our advancement." The United States could "not in silence permit any European interference on the North American continent, and should any such interference be attempted will be ready to resist it at any and all hazards."[49]

The message drew support from both the press and the president's associates. The press remained concerned that negotiations had failed but favored the administration's articulation of an aggressive approach to the problem. Caught up in the fervor of manifest destiny, some observers saw it as an opportunity to move that destiny even farther north. If it came to a fight for Oregon, *Niles' National Register* hotly asserted, the United States should take the Canadas too. Polk's message drew additional praise from friends and colleagues who called on the White House over the following days. Senator George McDuffie of South Carolina declared his determination to "draw the sword . . . in support of the doctrines of the message." Benton reminded Polk of Britain's legitimate position in the Fraser River Valley but conceded to the president's directives calling for congressional action. "Well!" he shrugged to Polk, "you have sent us your message; I think we can all go it as we understand it."[50]

How did Congress understand Polk's Oregon directives? The president had not specified how to implement his recommendations but rather left it to the "wisdom" of Congress—a less than comforting notion. The most difficult feature for members to sort out was the notice resolution. It could take the form of a simple or "naked" notice that stood without explanation or qualification, or it could also express a U.S. desire to resume diplomatic efforts during the notice period. Attached to the question of form, of course, was the question of how the British might react. With relations in such a dangerous state, the London government might regard any resolution, and especially one without explanation, as a hostile act designed to provoke a confrontation. Most western extremists supported a simple notice followed by active occupation of the entire territory. Among those who favored such action were powerful lawmakers such as the hot-headed Lewis Cass of Michigan, Edward Hannegan of Indiana, David Atchison of Missouri, and the influential chairman of the Senate Foreign Relations Committee, William Allen of Ohio. The one notable defector from the western ranks was Benton, who now found himself allied with moderates led by his rival Calhoun and including Anglophile Daniel Webster. Benton, certainly an expansionist, joined the moderates because he had become convinced that American interests would be served south of

the 49th parallel. The unusual moderate coalition, primarily southern and eastern in nature, hoped to delay the notice or to frame it in
a fashion that invited compromise at 49 degrees.

The opening salvo came in the Senate about a week after Polk's
message and indicated that the Democratic majority would press
its leader's agenda. Cass, in what a colleague described as a "thundering declaration of war," demanded an assessment of readiness.
Would the United States, the Michigan senator inquired, be capable
of repelling an invasion? War with Britain, Allen joined in, was
inevitable. The United States must make appropriate preparations—
especially in guiding "the hearts of the people." Ignoring Archer's
pleas for caution, the Senate passed Cass's "preparedness" resolution. The actual notice appeared about a week later in an admonition by Kentucky Whig John J. Crittenden, who warned his fellow
legislators that such a hasty move could arouse the British. Allen,
aptly referred to as the Ohio Foghorn, introduced a simple resolution to abrogate the existing arrangement with Britain. Atchison
called for a territorial government that secured American citizens
west of the Rockies. It appeared that, despite the counsel of moderates, Congress would expedite the president's will. His vice president, George Dallas, had appointed three 54°40' men to the
five-member Senate Foreign Relations Committee with one of the
most vocal extremists as its chair. Surely, Polk's party would
deliver.[51]

Although a late arrival, John C. Calhoun returned to Washington determined to slow the reckless move to abrogate the 1827 convention. He had become impatient with the "folly" of Polk's Oregon
policy that had, he believed, put at risk territory that "would have
fallen into our hands." In the Senate he wielded his considerable
influence to draw together a coalition of moderates that included
many of his political opponents from tariff battles. The entire nation, Milwaukee newspaperman Rufus L. King implored, "now look
to you [Calhoun] as the one who can save us from a War with England." Within forty-eight hours of his arrival in Washington,
Calhoun met with Polk to plead for restraint and to ask him not to
press for a provocative notice resolution.

Polk must have been amused that the author of "masterly inactivity" was advising him to delay and probably thought that he could
have expected no more. The president, however, exhibited the same
resolve to Calhoun that he had consistently set forth during the past
weeks. The senator departed the meeting, realizing that he had no
alternative but to oppose his party chief and block the resolution—

which did not escape the observant Polk. Calhoun, the president recorded in his diary, could be counted in the opposition. If Polk had lost an important ally in the Senate, he might have felt relieved that a powerful voice had joined his cause in the House. Bancroft informed him early in the day that John Quincy Adams intended to champion the administration's position as a means toward completing his 1819 treaty's goal to establish control of the continent. In fact, the extremists' position was more solid in the House than in the Senate. There, expansionist Democrats were not only stronger but were also joined by a substantial number of Whigs.[52]

While Polk enunciated the American position on Oregon and chastised the Europeans for their alleged designs on North America, the Peel government faced troubles at home that made the Oregon dispute of secondary importance. In the summer of 1845 word came to London that a blight had ruined the potato harvest in Ireland. Within months the magnitude of the problem became evident in its broader ramifications for the Empire. Peel determined that the potato famine necessitated a final push to repeal the Corn Laws that had restricted the import of foreign grain for decades. Repeal, however, would be a difficult task because it challenged long-standing British commercial policy. Also, several members of the Peel ministry had come to office with the support of protectionists who viewed repeal as betrayal. Such a move, howled Lord Stanley, was harsh and unnecessary.[53]

By early December, Peel acknowledged that the Corn Laws issue had fragmented his cabinet, and he submitted his resignation to the queen. When Victoria asked Whig leader Lord John Russell to form a new government, he realized that his recent conversion to Corn Laws repeal had eroded the possibility of establishing anything but a minority government. Also, in an attempt to piece together a cabinet he found that essential members refused to serve with one another. Russell believed that his government required the services of both Palmerston and Lord Grey. This duo presented an insurmountable obstacle. Palmerston agreed to join only as head of the Foreign Office, while Grey adamantly refused to join a cabinet in which the volatile Palmerston guided foreign policy. With the queen equally concerned about French apprehension over Palmerston's return to Whitehall, Russell tried to persuade him to take another office. Palmerston graciously declined, stating that he would support Russell's government from outside the cabinet. Russell was discouraged by the prospects of a weak and divisive cabinet and returned to the queen with his regrets. If he had thought his colleagues unreasonable in their reaction to a prospective Palmerston Foreign Office, he had only to observe initial reactions to appreciate their acumen. The mere mention of Palmerston back behind the desk at Whitehall had had a substantial negative impact on London securities and on both political and financial leaders in France.[54]

In the week before Christmas, Queen Victoria asked Peel to form another cabinet and reclaim the reins. Although he undoubtedly knew that his government would not last long, he was much invigorated by the opposition's failure to replace him. "I resume power," he wrote Princess Lieven in Paris, "with greater means of rendering public service than I should have had if I had not relinquished it." The "Whig abortion" not only exposed the vulnerability of his opposition but also permitted him to change the makeup of the cabinet. Peel brought in members more in line with his agenda, which not only strengthened his domestic hand but, in allowing him to appoint Lord Ellenborough to head the Admiralty, also gave Lord Wellington crucial support for his rearmament effort and consequently enhanced the government's international posture. Fortunately, Aberdeen continued at the Foreign Office; and, since Peel was occupied with fiscal problems and repeal of the Corn Laws, the Scottish peer had far greater latitude in conducting foreign policy. Aberdeen would use the specter of Palmerston's imminent return and the stern posture of a more militant cabinet to press for settlement. "In the course of the year," he boldly wrote Peel on Christmas Day, the Oregon dispute would be settled "either by arbitration or by direct negotiation."[55]

If the foreign secretary believed that arbitration remained an option, he had misread the Polk administration. Pakenham might continue to propose the method, but Polk had determined to stand pat on Jackson's admonition to yield to arbitration only "at the cannon's mouth." The president, Pakenham complained, had not even mentioned British offers of arbitration in his annual message, which confirmed his belief that the July offer had been nothing more than "a feint on the part of the U.S. government." The speech had generated great excitement and had driven down stocks by 3 percent. If Calhoun's moderate forces could not be mustered to stall the president's plans, Congress would likely move forward with the notice to abrogate the open-access arrangement.[56]

For the remainder of 1845 advocates of compromise worked to persuade an obstinate Polk to end the impasse. The president, however, seemed determined to wait for Congress to act on his instructions. Shortly after the annual message, Benton approached him with a British plan for settlement that Pakenham had conveyed to the senator, which partitioned the territory at 49 degrees and awarded Britain all of Vancouver Island and free navigation of the Columbia River. Perhaps, Benton thought, they could include a reciprocal arrangement for the United States on the St. Lawrence River. Although Attorney General Mason interrupted the conversation before Benton could pursue the matter, Buchanan asked Polk at a subsequent cabinet meeting if such a proposal might go to the Senate. When Polk responded in the negative, the secretary of state engaged in a rare attempt to force the issue. He drafted instructions to McLane to tell Aberdeen that "the president would be strongly inclined to submit" a British offer to compromise at 49 degrees "to the Senate for their advice." Polk predictably rejected the draft, and he conceded only to a modified version that made the oblique promise that the administration would "judge of the character of any new proposition." The president, however, directed Buchanan not to invite a proposal from the British minister.[57]

The secretary completed his instructions to McLane a few days later and added that Polk was concerned about recent British military movements. With the Oregon dispute "approaching a crisis," the administration assumed that the United States was the probable target of the buildup. McLane should determine the intent and extent of these preparations. Putting the best face on the situation, Buchanan left the way open for conciliation by declaring that the crisis had been "necessary" to convince the American people of the "magnitude and importance" of the Oregon dispute.[58]

The new instructions crossed a despatch from London that diluted Buchanan's already thin optimism. Aberdeen, McLane stated, had expressed frustration with Polk's unorthodox handling of the recent negotiations and assumed that the administration meant to close "the door to further attempts at compromise." The Peel government would not present a proposal to a closed door. Although the British did not seek war, McLane insisted, they would back the government in a call to arms. Aberdeen had exhausted "all peaceful attempts" and told Pakenham to offer arbitration one last time. If rejected again, the Peel ministry would be prepared for dire consequences. Since the intimation elevated the arbitration offer to the level of an ultimatum, McLane warned, the administration should be careful in its response. If the president turned down the offer, he should do so with a clear intimation that the way remained open to a negotiated settlement. The implication seemed to be that even though the British preferred a partition resembling that of the July offer, their patience was not inexhaustible.[59]

At the next cabinet meeting, McLane's despatch precipitated what Polk called a "grave discussion" concerning the prospects of war with Britain over Oregon. Either war or peace, Buchanan predicted, would emerge from the actions of the next two weeks. Despite the consensus of the cabinet that this prediction had sufficient merit to necessitate military preparations, the administration remained skeptical of the likelihood of an impartial arbiter and thus intransigent on arbitration. Buchanan, however, sought to prompt a compromise offer from Pakenham assuring him that it would pass to the Senate. Still unable to fully sway the president, the secretary nonetheless secured his qualified promise to discuss with a few senators a British offer to partition at 49 degrees as long as the United States received adequate ports north of that line to permit access to the Juan de Fuca Strait. This arrangement *might* lead him to submit the matter to the Senate for advice.[60]

Indeed, the president called in Allen to obtain his reaction to McLane's despatch. Allen, not surprisingly, agreed with the rejection of arbitration but declared that a British compromise offer should go before the Senate. Fellow Tennessee Senator Hopkins Turney, who had come to Polk to warn him of the Benton and Calhoun collusion on Oregon, asked if a British offer would go to that body. But Polk, still not fully decided, promised only a confidential consultation with its members. By the end of the month, however, Polk wrote McLane that a British proposal resembling the July offer would go to the Senate where a favorable response was possible. The persistence of moderate Democrats and the increasingly threatening news from McLane moved Polk to expose the first sign of a crack in his rigid demeanor. A crack was all he would allow at this stage, however. Arbitration was out of the question.[61]

Pakenham remained true to his instructions and prepared to embark on a new and innovative attempt to win arbitration. Shortly after the December cabinet meeting at which Polk had left no doubt of his opposition to arbitration, Buchanan met with the British minister to hear the ill-fated proposal. After Buchanan once again declared that there was no chance of salvaging the negotiations, Pakenham urged arbitration. The entire territory and not the question of title, he proposed, should go before an arbiter. Knowing the administration's fear that an impartial arbiter could not be found, the minister suggested an alternative to the customary inclusion of a European sovereign—perhaps an independent state such as Switzerland, Hamburg, or Bremen could proffer a decision. Maybe, a facetious Buchanan interrupted, the Pope should lend his services. Pakenham either missed his associate's strained attempt at humor or was so intense that he was in no mood to appreciate it. He would gladly, the British minister submitted, forfeit half of his possessions to see the dispute resolved. The United States, he implied, was not committed to maintaining peace. His government, for the sake of amicable relations, would accept an arbiter's award of the entire region to the United States just "to get clear of the question." Of course the administration wanted peace, Buchanan responded defensively, especially when facing a British navy capable of commanding the Pacific coast. If the United States restricted a conflict to the west coast, the usually sober Pakenham chided, he "would willingly make a bargain to fight it out" there.[62]

The secretary could not accept arbitration under any scheme. Acceptance of arbitration, Buchanan argued, implied a tacit admission to the validity of British claims. After an almost token presentation of the new offer to Polk and Bancroft, the secretary penned a tactful rejection. Despite U.S. inability to accept arbitration, the president nonetheless "cherishes the hope that this long-pending controversy may yet be finally adjusted in such a manner as not to disturb the peace, or interrupt the harmony now so happily subsisting between the two nations."[63]

Although judiciously constructed, the rejection did not impress the British minister. Its bases, he wrote Aberdeen, were groundless. The United States had acknowledged the validity of Britain's claims since the early negotiations that had produced open access and partition offers. While Pakenham hoped that the Americans would come around to this reasonable approach, his despatch betrayed his doubt with the skeptical phrase, "we might perhaps imagine." These tentative words from the British minister ended the diplomatic communication of 1845. But unlike earlier rejections and frustrated talks, the climate had changed. A rejection now, if McLane was correct, would be tantamount to an ultimatum issued by a nation that was not only honor-bound to defend its prestige but was also preparing to do so by force of arms.[64]

CHAPTER TEN

From Crisis to Compromise: The Oregon Treaty

Pshaw! Who seriously dreams of insisting . . . at all hazard, upon
54°40'? I conscientiously believe no body.
—Louis McLane, May 3, 1846

The first year of the Polk administration had witnessed crises
over the U.S. southern and western boundaries, neither of which
had been satisfactorily resolved. Eighteen forty-five had ended with
Texas formally annexed and the Lone Star Republic retired to
America's expansionist archives. The question remained of where
the new state of Texas ended and the Mexican republic began and
only added fuel to the dangerous sparks of America's relations with
its southern neighbor. Equally dangerous was the crisis over Oregon. The new year, Pakenham believed, had approached with Britain moving more assertively toward an Anglo-American altercation
resulting from the rejection in Washington of what his counterpart
in London had deemed an ultimatum. Circumstances might yet move
the two sides to salvage the negotiations—a move that both Aberdeen and Polk, in fact, preferred but dared not initiate as long as
national honor was at stake.

Unfortunately, Aberdeen's pressure to make arbitration the
method of resolution and Polk's determination to reject it perpetuated an impasse that was next to impossible for the diplomats to
overcome. As they struggled to do so, Polk balanced alternating
pressures from Mexico City and London against his party's quest
for expansion and its desire for free trade with Britain. In London,
changed political conditions for the Peel ministry gave Aberdeen
more latitude and a stronger hand in dealing with Washington. He
too, however, did not wish to jeopardize the potential benefits of
relaxed trade with an Anglo-American break. Ironically, national

233

honor might provoke both governments to pursue a war that neither side wanted.

I

Both Polk and Aberdeen had done little to calm the storm swirl-
ing around the Oregon Question in the aftermath of the fall diplomatic disaster. Polk had not only withdrawn his compromise offer
but had also flatly rejected arbitration without providing an opening for further negotiation. In so doing, he had ignored what appeared to be an ultimatum—the final British offer. The consequences
of allowing the dispute to fester much longer were becoming increasingly clear. Correspondence from Louis McLane in London
verified the more militant attitude of even the usually pacific Aberdeen, who likewise contributed to the problem by relying on the
proved ineffective tactic of arbitration. Each time it was suggested
over the history of the dispute it had been summarily rejected. If
Aberdeen meant to be subtle, it was a dangerous ploy. Polk was the
last person to appreciate the delicate nuances of diplomacy. Only
an outright counter to the withdrawn July offer would impress him.
If the foreign secretary wished to jump-start the stalled negotiations, he should have instructed Pakenham to extend an offer while
relying on the unofficial, and at times indiscreet, assurances of
Edward Everett and others that Polk would issue a favorable response. Perhaps Aberdeen had turned to a legalistic principle of
negotiation when he told his man in Washington that Polk had released Britain from any obligation to submit a counteroffer by with-
drawing the July offer. But if Aberdeen was of the mind that war
clouds would make arbitration more palatable, he was wrong.[1]

Although Pakenham did not place much faith in his arbitration
proposal, he expressed renewed hope for direct negotiation. Secretary of State Buchanan, the minister told Aberdeen, seemed disappointed that the British had put forward arbitration rather than a
counteroffer. Senators Archer and Benton as well as a prominent
Washington banker had told Pakenham that the United States would
accept a partition at the 49th parallel that left Britain the full extent
of Vancouver Island and free use of the Columbia River. If the British minister made such an offer, these Americans assured him, the
president would "refer it to the Senate" where "it would be approved without much opposition." This overture hinted at an encouraging shift in the fixed American posture. A mere three months
before, Pakenham knew, the United States would not have consid-

ered such a suggestion. A negative impact on commerce and the specter of an Anglo-American conflict, he explained, had led many Americans to realize that the dispute "was no longer to be trifled with." The Calhoun and Benton forces in the Senate would mold that opinion into a barrier against any rash move that might provoke war. And, at the same time, overt resistance to hostile rhetoric or resolution by the congressional moderates would bolster the British position by allowing them more flexibility to compromise "by removing that appearance of bullying, and threatening" by the United States.[2]

Calhoun indeed resisted the extremist assault. After the return from Christmas break, Senator Hannegan led westerners in a call for renewing the administration's all-Oregon pledge. Polk, they asserted, was bound by the Constitution to guarantee U.S. interests in the entire territory. Calhoun defended the president's prerogative to partition the territory in accordance with the line offered by the British in previous negotiations. Responding to Hannegan, the South Carolina senator joined Benton and Archer in tabling all the problematic resolutions except for William Allen's simple notice draft. That lone survivor they managed to divert to committee, delaying a Senate debate until the second week in February.[3]

Meanwhile, the president gave every indication that he remained firmly entrenched against compromise. Calhoun's South Carolina colleague, James A. Black, went to the president to solicit his support for a plan to mediate between the moderates and extremists. The extremists would yield on the notice resolution if the moderates agreed to the extension of federal law and protection for American settlers as well as land grants and a rejection of partition. To Black, Polk offered the famous retort that the "only way to treat John Bull was to look him straight in the eye." Anything less would encourage the British to "become arrogant and more grasping." When a week later Calhoun appealed to the president not to force the notice resolution, the senator received a similar dose of Polk's intransigence. Contrary to Calhoun's sense that many of his congressional colleagues viewed notice as a prologue to armed confrontation, Polk believed that McLane's recent communication showed that the step might promote peace. Calhoun did not think so. He was determined to block the notice resolution in the Senate. But in the House the extremists were strong enough to force the issue. Pakenham conceded that notice would "carry in the end."[4]

Polk must have believed that notice would yield peace because he made no move to prepare for war. The December report of his war secretary, William Marcy, showed that the army could field only a modest force. Nevertheless, Marcy asked for very little augmentation, opting instead to wait until the demand arose. No action by the administration suggested concern over the recent war furor. And although Marcy confided to Benton that Polk would have to call up fifty thousand troops from the states in the event of an emergency, the secretary of war remained so frugal in his request that it seemed at odds with the president's pledge to stare down John Bull. About the only signs that Polk appreciated the gravity of the British military threat were his diversion of Commodore John Sloat's squadron from off Mexico to the Northwest and his authorization to distribute small arms and anti-British propaganda to Americans in Oregon.[5]

In the meantime, London received the president's message to Congress with surprisingly little uproar, considering the explosion that had greeted the Inaugural Address. The British were preoccupied with the food crisis, the trade reform movement, and the "Whig abortion," but they also remembered that the president's March bluster had been followed by a reduction in tension and an offer to compromise. The mild reaction did not surprise McLane. He had predicted before the speech that the British would temper their response, partly because they had been conditioned by Polk's earlier rhetoric and also because they anticipated a move to abrogate the 1827 agreement. As it happened, the British press heaped praise on the president's move to reform the tariff and so assigned little importance to the December comments on Oregon. Even the attention given to the dispute focused on commerce. Repeal of the Corn Laws, the *Economist* predicted, would prompt Polk to leave Oregon to arbitration. In the words of the London *Illustrated News*, Oregon was not worth "the expense of one year's war."[6]

As the British people learned more of the basis for U.S. claims from documents published with the president's message, they tempered their enthusiasm for their earlier position. British commercial leaders, McLane wrote Calhoun in early January of 1846, would not support a war over Oregon, especially that part south of 49 degrees. Further, there was every reason to expect that anticipated changes in the trade policies of both nations would ensure peace. When the *Times* of London put forth a possible compromise, there was little doubt of the prospects for an amicable settlement. Most of those who knew the London press understood that Aberdeen had groomed the young editor of the *Times*, John Delane, to advance the ministry's position on critical issues. In fact, Delane had been privy to a "leak" that allowed the *Times* to break the news of the Peel resignation the previous year. So the paper's suggestion that the British minister in Washington receive instructions to offer the line that Albert Gallatin had proposed in the 1820s—a boundary at 49 degrees that left Britain with Vancouver Island, access to the Juan de Fuca Strait, and navigation of the Columbia—affirmed the Peel government's wish to settle the dispute on friendly terms.[7]

The London government actually viewed the president's message as far less belligerent than it had expected. Indeed, Aberdeen told McLane that the twelve-month notice should encourage negotiations by establishing clear time parameters. The recent British military preparation "had no direct reference to such a rupture." McLane was convinced, he wrote Calhoun, that although the British were "better prepared for war than they have ever been at any antecedent period, this government is, I am persuaded, sincerely desirous of peace, and, short of the point of honor, will make great concessions to maintain it." Calhoun, McLane counseled, should move the United States toward compromise. A concession that secured the Hudson's Bay Company's rights for a certain period would assuage British honor and make compromise admissible.[8]

Indeed, apart from the determination to safeguard honor, a truly conciliatory tone now emanated from most government members in London. Not only did the desire for peace proceed from the Royal Speech but so also did the discussions in both houses of Parliament. The Marquess of Lansdowne told the House of Lords that the government should "maintain what is of so much importance to the interests of the world, a peace between this country, and the United States, without sacrificing any of the honor of this country." Likewise, Lord Francis Egerton in the House of Commons, while respecting the need to protect honor, heralded the strong union of blood and language that connected the two nations.[9]

The conciliatory attitude of Lord John Russell as leader of the Whig opposition was crucial to the prospects for peace. That a compromise offer from Polk had stood with no counter extended by Britain was, in Russell's view, highly improper. The July offer of the United States, he asserted in the House of Commons, necessitated a British statement "of the terms on which they would be satisfied to settle the question." Everett had cautioned Russell that his public position would help determine war or peace between the United States and Britain. If the conservatives knew that the opposition would not turn the British public against compromise, Aberdeen would probably move to settle the dispute. This possibility, combined with Russell's recognition that he could achieve repeal of the Corn Laws only in concert with the Peel ministry, transformed him into an advocate for compromise. Russell's decision was critical. As leader of the opposition, he had hinted at support for a compromise boundary extended by the Peel government. Aberdeen was free to make such a move without having to undergo another venomous charge similar to that of the "Ashburton capitulation."[10]

And yet, McLane's despatch communicating the friendly pronouncements from London also included comments that threatened to dilute its positive intention. Overshadowing the conciliatory expression was his warning that the unpredictable variable of national honor had appeared in the Royal Speech and those speeches that followed. Such an intangible was so "susceptible of being stretched to cover inadmissible demands" that the administration should not confuse a British desire for peace with a guarantee against war. He reinforced his warning with an unsettling report of the British military buildup. At the height of tension in early December, when Peel was in the nebulous state of temporary abdication, he had warned Queen Victoria that whoever replaced his government must support military increases that were at least in part due to "our relations with the United States." The move to do so upon Peel's return to power had contributed to the preparedness remarks in the Royal Speech. If there was any comfort in Aberdeen's assurances to McLane that the action had no connection with Washington-London relations, the pronouncements of the pugnacious Lord Ellenborough undercut such a feeling. Although rejected by Peel, Ellenborough proposed shoring up Canadian defenses and positioning warships in the Chesapeake to lure British-born seamen from American service. Such abrasive expressions nonetheless were central to McLane's meeting with Aberdeen in late January.[11]

McLane faced a foreign secretary who, though supportive of the recent amicable gestures, was disappointed at word from Pakenham that the Polk administration had turned down arbitration without making any provision for restarting the negotiations. Contrary to what Buchanan had intended, Aberdeen viewed the rejection of arbitration as a sign that Polk did not desire a British proposal and, in fact, did not seek a compromise. Although McLane reminded Aberdeen that Polk had never viewed arbitration as a viable option, the foreign secretary was not moved. In what was clearly an attempt to impress McLane with the gravity of the situation, Aberdeen announced that he would no longer oppose his colleagues' push for military preparations "founded upon the contingency of war with the United States." Such measures were "not only for defense and protection of the Canadas, but for offensive operations." McLane's despatch indeed conveyed an appreciation of the bellicose implications of the meeting. British preparations included the "immediate equipment of thirty sail of the line, besides steamers and other vessels of war."[12]

Despite the highly charged nature of his meeting with Aberdeen, McLane came away far less intimidated than the foreign secretary had intended. Aberdeen wrote Pakenham shortly afterward that the American minister should have recognized the dangerous state of affairs. But McLane was convinced that London had moved toward repeal of the Corn Laws in anticipation of better relations with Washington. The British would not pursue an inflammatory posture which "for the sake of a degree of latitude on the Pacific" would jeopardize their commerce with the United States. Perhaps McLane's judgment was affected by a certain wishfulness imposed by his desire to keep British commerce rolling on American rails. Regardless of his motivation, he felt confident that London would put forward a compromise offer resembling that recommended by Polk in July.[13]

II

Meanwhile, U.S. congressmen stumbled all over each other to participate in the notice debate. Such a potential backlog ensued that the House imposed a one-hour limit on members' perorations. In early January, Robert Winthrop of Massachusetts implied that the two nations should resort to arbitration or negotiations. Since neither government would jeopardize honor by conceding to previously rejected terms, the unfortunate alternative was armed confrontation. Joshua R. Giddings from Ohio chided his southern colleagues for retreating from the "all Oregon" commitment of the Baltimore platform. Not only should the United States annex the entire territory, but the process also should reach beyond 54°40' and take in the Canadas as well. Pennsylvania Congressman Charles Ingersoll offered a resolution to serve notice to Great Britain to "annul and abrogate" the 1827 arrangement. The two nations had tied a "Gordian knot," he lamented, "which that oracle of public opinion in both hemispheres, the press, now announced could only be cut by the sword." Other legislators proposed a territorial government and the retention of Oregon as an essential outlet for the

Mississippi Valley—"the garden of the world and the granary of the universe"—and a necessary entrepôt for growing Pacific commerce.[14]

Some congressmen wrapped Oregon in the broader concept of national destiny by contending that their nation should thwart the encroachment of European monarchies with the barrier of democracy. The United States, they argued, had an obligation to secure land contiguous to its borders to provide for an expanding populace and to secure its "inherent and pre-existent right" to the continent. Oregon belonged to the United States, Frederick P. Stanton of Tennessee asserted in a clever turn of phrase, not because destiny made it right but rather it was "our destiny because it is right." No one, however, outdid the aged statesman from Braintree, John Quincy Adams. To the privacy of his diary he confided that he had only offered a compromise on Oregon when at the State Department two decades earlier because he was certain the British would reject it, but he now boldly and publicly proclaimed the entire region America's. Adams went well beyond the rhetoric of his fellow legislators and solicited the sanction of God. Holding aloft the words of Genesis, Adams entreated the nation's leaders to heed the admonition to "be fruitful and multiply, and replenish the earth, and subdue it," by "effectively" occupying the Oregon Territory. Congressman George Fries of Ohio proclaimed that, on the power and authority of God, the United States would move ahead " 'til the stars and stripes wave over Oregon, every inch of Oregon."[15]

Fortunately, sufficient calm prevailed in the House to ease the truculent atmosphere surrounding the Oregon debate and to convert the simple notice resolution to one with assurances of its peaceful intent. Congress, an amendment made clear, did not intend to block an "amicable settlement" by its notice to abrogate the 1827 agreement. A resolution with the pacific amendment passed handily on February 9 by a margin of 163 to 54. The House had expedited the president's directive and had couched the notice in such a way that might jog, as Aberdeen had conjectured, the stalled negotiations. Senate action, however, was throttled by Calhoun's now-famous delay tactics.

Pakenham closely monitored the movement of the notice resolution and saw very little to concern him in either the Senate or the press. After Senator Crittenden failed in his efforts to hold Polk's political feet to the fire of responsibility by leaving notice to the discretion of the Executive Office, Senator John Fairfield of Maine pushed for a military buildup and an expansion of U.S. naval capa-

"ULTIMATUM ON THE OREGON QUESTION." James Baillie, New York, April 5, 1846. *Courtesy Library of Congress.*

bility. This effort, Benton argued, smacked of war. Pakenham seemed pleased that Benton was trying to control the more hot-headed members of the Senate and opined that Senate Democrats would hedge on military expenditures as a matter of fiscal respon-sibility. The Whigs, however, might align with the preparedness contingent because they could hold up the whole campaign to the American people as "practical proof of the expence attending such warlike Demonstrations." In this dangerous fashion they hoped to manipulate the war talk toward the "maintenance of peace."[16]

Indeed, peace seemed to be the order of the day. Perhaps a re-sult of Britain's tempered reaction to Polk's address, an equally mild mood prevailed in the United States that was reflected in a rise in public securities as well as in a noncombative press. The war panic, the New York *Herald* reported, had subsided; and, in the wake of Polk's July offer, the British had realized that only the greed of the Hudson's Bay Company stood in the way of an ami-cable settlement. "Peace! Peace!" declared a Baltimore newspa-per; it has just been "found out that nobody wants war, and that there is no need of one." The New York *Journal of Commerce* pre-dicted a British offer to compromise at 49 degrees. And the *Na-tional Intelligencer* reported that Gallatin, another veteran of the Oregon Question, opposed America's extreme claims and called for compromise. The U.S. claim to the territory, he contended, was neither clear nor unquestionable. It seemed that the anxious Christmas season had emboldened advocates of compromise and softened the general posture of the nation.[17]

A more reasonable mood even seemed to be circulating within the halls of the White House. Although Allen's call for "Fifty-four Forty or Fight!" had captured the imagination of opportunistic editors and was chanted by a large number of people in church and tavern alike, there was a growing mood for compromise. If the United States could fulfill manifest destiny below the 49th parallel without a fight with the powerful British lion, then that should be the path pursued. Would not a compromise along the lines outlined by the *Times* give the United States all it required and, as some congressmen stated, bring all American settlements within the Union? If so, it would not only be foolish to fight but would also be costly in the face of the Peel ministry's determination to open Brit-

"RIDICULOUS EXHIBITION; OR, YANKEE-NOODLE PUTTING HIS HEAD INTO THE BRITISH LION'S MOUTH." *Punch* (London), April 25, 1846.

ish markets to American grain. Surely no one could object to an arrangement that secured for the nation a significant piece of land fulfilling the call of manifest destiny and a critical stake in the Atlantic free trade—not even Young Hickory.

Before the first of the year, Polk had written McLane that the Senate would welcome a British compromise offer resembling his own of July. The president told his cabinet during the third week of January that U.S. adjustments in trade policy and a possible indemnity to pacify the Hudson's Bay Company might entice Britain to yield on Oregon. Such a proposition, he believed, gave Peel room to compromise without sacrificing national honor. Although Polk expressed reservations about the potential success of the scheme, he thought that British interest in preserving commerce with the United States might override any value placed on the Oregon Territory. McLane, Polk directed, should test Aberdeen with this reciprocity notion and determine whether he was agreeable to an Oregon settlement combined with a trade treaty. Now that Peel had openly expressed his willingness to compromise, Polk explained that he was prepared to hear a British proposal. The president, however, would not entertain such an offer without involving the Senate. His own political position and the high ground he had taken in his annual message prohibited him from doing so.[18]

Polk was now willing to partition the territory as long as he did not have to bear the brunt of the political fallout. Like Peel, the president had more than Oregon to consider; he had to maintain his loyal ranks to achieve his domestic agenda. To win a tariff reduction and an independent treasury, Polk required the support of the same western Democrats who opposed an Oregon partition. But while plotting a politically cautious path, Polk also seemed impressed by British military preparations.

Several factors determined the president's more expedient path. The Peel government's move toward free trade appealed to Polk who saw, as a true protégé of Old Hickory, the potential for mutual commercial rewards between the Atlantic nations. He also realized that the hostile reaction of the French to his annual message diluted any chance of their restraining the British in any Anglo-American row. Added to the mix was the increased tension with Mexico following the formal annexation of Texas at the end of the previous year.[19] Peace was Polk's only viable option.

While both Atlantic nations attempted to ascertain each other's sincerity for peace, Pakenham pushed for arbitration of the entire territory. This new refrain on an old anthem, he believed, should appeal to an administration confident in its position. The new refrain, however, ended with the same chorus of earlier proposals. If an arbiter could not agree upon a unilateral award of the territory to the superior claimant, the territory would be partitioned in such a manner that reflected a "just appreciation of the respective claims" of both nations. Pakenham knew that the prospect of partition and the consequent admission of a legitimate British claim would most likely dash this proposal on the same rocks as its predecessors. Had he been privy to Buchanan's simultaneous despatch to McLane, his lack of faith in arbitration would have been affirmed. Although the Senate, in its trepidation over a possible breach with Britain, would probably sacrifice some of America's rights, the president, Buchanan believed, would never put at risk the territory south of 49 degrees. Polk would not permit a third party "to deprive us of a foot of the soil on the continent south of the 49th parallel of latitude, and of the valuable harbors of Puget's Sound." Perhaps to encourage the British to hurry a compromise proposal, Buchanan told McLane that they should not persist with ineffective arbitration proposals. With passion in the United States still running to 54°40', the British "have not an hour to lose, if they desire a peaceful termination of the controversy."[20]

The secretary of state officially rejected Pakenham's latest arbitration proposal in early February. Since even an unbiased arbiter would favor pleasing both claimants, Buchanan correctly asserted, the United States would not and indeed could not submit a region as important as Oregon to the uncertainty of arbitration. To Britain, the territory amounted to no more than a "distant colonial possession of doubtful value." To the United States, in contrast, the territory constituted "an integral and essential portion of the Republic. The gain to Great Britain," Buchanan assessed, "she would never sensibly feel; whilst the loss to the United States would be irreparable." The secretary foresaw several prosperous states arising from the Oregon Territory that would not only host the growing American population but would also prove critical to U.S. commerce in the Pacific. According to Buchanan, the president believed that the United States and Great Britain, who were "more closely bound together by the ties of commerce" than any others, should resolve this problem through direct negotiation and "without the interposition of any arbitrator."[21]

Later in the month McLane's despatch of February 3 arrived, and although Polk had already acknowledged Britain's "warlike preparations," the new information about "thirty sail of the line" destined for service in North American waters generated considerable worrisome activity within the administration. The despatch arrived late on a Saturday, but Buchanan was unwilling to wait until morning and delivered it to the White House that same evening. The rapid pace continued the next day as cabinet members met with the president after church services to discuss the despatch. After an inconclusive meeting of Polk, Bancroft, and Buchanan on Monday, the president brought the despatch before the entire cabinet at its regular meeting on the following day. The ensuing discussion moved the administration to provide an opening for a British offer—a position that the president had tenaciously opposed throughout the crisis. The United States, Buchanan recommended, should notify Aberdeen that the administration would entertain a British offer of partition at 49 degrees that authorized British navigation of the Columbia River and a ten-year guarantee of the Hudson's Bay Company's property. The cabinet unanimously approved the suggestion and agreed that such a proposal, once made, should go before the Senate for consideration. After the cabinet adjourned,

"POLK'S DREAM." James Baillie, New York, April 8, 1846. *Courtesy Library of Congress.*

Buchanan drafted a despatch to McLane instructing him to inform Aberdeen of the administration's new stand on Oregon.[22]

Rumors of a possible Oregon compromise began to circulate throughout the capital. Senator William Haywood from North Carolina called on Polk to apprise him of a scheme forwarded by Calhoun's Senate contingent that called for a resolution urging the administration to seek a compromise. Instead of that step, Haywood intended to join Benton and others in pushing for a notice resolution aimed at drawing a compromise offer from Whitehall. Calhoun's bloc, Allen told Polk that same evening, had concocted this plan to undercut the president by forcing him to yield to the British. Allen was perplexed that Polk seemed poised to compromise and tried to enlist the president's southern pride. A compromise, Allen warned, would cost Polk the support of perhaps ten western and southwestern states. The president recalled his earlier pledge against a second term and indicated that the favor of the states made little difference to his political survival. Besides, Polk chided his visitor tongue in cheek, the good senator had previously supported the transmission to the Senate of a British proposal reflecting that of the administration's July offer. Allen had contradicted his earlier position. The blistering rhetoric on the floor of the Senate left no doubt that he had taken up the all-Oregon crusade. As noted earlier, Allen is credited with coining the most vitriolic of challenges to compromise—"Fifty-four Forty or Fight."[23]

The Senate's debate on notice finally began on February 10. Allen opened the discussion with a two-day speech demanding the eviction of Britain from the territory. The United States, he insisted, must not permit the British bully to rule American soil. Just ask the citizens of this country if they were willing to forfeit the territory out of "dread of invasion by a rabble of armed paupers, threatened to be sent by a bankrupt government, whose whole power of the sword and the dungeon is required to stifle the cries of famine at home, or to protect its own life against the uplifted hands of starving millions." The answer would be such a defiant *no*, he confidently declared, that it would "make the British empire tremble throughout its whole frame and foundation." While western Democrats decried the surrender of any part of the territory, Whig and Democratic moderates from the East and the South held out for negotiation—toward even partition to preserve the peace.

From this nest of political infighting, Calhoun emerged with a plan to urge the administration to reopen the negotiation with a compromise offer. His plan encountered a struggle from within the Senate because the Whigs did not want to give the president any room to abdicate responsibility for breaking his campaign pledge. Calhoun soon decided that the scheme was a dead issue because the president had not softened sufficiently to extend a compromise in the same hand bitten by the British lion the previous summer.

Calhoun and Georgia's Walter Colquitt braved a snowstorm to secure this disheartening information from Polk. The president assured his visitors only that he would involve the Senate in any deliberation over a reasonable British offer. The senators then tried to convince their intransigent host to "repropose" the July offer. Polk rejected this suggestion and added that he would continue to oppose any compromise that placed no constraints on British navigation of the Columbia River.[24]

Later on the 25th the cabinet met and approved Buchanan's instructions to McLane. News of the deployment of British ships to North America, the secretary wrote, would lead the American public into believing that a conflict was imminent. McLane should discourage the Peel ministry from advancing this tactic. Perhaps as an incentive to the British to do so, Buchanan instructed McLane to inform Aberdeen that a proposed division of the territory at 49 degrees with British retention of all of Vancouver Island and limited navigation of the Columbia would go to the Senate. Aberdeen should act quickly, the secretary warned in an accompanying letter, because the turbulence in domestic politics could present Britain and Polk with an even less friendly Congress after the November elections. Aberdeen should not assume that he could intimidate the United States with further delay.[25]

Buchanan was rightfully concerned at the misperception gaining currency in the Foreign Office. The mood in the United States, Pakenham reported, had become decidedly more amiable. Calhoun's efforts toward compromise had convinced the British minister that the Senate favored a partition of the territory. Calhoun had told him that no more than seven senators would block a compromise. Pakenham thought that the Peel government had played it well. The projected repeal of the Corn Laws offered an enticement for the preservation of peace through compromise and, combined with the demonstration of British willingness to defend honor by force, had convinced the Americans that they had "put themselves in the wrong by trifling too far with the forbearance of England." A New York correspondent for the London *Morning Post* said it best. The zealous patriots in the U.S. Congress had mounted "their war-horses and charged upon St. George with the certainty of the American people following them" only to find that they now rode "all alone in their glory, whilst the nation has either forgotten them in their profound contempt or made merry at their ludicrous pranks." Rest assured, Pakenham confidently advised the Foreign Office, that no further intimidation through military preparations was necessary.[26]

III

An objective observer, neglecting the intangible but critical factor of national honor, might have been amused at the posturing that both sides adopted to reach terms that were mutually acceptable. Buchanan had reversed his pacific position and now urged Polk to raise the nation's military capability. Was this due to a belief that war was inevitable? Probably not. But he did understand that the Peel government had decided to negotiate from a more pugnacious stance. The best way to ensure America's bargaining position was to meet the British with an equal show of resolve. Buchanan also knew that the noise from the Senate was one of conciliation and that the administration had to project a defiant voice to balance it. Otherwise, his instructions to warn Aberdeen not to delay would fall on incredulous ears.[27]

The advocates of conciliation had not yet won the day because the president still appeared to be in the expansionist camp. In early March, Haywood startled his colleagues by declaring that both he and his old college friend Polk backed a compromise at the 49th parallel. Democratic politicos immediately rushed to the White House to wrest the administration's intent from the president himself. Hannegan, who appeared to Polk to be excited, demanded to know if Haywood spoke for the administration. No individual, Polk assured the Indiana senator, was authorized to speak on his behalf. After all, he asserted, he had clearly presented his position in his congressional message of December. Polk held his cards close to his chest and revealed very little to Hannegan, who had hoped for a renewed commitment to all Oregon. And those who approached the president after Hannegan left did no better at extracting information. Polk, however, feared the repercussions of party division on his domestic slate and took the opportunity to call for "harmony on the Oregon question." When he finally had a quiet moment to assess the day's events, Polk concluded that much of what he had observed was more reflective of jockeying for the wide-open Democratic nomination for 1848 than of any deep-rooted position on policy.[28]

Perhaps Hannegan had stewed through the night over Polk's rebuff, because as soon as Haywood relinquished the floor the following day the Hoosier blasted both the senator and the president. If, as Haywood contended, Polk supported compromise, he was an "infamous man," Hannegan bitterly remarked, "with the tongue of a serpent." This testy exchange involved several senators and sent more anxious visitors to the White House. But even the stern and persuasive Michigan senator, Lewis Cass, learned no more of the president's mind than his colleagues had on the previous day.[29]

Expansionist Democrats were not to be denied, however. Concerned that Polk was poised to jettison the all-Oregon plank of his 1844 platform, western Democrats met in caucus and directed a committee to draw out the president's aim. Committee envoys David Atchison and Hannegan appeared at Polk's door immediately after Mississippi Senator Jesse Speight had warned him of the caucus. Hannegan demanded that Polk state his position. "I would answer no man," Polk hotly declared, "what I would do in the future." As for what I might do, he continued in pious indignation, "I would be responsible to God and my country." Polk must have been exasperated when Allen appeared on the heels of Hannegan and Atchison and continued the probe. The president assured his visitor that he had every intention to forward a British offer to the Senate, but this promise did not pacify the senator. Fortunately for Polk, as Allen doggedly pressed him, the First Lady mercifully rescued her husband with a deputation of White House guests who maneuvered him out of Allen's clutches to a more relaxed gathering in the parlor.[30]

The stream of lawmakers was only temporarily slowed as the parade continued over the next several days. When Benton met with the president about a week later, Polk told him of McLane's latest instructions and the senator cautioned him that a notice resolution sponsored by Crittenden would lay responsibility for serving notice at the doorstep of the White House. Perhaps, Polk said, it would be dangerous in the present state of the party to oppose Crittenden. It might be expedient to hammer out a more acceptable version of his resolution. Toward this end, Buchanan was to work behind the scenes to influence Senate Democrats.[31]

It still remained uncertain if the administration could mollify Calhoun's bloc. Unlike Polk's machinations, Calhoun let it be known that he would declare his position in a prearranged address to the Senate. On March 16 the expectations of the powerful senator's address drew a capacity crowd to the gallery and emptied the House. The Richmond *Enquirer* reported that "the ladies had complete possession of the gallery by eight o-clock A.M." and that a trainload of citizens "journeyed all the way from New York City, solely for the purpose of hearing him." As anticipated, Calhoun was dynamic. Due to a recent relaxation in Anglo-American tension, he stated, it was incumbent on him to serve notice to abrogate the 1827 convention. Far from triggering a war as he had previously feared, a notice resolution drafted in a moderate form would encourage an amicable settlement of the dispute. Since a majority of the public on both sides of the Atlantic favored a compromise, the Senate should deal with the issue now rather than subjecting it to the campaign cauldron of the coming election season.[32]

Reasonable statesmen on both sides had come to appreciate the benefits likely to accrue from compromise. As Calhoun prepared Americans for settlement, Lord Clarendon, a close associate of Aberdeen and prominent Whig, did the same in Britain. Parliament's failure to address the subject, he cautioned, might stir up the zealots. Despite his acknowledgment that much of the blustering of Washington lawmakers was nothing more than electioneering, he admonished his peers to recognize the seriousness of the situation. In the current climate of commercial accommodation, he continued, it was unlikely that the United States would choose war. "Of all the countries in the world," that nation would be the primary beneficiary of the "enlightened system of commerce" that the London government had determined to construct. Since nothing positive could result from war, the British should view an American notice to end the present arrangement not as a hostile gesture but rather as a desire to settle the Oregon Question within a year.[33]

Aberdeen agreed with Clarendon's assessment and accepted his call for documents relative to the Oregon dispute. Both he and Lord Brougham assured Parliament that Britain did not seek war and that war was not imminent. Ashburton, however, injected the cautious reminder of the unpredictable factor of national honor. The issue on its own merits, the elderly banker declared, was "worthless," but honor could throw the two nations into a war that neither side wanted.[34]

Honor remained the critical issue, and the longer the Senate debated the matter the more convinced Aberdeen became that he could preserve it. When McLane informed him that Polk had agreed to put a proposal before the Senate but that the president, if left to his own devices, would hold out for all Oregon, Aberdeen responded that he would issue any further proposition through McLane. Such a proposal, the latter believed, would partition the territory at 49 degrees while reserving British rights to all of Vancouver Island and perpetual navigation of the Columbia. Aberdeen had planted national honor on the bank of the river that had provoked the controversy in the beginning. The genteel Scottish peer, McLane wrote

"YOUNG YANKEE-NOODLE TEACHING GRANDMOTHER BRITANNIA TO SUCK EGGS." *Punch* (London), March 14, 1846.

Calhoun, would not yield on the point of honor and, in fact, did not see the need to do so in light of the languishing U.S. position evident in the Senate debates.[35]

Although Aberdeen was confident that he could secure British honor, he continued to seek a compromise settlement. Several recent developments encouraged him to believe that compromise was the most reasonable approach. Americans in Oregon far outnumbered those loyal to the crown and were reaching farther north, to Puget's Sound where Americans had already established a settlement. The Hudson's Bay Company had moved its headquarters from

Fort Vancouver to the island and had plans to evacuate the fort altogether. Probably the most effective consideration, however, was that the territory Aberdeen contemplated surrendering—between the Columbia and 49 degrees—was nearly worthless to the crown. The Peel government's recognition of its limited value, combined with Whig leader Russell's assurance that the opposition would not contest a compromise, allowed Aberdeen considerable latitude to resolve the long-standing dispute.[36]

As British statesmen optimistically predicted a Senate opening encouraging direct negotiations, that body indeed moved toward a modest resolution. But the all-Oregon crusade would not die quietly. Even though zeal waned in the Senate, it had not diminished in the hinterland. The passion for manifest destiny that eventually took Americans into a war of conquest with Mexico had captured Oregon. Many lawmakers' mailboxes continued to show that Americans viewed a retreat from the all-Oregon demand as a betrayal. This opinion was especially true among their western constituents. Partly due to their own sentiments and partly due to the swelling objection to forfeiting any territory, pro-Oregon senators attempted to throw up last-minute barricades to preserve their 54°40' hopes. Lewis Cass aggressively challenged recently published documents substantiating Britain's claims and affirmed stiff objection to compromise. It must have seemed to veterans of the Maine-New Brunswick border dispute a case of déjà vu when the Michigan senator pointed to the cartographic errors that characterized the history of North American boundaries. The line of 49 degrees, he asserted, was not the result of terms established at Utrecht in 1713, as many had assumed, but rather a myth perpetuated by mapmakers. There was, in fact, no foundation for such a partition across the Pacific Northwest. Indeed, McLane had a member of his legation go to Paris to check Cass's argument and found it correct. This information the U.S. minister withheld, however. With the Senate more receptive to Benton's defense of the Utrecht line and hence favoring compromise, it seemed wise to allow that body to proceed with the notice resolution toward that end.[37]

Calhoun's support for a notice resolution that invited negotiation, underpinned by Benton's call to compromise, doomed the all-Oregon movement. When Benton issued his response to Cass, any hope for the reappearance of the spirit of the youthful Missouri expansionist of the 1820s was dashed. Most Americans seemed resigned to compromise. "We are at a loss," a Missouri newspaper chided, "to know what the little squad of politicians from this section, who have been crying for the 'whole of Oregon or none' will do now." In an election year, the paramount issue to politicians became not whether the moderate notice resolution would pass but how best to package their role. To some, it was wiser to rant even louder and go down as the last defender of a lost cause. To others, the political winds indicated that the more expedient path was to join the compromise. There was little chance of pursuing what Pakenham feared—a procedural delay until the November elections brought in a more sympathetic Congress.[38]

The politics of the day focused more on exploiting manifest destiny for the 1848 presidential election than toward affecting the outcome of the notice debate. American statesmen, Polk sarcastically observed, were more committed to "forty-eight" than either "forty-nine" or "fifty-four forty." Even his secretary of state was caught up in "presidential fever." Buchanan was aware of the political capital that Cass had garnered with his bold expansionist agenda and had adopted a surprisingly militant posture. Reversing in late March his long-standing pressure on Polk to compromise, he began to support military preparedness. Polk had to rein him in. Buchanan's changed position portended serious repercussions because it affected his credibility with his chief. It was distressing, Polk confided to his diary, "that a member of the cabinet should be an aspirant for the presidency, because I cannot rely upon his honest and disinterested advice."[39]

Any balance that Polk hoped to strike between preservation of honor and pacification of party had to take place with one eye on John Bull. The British were encouraged by the bickering among America's spokesmen. If their tongues continued unrestrained, Polk's bargaining position would surely erode. Further, the extremists might raise the hackles of British nationalists who, according to McLane, were ripe for "the war spirit." *Blackwood's Edinburgh Review* offered support for McLane's observation in an article cynically entitled "How they Manage Matters in 'The Model Republic.'" The author found the "rhetorical flourishes" of Washington's leaders "without parallel in the history of civilized senates," both "outrageous and absurd." The declarations should arouse British consternation and expose the hazardous predicament that Polk and his party had created.[40] McLane was at times more concerned with the effect of the moderates than the extremists. The British, he fretted, had taken to appropriating the arguments of American apologists to defend the crown's position. Elder diplomat Albert Gallatin's letters to the press, for example, appeared among the most convincing British challenges to the U.S. case.[41]

The moderate climate convinced the Peel government that it could patiently await an American overture before extending an offer. All talk of compromise, McLane complained, was open to the scrutiny of the entire world and gave the impression that "Congress had been constituted a joint-commission for the conduct of the whole negotiation." It would bode better for resolution if the dispute was left to the officials "to whom the constitution" had entrusted such matters. Polk was aware of the dangerous impact of congressional intrusion into foreign policy. "The great error of the whole debate in both Houses," he lamented to Benton in early April, "had been that whatever had been said was spoken not only to our own people but the Brittish [sic] Government; that we thereby exposed our hand, whilst our adversary kept hers concealed." But one could hardly fault the lawmakers. After all, in his desire to share responsibility, Polk had invited Congress to participate in the process.[42]

The exposure of the U.S. hand seems to have encouraged the British to delay. Every report from Congress supported this strategy. Pakenham saw no need for a further display of strength, and Peel was so certain of this stand-pat position that he hardly considered Ellenborough's push for continued preparation. British readiness, the prime minister had assured Ellenborough in mid-March, was already "far in advance" of that of the United States and was sufficient to facilitate a settlement of the dispute. Encouraged by influential Americans such as Daniel Webster, the Peel government saw only one obstacle to delay—the impending return to the Foreign Office of the saber-rattling Palmerston.[43] Fortunately, the Senate had picked up the pace toward negotiations by working out a final version of the notice resolution. By a 40-to-14 margin, the Senate overrode the protests of Allen and Hannegan and approved Crittenden's proposal to have the president, at his discretion, serve notice to Britain. Although Polk would have preferred a version that more cleanly diverted responsibility for compromise to the senators, he encouraged its adoption. Otherwise the Senate might postpone it indefinitely or table it "to await the arrival of more Brittish [sic] Steamers."[44]

Timing was crucial. As the Senate voted on Crittenden's resolution, troubling news arrived from the southern border. Special envoy John Slidell returned from Mexico to report that relations with that nation had so soured that peaceful adjustment of outstanding problems seemed unlikely. Since Mexico had rebuffed Slidell's mission, Polk now had two crises to face and must have gained a new appreciation for expediting the notice resolution.[45] As tension continued to rise on the Rio Grande, Congress presented to Polk in the last week of April the long-awaited directive to transmit notice to London. Reflecting the influence of the moderates, the resolution indicated that the United States sought to end the present arrangement with Britain in an effort to "more earnestly and immediately" clear impediments to an "amicable settlement of all their differences and disputes" regarding Oregon.[46]

Although Polk now had the method for breaking the diplomatic impasse, he still faced a major obstacle. As he told South Carolinian George McDuffie and the elderly Richard Rush, who both wanted him to attach a compromise offer with the resolution, there was still a point beyond which he could not honorably go. Ironically and perhaps dangerously, Aberdeen had set his jaw rigidly on the precise point that Polk had in mind—navigation of the Columbia.[47]

Within the week Polk directed McLane to serve notice of the U.S. intention to abrogate the 1827 convention and to resolve the Oregon Question. In an attached letter, which Buchanan showed to Pakenham, the president told his minister in London to transmit this directive to the Foreign Office with "the kindest manner." The materials en route to London, Pakenham wrote Aberdeen, were "unobjectionable" because they confirmed the Senate's desire to end the dispute on friendly terms. The transmission of notice revealed that among many moderates who viewed the world from the commercial desks of the Northeast, there was a sense that peace with Britain was assured. "Let the dogs of war bawl & go to 54°40'," a New York newspaper declared; "the prey has escaped them. The 'national heart' needs not now to 'be prepared for war.' "[48]

As the packet departed for London with the hope of silencing the "dogs of war," war came from the south. Polk's cabinet sifted through the April reports of General Zachary Taylor and found no comfort. The fiery military chieftain anticipated a confrontation at the Rio Grande. In the second week of May, news arrived that his prediction had been correct: hostilities had begun with Mexico. Within forty-eight hours, Polk delivered his war message to Congress. After heated debate and hand-wringing deliberation, that body returned a formal declaration of war. The Mexican problem that had vied with Oregon for Polk's attention since he took office had finally exploded. Polk must have sighed at his good fortune that the Oregon problem was on track for settlement—but his relief must have been somewhat restrained. What if Britain chose now to shelve the northwestern dispute and seize the opportunity to contain the United States by supporting Mexico? This notion was not far-fetched. The British had always opposed U.S. expansion into California.[49]

Buchanan was concerned that Britain might yield to temptation and asked Polk to issue a disclaimer to London, which promised that the United States had no territorial aspirations in California or New Mexico. Without such an expression, Buchanan feared, the United States would not only fail to end the Oregon dispute but would also probably "have war with England." An incredulous Polk must have been tempted to let slip an uncharacteristic chuckle. Was this not destiny beckoning the United States to the Pacific? The president at that moment stood to gain a respectable part of Oregon and perhaps all remaining contiguous territory between Texas and the Pacific. This was not the time to retire his early style of brinkmanship diplomacy. Word of Taylor's victories at Palo Alto and Resaca de la Palma affirmed Polk's decision. Early success in the war with Mexico should discourage Britain from any extravagant notions of intervention.[50]

IV

Meanwhile, as the U.S.-Mexican conflict grew into full-scale war, the notice resolution reached Aberdeen's desk, where it became entangled in matters of national honor and use of the Columbia River. Except for an obligatory caution by the *Morning Chronicle*, the British press did not react badly to the Washington initiative. Now that the United States had given Aberdeen his desired opening for a settlement, all that remained was to secure honor by gaining rights to the Columbia. McLane knew that Polk too had placed great emphasis on the river and worked to move Aberdeen off his position. But the American minister had been frustrated "by the pertinacity with which" Aberdeen insisted on navigation of the Columbia. Just as the two sides refused to assess the territory solely on merit, so too did they reckon the river beyond its inherent value. It was widely known that the Columbia with its sandbar and rapids would not accommodate Pacific traffic. Observers for decades had reported its limitations. In fact, the Wilkes expedition in the early

1840s had offered one of the most definitive and critical appraisals of the river. So the only remaining argument for the river was national honor.[51]

Appreciating the significance of the navigation problem, McLane had tried in February 1846 to appease Aberdeen and assuage British honor with the promise of navigation for a specified period. By May, however, the foreign secretary was more confident of his position and demanded perpetual navigation in addition to portage rights—rights offered by Gallatin in the 1820s. McLane reminded Aberdeen that the offer had been rejected and, as Gallatin had said at the time, could not be considered binding in subsequent negotiations. The American minister could not sway Aberdeen from his position. He might compromise the territory but he would not compromise honor. In the foreign secretary's mind, British honor in the Oregon dispute and retention of navigation on the Columbia had become synonymous.[52]

McLane believed that Polk would reject any offer that included navigation of the river and so continued working to soften Aberdeen's position. The foreign secretary stood firm because he was convinced that the Senate would find the navigation concession reasonable. McLane knew that the opinion of the Senate was meaningless if the president, in exercising his foreign policy prerogative, did not ask for it. The obdurate Polk, McLane believed, would not let a proposal that included navigation get past his office. But when the American minister reported the likely terms of a British proposal, he predicted that Aberdeen would concede no more on the river than a possible narrowing of the navigation clause to the Hudson's Bay Company.[53]

On May 19, Aberdeen, supported by colleagues who called for a timely resolution of the dispute, transmitted official instructions to Pakenham clearly intimating that the moment had arrived for settlement. Circumstances in Britain made it expedient to resolve the affair. In the broader view of London's foreign policy, Oregon was only an irritant to the crown. "For God's sake, end it," John Croker admonished, "for if anything were to happen to Louis Phillippe [*sic*, king of France], we shall have an American war immediately, and a French one just after, a rebellion in Ireland, real starvation in the manufacturing districts, and a twenty per-cent complication in the shape of Income Tax." Aberdeen wrote Pakenham that the British government wanted to settle the dispute amicably and would lay aside "punctilio and etiquette." But, he added, the United States would bear the onus of war if it did not now seize the opportunity that he provided. Aberdeen's despatch then outlined the terms of this presumably crucial opportunity. It appeared virtually the same as that predicted by McLane except for the sensitive navigation clause. Aberdeen called for navigation of the Columbia for all British subjects engaged in trade with the Hudson's Bay Company.[54]

The issue of who would navigate the Columbia and for how long was more important than has been generally acknowledged. Its importance, however, lies more in McLane's perception of the Polk administration's position than in Aberdeen's insistence on navigation. Convinced that his chief would not compromise, McLane persisted in his efforts to win the point in London. If navigation rights went only to the Hudson's Bay Company, McLane reasoned, its value as a point of honor would diminish. After all, he wrote Buchanan, "no English statesman" would take the nation to war to preserve a benefit to so narrow a constituency. Operating from this assumption along with a belief that he had won over Aberdeen to restricted navigation, McLane issued a dangerous recommendation to Washington. The Senate, he wrote both Buchanan and Polk, should not view Pakenham's offer as an ultimatum but merely as an opening offer to reestablish negotiations. That done, the administration should make a counterproposal that restricted the terms of navigation and limited the rights to a defined period. If Polk truly opposed perpetual navigation of the Columbia as he had told Benton as late as May 3, McLane's advice might have tempted him to prolong the negotiations. Further, Buchanan might have viewed a U.S. counterproposal as a means of recovering lost political ground with his western colleagues. Holding out this possibility to Polk and Buchanan was indeed hazardous.

The critical problem was that Pakenham's instructions did not allow the flexibility implied by McLane. Contrary to the latter's intimation, the despatch to his counterpart in Washington contained terms that had every appearance of an ultimatum. You are directed, Aberdeen told Pakenham, to "make another, and I trust, final proposition to the Secretary of State, for the solution of these long-existing difficulties." In addition, Pakenham was again permitted to judge for himself as to the time and circumstances for presenting the offer. Indeed, he could withhold the new proposition if he thought delay warranted by changed conditions. If, however, he made the offer and the United States responded with a counter, he was to send it to London.[55]

If Pakenham's judgment had earlier led to bad results, this time it could have been devastating. To say that Pakenham witnessed "changed conditions" in early June when he received his instructions is an understatement. The United States was now at war with Mexico. He therefore had more than ample justification to delay his offer. But if he delayed, or if the Polk administration opted to follow McLane's advice, the dispute—so near settlement—would have returned to London to be reviewed not by Aberdeen but by his successor at Whitehall, the mercurial Palmerston. As anticipated, the Peel government would yield power to a Whig ministry following the repeal of the Corn Laws. Also as anticipated, the new Russell ministry would name Palmerston to the Foreign Office. In July, Pakenham noted that if Washington had followed McLane's advice to counter rather than accept the crown's offer, it would have derailed the entire process and "all would have been spoiled."[56]

Meanwhile, Polk met with his cabinet and voiced disapproval of the British proposal outlined in McLane's despatch. The president's cabinet, however, advised forwarding a British offer to the Senate along with a message stating the administration's position. Polk's advisers argued that since McLane thought that the offer would restrict navigation to the Hudson's Bay Company, the issue of the river should not hinder settlement. After all, the navigation rights under those terms should not outlive the expiration of the company's charter in 1859.[57]

During the first week of June, Pakenham, doubtless influenced by Taylor's victories in the field and a sense that settlement of the exasperating Oregon issue was in sight, presented the new proposal to Buchanan. The British minister wanted him to understand that this was a proposition with little or no flexibility and so read to him from his official instructions. That afternoon the secretary of state presented the proposal to the cabinet; and, after a brief deliberation to determine that navigation rights on the Columbia would terminate with expiration of the Hudson's Bay Company's charter, it responded favorably. To avert the threat of a war with Britain, the cabinet concluded, the proposal should go to the Senate with an addendum that reasserted the president's confidence in the strength of America's Oregon claim. The secretary of state, to the chagrin of his colleagues, declared that he would withhold his opinion until he saw the message. The all-Oregon legislators, he declared, "were the true friends of the administration and he wished no backing out on the subject."[58]

Polk and members of the cabinet must have glared in disbelief at Buchanan's statement. The secretary had been the most vocal advocate of compromise throughout the long deliberations over the Oregon Question. But now that compromise was virtually certain, he reversed his position and assumed a hard-line stance. Polk swallowed hard and sketched out his proposed message. He still held the position that he had articulated in December, but, in view of the sentiments expressed by Congress and in deference to the offers of his predecessors, he would take the Senate's advice on the British proposal. Left to him, however, the offer would be rejected. When Buchanan stated that he did not approve and would not draft the message, it is no wonder that Polk recorded in his diary that the secretary of state was trying to distance himself from the compromise. In his defense, however, Buchanan's biographer argues that the secretary had determined that total responsibility for the loss of the northern half of Oregon was about to rest at his feet. He hesitated only because he was confident that his opposition would not affect the progress toward settlement of the dispute but would save him from the brunt of the anticipated attack for capitulation.[59]

Whatever underlay the Buchanan switch, his new position held steady throughout the drafting of the administration's message to the Senate. Buchanan, on June 8, refused for a second time to help draft the message. The president, at his rope's end with Buchanan, accused him of working at cross purposes, shirking his duties, and deliberately attempting to make an issue with his president. Buchanan was "struck to the heart" by this last accusation and tried to mend the emotion-charged complication. Nevertheless, still complaining about the message the following day, Buchanan took the draft aside for about an hour and returned with an edited version. This, too, the cabinet rejected. Polk seized control of the meeting and worked out a compromise draft which he had delivered with the British offer to the Senate the next day. In this final draft, Polk emphasized his December position but volunteered his intention to act on the advice of a two-thirds' Senate majority. To guarantee that the Senate took appropriate action, Polk worked behind the scenes to clear the way for the treaty. The president, Pakenham keenly observed, added his stern message to the British offer only because he was certain that it would not jeopardize passage. It was hoped that the submission to the Senate would not set off yet another round of debate.[60]

Fortunately for the prospects of expeditious action, the Senate had not only exhausted the Oregon issue but now also had to contend with a war with Mexico. As a result, the long-delayed struggle over the Oregon Question expended only a few hours of Senate time over three days. Not even the inclusion of McLane's recommendation that a modified proposal placing a limit on the navigation of the Columbia River elicited new discussion. Pakenham assured key senators that navigation of the river would not extend beyond the life of the Hudson's Bay Company's charter. There was no passion for prolonging the dispute over what appeared to be an inconsequential point. Allen failed in his last-gasp attempt to have the issue abducted by committee or hindered by amendment.[61]

After the Senate resolution recommended acceptance of the British proposal, Pakenham joined Buchanan in drafting a treaty reflecting the recent events. It must have been an easy task, since Pakenham reported that they did not alter "a single word" of the Foreign Office proposal. The boundary delineating British and U.S. territory in the Northwest would continue westward from the previously established line of 49 degrees at the Rocky Mountains to the middle of the channel separating Vancouver Island from the continent. The line would then turn south and track the middle of the Juan de Fuca Strait to the Pacific. South of the 49th parallel this waterway would "remain free and open to both parties." On the issue of navigation, the final treaty language stated that the Columbia River from the intersection of the 49th parallel with the "great northern branch shall be free and open to the Hudson's Bay Company, and to all British subjects trading with the same" to the Pacific. This section of the second article of the treaty assured its acceptance by the Foreign Office by meeting Aberdeen's honor-saving desideratum.[62]

On June 15, Polk quickly forwarded the treaty back to the Senate, where some of the westerners took another jab at the agreement. After Allen failed to attach an amendment proclaiming that the treaty forfeited U.S. territory, he expressed his indignation by stepping down as chairman of the Foreign Relations Committee. Before emotions could stir up the debate, however, Benton made his senior presence felt by curtailing his longtime Anglophobia and lauding the generosity of Britain's offer. The British, he declared, had legitimate claims to all the area between the Columbia and the 49th parallel. It was not unreasonable, therefore, that they considered navigation of the river only modest compensation for their release of the entire disputed territory to the United States. With America at war with Mexico and the nation's economy demanding peaceable commerce, Benton saw no profit in drawing out the

Oregon dispute. His colleagues agreed. On June 18 the Senate endorsed the Oregon Treaty by a 41-to-14 margin.[63]

Ironically, McLane remained convinced that the negotiations were not ending but just beginning. The American minister believed that he had uprooted his family and interrupted his business to go to London for one purpose—to settle the Oregon dispute. If this latest attempt proved unsuccessful, it would probably mean the failure of his mission. He was afraid that the war with Mexico would delay or derail the Oregon negotiations. The British, he reported to Washington, saw the Mexican War as a prelude to an Anglo-American conflict. Any military forces fielded for the war in the Southwest, they feared, would ultimately be turned on Britain. Further, some London circles speculated that U.S. conquest of the Southwest would encourage Polk to pursue his Oregon folly. In fact, the *Morning Chronicle* conjectured, there was every reason to believe that the voracious Americans would absorb both California and Canada. British arms, McLane reported, were en route to Canada to prepare for such an eventuality.[64]

Contrary to the recommendations of his previous despatch, McLane now warned that Washington should accept the offer and that it would be dangerous to delay with a counterproposal. If the Mexican War went badly, Britain might launch a preemptive assault on the United States out of Canada. Besides, McLane fretted, the Peel ministry could fall at any moment with the expected repeal of the Corn Laws. The American minister was so concerned over this last point that he asked Aberdeen if repeal might be delayed until the next packet brought news from the United States. Perhaps, McLane confided, a treaty would be among the correspondence from Washington. Obviously, Aberdeen could do little more with this unorthodox suggestion than to promise to pass it on to Peel and to assure McLane that a new Whig government under Russell would support the settlement now that it was on track. Lord Clarendon had recently confirmed for the foreign secretary that a new government would accept the Oregon Treaty. But McLane's concern was understandable. With the certain prospects of a Palmerston Foreign Office coming in with a Whig government, nothing would calm McLane short of a signed and accepted treaty.[65]

On June 29 the long-awaited news of the treaty reached Whitehall. The timing was crucial. The treaty arrived concurrent with the repeal of the Corn Laws, the resignation of the Peel ministry, and the creation of a Whig government under Russell. Approximately two weeks later, McLane made the formal exchange of the

Oregon Treaty with Lord Palmerston at the Foreign Office. It must have satisfied McLane that the loudest critic of the Ashburton capitulation had no choice but to relinquish Oregon.[66]

In the autumn the news of the treaty finally reached the territory. Despite the propaganda that had permeated the debate, the Oregon settlers responded favorably and with a certain amount of relief. Although they would not enjoy a contiguous wilderness north to Alaska, their birthright as U.S. citizens in the Pacific Northwest was secured. This was indeed cause for celebration. The local newspaper, the *Spectator,* reported that "the only piece of ordnance owned . . . by the territory—a twelve-pounder . . . was quickly mounted upon the rocks" overlooking the river and fired in salute. The bursts were "the loudest and the rejoicing echoes of the hills of the Willamette the longest, that the patriotic could wish to hear."[67]

Afterword

> We are two people, but we are of one family. We have fought, but
> we have been reconciled.
>
> —London *Times*, January 1846

While the hills of the Columbia River Country resonated with the celebratory salutes to the peaceful resolution of the Oregon dispute, the rumble of artillery in the Southwest signaled the failure of diplomacy in that region. Characters such as Charles Wilkes and Stephen Kearny had colored the narrative of America's northern adventures, and now they reappeared in the Mexican War in pursuit of expansion not by exploration or negotiation but by the sword. In the autumn of 1846, General Winfield Scott, who had been dispatched on more than one occasion to preserve the peace on the northern frontier, was issued command of troops to conduct war on the southern border. America's destiny now advanced by force of arms.

As clumsy as President Polk had been with his administration's foreign policy, his timing was nearly providential. In the spring he had concluded the Oregon Treaty and mobilized congressional efforts at tariff reform (achieved in the summer) at precisely the same moment that hostilities erupted with Mexico. These fortuitous actions helped to neutralize appeals from the Mexican minister to London, Tomás Murphy, and pressure from Lord Ellenborough and others in Peel's cabinet to protect California from American intrusion. Although tempting schemes were presented to British Minister George Bankhead in Mexico City that would have increased London's influence, Aberdeen prevailed upon Her Majesty's Government to choose rapprochement with the United States.

Forces on both sides of the Atlantic had worked for years to erase the memory of two bitter wars and counter a steady barrage of acrimonious rhetoric. Since Richard Pakenham's cousin Edward's body had been ingloriously pickled in a rum barrel following General Andrew Jackson's victory at the Battle of New Orleans in 1815, the efforts of statesmen had yielded promising results. In 1817, Richard Rush and Charles Bagot reduced the risk of altercation on

265

the Great Lakes, reflecting Lord Castlereagh's tacit acceptance of the growing power of the United States in North America. In the following year, in the friendly confines of Castlereagh's country cottage in Kent, diplomats sorted out a host of outstanding issues that included a portion of the disputed U.S.-Canadian border. During the 1820s even the implacable George Canning acknowledged America's position in the Western Hemisphere by inviting Washington to join London in opposing European schemes to restore Spain's Latin American colonies. Likewise, the bitterly Anglophobic President Andrew Jackson accepted the mutual benefits of Anglo-American trade and had his minister to London, Louis McLane, negotiate a reciprocity treaty in 1830. An abolitionist movement in Britain, a separatist movement in Canada, and the just plain movement of Americans to the "shared" Oregon Territory, however, exposed the frailty of the Anglo-American accord. When the powerful ingredients of national honor and manifest destiny joined the mix, a violent reaction seemed probable.

Upon his arrival at Whitehall in 1841, Aberdeen faced a stack of unresolved differences with the United States that ranged from maritime disputes to border crises. These problems needed the utmost attention because they involved more than appearances indicated. Beneath the squabbles over the *Caroline*, the *Creole*, the McLeod affair, the African slave trade, and, most vexing of all, the northern border lay a sensitive and sometimes raw nerve called national honor. The United States believed that it had earned the respect of its former imperial master and had determined to hold the high ground in the face of traditional British disdain. The crown, likewise, had to protect national honor against the impertinent assault of the young American republic. When the diplomats met in 1842 and in fits and starts over the next four years, their task was difficult and their responsibility great: any misstep might have turned a budding relationship into another costly war.

Astute diplomacy, sometimes at the eleventh hour and frequently in opposition to powerful forces, not only arrested the unraveling of Anglo-American relations but also repaired and strengthened the relationship in the process. Webster and Ashburton adroitly maneuvered sensitivities in the North and South and manipulated facts and finances to delineate the Maine-New Brunswick border and resolve the slave trade and maritime controversies. Their accomplishment, branded capitulation by opponents, edged rapprochement forward. Over the following four years, however, America's grand designs in the West ran headlong into Britain's long-held desire to contain the Americans and legitimize its own interests in the Pacific. Once again, honor became the central issue as the Jacksonians regained the White House with Young Hickory and challenged the British in the Pacific Northwest. But in the midst of war talk that threatened "Fifty-four Forty or Fight," diplomats returned to negotiation. Overcoming Polk's recalcitrance combined with Democratic electioneering, the two Atlantic nations secured a compromise that preserved honor for both sides, granted to the United States essential harbors and settlements in the Oregon Territory, cleared the way for the war with Mexico, and firmly established the preference for rapprochement. The economic interdependence of the two English-speaking nations had convinced both peoples that their interests ran parallel.

Although the crown had not forsaken hopes of restraining America's expansion and would keep a vigilant eye on its adventures in the Caribbean, the British concessions along the U.S.-Canadian boundary and subsequent neutrality in the Mexican War indicated acceptance of a continental United States and the failure of containment. Settlement of the border crises of the 1840s by the Webster-Ashburton and Oregon treaties strengthened the Atlantic relationship and, in so doing, provided the United States with the essential prologue to manifest destiny.

Notes

Chapter 1: The Search for National Honor, 1–20

1. "The United States," *Blackwood's Edinburgh Magazine* (London) [n.d.], 814–23.

2. Myron F. Brightfield, *John Wilson Croker* (Berkeley, 1940), 393–95.

3. Frank Thistlethwaite, *America and the Atlantic Community: Anglo-American Aspects, 1790–1850* (New York, 1963), 9, 11–12; H. C. Allen, *Conflict and Concord: The Anglo-American Relationship since 1783* (New York, 1959), 58–60; Charles S. Campbell, *From Revolution to Rapprochement: The United States and Great Britain, 1783–1900* (New York, 1974), 52.

4. Hunter Miller, ed., *Treaties and Other International Acts of the United States of America, 1776–1863,* 8 vols. (Washington, DC, 1931–1948), 2:152.

5. For a discussion of the northeastern boundary issue from 1783 through the mid-1830s see Howard Jones, *To the Webster-Ashburton Treaty: A Study in Anglo-American Relations, 1783–1843* (Chapel Hill, 1977), 3–19.

6. Alfred L. Burt, *The United States, Great Britain, and British North America from the Revolution to the Establishment of Peace after the War of 1812* (New Haven, 1940), 71, 165, 423–26; Samuel F. Bemis, *Jay's Treaty: A Study in Commerce and Diplomacy* (New York, 1923), 320; Bradford Perkins, *The First Rapprochement: England and the United States, 1795–1805* (Berkeley, 1955), 48–49; George Dangerfield, *The Era of Good Feelings* (New York, 1952), 64–65, 368; Bradford Perkins, *Castlereagh and Adams: England and the United States, 1812–1823* (Berkeley, 1964), 104n.4; Samuel F. Bemis, *John Quincy Adams and the Foundations of American Foreign Policy* (New York, 1949), 215; Fred L. Engelman, *The Peace of Christmas Eve* (New York, 1960), 231, 246, 262, 263, 266–79, 299; *American State Papers, Foreign Relations*, 6 vols. (Washington, DC, 1832–1859), 5:50–51 (hereafter cited as *ASPFR*); Kenneth Bourne, *Britain and the Balance of Power in North America, 1815–1908* (Berkeley, 1967), 59, 60; Henry S. Burrage, *Maine in the Northeastern Boundary Controversy* (Portland, 1919), 108, 111.

7. Bemis, *Adams and Foundations*, 471–72; John T. Faris, *The Romance of the Boundaries* (New York, 1926), 48; John B. Moore, *History and Digest of the International Arbitrations to Which the United States Has Been a Party*, 6 vols. (Washington, DC, 1898), 1:80–82, 112; Bourne, *Balance of Power*, 60.

8. Moore, *International Arbitrations*, 1:132–36; Miller, ed., *Treaties*, 3:359–69. President John Quincy Adams objected to William I because he was a cousin of the king of England and an honorary general in the British army. But, in June 1828, Adams finally agreed to the appointment. Bemis, *Adams and Foundations*, 472, 475, 477–78; Jones, *Webster-Ashburton Treaty*, 13.

9. Burrage, *Maine*, 174, 195–96, 198, 199, 201, 204, 206; Gallatin to Henry Clay, Oct. 30, 1826, *ASPFR*, 6:649; Moore, *International Arbitrations*, 1:138–

39; Frederick Merk, *Fruits of Propaganda in the Tyler Administration* (Cambridge, 1976), 50–51.

10. Burrage, *Maine*, 210–11, 215; Merk, *Fruits of Propaganda*, 51.

11. Robert Dunlap to Forsyth, July 3, 1837, William R. Manning, ed., *Diplomatic Correspondence of the United States. Canadian Relations, 1784–1860*, 4 vols. (Washington, DC, 1940–1945), 3:29n.3 (hereafter cited as *DCUSCR*); MacLauchlan to Sir John Harvey, June 10, 1837, ibid., 27–28n.3; Harvey to Dunlap, June 12, 1837, ibid., 28n.3; Charles Peters to Harvey, June 5, 1837, Great Britain, Parliament, *British Sessional Papers, 1801–1900*, 39 (1837–38): 57 (hereafter cited as *HCSP*); New Brunswick solicitor general to Harvey, Sept. 5, 1837, ibid., 68; Thomas C. Hansard, ed., *Hansard's Parliamentary Debates*, 3d series, 356 vols., London, 1830–1891, 38:251 (hereafter cited as *Parl. Debates*); Report to Maine's land agent, May 7, 1838, *HCSP* 32 (1840): 49–50; Elijah Hamlin to Fairfield and council, Jan. 22, 1839, William S. Jenkins, ed., *Records of the States of the United States, 1836–41. Maine: Legislative Records, Journal of the State of Maine, Appendix* [Joint meeting of House and Senate] (Washington, DC, 1949), 19 Legis., 1–33; Fairfield's message to assembly, Jan. 4, 1839, ibid., 35–53; Fairfield's confidential message to assembly, Jan. 23, 1839, ibid., 56–58. See also Jones, *Webster-Ashburton Treaty*, 33–47; Howard Jones, "Anglophobia and the Aroostook War," *New England Quarterly* 48 (Dec. 1975): 519–39; Thomas LeDuc, "The Maine Frontier and the Northeastern Boundary Controversy," *American Historical Review* 53 (Oct. 1947): 30–41; and Burrage, *Maine*, 258–62.

12. Harvey to Fox, Feb. 13, 1839, Great Britain, Foreign Office, America, United States, Public Record Office, Kew, 5/331 (hereafter cited as FO, PRO); Proclamation by Harvey, Feb. 13, 1839, ibid.; MacLauchlan to Harvey, Jan. 17, 1839, New Brunswick, Dispatches, Public Archives of Canada, Ottawa (hereafter cited as N.B., Disp., PAC); *Whig* (Bangor) [n.d.], cited in David Lowenthal, "The Maine Press and the Aroostook War," *Canadian Historical Review* 32 (Dec. 1951): 315–36; Burrage, *Maine*, 259–60; John F. Sprague, "The North Eastern Boundary Controversy and the Aroostook War," *Historical Collections of Piscataquis County, Maine* (Dover, ME, 1910), 216–81.

13. Harvey to Fairfield, Feb. 13, 1839, *HCSP* 32 (1840): 38; Sprague, "North Eastern Boundary," 274; *Whig* (Bangor), Feb. 17, 1839, cited ibid., n.*; *Advertiser* (Portland) [n.d.], quoted in *Journal* (Augusta), April 9, 1839; Jarvis to Harvey, Feb. 19, 1839, N.B., Disp., PAC; Fairfield's special message to house, Feb. 15, 1839, Jenkins, ed., *Records . . . Maine: Journal of Senate, Append.*, 19 Legis., 61–63; Fairfield's message to assembly, Feb. 18, 1839, ibid., 63–67; *Herald* (New York), Feb. 20, 1839; Fairfield to Everett, Feb. 18, 1839, Jenkins, ed., *Records . . . Maine: Executive Records*, 104–5; Fairfield to Van Buren, Feb. 18, 19, 1839, ibid., 115–19; Fairfield to Harvey, Feb. 19, 1839, ibid., 106–10; Jenkins, ed., *Records . . . Maine: Journal of Lower House*, 19 Legis., 265 (Feb. 18, 1839); ibid., *Journal of Senate*, 19 Legis., 273–74 (Feb. 19, 1839); Burrage, *Maine*, 260–63. For the long roster of men called to military duty see *Aroostook War: Historical Sketch and Roster of Commissioned Officers and Enlisted Men Called into Service for the Protection of the Northeastern Frontier of Maine. From February to May, 1839* (Augusta, ME, 1904).

14. *Royal Gazette* (New Brunswick), March 6, 1839; *Observer* (St. John), Feb. 19, 1839, cited in *Gleaner* (Miramichi, New Brunswick), Feb. 26, 1839; *Herald* (St. John), March 13, 1839, cited in *Gleaner*, March 19, 1839; Col. A. Maxwell's address to New Brunswick militia, cited in *Gleaner*, March 5, 1839; *Sentinel* (Fredericton), Feb. 16, 1839, quoted in *Gleaner*, Feb. 26, 1839; *Times* (London), March 20, 1839; *Morning Herald* (London), March 21, 1839, cited in

Gleaner, April 30, 1839; Deposition of Nicholas Cunliffe, Feb. 16, 1839, N.B., Disp., PAC; Sir John Colborne to Harvey, Feb. 18, 22, 1839, N.B., Disp., PAC; Sir Colin Campbell to Harvey, Feb. 27, 1839, ibid.; Maxwell to Harvey, March 7, 1839, ibid.; MacLauchlan to Harvey, Feb. 27, 1839, ibid.; Joseph Sherwood to Harvey, Feb. 18, 26, March 2, 1839, ibid.; Colborne to Campbell, Feb. 27, 1839, FO 5/331, PRO; Colborne to Harvey, Feb. 27, 1839, ibid.

15. Fairfield to Van Buren, Feb. 19, 1839, Jenkins, ed., *Records . . . Maine: Executive Records*, 118–19; Fairfield to Harvey, Feb. 21, 1839, ibid., 114–15; Harvey to Fairfield, Feb. 18, 1839, *HCSP* 32 (1840): 43; Fairfield's message to house, Feb. 21, 1839, ibid., 42; Harvey to Lord Glenelg, Feb. 24, 1839, ibid., 161; Sprague, "North Eastern Boundary," 275–76; Albert B. Corey, *The Crisis of 1830–1842 in Canadian-American Relations* (New Haven, 1941), 114–15.

16. *Sun* (Pittsfield, MA), March 28, 1839; letter of Feb. 26, 1839, cited in Lowenthal, "Maine Press," 321; Leonard B. Chapman, ed., "Rev. Caleb Bradley on the Madawaska War," *Collections and Proceedings of the Maine Historical Society*, 2d ser., 9 (Portland, 1898): 418–25.

17. *Whig* (Bangor) [n.d.], cited in Sprague, "North Eastern Boundary," 275; *Republican* (Belfast) [n.d.], cited in Lowenthal, "Maine Press," 323; *Southwick's Family Paper*, March 17, 1839, cited ibid., 329; *Journal* (Augusta), Feb. 19, 26, 1839; Fairfield's speech, ibid., March 5, 1839; *Age* (Augusta) [n.d.], cited ibid.; *Courier* (Northampton, MA), Feb. 27, 1839; "Maine Battle Song" in "Documentary History of the North Eastern Boundary Controversy," *Historical Collections of Piscataquis County, Maine* (Dover, ME, 1910), 282–327.

18. *Sun* (Pittsfield), March 7, 28, 1839.

19. U.S., Congress, *Congressional Globe*, 25 Cong., 3 sess., 216–19 (hereafter cited as *CG*); J. C. Bennett of Illinois militia to Fairfield, [?] 1839, in Arthur G. Staples, ed., *The Letters of John Fairfield* (Lewiston, ME, 1922), 253; S. T. Carr of New York to Fairfield, [?] 1839, ibid.; *Advertiser* (Boston), Feb. 21, 1839, *Albion* (New York), Feb. 23, 1839, *Commercial Advertiser* (New York), Feb. 21, 22, 1839, *Gazette* (New York), March 5, 1839, all cited in *Royal Gazette* (New Brunswick), March 27, 1839; *Enquirer* (Richmond), March 2, 1839; *Courier* (Northampton, MA), March 20, 1839; *Advertiser* (Boston) [n.d.], cited in *Gleaner* (Miramichi, New Brunswick), March 26, 1839; *Patriot* (Boston), March 16, 1839, cited in Lowenthal, "Maine Press," 329; *National Intelligencer*, Feb. 24, 1839; *Herald* (New York), Feb. 25, March 1, 1839.

20. Fairfield to Van Buren, Feb. 22, 1839, Martin Van Buren Papers, Library of Congress, Washington, DC (hereafter cited as Van Buren Papers); Lowenthal, "Maine Press," 327–36; James C. Curtis, *The Fox at Bay: Martin Van Buren and the Presidency, 1837–1841* (Lexington, KY, 1970), 184–85.

21. Forsyth to Fox, Feb. 25, 1839, Department of State, Notes to Foreign Legations in the United States from the Department of State, 1834–1906, Great Britain, National Archives, Washington, DC (hereafter cited as NTFL, GB, NA); Forsyth to Fairfield, Feb. 26, 1839, *HCSP* 32 (1840), 41; James D. Richardson, ed., *A Compilation of the Messages and Papers of the Presidents*, 11 vols. (New York, 1896–1910), 3:517, 518; *CG, App.*, 25 Cong., 3 sess., 211, 213, 260, 312, 315, 316; *CG*, 25 Cong., 3 sess., 229, 231, 233, 239, 242; Fox to Palmerston, March 7, Aug. 10, 1839, FO 115/69, PRO; Curtis, *Fox at Bay*, 184–85; Burrage, *Maine*, 265–66; Claude M. Fuess, *Daniel Webster*, 2 vols. (Boston, 1930), 2:72.

22. *CG*, 25 Cong., 3 sess., 229, 232, 238, 242; Palmerston to Fox, May 1, 1839, *HCSP* 32 (1840), 80; Burrage, *Maine*, 266–67. Forsyth had first recommended Webster for the position as special minister to Britain, but Democrats in Van Buren's party staunchly opposed the choice. Webster called for a

compromise. See his "Memorandum on northeastern boundary, 9 March 1839," Charles M. Wiltse, ed., Daniel Webster Papers, Dartmouth College, Hanover, New Hampshire (F12/15393) [hereafter cited as WP]; Reuel Williams et al. to Van Buren, March 9, 18, 1839, Van Buren Papers; George Evans of Maine to Van Buren, March 20, 1839, ibid.; Fairfield to Van Buren, March 22, 1839, ibid.; Isaac Hill on Webster for English mission, March 21, 1839, ibid.; memorandum by Van Buren, [?] March 1839, ibid.; H. J. Anderson to Van Buren, April 6, 1839, ibid.; and Fox to Palmerston, Feb. 23, March 7, May 16, 1839, FO 115/69, PRO.

23. Richardson, ed., *Messages and Papers*, 3:526, 527; memorandum by Fox and Forsyth, Feb. 27, 1839, in Department of State, folder marked "NE. Bdry. Negot.," E89, NA; Fox to Harvey, Feb. 27, 1839, FO 5/331, PRO; Palmerston to Fox, April 6, 1839, Palmerston Papers, General Correspondence, FO 168/1–2, University of Southampton, Southampton, England (hereafter cited as Palmerston Papers, GC); Fox to Palmerston, March 7, 1839, FO 115/69, PRO; Lowenthal, "Maine Press," 329.

24. Poinsett to Scott, Feb. 28, 1839, *DCUSCR*, 3:108; Winfield Scott, *Memoirs of Lieut.-General Scott, LL.D., Written by Himself*, 2 vols. (New York, 1864), 2:333–34.

25. Col. A. Maxwell to Harvey, Feb. 26, 1839, N.B., Disp., PAC; "Statement of Melvin House," 1839, ibid.; Lowenthal, "Maine Press," 323, 333.

26. Scott, *Memoirs*, 2:334, 336–40; Maine senator's speech quoted in Charles W. Elliott, *Winfield Scott, The Soldier and the Man* (New York, 1937), 360.

27. Burrage, *Maine*, 271–72.

28. Curtis, *Fox at Bay*, 186; Burrage, *Maine*, 273–74; Scott, *Memoirs*, 2:336–45; Elliott, *Winfield Scott*, 362–65.

29. Scott to Harvey, March 21, 1839, *HCSP* 32 (1840), 164; "Documentary History," 322–23; Fairfield's message to assembly, March 12, 1839, in Jenkins, ed., *Records . . . Maine: Journal of Senate, Append.*, 19 Legis., 70–86; Harvey to Fox, March 6, 1839, FO 5/331, PRO; Marcus T. Wright, *General Scott* (New York, 1894), 143–44.

30. Fox to Palmerston, March 7, April 20, Aug. 10, Sept. 28, 1839, FO 115/69, PRO; Richard Rush to Van Buren, April 14, 1840, Van Buren Papers; Benjamin Rush to Forsyth, Oct. 16, 1839, *DCUSCR*, 3:540–41; Francis P. Wayland, *Andrew Stevenson: Democrat and Diplomat, 1785–1857* (Philadelphia, 1949), 144; Herbert C. F. Bell, *Lord Palmerston*, 2 vols. (London, 1936), 1:251, 252.

31. Forsyth to Fox, July 29, Dec. 24, 1839, March 25, 1840, NTFL, GB, NA; Aaron Vail to Fox, Aug. 19, 1839, ibid.; Jenkins, ed., *Records . . . Maine: Journal of Senate*, 19 Legis., 433–36 (March 21, 1839); Harvey memorandum for warden of disputed territory, Aug. 30, 1839, *HCSP* 32 (1840): 95; Palmerston to Fox, Oct. 14, 1839, ibid., 94; Fairfield to Vail, Nov. 21, 1839, ibid., 141–43; Instructions to British survey team in Palmerston to Fox, July 9, 1839, ibid., 85; British surveyors' report, April 16, 1840, ibid., 56–57; Palmerston to Melbourne, April 22, 1840, ibid., 61 (1843), 18; Fox to Forsyth, Jan. 26, March 7, July 28, 1840, *DCUSCR*, 3:553–55, 559–61, 582–87; Fox to Vail, July 30, 1839, ibid., 519–20; James Stephen to Lord Teveson, Aug. 30, 1841, FO 5/374, PRO; Williams, C. S. Daveis, Fairfield, and Kent to Forsyth, June 19, 1839, in "NE. Bdry. Negot."; Forsyth to Van Buren, June 20, 1839, ibid.; Fox to Palmerston, April 20, Sept. 28, 1839, FO 115/69, PRO; Fairfield to Van Buren, Dec. 23, 1839, in Jenkins, ed., *Records . . . Maine: Executive Records*, 141–43; Bourne, *Balance of Power*, 84n.2, 85; Bell, *Lord Palmerston*, 1:251; Alvin L. Duckett, *John Forsyth: Political Tactician* (Athens, GA, 1962), 205.

32. MacLauchlan to officer in charge of American armed posse on Fish River, April 21, 1839, N.B., Disp., PAC; Lord Sydenham to Russell, March 13, Nov. 24, Dec. 20, 1840, in Paul Knaplund, ed., *Letters from Lord Sydenham, Governor-General of Canada, 1839–1841, to Lord John Russell* (London, 1931), 52–53, 102, 108; Palmerston to Russell, Jan. 19, 1841, Lord John Russell Papers, PRO, Kew (hereafter cited as Russell Papers).

Chapter 2: Remember the Caroline! 21–41

1. On the *Caroline* affair see Howard Jones, "The *Caroline* Affair," *The Historian* 38 (May 1976): 485–502; Jones, *Webster-Ashburton Treaty*, 20–32; and Kenneth R. Stevens, *Border Diplomacy: The Caroline and McLeod Affairs in Anglo-American-Canadian Relations, 1837–1842* (Tuscaloosa, 1989), 1–41.

2. Reginald C. Stuart, *United States Expansionism and British North America, 1775–1871* (Chapel Hill, 1988), 131–32; *North American Review*, cited in Corey, *Crisis of 1830–1842*, 15, 16.

3. R. A. Mackay, "The Political Ideals of William Lyon Mackenzie," *Canadian Journal of Economics and Political Science* 3 (Feb. 1937): 1–22; Augustus N. Hand, "Local Incidents of the Papineau Rebellion," *New York History* 15 (Oct. 1934): 376–87.

4. Edwin C. Guillet, *The Lives and Times of the Patriots: An Account of the Rebellion in Upper Canada, 1837–1838, and of the Patriot Agitation in the United States, 1837–1842* (Toronto, 1968; originally published in 1938), 132; Edgar W. McInnis, *The Unguarded Frontier: A History of American-Canadian Relations* (Garden City, NY, 1942), 150; Orrin E. Tiffany, "The Relations of the United States to the Canadian Rebellion of 1837–38," *Buffalo Historical Society Publications* 8 (1905): 1–147; Chester W. New, "The Rebellion of 1837 in Its Larger Setting," *Canadian Historical Association, Report, 1937*, 5–17; D. G. Creighton, "The Economic Background of the Rebellions of Eighteen Thirty-Seven," *Canadian Journal of Economics and Political Science* 3 (Aug. 1937): 322–34; Wilson P. Shortridge, "The Canadian-American Frontier during the Rebellion of 1837–1838," *Canadian Historical Review* 7 (March 1926): 13–26; Corey, *Crisis of 1830–1842*, 34–35; R. S. Longley, "Emigration and the Crisis of 1837 in Upper Canada, 1837–1842," *Canadian Historical Review* 17 (March 1936): 29–40.

5. *Argus* (Albany), Dec. 9, 1837; *National Intelligencer*, April 11, Dec. 5, 7, 1837.

6. Richardson, ed., *Messages and Papers*, 3:485–87; C. P. Stacey, ed., "A Private Report of General Winfield Scott on the Border Situation in 1839," *Canadian Historical Review* 21 (Dec. 1940): 407–14; *CG*, 25 Cong., 2 sess., 77, 78, 83, 248–49; Curtis, *Fox at Bay*, 171; John K. Mahon, *History of the Second Seminole War, 1835–1842* (Gainesville, FL, 1967), 225–26. On Van Buren see also Robert V. Remini, *Martin Van Buren and the Making of the Democratic Party* (New York, 1970); John Niven, *Martin Van Buren: The Romantic Age of American Politics* (New York, 1983); Donald B. Cole, *Martin Van Buren and the American Political System* (Princeton, NJ, 1984); and Major L. Wilson, *The Presidency of Martin Van Buren* (Lawrence, KS, 1984).

7. Stevens, *Border Diplomacy*, 8, 9–10; William Kilbourn, *The Firebrand: William Lyon Mackenzie and the Rebellion in Upper Canada* (Toronto, 1956), 10–11, 13.

8. Head to Fox, Dec. 23, 1837, Colonial Office, Public Archives of Canada, Ottawa (hereafter cited as CO, PAC); Head to Fox, Jan. 8, 1838, FO 881/9, PRO;

Deposition of John Elmsley, Nov. 27, 1841, Department of State, Despatches from U.S. Ministers to Great Britain, 1791–1906, National Archives, Washington, DC (hereafter cited as Desp., GB, NA); Head to MacNab, Dec. 21, 1837, Sir Allan MacNab Papers, Albemarle Manuscripts, Public Archives of Canada, Ottawa (hereafter cited as MacNab Papers); *Niles' Register* 53 (Jan. 27, 1838): 337; Guillet, *Lives and Times of the Patriots*, 73; Stevens, *Border Diplomacy*, 10, 11, 21.

9. Shepard McCormack to MacNab, [?] 1838, MacNab Papers; Forsyth to Stevenson, March 12, 1838, *DCUSCR*, 3:48; Head to Fox, Jan. 8, 10, 1838, FO 5/328A, PRO; Deposition of William Merritt, April 19, 1838, encl. in Palmerston to Stevenson, Aug. 27, 1841, Desp., GB, NA; Stevens, *Border Diplomacy*, 10–11.

10. Deposition of Wells, Dec. 30, 1837, U.S. Congress, *House Exec. Docs.*, 25 Cong., 2 sess., 46; Stevens, *Border Diplomacy*, 13.

11. Deposition of Wells, Dec. 30, 1837; Jones, *Webster-Ashburton Treaty*, 23.

12. Elmsley to MacNab, Dec. 29, 1837, *DCUSCR*, 3:421; MacNab to Drew, Dec. 29, 1837, ibid.; MacNab to Rogers, Dec. 29, 1837, FO 881/9, PRO; Jones, *Webster-Ashburton Treaty*, 23, 29; Stevens, *Border Diplomacy*, 11, 13.

13. Stevens, *Border Diplomacy*, 13, 14; Guillet, *Lives and Times of the Patriots*, 79.

14. Drew's report to MacNab, Dec. 30, 1837, FO 881/9, PRO; Stevens, *Border Diplomacy*, 14. Since the area had only one hotel, twenty-three people had been allowed to take lodging on the *Caroline* along with its officer and nine crew members.

15. Stevens, *Border Diplomacy*, 14, 15, 146.

16. John C. Dent, *The Story of the Upper Canadian Rebellion; Largely Derived from Original Sources and Documents*, 2 vols. (Toronto, 1885), 2:214; Drew to Sir John Barrow, Jan. 1, 1838, FO 5/328A, PRO; statement of claims for losses of *Caroline*, Dec. 30, 1837, *House Exec. Docs.*, 25 Cong., 2 sess., 61; Milledge L. Bonham, Jr., "Alexander McLeod: Bone of Contention," *New York History* 18 (April 1937): 189–217; Guillet, *Lives and Times of the Patriots*, 71–87.

17. Deposition of Samuel Longley, Dec. 30, 1837, *House Exec. Docs.*, 25 Cong., 2 sess., 19; Appleby to New York grand jury, ibid., 34; other depositions encl. in Palmerston to Stevenson, Aug. 27, 1841, Desp., GB, NA; Forsyth to Stevenson, March 12, 1838, *DCUSCR*, 3:49.

18. *Niles' Register* 53 (Jan. 20, 1838): 323; *National Intelligencer*, Jan. 5, 1838; *Republican* (Rochester), Jan. 2, 1838; *Argus* (Albany), Jan. 3, 1838; *Star Extra* (Buffalo) [n.d.], quoted in *Herald* (New York), Jan. 4, 1838; *Herald* (New York), Jan. 4, 5, 6, 1838; Guillet, *Lives and Times of the Patriots*, 80n.9; Kilbourn, *Firebrand*, 202.

19. Poem from Robert H. Ferrell, *American Diplomacy: A History* (New York, 1959; 3d ed., 1975), 207; New Yorker quoted in Stevens, *Border Diplomacy*, 16.

20. "Minutes of the Niagara Sessions relative to the murder on board the *Caroline*," Jan. 25, 1838, FO 881/9, PRO; Rogers to Van Buren, Dec. 30, 1837, *DCUSCR*, 3:456; *Herald* (New York), Jan. 9, 16, 1838; *National Intelligencer*, Jan. 19, 1838; Head to MacNab, Jan. 1, 1838, MacNab Papers; Stevens, *Border Diplomacy*, 20; Guillett, *Lives and Times of the Patriots*, 80n.10.

21. Jacob Gould to Van Buren, Jan. 8, 1838, Van Buren Papers; *Herald* (New York), Jan. 5, 8, 1838.

22. *Herald* (New York), Jan. 4, 5, 16, 1838.

23. Scott, *Memoirs*, 1:307.

24. Jones, *Webster-Ashburton Treaty*, 27; Stevens, *Border Diplomacy*, 12, 27.

25. Thomas Hart Benton, *Thirty Years' View; or, A History of the American Government for Thirty Years from 1820 to 1850*, 2 vols. (New York, 1856), 2:280–81, 293; MacNab to Col. J. M. Strachan, Jan. 1, 1838, FO 881/9, PRO; *CG*, 25 Cong., 2 sess., 76–78, 82–83, 87, 248–49.

26. Jones, *Webster-Ashburton Treaty*, 28; Stevens, *Border Diplomacy*, 27–28.

27. Forsyth to Fox, Jan. 5, 1838, NTFL, GB, NA; Stevens, *Border Diplomacy*, 19; Jones, *Webster-Ashburton Treaty*, 28.

28. Fox to Forsyth, Feb. 6, 1838, Department of State, Notes from the British Legation in the United States to the Department of State, 1791–1906, National Archives, Washington, DC (hereafter cited as NFBL, NA); Law officers' opinion, Feb. 21, 1838, in FO 881/9, PRO; Fox to Palmerston, Feb. 25, 1838, Jan. 26, 1841, FO 5/322 and FO 115/69, PRO; Stevens, *Border Diplomacy*, 25.

29. Stevens, *Border Diplomacy*, 22–23, 24–25.

30. Forsyth to Fox, Feb. 13, 1838, NTFL, GB, NA; Forsyth to Stevenson, March 12, 1838, *DCUSCR*, 3:50–51.

31. Stevenson to Palmerston, May 22, 1838, *DCUSCR*, 3:449–56.

32. Lord Glenelg to Palmerston, [June?] 1838, CO 537/139, PAC; Sir George Arthur to Glenelg, Dec. 17, 1838, FO 5/339, PRO; Head to MacNab, Jan. 1, 1838, MacNab Papers. Palmerston instructed Fox to declare that "the attack upon the *Caroline* was the publick Act of persons in Her Majesty's Service, and, according to the usages of nations, that proceeding can only be the subject of negotiations between the two governments, and cannot be made the ground of proceedings against individuals." Palmerston to Fox, Nov. 6, 1838, FO 5/321, PRO.

33. *Herald* (New York), Jan. 11, 1838; Scott, *Memoirs*, 1:308–17; Stacey, ed., "Private Report of Scott," 408; Curtis, *Fox at Bay*, 174–75; Elliott, *Winfield Scott*, 338–57.

34. Buffalo resident quoted in Elliott, *Winfield Scott*, 340; ibid., 338–57; Scott, *Memoirs*, 1:308–17.

35. Stevens, *Border Diplomacy*, 20–21, 36; Marcy quoted ibid., 21.

36. Jones, *Webster-Ashburton Treaty*, 31. A New York grand jury indicted Van Rensselaer, Mackenzie, and twelve other Patriots in the summer of 1838. Stevens, *Border Diplomacy*, 42.

37. Scott, *Memoirs*, 313–17; Stevens, *Border Diplomacy*, 21.

38. Stevens, *Border Diplomacy*, 37.

39. Ibid., 50–53; McInnis, *Unguarded Frontier*, 154; Corey, *Crisis of 1830–1842*, 82–90. After arriving in Quebec in early 1838, Durham sent his wife's brother, Col. Charles Grey, to Washington for the purpose of resolving these border issues. See Charles Grey to his father, June 11, 1838, in William G. Ormsby, ed., *The Grey Journals and Letters; Crisis in the Canadas, 1838–1839* (London, 1965), 32.

40. Chester W. New, *Lord Durham: A Biography of John George Lambton, First Earl of Durham* (Oxford, 1929), 378–80; C. P. Stacey, "The Myth of the Unguarded Frontier, 1815–1871," *American Historical Review* 56 (Oct. 1959): 1–18.

Chapter 3: The Strange Case of Alexander McLeod, 43–70

1. On the McLeod affair see Jones, *Webster-Ashburton Treaty*, 48–68; and Stevens, *Border Diplomacy*, 71–155.

2. *Herald* (New York), March 23, 1841.

3. Alastair Watt, "The Case of Alexander McLeod," *Canadian Historical Review* 12 (June 1931): 164,n.1; Manchester incident recounted in McLeod's letter reprinted in *Examiner* (London), Oct. 30, 1841. See also Stevens, *Border Diplomacy*, 72.

4. McLeod's memorial to Sir Charles Bagot, May 2, 1842, cited in Watt, "McLeod," 163; first Arthur quote in Stevens, *Border Diplomacy*, 73,n.5; second Arthur quote, ibid., 73,n.6; Jackson quote, ibid., 73–74,n.6. See also ibid., 73, 81.

5. Fox to Forsyth, Dec. 13, 1840, NFBL, NA; Fox to Palmerston, Dec. 27, 1840, Jan. 10, 26, 1841, FO 115/69, PRO.

6. Stevens, *Border Diplomacy*, 75–76.

7. Fox to Palmerston, Jan. 10, 1841, FO 115/69, PRO. See also Jones, *Webster-Ashburton Treaty*, 50.

8. *CG*, 26 Cong., 2 sess., 74, 80–81; Benton, *Thirty Years' View*, 2:294.

9. Edition of Dec. 21, 1840.

10. Russell to Stevenson, Feb. 2, 1841, cited in Corey, *Crisis of 1830–1842*, 137; *Parl. Debates,* 66:364–66; Fox to Palmerston, Jan. 10, 1841, FO 115/69, PRO; Palmerston to Fox, Feb. 9, 1841, Palmerston Papers, GC; Palmerston to Fox, Feb. 9, 1841, Lord Palmerston's Letter-Books, Additional Manuscripts, British Library, London (hereafter cited as Palmerston, Letter-Books); Palmerston to Fox, Feb. 9, 1841, FO 5/358, PRO; Palmerston to William Temple, Feb. 9, 1841, in Stevens, *Border Diplomacy*, 88,n.35; Stevenson to Van Buren, Feb. 9, 1841, Van Buren Papers.

11. *Herald* (New York), Feb. 4, 10, 1841; Jones, *Webster-Ashburton Treaty,* 51–52; Stevens, *Border Diplomacy*, 81. Fox had earlier made this proposal to jump bail and Arthur welcomed it except for two considerations: posting bail would legitimize the judicial actions in New York, and forfeiting bail would be tantamount to a ransom payment. Governor-General Lord Sydenham only reluctantly supported the intentional forfeiture of bail as a way to avoid a trial, because he believed it "impossible to act with the Americans as you would do with a civilized people." Stevens, *Border Diplomacy*, 80–81.

12. Emissary quoted in Stevens, *Border Diplomacy*, 82; Fox quoted ibid.; *Times* quoted ibid.

13. Marcus T. C. Gould, *Gould's Stenographic Reporter*, 2 vols. (Washington, DC, 1841), 2:17–18 (hereafter cited as *Gould*); Stevens, *Border Diplomacy*, 80.

14. *CG*, 26 Cong., 2 sess., 171–75; U.S. Congress, *House Reports*, 26 Cong., 2 sess., 2–3, 5; *CG, App.,* 26 Cong., 2 sess., 374–75. See also Stevens, *Border Diplomacy*, 83–84; and John B. Edmunds, *Francis W. Pickens and the Politics of Destruction* (Chapel Hill, 1986), 61–63.

15. Fox to Palmerston, Feb. 7, 1841, FO 115/69, PRO; Sydenham to Russell, April 10, 1841, in Knaplund, ed., *Letters from Lord Sydenham*, 128; *Times* quoted in Stevens, *Border Diplomacy*, 86; Adams and Everett cited ibid., 85.

16. Webster's 1846 speech before Congress in James M. McIntyre, ed., *The Writings and Speeches of Daniel Webster*, 18 vols. (Boston, 1903), 9:123; Webster to Crittenden, March 15, 1841, ibid., 11:264–66; Seward's message to New York legislature, Jan. 4, 1842, in George E. Baker, ed., *The Works of William H. Seward*, 5 vols. (New York, 1884), 2:302; Harrison to Crittenden, March 15, 1841, Department of State, Domestic Letters, National Archives, Washington, DC (hereafter cited as Dom. Letters, NA). See also Stevens, *Border Diplomacy*, 94–95.

17. Critic quoted in Jones, *Webster-Ashburton Treaty*, 54; Palmerston to Queen Victoria, June 15, 1839, quoted in Bell, *Lord Palmerston*, 1:247; Webster to Thomas Ward of Baring Bros. of London, Feb. 29, 1840, Baring Papers, Public Archives of Canada, Ottawa (hereafter cited as Baring Papers); Webster to Joshua Bates of Baring Bros., March 26, 1840, ibid.; Fox to Palmerston, March 7, 1841, FO 115/69, PRO; Ralph W. Hidy, *The House of Baring in American Trade and Finance* (Cambridge, 1949), 100, 283–84, 293, 316, 320–21, 327.

18. *Times, Morning Chronicle,* and *Morning Herald* cited in Corey, *Crisis of 1830–1842,* 138–39. For Peel's speech see Russell to Queen Victoria, March 6, 1841, in Arthur C. Benson and Viscount Esher, eds., *The Letters of Queen Victoria: A Selection from Her Majesty's Correspondence Between the Years 1837 and 1861,* 3 vols. (London, 1908), 1:260. Cass to Webster, March 5, 1841, cited in George T. Curtis, *Life of Daniel Webster,* 2 vols. (New York, 1870), 2:62; John Powell to Hull, March 11, 1841, U.S. Cong., *Senate Docs.,* 27 Cong., 1 sess., no. 33, 4–5; Stevenson to Hull, March 8, 12, 1841, Desp., GB, NA; Stevenson to Webster, March 9, 18, April 7, 1841, ibid.; Joseph H. Parks, *John Bell of Tennessee* (Baton Rouge, LA, 1950), 190. See also Stevens, *Border Diplomacy,* 97–98; and Linda M. Maloney, *The Captain from Connecticut: The Life and Naval Times of Isaac Hull* (Boston, 1986), 470–76.

19. Jones, *Webster-Ashburton Treaty,* 55. Webster's later note to the British has become a classic explanation of the right of self-defense. According to the secretary, the British would have been justified in launching a preemptive attack on the *Caroline* if they could prove "a necessity of self-defence, instant, overwhelming, leaving no choice of means, and no moment for deliberation." Webster to Fox, April 24, 1841, in Kenneth E. Shewmaker, ed., *The Papers of Daniel Webster: Diplomatic Papers, 1841–1843,* 2 vols. (Hanover, NH, 1983), 1:67. See also Stevens, *Border Diplomacy,* 102–4.

20. Stevens, *Border Diplomacy,* 93; Seward's first quote, ibid., 95; Seward's second quote in Jones, *Webster-Ashburton Treaty,* 55. See also Seward to Webster, March 22, 1841, in Baker, ed., *Works of Seward,* 2:558; Albert D. Kirwan, *John J. Crittenden* (Lexington, KY, 1962), 145; Glyndon G. Van Deusen, *William Henry Seward* (New York, 1967), 77; Elliott, *Winfield Scott,* 398; Samuel F. Bemis, ed., *American Secretaries of State and Their Diplomacy* (New York, 1928), 5:16; and Seward to Richard Blatchford, March 23, 1846, WP (F20/26798).

21. McIntyre, ed., *Writings and Speeches of Webster,* 9:133.

22. Bell to Scott, March 12, 1841, "Military Book No. 23," War Office, No. 210, 266, Military Division, National Archives, Washington, DC; Robert Anderson to Bell, March 17, 1841, Department of War, National Archives, Washington, DC (hereafter cited as War Dept., NA); Anderson to Lt. Col. J. B. Crane, March 17, 1841, ibid.; Scott to Bell, March 26, April 6, 1841, ibid.; Secretary of War Spencer to President John Tyler, April 29, 1842, ibid.

23. Adams and Poinsett quoted in Stevens, *Border Diplomacy,* 101.

24. Fuess, *Daniel Webster,* 2:96–100; Oliver P. Chitwood, *John Tyler: Champion of the Old South* (New York, 1939), 272–73, 278; Robert F. Dalzell, Jr., *Daniel Webster and the Trial of American Nationalism, 1843–1852* (Boston, 1973), 37–39, 85.

25. Webster quoted in Stevens, *Border Diplomacy,* 105. See also ibid., 106.

26. Webster to Spencer, March 11, April 19, 1841, Dom. Letters, NA; Webster quote of April 16, 1841, in Stevens, *Border Diplomacy,* 106.

27. Seward quoted in Stevens, *Border Diplomacy,* 107; Webster quoted ibid., 109. For evidence that the British paid Spencer's $5,000 fee see Lord Aberdeen

to Fox, May 18, 1842, Aberdeen Papers, Additional Manuscripts, British Library, London (hereafter cited as Aberdeen Papers); Fox to Aberdeen, June 28, 1842, FO 115/79, PRO. Sydenham claimed the money came from the "Military Chest" of Canada. See Sydenham to Russell, May 25, 1841, in Knaplund, ed., *Letters from Lord Sydenham*, 138.

28. Stevens, *Border Diplomacy*, 108–9; first Tyler quote, ibid., 106; Tyler to Seward, May 15, 1841, in Lyon Gardiner Tyler, ed., *The Letters and Times of the Tylers*, 3 vols. (Richmond, 1884–1896, reprint. New York, 1970), 2:208–9.

29. *CG*, 27 Cong., 1 sess., 115; *CG, App.*, 27 Cong., 1 sess., 77, 79.

30. *CG*, 27 Cong., 1 sess., 14; *CG, App.*, 27 Cong., 1 sess., 14–18, 44–46, 66–69, 82–83; Benton, *Thirty Years' View*. See also Stevens, *Border Diplomacy*, 115–20.

31. *The People* v. *Alexander McLeod*, May 6, 1841, in Nicholas Hill, Jr., *New York Common Law Reports, Vol. 15* [4 vols. in one] (Newark, NY, 1885), 1:164–84; detailed account of prosecution and defense arguments in John L. Wendell, *Reports of Cases Argued and Determined in the Supreme Court of . . . New York, Vol. 25* (Newark, NY, 1885), 917–60; Cowen's entire decision, ibid., 567–603.

32. Stevens, *Border Diplomacy*, 113, 121; Webster and Story quoted ibid., 122; *Herald* (New York), July 13, 24, 1841; *Courier* (Montreal) [n.d.], cited in *Niles' Register* 60 (Aug. 7, 1841): 368; *Times* (London), Aug. 11, 18, 1841; *Mail* (Liverpool) [n.d.], cited in Corey, *Crisis of 1830–1842*, 140; Stevenson to Webster, Aug. 18, 1841, Desp., GB, NA; Fox to Palmerston, Aug. 5, 8, 1841, FO 5/362, PRO. Americans disagreeing with Cowen included Daniel Tallmadge of the Superior Court of New York City, Chancellor James Kent of New York, Roger Sherman of the Supreme Court of Connecticut, and Simon Greenleaf, professor of law at Harvard. Wendell, *Reports*, 1205–18; Kent to Webster, Dec. 21, 1842, in Shewmaker, ed., *Daniel Webster: Diplomatic Papers*, 2:708–9.

33. Fox to Palmerston, Aug. 28, 1841, FO 5/362, PRO; Samuel S. Nicholas to Crittenden, June 13, 1841, John J. Crittenden Papers, Library of Congress, Washington, DC (hereafter cited as Crittenden Papers); Gardner and Bradley to William H. Draper, July 19, 1841, FO 5/374, PRO; Sydenham to Fox, Aug. 3, 1841, ibid.; Webster to Spencer, Aug. 6, 1841, Dom. Letters, NA; Webster to Fox, Sept. 20, 1841, NTFL, GB, NA; Stevens, *Border Diplomacy*, 129.

34. Palmerston to Fox, June 29, Aug. 18, 1841, Palmerston's Letter-Books; Wellington to Peel, May 17, 1841, Sir Robert Peel Papers, Additional Manuscripts, British Library, London (hereafter cited as Peel Papers); Sydenham to Russell, April 10, 12, 1841, in Knaplund, ed., *Letters from Lord Sydenham*, 129, 133; Sydenham to Russell, July 27, 1841, Russell Papers; Corey, *Crisis of 1830–1842*, 139; Jones, *Webster-Ashburton Treaty*, 60.

35. Fox to Webster, Sept. 5, 1841, NFBL, NA; *Herald* (New York), Sept. 17, 1841; Tyler to Webster, ca. Sept. 8, 1841, in Shewmaker, ed., *Daniel Webster: Diplomatic Papers*, 2:116. For the Peel ministry's concern about relations with France see Wilbur D. Jones, *The American Problem in British Diplomacy, 1841–1861* (Athens, GA, 1974), 8, 18.

36. Fletcher Webster to Fox, Sept. 28, 1841, NTFL, GB, NA; Fox to Fletcher Webster, Oct. 21, 1841, NFBL, NA; Fox to Daniel Webster, Nov. 26, 1841, ibid.; Daniel Webster to Fox, Nov. 27, 1841, NTFL, GB, NA; *Globe* (Washington), Sept. 29, 1841; Frederick W. Seward, ed., *William H. Seward: An Autobiography from 1801–1834. With a Memoir of His Life, and Selections from His Letters, 1831–1846*, 3 vols. (New York, 1891), 1:551, 556–57; Wellington to Peel, Oct. 19, 1841, Peel Papers; Peel to Lord Stanley, Oct. 20, 1841, ibid.; Peel to Wellington, Oct. 20, 1841, ibid.; Aberdeen to Fox, Nov. 3, 1841, FO 5/358, PRO;

Notes

Albert B. Corey, "Public Opinion and the McLeod Case," *Canadian Historical Association Report, 1936* (Toronto, 1936), 53–64. On Grogan see Stevens, *Border Diplomacy*, 138–43.

37. Webster to Spencer, Aug. 24, 1841, Dom. Letters, NA; Webster to Spencer, Sept. 9, 1841, in Shewmaker, ed., *Daniel Webster: Diplomatic Papers*, 2:117; Seward to Webster, Sept. 3, 16, 17, 22, 1841, ibid., 109–14, 119–20, 120–21, 148–50; Webster to Seward, Sept. 23, 1841, ibid., 150–51; Tyler to Webster, [?] 1841, WP (F16/02178); Seth Hawley to Seward, Sept. 17, 20, 1841, WP (F16/20381); Seward, ed., *William H. Seward*, 1:566; Webster to Seward, Sept. 14, 1841, Dom. Letters, NA; Seward to Webster, Sept. 23, 1841, in Baker, ed., *Works of Seward*, 2:579–83; Seward to Oneida sheriff, Sept. 24, 1841, ibid., 585–86; Seward to Rev. Eliphalet Nott, Sept. 17, 1841, ibid., 3:453; *Herald* (New York), Sept. 22, 1841; Proclamation by President Tyler, Sept. 25, 1841, in Richardson, ed., *Messages and Papers*, 4:73; Wool to Scott, Sept. 24, 29, 1841, War Dept., NA; Scott to H. Underwood, Sept. 27, 1841, ibid.; Scott to Lt. Horace Brooks, Sept. 29, 1841, ibid.; Wool to Judge F. C. White, Sept. 30, 1841, ibid.; Wool to Brooks, Oct. 1, 1841, ibid. On Mackenzie's pardon see Stevens, *Border Diplomacy*, 45–47.

38. Aberdeen to Fox, Sept. 14, 1841, FO 5/358, PRO; Hughes to Webster, Sept. 18, 1841, in Harold D. Moser, ed., *The Papers of Daniel Webster: Correspondence, 1840–1843* (Hanover, NH, 1982), 5:154–55; "McLeod Resolutions" to Aberdeen, Aug. 20, 1841, FO 5/374, PRO; Aberdeen to Colonial Society, Aug. 31, 1841, ibid.; *Parl. Debates,* 59:1129; Peel's memorandum to Lords Aberdeen, Haddington, and Stanley, Oct. 17, 1841, in Charles S. Parker, ed., *Sir Robert Peel, From His Private Papers*, 3 vols. (London, 1891–1899), 3:387–88; Peel to Wellington, Oct. 18, 1841, Peel Papers; Peel to Stanley, Sept. 20, 1841, ibid.; Stevens, *Border Diplomacy*, 132–33, 144–45.

39. Fox to Aberdeen, Sept. 30, 1841, cited in Watt, "McLeod," 157; Aberdeen to Fox, Nov. 18, 1841, FO 5/358, PRO; Peel to Queen Victoria, Oct. 28, 1841, in Benson and Esher, eds., *Letters of Queen Victoria*, 1:355–56; Fox to Aberdeen, Oct. 1, 12, 1841, FO 115/76, PRO; Scott quoted in Stevens, *Border Diplomacy*, 133.

40. Everett to Webster, March 30, 1842, in Moser, ed., *Daniel Webster: Correspondence*, 5:197; Aberdeen to Queen Victoria, Oct. 20, 1841, Aberdeen Papers; Queen Victoria to Aberdeen, Oct. 20, 1841, ibid.; Webster to Everett, Nov. 20, 1841, Department of State, Diplomatic Instructions, Great Britain, National Archives, Washington, DC (hereafter cited as Dip. Instr., GB, NA); Jones, *Webster-Ashburton Treaty*, 61.

41. Spencer to Webster, Sept. 24, 1841, in Shewmaker, ed., *Daniel Webster: Diplomatic Papers*, 2:151–52; Spencer to Webster, Sept. 27, 29, Oct. 1, 1841, WP (F16/20421, 20441, 20477); Stevens, *Border Diplomacy*, 144.

42. *Herald* (New York), Sept. 13, 21, 1841; *Gould,* 2:11, 16, 40–41, 66; New York *Sun, Trial of Alexander M'Leod for the Murder of Amos Durfee and as an Accomplice in the Burning of the Steamer Caroline in the Niagara River, during the Canadian Rebellion[s] in 1837–8* (New York, 1841), 3; *Observer* (Utica), May 11, 1841, cited in Bonham, "McLeod," 201.

43. Hall quoted in *Gould*, 2:21, 24, 42.

44. Barroom quotes, ibid., 72; Bradley quoted ibid., 243; Appleby quoted ibid., 61. See also ibid., 50, 61, 63, 77, 259.

45. First Bradley quote, ibid., 244; second Bradley quote, ibid., 236.

46. Ibid., 233; Hall quoted in New York *Sun, Trial of Alexander M'Leod*, 26. See also Stevens, *Border Diplomacy*, 150–51.

47. *Gould*, 2:6, 145, 358; Gridley quoted ibid., 341. Although McLeod did not testify during the trial, his deposition was read.

48. Seward to David Moulton, Sept. 24, 1841, in Baker, ed., *Works of Seward*, 2:585–86; Wool to Scott, Oct. 11, 18, 1841, War Dept., NA; Bonham, "McLeod," 215; Stevens, *Border Diplomacy*, 155.

49. *Gould*, 2:6, 41; quote, ibid., 145.

50. Fox to Sir Richard Jackson, Oct. 11, 25, 1841, cited in Watt, "McLeod," 158; Fox to Palmerston, March 28, 1841, FO 115/69, PRO; Fox to Aberdeen, Sept. 28, Oct. 28, 1841, ibid.; Seward's message to New York assembly, May 10, 1841, in Baker, ed., *Works of Seward*, 2:407; Charles Z. Lincoln, ed., *Messages from the Governors, Comprising Executive Communications to the Legislature and Other Papers Relating to Legislation from the Organization of the First Colonial Assembly in 1683 to and Including the Year 1906, with Notes*, 11 vols. (Albany, 1909), 3:932–33.

51. *CG*, 29 Cong., 1 sess., 344, 419, 422; Aberdeen to Fox, May 18, 1842, Aberdeen Papers; Fox to Aberdeen, June 28, 1842, FO 115/79, PRO; Stevens, *Border Diplomacy*, 154–55; Howard Jones, "The Attempt to Impeach Daniel Webster," *Capitol Studies* 3 (Fall 1975): 31–44.

52. Tyler's message to Congress, Dec. 7, 1841, in Richardson, ed., *Messages and Papers*, 4:75; Everett to Webster, Dec. 15, 1841, in Shewmaker, ed., *Daniel Webster: Diplomatic Papers*, 2:167; Senator John Berrien to Webster, Jan. 10, 1842, ibid., 706–7; Webster to Berrien, Jan. 14, 1842, ibid., 707–8; *U.S. Statutes at Large* (Boston, 1852–   ), 5:539; Fox to Aberdeen, Nov. 28, 1841, FO 115/76, PRO.

53. Aberdeen to Fox, Nov. 18, 1841, FO 5/358, PRO; Everett to Webster, Dec. 15, 1841, in Shewmaker, ed., *Daniel Webster: Diplomatic Papers*, 2:167; Watt, "McLeod," 160–61; Guillet, *Lives and Times of the Patriots*, 189,n.13; "Draft Note in Colonial Office" by Aberdeen, June 2, 1842, FO 5/388, PRO; Moore, *International Arbitrations*, 1:391–425, and 3:2419–28; William M. Malloy et al., eds., *Treaties, Conventions, International Acts, Protocols, and Agreements Between the United States and Other Powers, 1776–1937*, 4 vols. (Washington, DC, 1910–1938), 1:664–68; John B. Moore, *A Digest of International Law*, 8 vols. (Washington, DC, 1906), 6:1014.

Chapter 4: Honor at Sea or Slavery at Home? 71–96

1. Peter Kolchin, *American Slavery, 1619–1877* (New York, 1993), 80–81.

2. Treaty of Ghent in Malloy et al., eds., *Treaties and Agreements*, 1:618; Perkins, *Castlereagh and Adams*, 275–76. See James A. Rawley, "Captain Nathaniel Gordon, the Only American Executed for Violating the Slave Trade Laws," paper delivered before Tenth Naval History Symposium, U.S. Naval Academy, Annapolis, Maryland (Sept. 13, 1991).

3. *U.S. Statutes at Large*, 3:532–34; Adams to Stratford Canning, Dec. 30, 1820, *ASPFR*, 5:76, 90–93, 140–41; Adams to Rush, June 24, 1823, ibid., 333–35; Adams to Stratford Canning, Aug. 15, 1821, in Worthington C. Ford, ed., *Writings of John Quincy Adams*, 7 vols. (New York, 1913–1917), 7:171; Philip D. Curtin, *The Atlantic Slave Trade: A Census* (Madison, WI, 1969), 250; Perkins, *Castlereagh and Adams*, 276–77.

4. Duckett, *Forsyth*, 182–83, 192; Charles F. Adams, ed., *Memoirs of John Quincy Adams, Comprising Portions of His Diary from 1795 to 1848*, 12 vols. (Philadelphia, 1874–1877), 6:328.

5. Liberia's governor quoted in Hugh G. Soulsby, *The Right of Search and the Slave Trade in Anglo-American Relations, 1814–1862* (Baltimore, 1933), 46; Adams to Albert Gallatin and Richard Rush, Nov. 2, 1818, *ASPFR*, 5:73; Adams to Stratford Canning, June 29, 1822, in C. F. Adams, ed., *Memoirs of John Quincy Adams*, 3:557; Jones, *Webster-Ashburton Treaty*, 72.

6. Soulsby, *Search and the Slave Trade*, 42, 49; Jones, *Webster-Ashburton Treaty*, 72.

7. Paine-Tucker agreement encl. in Fox to Forsyth, Aug. 15, 1840, NFBL, NA; Stevenson to Webster, March 3, 1841, John Rutherfoord Papers, Perkins Library, Duke University, Durham, North Carolina; Great Britain, *British and Foreign State Papers*, 116 vols. (London, 1812–1925), 30 (1841–42):1138, 1145 (hereafter cited as *BFSP*); Palmerston to Stevenson, Aug. 5, 1841, Desp., GB, NA; Everett to Aberdeen, Feb. 21, 1842, ibid.

8. Stevenson to Webster, May 18, 1841, Desp., GB, NA; Palmerston to Stevenson, Aug. 27, 1841, ibid.; Stevenson to Palmerston, April 16, 1841, ibid.; Stevenson to Aberdeen, Sept. 10, Oct. 21, 1841, ibid.

9. Peel to Aberdeen, Oct. 25, 1841, Peel Papers; Aberdeen to Stevenson, Oct. 13, 1841, Desp., GB, NA.

10. Croker to Peel, Oct. 26, 1841, Aberdeen Papers; Peel to Croker, Oct. 29, 1841, ibid.; Peel to Aberdeen, Nov. 1, 1841, ibid.

11. Aberdeen to Everett, Dec. 20, 31, 1841, Desp., GB, NA; Everett to Webster, Dec. 28, 1841, ibid.; Wilbur D. Jones, *Lord Aberdeen and the Americas* (Athens, GA, 1958), 15.

12. Everett to Aberdeen, Dec. 27, 1841, Desp., GB, NA; Aberdeen to Everett, Dec. 31, 1841, ibid.

13. Everett to Webster, Jan. 3, 1842, in Shewmaker, ed., *Daniel Webster: Diplomatic Papers*, 488–89; Everett to Webster, March 1, 1842, Desp., GB, NA.

14. Cass to François P. G. Guizot, Feb. 13, 1842, Department of State, Despatches from U.S. Ministers to France, 1791–1906, National Archives, Washington, DC (hereafter cited as Desp., France, NA); Cass to Webster, Feb. 15, 25, April 29, Dec. 11, 1842, March 7, 1843, ibid.; Cass to Webster, March 14, 1842, Lewis Cass Papers, Clements Library, University of Michigan, Ann Arbor (hereafter cited as Cass Papers); Varina (Howell) Davis, *Jefferson Davis, Ex-President of the Confederate States of America: A Memoir by His Wife*, 2 vols. (New York, 1890), 1:277; British Consul William Peter to Aberdeen, April 20, 1842, Aberdeen Papers; Kenneth E. Shewmaker, "The 'War of Words': The Cass-Webster Debate of 1842–43," *Diplomatic History* 5 (Spring 1981): 151–63; Frank B. Woodford, *Lewis Cass: The Last Jeffersonian* (New Brunswick, NJ, 1950), 215.

15. Cass's pamphlet printed in William T. Young, *Sketch of the Life and Public Services of General Lewis Cass. With the Pamphlet on the Right of Search, and Some of His Speeches on the Great Political Questions of the Day* (Philadelphia, 1853), 136–55. The *Republican Banner* (Nashville) praised Cass's actions on behalf of the South. See edition of Nov. 30, 1842.

16. Cass to Guizot, Feb. 13, 1842, Desp., France, NA.

17. Cass to Webster, Feb. 13, 15, 20, 22, 24, 25, April 29, 30, May 17, 26, Oct. 3, Dec. 11, 1842, March 7, 1843, ibid.; Cass to Webster, Sept. 17, 1842, U.S. Congress, *Senate Docs.*, 17 Cong., 3 sess., 34; Webster to Cass, Nov. 14, Dec. 20, 1842, ibid., 6–8, 14, 18; Webster to Cass, April 25, 1842, Cass Papers; Webster quote on Cass in Webster to George Ticknor, Feb. 18, 1842, in Shewmaker, ed., *Daniel Webster: Diplomatic Papers*, 1:26; Tyler to Webster, Feb. [March?] 1842, WP (F16/21734); Webster to son Fletcher, Oct. 5, 1842, WP (F18/

23526); Webster to Everett, April 26, 1842, Edward Everett Papers (F7/1058), Massachusetts Historical Society, Boston (hereafter cited as EP). Cass also received praise from Hugh Legaré, Tyler's attorney general from South Carolina. See Legaré to Cass, April 5, 1842, Cass Papers. Cass did not win the Democratic presidential nomination in 1844.

18. Everett to Webster, Jan. 31, 1842, WP (F16/21455); Everett to Webster, March 3, 1842, in Shewmaker, ed., *Daniel Webster: Diplomatic Papers*, 1:713–14.

19. Guizot to Cass, May 26, 1842, Desp., France, NA; Cass to Webster, April 30, 1842, Cass Papers; Everett to Webster, Jan. 29, 1842, WP (F16/21434); Jones, *American Problem*, 8, 18; William L. Langer, *Political and Social Upheaval, 1832–1852* (New York, 1969), 309; Norah Lofts and Margery Weiner, *Eternal France: A History of France, 1789–1944* (Garden City, NY, 1968), 133–34. Everett believed that France's primary motivation was its strong anti-British sentiment. In 1845 the French government agreed to station a fleet along the African coast to suppress the slave trade.

20. The British government renounced visit-and-search in 1858.

21. On the *Creole* affair see Jones, *Webster-Ashburton Treaty*, 78–86; and Howard Jones, "The Peculiar Institution and National Honor: The Case of the *Creole* Slave Revolt," *Civil War History* 21 (March 1975): 28–50.

22. See Clement Eaton, *The Freedom-of-Thought Struggle in the Old South* (New York, 1964), 162–95; idem, "The Freedom of the Press in the Upper South," *Mississippi Valley Historical Review* 18 (March 1932): 479–99; *Enquirer* (Richmond), Feb. 4, March 1, May 4, 1832; William W. Freehling, *Prelude to Civil War: The Nullification Controversy in South Carolina, 1816–1836* (New York, 1965), 255, 257, 259.

23. A fairly complete documentary collection on the *Creole* affair is in U.S. Congress, *Senate Docs.*, 27 Cong., 2 sess., 1–46. See depositions by Merritt, Nov. 9, 1841; Gifford, Nov. 9, 1841; and Lucius Stevens (second mate), Nov. 10, 1841, all in Dispatches from U.S. Consuls in Nassau, New Providence Island, 1821–1906, roll 5, vol. 5: Jan. 9, 1840–Dec. 28, 1841, Amistad Research Center, Tulane University, New Orleans, Louisiana (hereafter cited as Nassau Disp., ARC); deposition by Gifford and crew, Nov. 17, 1841, *Senate Docs.*, 27 Cong., 2 sess., 16; Helen T. Catterall, ed., *Judicial Cases Concerning American Slavery and the Negro*, 5 vols. (Washington, DC, 1926–1932), 3:565. See also Edward D. Jervey and Edward C. Huber, "The *Creole* Affair" (unpublished essay). Male slaves on the *Creole* were permitted to roam the deck both night and day.

24. Depositions by Merritt, Nov. 9, 1841; Gifford, Nov. 9, 1841; and Stevens, Nov. 10, 1841, all in Nassau Disp., ARC.

25. Bacon to Webster, Nov. 17, 1841, ibid.; deposition by Gifford and crew, Dec. 2, 1841, *Senate Docs.*, 27 Cong., 2 sess., 40; Catterall, ed., *Judicial Cases*, 3:565.

26. Depositions by Gifford, Nov. 9, 1841; Stevens, Nov. 10, 1841; Blin Curtis, Nov. 10, 1841; Theophilus J. D. McCargo, Nov. 10, 1841; Jacob Lietener, Nov. 15, 1841, all in Nassau Disp., ARC; Bacon to Webster, Nov. 17, 1841, ibid.

27. Depositions by Merritt, Nov. 9, 1841; Gifford, Nov. 9, 1841; Stevens, Nov. 10, 1841; Curtis, Nov. 10, 1841; McCargo, Nov. 10, 1841; Lietener, Nov. 15, 1841; Gifford and crew, Nov. 17, 1841, all ibid.; Bacon to Webster, Nov. 17, 1841, ibid.

28. Ibid., all references.

29. Ibid.

30. Ibid.; deposition of Ensor, Nov. 18, 1841, ibid. The black injured in the mutiny eventually died along with another one of the nineteen sometime later from natural causes.

31. Deposition by Gifford and crew, Dec. 2, 1841, *Senate Docs.*, 27 Cong., 2 sess., 37, 40; Jones, "Peculiar Institution," 31.

32. Deposition by Gifford and crew, Dec. 2, 1841, *Senate Docs.*, 27 Cong., 2 sess., 41–42; deposition by same, Dec. 7, 1841, quoted in *Advertiser* (New Orleans), Dec. 8, 1841. *Advertiser* cited in *Liberator* (Boston), Dec. 31, 1841.

33. Nassau Council and governor to Bacon, Nov. 9, 1841, encl. in Brit. Colonial Secretary C. R. Nesbitt to Bacon, Nov. 19, 1841, Nassau Disp., ARC; Nesbitt's statement to Cockburn, Nov. 9, 1841, *Senate Docs.*, 27 Cong., 2 sess., 6; Bacon to Webster, Nov. 30, 1841, ibid.

34. Depositions by Stevens, Nov. 13, 1841; Captain William Woodside, Nov. 13, 1841; Gifford, Stevens, and Curtis, Nov. 17, 1841, all in Nassau Disp., ARC; memorial by John Hagan and others (owners of some of the slaves aboard), seeking compensation for loss of slaves on *Creole*, Feb. 20, 1847, *Creole* Affair Collection, ARC; Bacon to Cockburn, Nov. 12, 1841, *Senate Docs.*, 27 Cong., 2 sess., 6; Cockburn to Bacon, Nov. 12, 1841, ibid., 7; Anderson's report to Cockburn, Nov. 13, 1841, Nassau Disp., ARC; Jones, "Peculiar Institution," 31.

35. Deposition by Gifford and crew, Dec. 2, 1841, *Senate Docs.*, 27 Cong., 2 sess., 42, 45; Bacon to Webster, Nov. 30, 1841, Nassau Disp., ARC; memorial by Edward Lockett (owner of some of the slaves aboard) seeking compensation, March 13, 1854, *Creole* Affair Collection, ARC; Catterall, ed., *Judicial Cases*, 3:566.

36. Deposition by Woodside, Nov. 13, 1841, Nassau Disp., ARC; deposition by Gifford and crew, Dec. 2, 1841, *Senate Docs.*, 27 Cong., 2 sess., 44–45.

37. Lockett memorial, March 13, 1854, *Creole* Affair Collection, ARC; deposition by Gifford, Nov. 13, 1841, Nassau Disp., ARC; Catterall, ed., *Judicial Cases*, 3:567,n.1.

38. Ibid., all references. Of the five slaves who returned to the United States, three were women, one was a mulatto girl of about thirteen years of age, and the other was a young boy, the son of one of the women.

39. Bacon to Webster, Nov. 30, 1841, Nassau Disp., ARC; Anderson's report to Cockburn, Nov. 13, 1841, ibid.; depositions by Gifford, Stevens, and Curtis, Nov. 17, 1841, ibid.; Nesbitt's statement to Cockburn, Nov. 9, 1841, *Senate Docs.*, 27 Cong., 2 sess., 6; Bacon to Cockburn, Nov. 12, 1841, ibid.; Cockburn to Bacon, Nov. 12, 15, 1841, ibid., 7, 8; deposition by Gifford and crew, Dec. 2, 1841, ibid., 37, 40, 41–45; Aberdeen to Everett, April 18, 1842, Desp., GB, NA; *Niles' Register* 61 (Jan. 8, 1842): 304; *Observer* (Nassau) [n.d.], cited in New Orleans *Picayune*, Dec. 30, 1841; Gifford quote in Jervey and Huber, "The *Creole* Affair," 12.

40. *Commercial Bulletin* (New Orleans), quoted in *Enquirer* (Richmond), Dec. 16, 1841; *Advertiser* (New Orleans), Dec. 4, 1841, cited in *Liberator* (Boston), Dec. 24, 1841; *Liberator* (Boston), Dec. 31, 1841; *National Intelligencer*, Dec. 15, 1841; *Mercury* (Charleston), Dec. 14, 1841; *Register & Journal* (Mobile), Dec. 6, 1841; *Union* (Nashville), Dec. 15, 1841; *Southron* (Jackson), Dec. 9, 1841; Louisiana Res., Jan. 14, 1842, in U.S. Congress, *House Docs.*, 27 Cong., 2 sess., 1; Mississippi Res., March 15, 1842, in Department of State, Miscellaneous Letters, National Archives, Washington, DC (hereafter cited as Miscellaneous Letters, NA); Virginia Res., Feb. 1842, in *Enquirer* (Richmond), Feb. 22, 1842; *Sun* (Baltimore), Dec. 20, 1841; *Courier* (Charleston) [n.d.], cited in *Picayune* (New Orleans), Jan. 5, 1842; Benton, *Thirty Years' View*, 2:411; *CG*,

27 Cong., 2 sess., 47, 116, 203–4; ibid., 26 Cong., 1 sess., 233; *CG, App.*, 26 Cong., 1 sess., 266–70; Richard K. Crallé, ed., *The Works of John C. Calhoun*, 6 vols. (New York, 1854–1860), 3:560–83. Charles M. Wiltse believes that the South feared that British interference with the interstate slave trade was evidence of a "plot" to destroy slavery itself. See his *John C. Calhoun*, 3 vols. (Indianapolis, 1944–1951), 3:63–64.

41. *U.S.* v. *Amistad* in Richard Peters, ed., *Reports of Cases Argued and Adjudged in the Supreme Court of the United States*, 90 vols. (Philadelphia, 1828–1874), 15 (1841): 519–98; William W. Story, ed., *Life and Letters of Joseph Story*, 2 vols. (Boston, 1851), 2:348; Charles G. Haines and Foster H. Sherwood, *The Role of the Supreme Court in American Government and Politics, 1835–1864* (Berkeley, 1957), 96–110. See also Howard Jones, *Mutiny on the Amistad: The Saga of a Slave Revolt and Its Impact on American Abolition, Law, and Diplomacy* (New York, 1987). Before the Supreme Court, John Quincy Adams appealed for the blacks' freedom on the basis of natural rights of liberty as stated in the Declaration of Independence. The Justices, however, dismissed this argument on the ground that American law condoned slavery. Ibid., 175–82, 188–94.

42. *National Intelligencer*, Dec. 23, 1841; *Journal* (Portsmouth) [n.d.], cited in *Liberator* (Boston), Jan. 7, 1842; *CG*, 27 Cong., 2 sess., 47–48.

43. Ibid., all references.

44. *Enquirer* (Richmond), Jan. 2, 1841; *Sun* (Baltimore), Dec. 14, 1841, March 23, 1842; *National Intelligencer*, Dec. 17, 1841; *Register & Journal* (Mobile), Dec. 4, 1841, March 1, April 11, 1842; *Picayune* (New Orleans), March 24, 1842; *American* (New York) [n.d.], cited in *Liberator* (Boston), March 11, April 8, 1842; *Liberator* (Boston), March 18, 1842; *Republican Banner* (Nashville), March 30, 1842; *Spy* (Worcester), Feb. 26, 1842, quoted ibid., March 11, 1842.

45. Birney's article cited in Betty Fladeland, *James Gillespie Birney: Slaveholder to Abolitionist* (Ithaca, 1955), 222; Whittier to Joseph Sturge, Jan. 31, 1842, in Annie Heloise Abel and Frank J. Klingberg, eds., *A Side-Light on Anglo-American Relations, 1839–1858; Furnished by the Correspondence of Lewis Tappan and Others with the British and Foreign Anti-Slavery Society* (New York, 1970; originally published in Lancaster, PA), 92; Simeon Jocelyn, April 1, 1842, cited in *Nonconformist*, April 27, 1842, 275–76, as cited in Abel and Klingberg, eds., *Side-Light*, 93,n.61; Tappan to John Scoble of British Society, April 1, 1842, cited ibid., 94; Jocelyn to Secretary of British Society, April 1, 1842, ibid., 94–95; ibid., 83; Wiltse, *Calhoun*, 3:69–70.

46. *CG*, 27 Cong., 2 sess., 342, 346, 373; ibid., 28 Cong., 1 sess., 534, 537–38; Samuel F. Bemis, *John Quincy Adams and the Union* (New York, 1956), 439–40; *Sun* (Baltimore), March 23, 1842; Gilbert H. Barnes, *The Antislavery Impulse, 1830–1844* (New York, 1933), 286,n.33; *National Intelligencer*, March 31, April 2, 1842. The gag rule in the House was in effect from 1836 to 1844.

47. Peters, ed., *Reports* 14 (1841): 540–98; Fox to Aberdeen, Dec. 28, 1841, *BFSP* 31 (1842–43): 673; *Enquirer* (Richmond), Dec. 21, 1841.

48. Webster to Everett, Jan. 29, 1842, Dip. Instr., GB, NA; Palmerston to Stevenson, Jan. 7, 1837, ibid.

49. Stanley to Cockburn, Jan. 7, 1842, CO File No. 42, April 30, 1842, Dept. of Archives, Nassau, Bahamas; Law Officers (Advocate General Sir John Dodson, Attorney General Sir Frederick Pollock, and Sir William Follett) to Stanley, Jan. 29, 1842, encl. in Stanley to Cockburn, Jan. 31, 1842, ibid.; Cockburn to Stanley, March 29, 1842, England's Despatches, 1839–1842, Folio 1489, ibid.

50. Law Officers to Stanley, Jan. 29, 1842, encl. in Stanley to Cockburn, Jan. 31, 1842, Dept. of Archives, Nassau, Bahamas; Cockburn to Stanley, March 29, 1842, England's Despatches, 1839–1842, Folio 1489, ibid.; Everett to Webster, Jan. 31, 1842, WP (F16/21448).

51. *Parl. Debates* 60: 318–26; Betty Fladeland, *Men and Brothers: Anglo-American Antislavery Cooperation* (Urbana, IL, 1972), 330–31. If Campbell had read farther into the work, he would have realized that Wheaton could not have believed the *Creole* ever came under British jurisdiction. Extradition had no bearing on the case because the master had the right to help from the American consul. See Henry Wheaton, *Elements of International Law*, ed. Richard Henry Dana, Jr. (Boston, 1836), 166,n.62. See also Arthur Nussbaum, *A Concise History of the Law of Nations* (New York, 1947), 234–35.

52. *Times* (London), Jan. 14, 19, Feb. 1, 16, May 18, June 3, 1842; *Liberator* (Boston), April 1, 1842; Abel and Klingberg, eds., *Side-Light*, 89–91; Aberdeen to Everett, April 18, 1842, Desp., GB, NA; Timothy Darling to Webster, April 16, 1842, encl. in Webster to Lord Ashburton, May 4, 1842, Lord Ashburton Papers, FO 5/379, PRO (hereafter cited as Ashburton Papers); *Compiler* (Richmond) [n.d.], cited in *Mercury* (Charleston), Dec. 23, 1842; *Courier* (New Orleans), Dec. 4, 1841, cited in *Liberator* (Boston), Dec. 24, 1841; Fox to Aberdeen, Feb. 25, 1842, *BFSP* 31 (1842–43): 692–93; Catterall, ed., *Judicial Cases*, 3:566,n.1.

53. Webster to Story, March 17, 1842, in Shewmaker, ed., *Daniel Webster: Diplomatic Papers*, 1:524–25; Everett to Aberdeen, March 1, 1842, Desp., GB, NA.

Chapter 5: Machiavellian Prelude to Negotiations, 97–119

1. Sir John Harvey to Fox, Jan. 11, 31, Feb. 10, 1840, N.B., Disp., PAC; Harvey to Gov.-Gen. A. Thomson, Jan. 17, 1840, ibid.; Harvey to Lt. Gen. Richard Jackson, Jan. 25, Feb. 3, 1840, ibid.; Lord Sydenham to Sir William Colebrooke, May 21, 1841, FO 5/362, PRO; "France, America, and Britain," *Edinburgh Review* (London), 1–48.

2. See Fox to Forsyth, Jan. 12, 26, March 7, 13, 26, June 22, July 28, Sept. 3, 1840, NFBL, NA.

3. Forsyth to Fox, Jan. 16, 28, 1840, NTFL, GB, NA; Harvey to Sydenham, Nov. 3, 13, 1840, *HCSP* 61 (1843): 43–45; Francis Rice to Warden James MacLauchlan, Nov. 3, 1840, ibid., 47; MacLauchlan to Harvey, Nov. 9, 1840, ibid., 46; Sydenham to Fox, Nov. 23, 1840, ibid., 49; Fox to Palmerston, Nov. 13, 1839, Jan. 11, 1840, FO 115/69, PRO; Palmerston to Fox, Feb. 19, 1840, Palmerston Letter-Books.

4. Kent to Maine legislature, Jan. 15, 1841, *HCSP* 61 (1843): 51–53; Maine Res., Feb. 15, 1841, Ala. Res., Jan. 15, 1841, Indiana Res., Feb. 24, 1841, Md. Res., March 23, 1841, all ibid., 129–33; Fox to Palmerston, March 30, July 30, 1840, ibid.; Palmerston to Russell, Jan. 19, 1841, quoted in Bell, *Lord Palmerston*, 1:253; Russell to Palmerston, Dec. 19, 1840, Palmerston Papers, GC; *Parl. Debates,* 61:1355–56.

5. Maine Report, March 30, 1841, in *HCSP* 61 (1843): 96–128; Sydenham to Colebrooke, May 21, June 8, 1841, ibid., 150–51; M. Langevin to Harvey, June 15, 1841, ibid., 156.

6. Webster to Fox, June 9, Sept. 4, 1841, ibid., 141–42, 164–65; Fox to Sydenham, July 27, 1841, ibid., 139–40; Fox to Webster, June 11, Sept. 6, 1841, ibid., 143–44, 166; Sydenham to Fox, Aug. 3, 1841, ibid., 162–63; Sydenham to Russell, Aug. 9, 1841, ibid., 52 (1845): 1; Palmerston to Fox, Aug. 31, 1841, ibid., 61 (1843): 163.

7. Smith had also acquired a substantial share in Samuel Morse's patent for a magnetic telegraph, and he would eventually make a fortune as the contractor for the telegraph line built between Washington and Baltimore in 1843–44. See Merk, *Fruits of Propaganda*, 9, 59–62.

8. Smith to Van Buren, Dec. 7, 1837, with enclosure: "Instructions proposed to be given to an agent on the n.e. boundary & c.," Van Buren Papers; Smith to Webster, June 7, 1841, in Shewmaker, ed., *Daniel Webster: Diplomatic Papers*, 1:94–95.

9. Merk, *Fruits of Propaganda*, 63; Shewmaker, ed., *Daniel Webster: Diplomatic Papers*, 1:xxiii; Smith to Webster, June 7, 1841, ibid., 96. A note dated July 19, 1842, concerning the secret-service fund account shows that Francis Smith received $2,000 for "services connected with the N.E. boundary." On February 1, 1845, he received an additional $500 "over the amount of $2,000 charged in former settlements." Two other men, "J Smith" and "A [Albert?] Smith," received $60 and $200, respectively, in matters relating to the "business of the boundary," while Albert Smith received $600 for his services. See note dated July 19, 1842, ibid., 637. For the law establishing the secret-service fund see *U.S. Statutes at Large*, 2:609.

10. Smith to Webster, Nov. 20, 1841, in Shewmaker, ed., *Daniel Webster: Diplomatic Papers*, 1:161–62; Smith's articles reprinted in U.S. Congress, *House Reports*, 29 Cong., 1 sess., 26–35; Merk, *Fruits of Propaganda*, 158,n.25; Joseph Griffin, ed., *History of the Press of Maine* (Brunswick, ME, 1872), 65. Under this act of separation, Massachusetts maintained a half interest in Maine's public lands.

11. Richard N. Current, "Webster's Propaganda and the Ashburton Treaty," *Mississippi Valley Historical Review* 31 (Oct. 1947): 187–200; *Eastern Argus* (Portland), July 29, Aug. 4, 1842, cited ibid., 190,ns.12, 14; *American* (Chicago), Aug. 5, 1842; *Democratic Free Press* (Detroit), Aug. 5, 1842; *Constitutional Democrat* (Detroit), Aug. 6, 1842; *Arkansas Times and Advocate* (Little Rock), Aug. 22, 1842, all cited ibid., 190,n.13; *Enquirer* (Richmond), Aug. 16, 1842.

12. "United States' Boundary Question," *Quarterly Review* 67 (Dec. 1840 and March 1841): 501–41; (author not identified), "Relations of Foreign Powers with the Present Conservative Cabinet," *Foreign Quarterly Review* 56 (Jan. 1842): 259–73; Palmerston to Fox, July 19, 1841, Palmerston Letter-Books; Sir Charles Graham to Peel, Aug. 1, 1841, in Parker, ed., *Peel, Private Papers*, 2:492–93. Graham was a close friend of Peel's. For the importance of France in the Peel ministry's policymaking see Jones, *American Problem*, 8, 18.

13. Robert C. Alberts, *The Golden Voyage: The Life and Times of William Bingham, 1752–1804* (Boston, 1969), 226, 423; Perkins, *First Rapprochement*, 12, 169; James E. Winston and R. W. Colomb, "How the Louisiana Purchase Was Financed," *Louisiana Historical Quarterly* 12 (April 1929): 189–237; Alexander DeConde, *This Affair of Louisiana* (New York, 1976), 172–73, 188; Peel to Aberdeen, Dec. 30, 1841, Peel Papers; Peel to Aberdeen, Nov. 17, 1841, Aberdeen Papers; Aberdeen to Fox, Jan. 3, 1842, ibid.; Fox to Palmerston, Aug. 16, 1840, FO 115/69, PRO; Fox to Aberdeen, Dec. 5, 1841, Jan. 28, 1842, ibid. The following letters show that the Baring lands in present-day Maine were not in the dis-

puted territory: Alexander Baring to William Bingham, Feb. 1, 15, 1796, Baring Brothers Papers, Private Docs., no. 2491, PRO (hereafter cited as Baring Brothers Papers); Bingham to Baring, Feb. 1, 1796, ibid. Webster's close ties with the House of Baring become clear in Webster to Thomas Ward of Baring Bankers of London, Feb. 29, 1840, Baring Brothers Papers; Webster to Joshua Bates, March 26, 1840, ibid.; Ward to Bates, Feb. 21, 1842, June 28, Dec. 1, 1843, Thomas Wren Ward Papers, Massachusetts Historical Society, Boston; Hidy, *House of Baring*, 100, 283–84, 293, 316, 320–21, 327.

14. Canto quoted in Alberts, *Golden Voyage*, 433; Bradford Perkins, *Prologue to War: England and the United States, 1805–1812* (Berkeley, 1961), 19–20, 31; Perkins, *Castlereagh and Adams*, 22; Dudley A. Mills, "British Diplomacy and Canada. The Ashburton Treaty," *United Empire: The Royal Colonial Institute Journal, New Series* 2 (Oct. 1911): 683–712. The government in London replaced Fox with Richard Pakenham as minister in February 1844.

15. Ashburton to Webster, Jan. 2, 1842, in Shewmaker, ed., *Daniel Webster: Diplomatic Papers*, 1:486–88; Everett to Webster, Jan. 3, 1842, ibid., 488; Lady Ashburton to Webster, Jan. 12, 1842, ibid., 490; Everett to Webster, Dec. 31, 1841, Desp., GB, NA; Peel to Aberdeen, Dec. 30, 31, 1841, Aberdeen Papers; Ashburton to Aberdeen, Dec. 28, 1841, ibid.

16. *Times* (London), Dec. 31, 1841; *Morning Chronicle* (London) [n.d.] and *Times* [n.d.], both quoted in *Enquirer* (Richmond), Jan. 27, 1842; *Examiner* (London), May 14, 1842; *Novascotian* (Halifax), June 2, 1842; "Relations of Foreign Powers," *Foreign Quarterly Review*, 265; Charles C. F. Greville, *The Greville Memoirs* (second part): *A Journal of the Reign of Queen Victoria from 1837 to 1852*, ed. Henry Reeve, 2 vols. (New York, 1885), 1:403; *National Intelligencer*, Jan. 26, March 1, 1842; *Register & Journal* (Mobile), Feb. 3, 8, 1842; *Madisonian* [n.d.], cited in *Mercury* (Charleston), Feb. 8, 1842; *Republican Banner* (Nashville), May 4, 1842; Winthrop to Everett, April 23, 1842, EP (F7/1034); *Enquirer* (Richmond), Jan. 27, 1842; Davis to Webster, April 27, 1842, WP (F17/22284); Mangum to Col. (C. S.) [?] Green, April 21, 1842, Adeline Ellery (Burr) Davis Green Papers, Perkins Library, Duke University, Durham, North Carolina; *Globe* (Washington) [n.d.], quoted ibid.; *Courier* (Boston), March 3, 1842; *Union* (Nashville), April 18, 1842.

17. Bayard Tuckerman, ed., *The Diary of Philip Hone*, 2 vols. (New York, 1910), 2:110; Webster to Everett, Jan. 29, 1842, EP (F7/0771); Everett to Aberdeen, Feb. 21, 1842, Desp., GB, NA; Gallatin to Ashburton, April 21, 1842, Aberdeen Papers; Ashburton to Gallatin, April 12, 1842, and Gallatin to Ashburton, April 20, 1842, both in Albert Gallatin Papers, New York University, New York.

18. LeDuc, "Northeastern Boundary Controversy," 30–41; Jones, *American Problem*, 18; instructions in Aberdeen to Ashburton, Feb. 8, 1842, Ashburton Papers; Ephraim D. Adams, "Lord Ashburton and the Treaty of Washington," *American Historical Review* 17 (July 1912): 764–82; Wilbur D. Jones, "Lord Ashburton and the Maine Boundary Negotiations," *Mississippi Valley Historical Review* 40 (Dec. 1953): 477–90; Hugh T. Gordon, *The Treaty of Washington, Concluded August 9, 1842, by Daniel Webster and Lord Ashburton. University of California, James Bryce Historical Prize Essays, 1905–07* (Berkeley, 1908), 173–257; Aberdeen to Ashburton, Feb. 9, 1842, Aberdeen Papers; memorandum by Wellington, Feb. 8, 1842, ibid.; Ashburton to Aberdeen, Feb. 10, 1842, ibid.

19. Aberdeen to Ashburton, Feb. 8, 1842, Ashburton Papers.

20. Ashburton to Aberdeen, Dec. 22, 28, 1841, ibid.

21. Ashburton to William Rives, Aug. 26, 1844, William Cabell Rives Papers, Library of Congress, Washington, DC (hereafter cited as Rives Papers); Jones, *Webster-Ashburton Treaty*, 102–3.

22. Sparks to Webster, Feb. 15, 1842, in Shewmaker, ed., *Daniel Webster: Diplomatic Papers*, 1:513–14; Franklin to Vergennes, Dec. 6, 1782, quoted ibid., and in Francis Wharton, ed., *The Revolutionary Diplomatic Correspondence of the United States*, 6 vols. (Washington, DC, 1889), 6:120. The letter read: "I have the honor of returning herewith the map your Excellency sent me yesterday. I have marked with a strong red line, according to your desire, the limits of the United States as settled in the preliminaries between the British and American Plenipotentiaries." Franklin's letter encl. in Sparks's letter to Webster.

23. Lawrence Martin and Samuel F. Bemis, "Franklin's Red-Line Map Was a Mitchell," *New England Quarterly* 10 (March 1937): 105–11; Bemis, *Adams and Foundations*, 479; Miller, ed., *Treaties*, 4:403–4; Sparks to Webster, Feb. 15, 1842, in Shewmaker, ed., *Daniel Webster: Diplomatic Papers*, 1:514.

24. Sparks to Webster, Feb. 15, 1842, in Shewmaker, ed., *Daniel Webster: Diplomatic Papers*, 1:514.

25. Webster to Sparks, March 4, 1842, ibid., 523; John Mulligan to Webster, July 13, 1838, WP (F40/55415); Webster's explanation of Steuben map, Nov. 27, 1844, in "Unpublished Testimony of the Select Committee of the House of Representatives," ibid.; Martin and Bemis, "Franklin's Map a Mitchell," 108; Merk, *Fruits of Propaganda*, 66; Miller, ed., *Treaties*, 4:403–4.

26. Everett to Aberdeen, May 17, 1842, FO 5/385, PRO; Everett to Webster, May 19, 1842, in Shewmaker, ed., *Daniel Webster: Diplomatic Papers*, 1:563.

27. Everett to Webster, May 31, 1843, WP (F18/24794); Miller, ed., *Treaties*, 4:407; Greville, *Memoirs*. 1:430.

28. Sparks to Everett, Jan. 30, 1843, in Herbert B. Adams, *The Life and Writings of Jared Sparks: Comprising Selections from His Journal and Correspondence*, 2 vols. (Boston, 1893), 2:405–6; Webster to Everett, June 14, Dec. 23, 1842, EP (F8a/0060 and 0756); Everett to Webster, June 16, 1842, WP (F17/22700); Bemis, *Adams and Foundations*, 479. The italicized words in the text were underlined in the original letter.

29. Martin and Bemis, "Franklin's Map a Mitchell," 107, 109; *Parl. Debates*, 57:1248, 1305. Sparks's red-line map disappeared after he saw it in Paris. Peel later claimed to have seen the d'Anville map around 1827 and doubted that it had been used in Paris in 1782–83, while Benjamin Disraeli told the House of Commons that he also had seen it and agreed that it was dubious. Apparently no one has seen it since 1842. Sparks's copy, entitled "Map of Maine," is with his letter to Webster of February 15, 1842, in the National Archives. The Steuben map is there also. Miller, ed., *Treaties*, 4:405; Burrage, *Maine*, 346,n.2; Sparks to Everett, Jan. 30, 1843, in Adams, *Life and Writings of Sparks*, 2:406; Sparks to George Gibbs, April 8, 1843, ibid., 409; Sparks to Rives, Feb. 23, 1843, Jared Sparks Letters, Clements Library, University of Michigan, Ann Arbor.

30. Webster to Williams, Feb. 2, 18, 1842, in Shewmaker, ed., *Daniel Webster: Diplomatic Papers*, 1:499–500, 518–19; Williams to Webster, Feb. 12, 1842, ibid., 501; Miller, ed., *Treaties*, 4:383.

31. Sprague to Webster, Feb. 17, 1842, in Shewmaker, ed., *Daniel Webster: Diplomatic Papers*, 1:516–17; Sprague to Webster, March 26, July 17, 1842, WP (F17/21980 and 22914). For Sprague's payment see "Copy of a Memorandum" of August 24, 1842, by disbursing agent of State Department, but in Webster's handwriting, in WP (F40/55375). For Smith's see secret-service fund account of February 1, 1845, in WP (F18/22959).

32. Merk questions the propriety of Daniel Webster's use of the executive fund. See his *Fruits of Propaganda*, 87–92. Critics who referred to Webster's newspaper campaign as propaganda include ibid.; and Current, "Webster's Propaganda and the Ashburton Treaty," 187–200.

33. Admiralty to Foreign Office, Jan. 21, 1842, FO 5/386, PRO; Greville to Henry Reeve, April 1, 1842, in Arthur H. Johnson, ed., *The Letters of Charles Greville and Henry Reeve, 1836–1865* (London, 1924), 62; *Enquirer* (Richmond), April 8, 1842; Ashburton to Aberdeen, April 8, 1842, Ashburton Papers.

34. *Herald* (New York), April 7, 10, 1842; Abel Upshur to Judge N. Beverley Tucker, April 20, 1842, in Tyler, *Letters*, 2:198; Benton, *Thirty Years' View*, 2:421; *Niles' Register* 62 (Aug. 6, 1842): 353; *CG, App.*, 27 Cong., 2 sess., 444.

35. Ashburton to Aberdeen, April 25, 1842, Ashburton Papers; Ashburton to Aberdeen, April 26, May 12, 29, 1842, Aberdeen Papers.

36. Webster to Fairfield and Davis, April 11, 1842, in Shewmaker, ed., *Daniel Webster: Diplomatic Papers*, 1:534–37; Webster to Fairfield, April 11, 1842, in McIntyre, ed., *Writings and Speeches of Webster*, 11:274; Smith to Webster, April 13, 1842, WP (F17/22153); Smith to Webster, April 16, 1842, in Moser, ed., *Daniel Webster: Correspondence*, 200; Webster to Bates and Rufus Choate, Feb. 15, 1842, WP (F16/21573); Mass. Resolves, March 3, 1842, U.S. Congress, *Senate Docs.*, 27 Cong., 3 sess., 63–64; Webster to Davis, April 16, 1842, WP (F17/22169); Davis to Webster, April 27, 1842, WP (F17/22282).

37. Webster to Sparks, May 14, 16, 1842, in Shewmaker, ed., *Daniel Webster: Diplomatic Papers*, 1:556–57; Adams, *Life and Writings of Sparks*, 2:400; Sparks to Everett, Jan. 30, 1843, ibid., 406–7; "Copy of a Memorandum," Aug. 24, 1842, in WP (F40/55375); Webster to Davis, April 16, 1842, WP (F17/22169); Martin and Bemis, "Franklin's Map a Mitchell," 106. Although Sparks reported expenses of only $20 for his trip to Augusta, Webster allotted him $250—again from the secret-service fund. The president refused the secretary's request to pay Sparks more. Sparks to Webster, May 16, 1842, WP (F17/22471); Webster to Tyler, Aug. 24, 1842, WP (F40/55375); Tyler to Webster, Aug. 25, 1842, WP (F40/55376).

38. Bemis, *Adams and Foundations*, 479–80.

39. Webster to Williams, May 7, 14, 1842, in Shewmaker, ed., *Daniel Webster: Diplomatic Papers*, 1:549–50, 557–60; Webster to Kavanagh, May 17, 1842, WP (F17/22474).

40. Sprague to Webster, May 18, 1842, WP (F17/22484); Sparks to Webster, May 19, 1842, WP (F17/22498); Maine Res., May 26, 1842, encl. in Fairfield to Tyler, May 27, 1842, in *DCUSCR*, 3:271,n.2; Jenkins, ed., *Records . . . Maine: Legislative Records*, 22 Legis. (May 26, 1842), 33–34.

41. Webster to Kent, May 28, 1842, WP (F17/22556); Maine commissioners to Webster, June 12, 1842, U.S. Congress, *House Docs.*, 27 Cong., 3 sess., 69; Mass. commissioners to Webster, June 13, 1842, ibid.; Webster to Everett, June 14, 1842, EP (F8a/0060).

42. Aberdeen to Sir James Kempt, Sir Howard Douglas, Lord Seaton, and Sir George Murray, Feb. 24, 1842, Aberdeen Papers; Aberdeen to Ashburton, March 3, 1842, ibid.; Kempt to Aberdeen, March 1, 1842, ibid.; Murray to Aberdeen, March 6, 1842, ibid.; Douglas to Aberdeen, March 7, 1842, ibid.; Seaton to Aberdeen, March 9, 1842, ibid.; Mildmay to Aberdeen, April 28, 1842, ibid.; revised instructions in Aberdeen to Ashburton, March 31, 1842, Ashburton Papers.

43. Aberdeen to Ashburton, April 1, 1842, Aberdeen Papers; Peel to Aberdeen, March 1842, ibid.

44. Colebrooke to Ashburton, May 12, 1842, FO 5/388, PRO; Ashburton to Aberdeen, May 12, 1842, Aberdeen Papers; Hamilton to Tyler, April 29, 1842, ibid.

45. Ashburton to Aberdeen, May 29, 1842, Aberdeen Papers; Aberdeen to Ashburton, June 3, 18, 1842, ibid.

46. Ashburton to Colebrooke, April 28, May 17, 24, 1842, N.B., Disp., PAC; Colebrooke to Ashburton, May 10, 27, 1842, FO 5/388, PRO.

47. Colebrooke to Ashburton, June 1, 1842, FO 5/388, PRO; Ashburton to Colebrooke, July 29, 1842, N.B., Disp., PAC; Ashburton to Aberdeen, June 29, 1842, FO 881/259, PRO. Thomas C. Grattan, British consul in Boston, implies that Webster was aware of New Brunswick's representatives in Washington. See his *Civilized America*, 2 vols. (London, 1859), 1:369.

Chapter 6: The Webster-Ashburton Treaty, 121–49

1. Ashburton to Webster, June 21, 1842, *HCSP* 61 (1843): 6–10; Ashburton to Aberdeen, July 13, 1842, Ashburton Papers; Julia G. Tyler (president's wife) to George T. Curtis, ca. late 1842, Lyon Gardiner Tyler, "The Ashburton Treaty, 1842," *Tyler's Quarterly Historical and Genealogical Magazine* 3, no. 4 (April 1922): 255–56; Tyler to son Robert, Aug. 29, 1858, in Tyler, *Letters*, 2:242. On the boundary negotiations see Jones, *Webster-Ashburton Treaty*, 121–38.

2. Webster to John Denison, April 26, 1842, in Moser, ed., *Daniel Webster: Correspondence*, 201; Ashburton to Webster, June 13, 1842, NFBL, NA. On the dinners see "information sheet" on St. John's Parish House, 1525 H Street, NW, Washington, DC.

3. Webster to Everett, April 25, 1842, EP (F7/1045); Ashburton to Webster, June 21, 1842, *HCSP* 61 (1843): 6–8.

4. Ashburton to Webster, June 21, 1842, *HCSP* 61 (1843): 6–8.

5. Aberdeen to Ashburton, May 16, 20, June 18, 1842, Aberdeen Papers; Peel to Aberdeen, May 16, 1842, ibid.

6. Ashburton to Aberdeen, July 13, 1842, ibid.

7. Webster to Everett, June 28, 1842, EP (F8a/0122); Tyler, *Letters*, 2:172, 218.

8. Maine commissioners to Webster, June 29, 1842, *HCSP* 61 (1843): 15–22; Webster to Ashburton, July 8, 1842, ibid., 10–15; Ashburton to Webster, July 11, 1842, ibid., 22–23; Aberdeen to Ashburton, July 2, 1842, Aberdeen Papers.

9. Ashburton to Aberdeen, June 29, 1842, Aberdeen Papers.

10. Ashburton to Webster, July 1, 1842, in Shewmaker, ed., *Daniel Webster: Diplomatic Papers*, 1:604.

11. Ashburton to Aberdeen, May 29, 1842, Ashburton Papers; Ashburton to Aberdeen, June 14, July 13, 1842, Aberdeen Papers.

12. Grattan to Aberdeen, June 14, July 30, 1842, Aberdeen Papers; Aberdeen to Ashburton, July 2, 1842, ibid.; Ashburton to Aberdeen, July 28, 1842, ibid.; Grattan, *Civilized America*, 1:365.

13. Grattan to Aberdeen, June 14, July 30, 1842, Aberdeen Papers; Aberdeen to Ashburton, July 2, 1842, ibid.; Ashburton to Aberdeen, July 13, 1842, Ashburton Papers.

14. Grattan, *Civilized America*, 1:367, 368, 371–72; Ashburton to Webster, July 11, 1842, *HCSP* 61 (1843): 23–26; Ashburton to Aberdeen, July 13, 1842, Ashburton Papers.

15. See J. R. Baldwin, "The Ashburton-Webster Boundary Settlement," *Canadian Historical Association, 1938* (Toronto, 1938), 121–33; and Bemis, *Adams and Foundations*, 479–80.

16. Webster to Everett, Aug. 25, 1842, Jan. 29, 30, March 10, 29, 1843, EP (F8a/0380, F8b/0949, 0955, 1139, 1190); Everett to Webster, Sept. 16, 1842, April 18, 1843, in Shewmaker, ed., *Daniel Webster: Diplomatic Papers*, 1:698–700, 911–12; Webster to Thomas Curtis, March 12, 1843, ibid., 899–900; Webster to Robert Letcher, Feb. 21, 1843, in Moser, ed., *Daniel Webster: Correspondence*, 5:274; Everett to Tyler, April 18, 1843, EP (F9a/0078).

17. Ashburton to Aberdeen, Aug. 9, 1842, Aberdeen Papers. Webster's staunchest critic is Bemis. See his *Adams and Foundations*, 479–80, 585–88.

18. Ashburton to Aberdeen, June 14, 1842, Aberdeen Papers; Aberdeen to Ashburton, July 2, 1842, ibid.; Aberdeen to Peel, Aug. 25, 1842, Peel Papers. Grattan claimed that one of the Maine commissioners informed him that Webster laid the Sparks map before the Maine commission on June 13. See Grattan to Aberdeen, Dec. 31, 1842, Aberdeen Papers.

19. Aberdeen to Ashburton, July 2, 1842, Aberdeen Papers.

20. See Bemis, *Adams and Foundations*, 585–88; and Ferrell, *American Diplomacy*, 210–11.

21. Ashburton to Aberdeen, June 14, Aug. 9, 1842, Aberdeen Papers.

22. For evidence that Webster was trying to borrow see Webster to Nathaniel Williams, Feb. 3, 4, March 13, Oct. 29, Dec. 8, 12, 1842, WP (F16/21499 and 21504; F17/21855; F18/23654, 23866, 23874). Bemis incautiously hazarded a "guess" that Ashburton gave Webster £2,998.1 "with only a general assurance that it would help out." *Adams and Foundations*, 588.

23. Ashburton to Aberdeen, Aug. 9, 1842, Aberdeen Papers. One might add that, technically, Ashburton did not say he paid money to anyone.

24. Ibid.

25. Ashburton to Aberdeen, April 25, Aug. 13, 1842, ibid.

26. Webster to Ashburton, July 8, 1842, *HCSP* 61 (1843): 10–15; Ashburton to Aberdeen, July 13, 1842, Ashburton Papers.

27. Webster to Maine commissioners, July 15, 1842, in McIntyre, ed., *Writings and Speeches of Webster*, 11:276–78; Ashburton to Webster, July 18, 1842, NFBL, NA; Webster to Ashburton, July 18, 1842, NTFL, GB, NA; Miller, ed., *Treaties*, 4:434.

28. Massachusetts commissioners to Webster, July 20, 1842, *DCUSCR*, 3:758; Maine commissioners to Webster, July 22, 1842, ibid., 760; "Memorandum," marked "A," encl. ibid., 765,n.1; Ashburton to Aberdeen, July 28, 1842, Aberdeen Papers. In September 1846 an agreement was reached on payment of the disputed territory fund. New Brunswick paid $14,893.45 to Maine and Massachusetts. Miller, ed., *Treaties*, 4:433.

29. Joseph Delafield to Major D. Fraser, July 20, 1842, U.S. Congress, *House Docs.*, 27 Cong., 3 sess., 101; Robert Stuart to Webster, July 7, 1842, ibid., 100; James Ferguson to Webster, July 25, 1842, ibid., 104.

30. Ashburton to Webster, July 16, 1842, in McIntyre, ed., *Writings and Speeches of Webster*, 11:280–82; Ashburton to Aberdeen, Aug. 9, 1842, Ashburton Papers.

31. Merk, *Fruits of Propaganda*, 75; Glyndon G. Van Deusen, *The Jacksonian Era, 1828–1848* (New York, 1959), 175,n.4; Corey, *Crisis of 1830–1842*, 168; Fremont P. Wirth, *The Discovery and Exploitation of the Minnesota Iron Lands* (Cedar Rapids, IA, 1937), 9–11; Tyler's message to Senate, Aug. 11, 1842, in Richardson, ed., *Messages and Papers*, 4:165. For a convincing argument that

Webster, Tyler, and Ashburton did not know of the mineral deposits along the northwestern section of the boundary see Thomas LeDuc, "The Webster-Ashburton Treaty and the Minnesota Iron Ranges," *Journal of American History* 51 (Dec. 1964): 476–81. The lack of official interest in the northwestern territory becomes evident on examination of the U.S. government's Land Office files. See General Land Office, Records: Letters to Surveyors General, 1796–1901, National Archives, Washington, DC.

32. Webster to Ashburton, July 27, 1842, in McIntyre, ed., *Writings and Speeches of Webster*, 11:284–87; Ashburton to Webster, Aug. 9, 1842, ibid., 289; Spencer to Webster, Aug. 11, 1842, in Department of State, envelope marked "Miscellaneous on Northeastern Boundary," E98, National Archives, Washington, DC; Ashburton to Webster, July 26, 1842, WP (F17/23005); Webster to Ashburton, Aug. 9, 1842, *HCSP* 61 (1843): 32; Webster to Senate (1846) in *CG*, 29 Cong., 1 sess., 617; Fox to Webster, April 25, 1843, NFBL, NA; Captain Andrew Talcott to Webster, July 14, 1842, *House Docs.*, 27 Cong., 3 sess., 82; Aberdeen to Peel, Aug. 15, 1842, Aberdeen Papers.

33. Webster to Sparks, March 11, 1843, in Shewmaker, ed., *Daniel Webster: Diplomatic Papers*, 1:786.

34. Despite the mutual gains from the treaty, Bemis maintains that "Webster achieved a diplomatic triumph—against his own country." *Adams and Foundations*, 481.

35. For these other issues discussed in the negotiations see Jones, *Webster-Ashburton Treaty*, 139–60.

36. Tyler to Webster, May 8, 1842, WP (F17/22413). See also Merrill D. Peterson, *The Great Triumvirate: Webster, Clay, and Calhoun* (New York, 1987), 321–22.

37. See Cass's pamphlet, *An Examination of the Question Now in Discussion Between the American & British Governments, Concerning the Right of Search*, in Young, *General Lewis Cass*, 136–65.

38. Ashburton to Aberdeen, Feb. 10, 1842, Aberdeen Papers; Peel to Aberdeen, Feb. 21, 1842, ibid.

39. Webster to Ashburton, July 30, 1842, WP (F17/23031); Tyler to Webster, [July, Aug.], Aug. 1, 1842, WP (F17/23070 and 23089); Webster to Ashburton, Aug. 8, 1842, in McIntyre, ed., *Writings and Speeches of Webster*, 11:318–25.

40. Everett to Webster, Jan. 31, 1842, WP (F16/21448); Ashburton to Webster, Aug. 9, 1842, in McIntyre, ed., *Writings and Speeches of Webster*, 11:326–27; Ashburton to Aberdeen, May 12, 1842, Ashburton Papers; Aberdeen to Ashburton, June 3, 1842, ibid.; Everett to Webster, April 15, 1842, Desp., GB, NA; Aberdeen to Ashburton, June 3, July 18, 1842, Aberdeen Papers.

41. Everett to Webster, April 15, 1842, Desp., GB, NA; Ashburton to Aberdeen, May 12, 1842, Ashburton Papers; Ashburton to Webster, Aug. 9, 1842, in McIntyre, ed., *Writings and Speeches of Webster*, 11:326–27; Aberdeen to Peel, Aug. 25, 1842, Aberdeen Papers. The British government finally renounced impressment in 1858.

42. Tyler to son Robert, Aug. 29, 1858, in Tyler, *Letters*, 2:240; Wilbur D. Jones, "The Influence of Slavery on the Webster-Ashburton Negotiations," *Journal of Southern History* 22 (Feb. 1956): 48–58; Webster to Everett, April 26, 1842, EP (F7/1058).

43. Ashburton to Aberdeen, April 25, 1842, *HCSP* 61 (1843): 4.

44. Everett to Webster, May 17, 1842, WP (F17/22479); Ashburton to Webster, [July?] 1842, WP (F17/23066); Aberdeen to Ashburton, May 26, 1842, *HCSP* 61

(1843): 4; Everett to Webster, June 1, 1842, Desp., GB, NA; Ashburton to Aberdeen, June 14, 1842, Aberdeen Papers; Aberdeen to Ashburton, July 2, 1842, ibid.; Ashburton to Aberdeen, June 29, 1842, Ashburton Papers; Alan R. Booth, "The United States African Squadron, 1843–1861," in Jeffrey Butler, ed., *Boston University Papers in African History* (Boston, 1964), 77–117, esp. 112–13; W. E. B. Du Bois, *The Suppression of the African Slave-Trade to the United States of America, 1638–1870* (New York, 1896), 183; Warren S. Howard, *American Slavers and the Federal Law, 1837–1862* (Berkeley, 1963), 42, 124–41; Peter Duignan and Clarence Clendenen, *The United States and the African Slave Trade, 1619–1862* (Stanford, 1962), 40–42; Richard W. Van Alstyne, "The British Right of Search and the African Slave Trade," *Journal of Modern History* 2 (March 1930): 37–47; Perkins, *Castlereagh and Adams*, 277; Moore, *Digest*, 2:946–47. The Anglo-American convention of April 7, 1862, allowed mutual search in suppressing the African slave trade.

45. Everett to Webster, Feb. 2, 1842, WP (F16/21486); Webster to [Edward?] Curtis, [Feb./March?] 1842, WP (F16/21724); Aberdeen to Ashburton, Feb. 9, March 3, 1842, Aberdeen Papers; Story to Webster, March 26, April 19, 1842, in Shewmaker, ed., *Daniel Webster: Diplomatic Papers*, 1:525–27, 537–38; Webster to Story, April 9, 1842, ibid., 532–33; Ashburton to Aberdeen, July 13, 1842, in McIntyre, ed., *Writings and Speeches of Webster*, 11:311.

46. Ashburton to Webster, July 31, 1842, in Shewmaker, ed., *Daniel Webster: Diplomatic Papers*, 1:657–58; Ashburton to Webster, Aug. 6, 1842, in McIntyre, ed., *Writings and Speeches of Webster*, 11:313–14, 316; Webster to Ashburton, Aug. 1, 1842, HCSP 61 (1843): 35–40; Aberdeen to Ashburton, May 26, 1842, Aberdeen Papers; Ashburton to Aberdeen, Aug. 9, 1842, ibid.; Ashburton to Aberdeen, April 28, Aug. 9, 1842, Ashburton Papers.

47. Hidy, *House of Baring*, 79–85; U.S. Congress, *Senate Docs.*, 34 Cong., 1 sess., 52, 241–45; Moore, *Digest*, 2:358–61; James B. Scott, ed., *Cases on International Law, Selected from Decisions of English and American Courts* (Boston, 1902), 252–55. The umpire was Joshua Bates, Boston banker and partner in the House of Baring.

48. Webster to Ashburton, July 27, 1842, NTFL, GB, NA; Ashburton to Aberdeen, July 28, 1842, Ashburton Papers; Ashburton to Webster, July 28, 1842, in McIntyre, ed., *Writings and Speeches of Webster*, 11:295–301; Webster to Ashburton, July 27, Aug. 6, 1842, ibid., 292–93, 302–3; Tyler to Webster, July 26, 1842, WP (F17/23009); Curtis, *Webster*, 2:121,n.1; *Caroline* doctrine in Stevens, *Border Diplomacy*, 102–5, 165–68; *U.S. Statutes at Large*, 5:539. The Remedial Justice Act of 1842 established federal jurisdiction over cases in which subjects are acting under government orders and authorized the removal of cases having international ramifications from state to federal courts.

49. Memorandum from Peel ministry to Ashburton, Jan. 1842, Ashburton Papers; Aberdeen to Ashburton, Feb. 8, 1842, ibid.

50. Memorandum by Wellington, Feb. 8, 1842, Aberdeen Papers; Ashburton to Aberdeen, April 25, 1842, Ashburton Papers; Ashburton to Aberdeen, June 29, 1842, ibid.; Aberdeen to Fox, Oct. 18, 1842, FO 115/79, PRO; Ashburton to Aberdeen, Jan. 1, 1843, Aberdeen Papers; Ashburton to Webster, Jan. 2, 1843, WP (F18/24063); Ashburton to Croker, Feb. 20, 1843, John Croker Papers, Clements Library, University of Michigan, Ann Arbor (hereafter cited as Croker Papers); Frederick Merk, "The Oregon Question in the Webster-Ashburton Negotiations," *Mississippi Valley Historical Review* 43 (Dec. 1956): 379–404; David M. Pletcher, *The Diplomacy of Annexation: Texas, Oregon, and the Mexican War* (Columbia, 1973), 100; Bourne, *Balance of Power*, 123.

51. Tyler quote in Allan Nevins, ed., *The Diary of Philip Hone, 1828–1851* (New York, 1927), 614.

52. *Globe* (Washington), June 9, Aug. 20, 22, 1842; *Times* (London), Aug. 13, 23–26, 29, 1842; *Morning Chronicle* (London), Sept. 19–22, 24, 26, 27, 1842, all cited in *National Intelligencer* (Washington), Jan. 26, 27, 31, Feb. 2, 4, 9, 16, 1843; *Morning Herald* (London) [n.d.], *Punch* (London) [n.d.], *Evening Star* (London) [n.d.], all cited in *Enquirer* (Richmond), Oct. 11, Nov. 22, Dec. 6, 1842; Everett to Webster, Aug. 19, 1842, Desp., GB, NA; Palmerston to Russell, Sept. [?] 1842, in G. P. Gooch, ed., *The Later Correspondence of Lord John Russell, 1840–1878*, 2 vols. (London, 1925), 1:58–59; Palmerston to Lord Monteagle, Oct. 28, 1842, Palmerston Papers, GC.

53. Everett to Webster, Feb. 10, March 31, 1843, in Shewmaker, ed., *Daniel Webster: Diplomatic Papers*, 1:779–80, 787–91; Sparks to Webster, Feb. 21, 1843, ibid., 783; Martin and Bemis, "Franklin's Map a Mitchell," 107–8.

54. Anthony Panizzi to Palmerston, March 29, 1839, FO 5/340, PRO; British warrant of April 1, 1839, ibid.; Ashburton to William Rives, Aug. 26, 1844, Rives Papers. In this letter to Rives, Ashburton explained his discovery of the Oswald map. I wish to thank Ann Liston for calling this letter to my attention.

55. Raymond Walters, Jr., *Albert Gallatin: Jeffersonian Financier and Diplomat* (New York, 1957), 343; Merk, *Fruits of Propaganda*, 48; Miller, ed., *Treaties*, 4:407–10; Ashburton to Aberdeen, Jan. 21, 1843, Aberdeen Papers; Ashburton to Croker, Feb. 7, 1843, Croker Papers; Webster to Everett, April 25, 1843, EP (F9a/0117). Other maps have appeared over the years. See Jones, *Webster-Ashburton Treaty*, 110–13. In an ironic twist, the historian who most criticizes Webster for hiding a map supporting the American claim was Bemis, who himself wrote that the Paris negotiators agreed during the preliminary talks to postpone the boundary issue until after the war, when a joint Anglo-American commission would deal with it. See his *The Diplomacy of the American Revolution* (New York, 1935), 228.

56. *CG*, 29 Cong., 1 sess., 636ff., 699, 729–30, 735; C. F. Adams, ed., *Memoirs of John Quincy Adams*, 12:266; Deposition of Stubbs, May 9–18, 1846, in "Unpublished Testimony of the Select Committee," in WP (F40/55279); "Statement of Moneys advanced to the Secretary of State and how accounted for by him," Feb. 1, 1845, WP (F40/55312); U.S. Congress, *House Reports*, 29 Cong., 1 sess., 1–4, 11–17; published portions of testimony, ibid., 9–11; Tyler's testimony, including expurgated sections, WP (F40/55212); Tyler to Webster, April 21, 1846, WP (F20/26855). See Jones, "Daniel Webster," 31–44. Ohio Democrat Jacob Brinkerhoff, Webster's longtime opponent, voted against exoneration. Brinkerhoff condemned the former secretary's "systematic electioneering" in Maine and thought it an "impeachable offence" to use federal money to influence a state legislature. Merk, *Fruits of Propaganda*, 210–14. See also Howard Jones, "Daniel Webster: The Diplomatist," in Kenneth E. Shewmaker, ed., *Daniel Webster: "The Completest Man"* (Hanover, NH, 1990), 203–29.

57. See Jones, *Webster-Ashburton Treaty*; Irving H. Bartlett, *Daniel Webster* (New York, 1978); and Maurice G. Baxter, *One and Inseparable: Daniel Webster and the Union* (Cambridge, 1984).

Chapter 7: Northwest to Oregon, 151–74

1. The name Oregon was not actually applied to the area until the 1820s. See T. C. Elliott, "The Origin of the Name Oregon," *Oregon Historical Quarterly 22*

(June 1921): 91–115; and Bernard DeVoto, *The Course of Empire* (Boston, 1952), 245–46.

2. F. W. Howay, ed., *The Dixon-Meares Controversy* (Toronto, 1929); William R. Manning, "The Nootka Sound Controversy," American Historical Association, *Annual Report, 1904* (Washington, DC, 1905), 279–478. For Vancouver's account of the river-colored water and meeting with Gray see W. Kaye Lamb, ed., *A Voyage of Discovery to the North Pacific Ocean and Around the World, 1791–1795,* 4 vols. (London, 1984), 2:497–511. See also John Scofield, *Hail, Columbia: Robert Gray, John Kendrick, and the Pacific Fur Trade* (Portland, 1993); John Meares, *Voyages Made in the Years 1788 and 1789, from China to the North West Coast of America,* 2 vols. (London, 1790), 1:270; and Alfred S. Green, "Memorandum Relative to the Territorial Rights Claimed by Great Britain in the Oregon Territory; and of the Negotiations between Great Britain and the United States which led to the Conclusion of the Convention of the 15th June, 1846," in Kenneth Bourne and D. Cameron Watt, eds., *British Documents on Foreign Affairs: Reports from the Foreign Office Confidential Print,* Part I, Series C, 6 vols. (Lanham, MD, 1986), 2:14 (hereafter cited as *BDFA*).

3. Lamb, *Voyage of Discovery,* 2:747–86.

4. Frederick Holman, Presidential Address delivered to the Oregon Historical Society Annual Meeting at Portland, Dec. 19, 1908, *Oregon Historical Quarterly* 10 (June 1909): 4; Sir Alexander Mackenzie, *Voyages from Montreal to the Frozen and Pacific Ocean* (London, 1801), 411; Dorothy O. Johansen, *Empire of the Columbia,* 2d ed. (New York, 1957), 74–81, 89–90; Donald D. Jackson, ed., *Letters of the Lewis and Clark Expedition, with Related Documents, 1783–1843* (Urbana, IL, 1962), 10–14.

5. Oscar Osburn Winther, *The Great Northwest: A History,* 2d ed. (New York, 1947; reprint, 1966), 37–40; Green, "Memorandum," *BDFA,* 2:38; Holman, Presidential Address, 13.

6. James Monroe and William Pinkney to James Madison, April 25, 1807, *ASPFR,* 3:162–64.

7. Johansen, *Empire of the Columbia,* 94–97; James Christy Bell, Jr., *Opening a Highway to the Pacific, 1838–1846* (New York, 1921), 23.

8. Green, "Memorandum," *BDFA,* 2:58, 41; Winther, *Great Northwest,* 47; Frederick Merk, *The Oregon Question: Essays in Anglo-American Diplomacy and Politics* (Cambridge, MA, 1967), 142–45.

9. Monroe and Pinkney in 1807 had negotiated in London with British commissioners Lords Holland and Auckland to draw a border at the 49th parallel from the Lake of the Woods westward "as far as their respective territories extend in that quarter," but they had not mentioned the area by name. See Monroe and Pinkney to James Madison, April 25, 1807, *ASPFR,* 3:162–64; Monroe to John Quincy Adams, James A. Bayard, Henry Clay, Jonathan Russell, and Albert Gallatin, March 22, 1814, *ASPFR,* 3:731, and *DCUSCR,* 1:218; Merk, *Oregon Question,* 7; and Joseph Schafer, "The British Attitude Toward the Oregon Question, 1815–1846," *American Historical Review* 16 (Oct. 1910–July 1911): 281.

10. Monroe to Anthony St. John Baker, July 18, 19, 1815, *DCUSCR,* 1:230–31, and *ASPFR,* 4:852; Green, "Memorandum," *BDFA,* 2:59; Baker to Lord Castlereagh, July 19, 1815, FO 5/107, PRO; Bell, *Highway to the Pacific,* 28; Merk, *Oregon Question,* 9.

11. Merk, *Oregon Question,* 11–18; Adams to John B. Prevost, Sept. 29, 1817, *DCUSCR,* 1:262; Bell, *Highway to the Pacific,* 29.

12. Merk, *Oregon Question,* 18; Simon M'Gillivray to Charles Bagot, Nov. 15, 1817, FO 5/123, PRO; Bagot to Adams, Nov. 26, 1817, *DCUSCR,* 1:831–

32; C. F. Adams, ed., *Memoirs of John Quincy Adams*, 4:24–25; Bagot to Castlereagh, Nov. 24, Dec. 2, 1817, FO 5/123, PRO. Also see Perkins, *Castlereagh and Adams*, 247; and Bemis, *Adams and Foundations*, 283–84.

13. Merk, *Oregon Question*, 19–20; Bagot to John C. Sherbrooke, Dec. 1, 1817, FO 5/123, PRO; Bagot to Castlereagh, Dec. 2, 1817, ibid.; Bagot to Castlereagh, Dec. 3, 1817, in Charles W. Vane, ed., *Memoirs and Correspondence of Viscount Castlereagh, Second Marquis of Londonderry*, 12 vols. (London, 1850–1853), 11:388–89; Perkins, *Castlereagh and Adams*, 247; Merk, *Oregon Question*, 19–20. For Castlereagh's interest in a period of peace see Castlereagh to Bagot, Nov. 10, 1817, FO 115/29, PRO; Richard Rush to Adams, Feb. 14, 1818, *DCUSCR*, 1:834–37; Green, "Memorandum," *BDFA*, 2:59–60; and Schafer, "British Attitude Toward the Oregon Question," 284. For M'Gillivray's argument in his "statement relative to the Columbia River (1815)" see M'Gillivray to Bagot, Nov. 15, 1817, FO 5/123, PRO; Katharine Judson, "The British Side of the Restoration of Astoria," *Oregon Historical Quarterly* 20 (Sept. 1919): 254–60; and George Canning to Lord Liverpool, July 7, 1826, in Edward J. Stapleton, ed., *Some Official Correspondence of George Canning*, 2 vols. (London, 1887), 2:71–75.

14. Merk, *Oregon Question*, 23–24. For the events concerning the restoration of Astoria see T. C. Elliott, "An Event of One Hundred Years Ago," *Oregon Historical Quarterly* 19 (Sept. 1918): 181–87; idem, "The Surrender of Astoria in 1818," *Oregon Historical Quarterly* 19 (Dec. 1918): 271–82; and Judson, "British Side of Restoration," 305–30.

15. Foreign Office to Admiralty, Jan. 26, 1818, in Green, "Memorandum," *BDFA*, 2:59–60; Judson, "British Side," 317–19; Castlereagh to Bagot, Feb. 4, 1818, FO 5/129, PRO; Merk, *Oregon Question*, 25–26. For the text of the British surrender see Prevost to Adams, Nov. 11, 1818, *DCUSCR*, 1:886. Castlereagh had directed that the post be restored but not the soil on which it stood. See Schafer, "British Attitude Toward the Oregon Question," 284.

16. Gallatin and Rush to Adams, Oct. 20, 1818, *DCUSCR*, 1:878; Green, "Memorandum," *BDFA*, 2:61–63; Protocol of the Third Conference, Sept. 17, 1818, *DCUSCR*, 1:865. Merk questioned Gallatin's short-sighted proposal of the line of the 49th parallel at the outset. Merk, *Oregon Question*, 39–40.

17. For a discussion of the Caledonia River controversy see Merk, *Oregon Question*, 46–71; and Protocol No. 7, Oct. 13, 1818, in Green, "Memorandum," *BDFA*, 2:61–62. The British proposal dated Oct. 6, 1818, appears in *DCUSCR*, 1:869. See also Merk, *Oregon Question*, 38–39.

18. Bemis, *Adams and Foundations*, 290–91. For the convention and the American negotiator's explanation to Adams see *DCUSCR*, 1:874–79; Green, "Memorandum," *BDFA*, 2:62–63; Rush, Journal, 2, "London 1818, British Negotiation (Oct. 16, 1818–Jan. 19, 1819)," Oct. 19, 1818, in Gallatin Papers; and Merk, *Oregon Question*, 54–55.

19. Gallatin and Rush to Adams, Oct. 20, 1818, *DCUSCR*, 1:879; Merk, *Oregon Question*, 26.

20. Bemis, *Adams and Foundations*, 317–40, 494, 516–19. See also Adams's diary entry for the evening of the treaty signing in C. F. Adams, ed., *Memoirs of John Quincy Adams*, 4:274; Johansen, *Empire of the Columbia*, 113–17; Monroe to Pinkney, May 10, 1816, *DCUSCR*, 1:243; Prevost to Adams, Nov. 11, 1818, ibid., 891; and Perkins, *Castlereagh and Adams*, 310.

21. Bemis, *Adams and Foundations*, 485–88; *Annals of Congress*, 16 Cong., 2 sess., 1820–21, 958–59.

22. C. F. Adams, ed., *Memoirs of John Quincy Adams*, 5:249–53.

23. The British government decided that this legislation did not violate the 1818 convention. Canning was instructed to drop the subject. See Castlereagh to Stratford Canning, April 10, 1821, FO 116/6, PRO; and Merk, *Oregon Question*, 174.

24. Verne Blue, "The Oregon Question, 1818–1828: A Study of Dr. John Floyd's Efforts in Congress to Secure the Oregon Country," *Oregon Historical Quarterly* 23 (Sept. 1922): 199, 203–4; *Boston Daily Advertiser*, Jan. 28, 31, Feb. 6, 20, 1822. See also Merk, *Oregon Question*, 120–21. William Sturgis added to the discussion later that year with his article "Examination of the Russian Claims to the North West Coast" in *North American Review*, Oct. 1822. See Bemis, *Adams and Foundations*, 511.

25. Blue, "Oregon Question, 1818–1828," 206–7.

26. Thomas Jefferson had suggested to John Jacob Astor that the territory on the Pacific coast would probably become an independent republic on the American model. See Thomas Jefferson to John Jacob Astor, Nov. 9, 1813, in Andrew A. Lipscomb and Albert E. Bergh, eds., *The Writings of Thomas Jefferson*, 20 vols. (Washington, DC, 1903–1904), 13:432–34; *Annals of Congress*, 17 Cong., 2 sess., 408, 414–22, 682–83; Merk, *Oregon Question*, 115–26; Bemis, *Adams and Foundations*, 511–16.

27. Johansen, *Empire of the Columbia*, 120; Protocol of the 12th Conference to Negotiate a Convention, April 2, 1824, *DCUSCR*, 2:407; Merk, *Oregon Question*, 129.

28. Richard Rush, *A Memoranda of a Residence at the Court of London* (Philadelphia, 1845), 468–69. See also J. H. Powell, *Richard Rush: Republican Diplomat, 1780–1859* (Philadelphia, 1942), 168–69.

29. Green, "Memorandum," *BDFA*, 2:71–72; Protocol of the 20th Conference to Negotiate a Convention, June 29, 1824, *DCUSCR*, 2:419–20.

30. Adams to Rush, July 22, 1823, *DCUSCR*, 2:55–66; Green, "Memorandum," *BDFA*, 2:72; Protocol of the 20th Conference to Negotiate a Convention, June 29, 1824, *DCUSCR*, 2:419–20.

31. *DCUSCR*, 2:419–20; Protocol of the 23d Conference to Negotiate a Convention, July 13, 1824, ibid., 421–22; Green, "Memorandum," *BDFA*, 2:73. See also Canning's reaction to Rush's message in Rush, *Residence at the Court*, 468–69. For Huskisson's denial of the noncolonization policy see Anna Lane Lingelbach, "Huskisson and the Board of Trade," *American Historical Review* 43 (July 1938): 769. See also Merk, *Oregon Question*, 136.

32. For details see Merk, *Oregon Question*, 46–71; and Winther, *Great Northwest*, 51. For Simpson's report on the Columbia Department see Frederick Merk, ed., *Fur Trade and Empire: George Simpson's Journal* (Cambridge, 1931), passim; and Winther, *Great Northwest*, 53. Simpson also suggested trapping out the southern area to block American encroachment. See Frederick Merk, "The Snake Country Expedition, 1824–1825: An Episode of Fur Trade and Empire," *Mississippi Valley Historical Review* 21 (June 1934): 49–62. See also Merk, *Oregon Question*, 72–98.

33. Merk, ed., *Fur Trade and Empire*, 257–66; Report of the Oregon Committee, May 15, 1826, U.S. Congress, *House Reports*, 19 Cong., 1 sess., 1–22; Canning to Liverpool, July 14, 1826, in Stapleton, ed., *Official Correspondence of Canning*, 2:115. For a discussion of the general mood of the British public and the cabinet see Merk, *Oregon Question*, 139–63.

34. Merk, *Oregon Question*, 107–13, 149; Clay to Gallatin, June 19, 1826, *ASPFR*, 6:644–46; Gallatin to Clay, June 20, 29, 30, 1826, in Henry Adams, ed.,

Writings of Albert Gallatin (New York, 1960), 2:307, 312–13, 319–20. For Clay's reply to Gallatin see Clay to Gallatin, June 23, 1826, *DCUSCR*, 2:105. Adams's "diplomatic administration" exercised caution because it was under attack for choosing negotiation over confrontation. See Mary W. M. Hargreaves, *The Presidency of John Quincy Adams* (Lawrence, KS, 1985), 115; and Canning Memorandum, Nov. 30, 1824, in Arthur R. Wellesley, ed., *Despatches, Correspondence and Memoranda of Field Marshal Arthur, Duke of Wellington* (London, 1867–1880), 2:358.

35. Henry Adams, ed., *Writings of Albert Gallatin*, 2:366–67. Later in the negotiations, Gallatin implied that the noncolonization doctrine was invalid. See William Huskisson and Henry U. Addington to Canning, Dec. 7, 1826, FO 5/219, PRO; Gallatin to Clay, Nov. 16, 1826, *ASPFR*, 6:650–52; and Green, "Memorandum," *BDFA*, 2:74.

36. Gallatin to Clay, Nov. 25, 1826, *ASPFR*, 6:652–55; Protocol of the Seventh Conference, Dec. 19, 1826, ibid., 666–71; Huskisson and Addington to Canning, Nov. 23, 1826, FO 5/219, PRO.

37. Gallatin to Clay, Nov. 25, Dec. 2, 1826, *ASPFR*, 6:654–56; Merk, *Oregon Question*, 167; Green, "Memorandum," *BDFA*, 2:74; Canning to Huskisson and Addington, Nov. 30, 1826, FO 5/219, PRO; Huskisson and Addington to Canning, Dec. 7, 1826, FO 5/219, PRO; Protocol of the Third Conference, Dec. 1, 1826, *ASPFR*, 6:660; Gallatin to Clay, June 20, 29, 30, 1826, in Adams, ed., *Writings of Albert Gallatin*, 2:307, 312–13, 319–20. For Clay's reply to Gallatin see Clay to Gallatin, June 23, 1826, *DCUSCR*, 2:105. For a discussion of the enclave offer see Merk, *Oregon Question*, 169.

38. For the draft of the Convention see *ASPFR*, 6:657; and Gallatin to Clay, Aug. 7, 9, 1827, ibid., 691–94.

39. Gallatin to Clay, Aug. 10, 1827, *DCUSCR*, 2:616.

40. T. C. Elliott, ed., "The Peter Skene Ogden Journals," *Oregon Historical Quarterly* 10 (Dec. 1909): 331–65; Gloria Griffin Cline, *Exploring the Great Basin* (Norman, OK, 1963); Merk, *Oregon Question*, 74–97; Johansen, *Empire of the Columbia*, 132–33. See also Fred Wilbur Powell, ed., *Hall J. Kelley on Oregon* (Princeton, 1932).

41. Johansen, *Empire of the Columbia*, 138–40. In 1825, Thomas Hart Benton, in his "Terminus Speech," contended that the Rocky Mountains would naturally block U.S. westward expansion. See Merk, *Oregon Question*, 117; Bell, *Highway to the Pacific*, 58, 70n, 77.

42. Winther, *Great Northwest*, 114–15; Robert Greenhow, *The History of Oregon and California* (Boston, 1844; reprint ed., Los Angeles, 1970), 361.

43. In 1847, Whitman found out how true this was when the Cayuse massacred his family and mission staff at Walla Walla. See Johansen, *Empire of the Columbia*, 172–73; John Forsyth to William A. Slacum, Nov. 11, 1835, *DCUSCR*, 2:294; Greenhow, *History of Oregon and California*, 361; and Slacum to Forsyth, March 26, 1837, *DCUSCR*, 3:390–91. See also Greenhow, *History of Oregon and California*, 363–64.

44. Alton (IL) *Telegraph*, Nov. 9, 1839. See also Bell, *Highway to the Pacific*, 86–87.

45. Report by Dr. Lewis F. Linn, June 6, 1838, *Senate Docs.*, 25 Cong., 2 sess., 1–23; Motion by Senator Linn, Jan. 2, 1839, *Senate Journal*, 25 Cong., 3 sess., 89; Res. by Senator Linn, Dec. 18, 1839, *Senate Journal*, 26 Cong., 1 sess., 12, 60. For the growing concern over law and order in the territory see Memorial from Citizens of Oregon Territory to U.S. Senate, Jan. 28, 1839, *Senate Journal*, 25 Cong., 3 sess., 161; Motion by Senator Linn, Jan. 2, 1839, ibid., 89; Winther,

Great Northwest, 142; and *Senate Journal*, 27 Cong., 2 sess., 81. For petitions see Cornelius J. Brosman, ed., "The Oregon Memorial of 1838," *Oregon Historical Quarterly* 35 (March 1933): 74–77; C. J. Pike, "Petitions of Oregon Settlers, 1838–1848," *Oregon Historical Quarterly* 35 (Sept. 1933): 216–35; *CG*, 25 Cong., 2 sess., Feb. 7, 1838, 169; ibid., May 11, 1838, 363; and Motion by Caleb Cushing, *House Journal*, Dec. 14, 1838, Jan. 4, Feb. 16, 1839, 25 Cong., 3 sess., 81, 195, 552.

46. In 1844 the mission board dispatched the Rev. George Gary in a vain attempt to reverse the secular trend. See Winther, *Great Northwest*, 117; Simpson to Governor, Deputy Governor, and Committee of the Hudson's Bay Company, Nov. 25, 1841, in Joseph Schafer, ed., "Letters of Sir George Simpson, 1841–1843," *American Historical Review* 14 (Oct. 1908–July 1909): 82; and Johansen, *Empire of the Columbia*, 164–72.

47. Johansen, *Empire of the Columbia*, 133–34; Stuart, *Expansionism*, 126–47; E. E. Rich, *History of the Hudson's Bay Company, 1670–1870*, 3 vols. (New York, 1961), 3:657–720 passim.

48. Forsyth to Andrew Stevenson, May 6, 1840, *DCUSCR*, 3:115; Stevenson to Forsyth, June 13, 30, July 3, 1840, ibid., 575, 579–81; Lord Palmerston to Stevenson, June 30, 1840, ibid., 580; George Simpson to London Office, July 8, 1839, cited in Merk, *Oregon Question*, 246. On Simpson's concern with the Farnham contingent see Simpson to McLoughlin, Sept. 11, 1840, in Glyndwr Williams, ed., *London Correspondents Inward from Sir George Simpson, 1841–42* (London, 1973), xxxv.

49. Charles Wilkes, "Document: Report on the Territory of Oregon," *Oregon Historical Review* 12 (Sept. 1911): 269–99; Simpson to Governor, Deputy Governor, and Committee of the Hudson's Bay Company, Nov. 25, 1841, in Schafer, ed., "Letters of Sir George Simpson," 82.

50. Schafer, ed., "Letters of Sir George Simpson," 70–89.

51. Donald A. Rakestraw, *For Honor or Destiny: The Anglo-American Crisis over the Oregon Territory* (New York, 1995), 42.

52. For Webster's explanation of this "tripartite" plan see Webster to Everett, Jan. 29, 1843, in Shewmaker, ed., *Daniel Webster: Diplomatic Papers*, 1:841–44; Green, "Memorandum," *BDFA*, 2:78; and Lord Ashburton to Lord Aberdeen, April 25, 1842, FO 5/379, PRO.

53. The British government had access to a collection of Oregon materials held by the Hudson's Bay Company that would have confirmed the diminished value of the territory. Unfortunately, the Foreign Office did not consult it. See Merk, *Oregon Question*, 203; Winther, *Great Northwest*, 122; Johansen, *Empire of the Columbia*, 164; Bell, *Highway to the Pacific*, 141; and Reginald Horsman, "American Indian Policy and the Origins of Manifest Destiny," *University of Birmingham Historical Journal* 11 (1968): 138–40. See also Horsman's "Scientific Racism and the American Indian in the Mid-Nineteenth Century," *American Quarterly* 27 (May 1975): 152–68, and *Race and Manifest Destiny: The Origins of American Racial Anglo-Saxonism* (Cambridge, 1981).

54. Jones, *Webster-Ashburton Treaty*, 154. Instructions for the northeastern problems accounted for more than triple those addressing the Oregon dispute. See Aberdeen to Ashburton, Feb. 8, 1842, FO 5/378, PRO; Merk, *Oregon Question*, 197–204; and House Res. Calling for Correspondence . . . Relating to Country West of Rocky Mountains, Feb. 20, 1828, *House Journal*, 20 Cong., 1 sess., 321.

55. Peter A. Brinsmade to Webster, April 8, 1842, in Shewmaker, ed., *Daniel Webster: Diplomatic Papers*, 1:863.

56. Ashburton to Aberdeen, July 13, 1842, Aberdeen Papers.

57. Ashburton to Webster, July 1, 1842, *DCUSCR*, 3:744–45; Ashburton to Aberdeen, June 29, 1842, ibid., 745n.

Chapter 8: Feed a Cold, Starve a Fever, 175–200

1. Bell, *Highway to the Pacific*, 89–90, 107.

2. Aberdeen to H. S. Fox, Oct. 18, 1842, *BDFA*, 2:122–23; Everett to Webster, Oct. 17, 1842, in Shewmaker, ed., *Daniel Webster: Diplomatic Papers*, 1:701–2.

3. Aberdeen to Fox, Oct. 18, 1842, *BDFA*, 2:122–23; Fox to Aberdeen, Nov. 15, 27, 1842, ibid., 124–25; Webster to Everett, Nov. 28, 1842, in Shewmaker, ed., *Daniel Webster: Diplomatic Papers*, 1:835.

4. Richardson, ed., *Messages and Papers*, 4:260–63. For contemporary commentary on Tyler's message see Greenhow, *History of Oregon and California*, 377; and Fox to Aberdeen, Dec. 12, 1842, FO 5/418, PRO.

5. Senate Bill No. 22, Dec. 20, 1842, *Senate Journal*, 27 Cong., 3 sess., 35, 148; Greenhow, *History of Oregon and California*, 378–80; Thomas R. Hietala, *Manifest Design: Anxious Aggrandizement in Late Jacksonian America* (Ithaca, NY, 1985), 65–79.

6. Everett to Webster, Jan. 2, 1843, in Shewmaker, ed., *Daniel Webster: Diplomatic Papers*, 1:838–39. Tyler's comment in his message about the right of search also agitated Aberdeen. See Everett to Webster, Feb. 1, 1843, ibid., 1:805–7. Aberdeen struggled throughout his tenure at the Foreign Office to change the traditionally hostile relationship between Great Britain and France and to create an entente cordiale. For a brief discussion see Murial Chamberlain, *Lord Aberdeen: A Political Biography* (New York, 1983), chaps. 21–22; and Jones, *American Problem*, 33–34.

7. Senate Bill No. 22, Dec. 20, 1842, *Senate Journal*, 27 Cong., 3 sess., 35, 148; Winther, *Great Northwest*, 144. There are numerous refutations of Benton's statement. The company was generally kind and hospitable to American settlers. For various testimonials see Bell, *Highway to the Pacific*, 144–48. Even Charles Wilkes admitted the generosity of the company in his report on Oregon in June 1842. See Wilkes, "Report on the Territory of Oregon," 299.

8. *CG*, 27 Cong., 3 sess., Jan. 25, 1843, 200; Greenhow, *History of Oregon and California*, 380–87; *CG, App.*, 27 Cong., 3 sess., Jan. 24, 1843, 138; Jesse S. Reeves, *American Diplomacy under Tyler and Polk* (New York, 1907; reprint ed., Gloucester, MA, 1967), 246; Crallé, ed., *Works of Calhoun*, 6:238.

9. Fox to Aberdeen, Jan. 29, 1843, FO 115/84, PRO; Aberdeen to Fox, Feb. 3, 1843, FO 5/418, PRO.

10. Fox to Aberdeen, March 4, 1843, FO 115/84, PRO.

11. Webster to Everett, Nov. 28, 1842, Jan. 29, 1843, in Shewmaker, ed., *Daniel Webster: Diplomatic Papers*, 1:834–43. For a discussion of Webster's views on Oregon see C. T. Johnson, "Daniel Webster, Lord Ashburton, and Old Oregon," *Washington Historical Quarterly* 1 (1906–1907): 208–16; and idem, "Daniel Webster and Old Oregon," *Washington Historical Quarterly* 2 (1907–1908): 6–11. For details on the Jones incident see George M. Brooke, Jr., "The Vest Pocket War of Commodore Jones," *Pacific Historical Review* 31 (1962): 217–33; Fox to Aberdeen, Feb. 24, 1843, FO 115/84, PRO; and Everett to Webster, Feb. 27, 1843, in Shewmaker, ed., *Daniel Webster: Diplomatic Papers*, 1:847.

12. Winther, *Great Northwest*, 125; Bell, *Highway to the Pacific*, 113.

13. Bell, *Highway to the Pacific*, 110–11; Greenhow, *History of Oregon and California*, 391. See also Johansen, *Empire of the Columbia*, 202. For details of

the convention see C. S. Kingston, "The Oregon Convention of 1843," *Washington Historical Quarterly* 22 (July 1931): 163–71; *Niles' National Register* 64 (July 29, 1843): 345; Pletcher, *Diplomacy of Annexation*, 215.

14. Greenhow, *History of Oregon and California*, 391–92; Richard Pakenham to Aberdeen, June 27, 1844, FO 5/406, PRO; James Douglas to Simpson, Oct. 23, 1843, in E. E. Rich, ed., *The Letters of John McLoughlin from Fort Vancouver to the Governor and Committee: Third Series, 1844–46* (Toronto, 1944), xxx–xxxi; Pletcher, *Diplomacy of Annexation*, 110.

15. Merk, *Oregon Question*, 257; Richard S. Cramer, "British Magazines and the Oregon Question," *Pacific Historical Review* 32 (May 1963): 371.

16. Aberdeen to Fox, June 3, 1843, FO 115/81, PRO. Fox believed that Tyler would not trust the matter to Everett because he was a holdover from the Whig appointments. See Fox to Aberdeen, Sept. 12, 1843, FO 5/418, PRO; and Everett to Abel P. Upshur, Aug. 17, 1843, *DCUSCR*, 3:823.

17. For Paulet's adventure in Hawaii see R. S. Kuykendall, *The Hawaiian Kingdom, 1778–1854* (Honolulu, 1938), 206–26; and John Tyler to Hugh S. Legaré, May 16, 1843, in Tyler, *Letters and Times*, 3:111–12. For Aberdeen's reversal of Paulet's action see Aberdeen to Fox, June 3, 1843, FO 115/81, PRO; Hietala, *Manifest Design*, 58–63; *Madisonian*, June 2, 1843; and John Tyler to Daniel Webster, July 8, 1843, in Tyler, *Letters and Times*, 2:272–73.

18. Everett to Upshur, Nov. 2, 14, Dec. 2, 1843, *DCUSCR*, 3:826–37; Green, "Memorandum," *BDFA*, 2:81–82.

19. Aberdeen to Pakenham, Dec. 28, 1843, FO 5/390, PRO.

20. Aberdeen to Pakenham, March 4, 1844, Aberdeen Papers. This letter has been reprinted in Robert C. Clark, ed., "Letter of Aberdeen to Pakenham, March 4, 1844, Concerning the Oregon Question," *Oregon Historical Quarterly* 39 (1938): 74–76.

21. Richardson, ed., *Messages and Papers*, 5:2111; Introduction of Atchison bill in U.S. Senate, Dec. 21, 1843, *Senate Journal*, 28 Cong., 1 sess., 43; Res. by R. D. Owen in U.S. House of Representatives, Jan. 4, 1844, *House Journal*, 28 Cong., 1 sess., 164; Res. by J. Semple in U.S. Senate, Jan. 8, 1844, *Senate Journal*, 28 Cong., 1 sess., 60, 182. Members of both parties expressed opposition, fearing that it would expose Everett's hand prematurely. Congressman J. Wentworth of Illinois introduced a similar resolution in the House; *CG*, 28 Cong., 1 sess., Jan. 4, 1844, 104. See Res., Jan. 4, 1844, *House Journal*, 28 Cong., 1 sess., 167, 198.

22. Fox to Aberdeen, Dec. 13, 1843, Jan. 19, 27, 1844, FO 5/390, PRO.

23. Claude H. Hall, *Abel Parker Upshur* (Madison, WI, 1963), 211–12.

24. *CG*, 28 Cong., 1 sess., March 18, 1844, 395.

25. Pakenham to Aberdeen, March 28, 1844, Aberdeen Papers; Hietala, *Manifest Design*, 65–79.

26. Charles Wiltse, *John C. Calhoun, Sectionalist, 1840–1850* (New York, 1951), 165–71.

27. Hietala, *Manifest Design*, 15–18; *Madisonian* quote in Pletcher, *Diplomacy of Annexation*, 124–25.

28. In the summer of 1844, Britain and France discussed a bilateral move to secure the status quo in the Pacific Southwest. See Pletcher, *Diplomacy of Annexation*, 157–60; Pakenham to Aberdeen, July 29, 1844, FO 5/407, PRO.

29. Pakenham to Aberdeen, June 27, 1844, FO 5/406, PRO; Pakenham to Aberdeen, April 14, 1844, FO 5/404, PRO.

30. Pletcher, *Diplomacy of Annexation*, 143; Pakenham to Aberdeen, May 13, 1844, FO 5/405, PRO.

31. Winther, *Great Northwest*, 123, 135–37. For a map of the county arrangement in the territory see Johansen, *Empire of the Columbia*, 233.

32. Merk, *Oregon Question*, 249; Bell, *Highway to the Pacific*, 163–79.

33. Johansen, *Empire of the Columbia*, 191.

34. *Globe* (Washington), April 27, 1844; *National Intelligencer*, April 27, 1844; Charles A. McCoy, *Polk and the Presidency* (Austin, 1960), 35–43. For a discussion of Walker's involvement see James P. Shenton, *Robert John Walker: A Politician from Jackson to Lincoln* (New York, 1961), 41–55; and Merk, *Oregon Question*, 367. The "Fifty-four Forty or Fight" slogan, contrary to tradition, was not the Democratic mantra in 1844. See Edwin A. Miles, " 'Fifty-four Forty or Fight': An American Political Legend," *Mississippi Valley Historical Review* 44 (Sept. 1957): 291–309.

35. Whig Robert Winthrop of Massachusetts announced to Congress that his section of the country would stand for U.S. rights in the territory. *CG*, 28 Cong., 1 sess., March 1844, *App.*, 318–19, 264–65. For a discussion of the expansionist theme of the period and its related components see Albert K. Weinberg, *Manifest Destiny: A Study of Nationalist Expansionism in American History* (Gloucester, MA, 1958); Anders Stephanson, *Manifest Destiny: American Expansionism and the Empire of Right* (New York, 1995), 28–65; and Paul H. Bergeron, *The Presidency of James K. Polk* (Lawrence, KS, 1987), 20. A bitter John Quincy Adams derided the election results: "The partial associations of Native Americans, Irish Catholics, abolition societies, liberty party, the Pope of Rome, the Democracy of the sword, and the dotage of a ruffian [Andrew Jackson] are sealing the fate of this nation, which nothing less than the interposition of Omnipotence can save." Quoted in Robert Remini, *Henry Clay: Statesman for the Union* (New York, 1991), 663.

36. Everett to Calhoun, April 1, 1844, Desp., GB, NA.

37. Travis L. Crosby, *Sir Robert Peel's Administration, 1841–1846* (London, 1976), 109–12; Government House, Kingston (Canada), to Lord Stanley, April 18, 1844, FO 5/419, PRO.

38. For more information on Anglo-American competition on the Lakes see Bourne, *Balance of Power*, 125–31; Pakenham to Aberdeen, July 29, 1844, FO 5/407, PRO; Foreign Office to Pakenham, July 3, 1844, FO 5/403, PRO; Barry M. Gough, *The Royal Navy and the Northwest Coast of North America, 1810–1914: A Study of British Maritime Ascendancy* (Vancouver, 1971), 65; R. C. Clark, *History of the Willamette Valley, Oregon*, 2 vols. (Chicago, 1927), 1:327–28; and Barry M. Gough, "HMS *Modeste* on the Pacific Coast, 1843–1847: Log and Letters," *Oregon Historical Quarterly* 61 (Dec. 1960): 408–36.

39. Pletcher, *Diplomacy of Annexation*, 149; Sam S. Phelps to Calhoun, March 6, 1844, in Chauncey S. Boucher and Robert P. Brooks, eds., "Correspondence Addressed to John C. Calhoun," *Annual Report of the American Historical Association for the Year 1929* (Washington, DC, 1930), 213. See also Francis W. Pickens to Calhoun, April 22, 1844, ibid., 222; and L. W. Hastings to Calhoun, May 20, 1844, ibid., 234–35; Pakenham to Aberdeen, June 13, 1844, Aberdeen Papers; and Bourne, *Balance of Power*, 132.

40. Pakenham to Aberdeen, No. 88, July 29, 1844, FO 5/407, PRO.

41. Calhoun to Pakenham, Aug. 22, 23, 26, Sept. 3, 5, 20, 1844, and Pakenham to Calhoun, Aug. 22, Sept. 12, 1844, *DCUSCR*, 3:254–71, 892–903. See Pakenham to Aberdeen, Aug. 29, 1844, FO 5/407, PRO; and Calhoun to Pakenham, Sept. 3, 1844, *DCUSCR*, 3:254–63.

42. Pakenham had anticipated Calhoun's contiguity argument in an earlier despatch. Notably, in this one, Pakenham promised to send any offer beyond his

instructions to the Foreign Office for consideration. It is unfortunate that he did not do this later, when communicating with his superiors might have prevented a crisis. See Pakenham to Aberdeen, Aug. 29, 1844, FO 5/407, PRO; Pakenham to Aberdeen, Sept. 28, 12, 1844, FO 5/408, PRO; Bourne, *Balance of Power*, 144; and Pakenham to Calhoun, [n.d.] (received Sept. 12, 1844), *DCUSCR*, 3:895–901.

43. Calhoun to Pakenham, Sept. 20, 1844, *DCUSCR*, 3:267–71; Memorandum of Sixth Conference Held with Calhoun and Pakenham, Sept. 24, 1844, ibid., 902–3; Aberdeen to Peel, Oct. 17, 1844, and Peel to Aberdeen, Oct. 19, 1844, Peel Papers.

44. Aberdeen to Pakenham, Nov. 1, 18, 1844, *BDFA*, 2:149–50.

45. Pletcher, *Diplomacy of Annexation*, 222–23.

46. Pakenham to Aberdeen, Dec. 12, 1844, *BDFA*, 151; Richardson, ed., *Messages and Papers*, 5:2191.

47. Bill introduced in U.S. House by Alexander Duncan, Dec. 16, 1844, *House Journal*, 28 Cong., 2 sess., 85–86; *CG*, App., 28 Cong., 2 sess., Dec. 19, 1844, 44; Pletcher, *Diplomacy of Annexation*, 223.

48. Pakenham to Aberdeen, Nov. 28, 1844, FO 5/409, PRO.

49. Pakenham to Aberdeen, Dec. 29, 1844, *BDFA*, 2:152–54; Pakenham to Aberdeen, Jan. 9, 29, 1845, FO 5/424, PRO; Pakenham to Calhoun, Jan. 15, 1845, *DCUSCR*, 3:912; Calhoun to Pakenham, Jan. 21, 1845, ibid., 271–72.

50. Pakenham to Aberdeen, Feb. 4, 1845, FO 5/424, PRO. See Pletcher, *Diplomacy of Annexation*, 223.

51. Everett to Calhoun, Feb. 28, 1845, Desp., GB, NA.

52. Ibid.

53. Ibid. Aberdeen had developed a close relationship with *Times* editor John Delane. The ministry would therefore use the *Times* to disseminate information. Merk, *Oregon Question*, 297–98; Everett to Calhoun, Feb. 28, 1845, in Clyde N. Wilson, ed., *The Papers of John C. Calhoun*, 22 vols. (Columbia, SC, 1995), 21:383–84.

54. *Niles' National Register* 64 (July 29, 1843): 345.

Chapter 9: Young Hickory Takes Charge, 201–32

1. On Polk's characteristics pertinent to his role as president there are a number of useful works. See Charles G. Sellers, *James K. Polk: Continentalist, 1843–1846* (Princeton, NJ, 1966); McCoy, *Polk and the Presidency*; and Bergeron, *Presidency of James K. Polk*. Also useful is Leonard D. White, *The Jacksonians: A Study in Administrative History, 1829–1861* (New York, 1954); Milo M. Quaife, ed., *The Diary of James K. Polk during his Presidency, 1845 to 1849*, 4 vols. (Chicago, 1910), 4:355. For Secretary of State Buchanan see Philip S. Klein, *President James Buchanan: A Biography* (University Park, PA, 1962). For Secretary of the Treasury Robert Walker see Shenton, *Robert John Walker*. For Secretary of War William Marcy see Ivor D. Spenser, *The Victor and the Spoils: A Life of William L. Marcy* (Providence, RI, 1959). Useful information on Secretary of the Navy George Bancroft can be found in Lilian Handlin, *George Bancroft: The Intellectual as Democrat* (New York, 1984); and Russell B. Nye, *George Bancroft: Brahmin Rebel* (New York, 1944).

2. The earlier drafts of the inaugural address are in the Polk Papers. Pletcher discusses the earlier drafts in his *Diplomacy of Annexation*, 236–37; Richardson, ed., *Messages and Papers*, 4:381.

3. Pakenham to Aberdeen, March 4, 1845, FO 5/425, PRO.

4. Pakenham to Aberdeen, March 29, 1845, ibid. For Pakenham's recollection of Buchanan's previous attitude toward arbitration see Pakenham to Aberdeen, Aug. 29, 1845, Aberdeen Papers.

5. Pakenham to Aberdeen, March 29, 1845, FO 5/425, PRO; Pletcher, *Diplomacy of Annexation*, 221.

6. Aberdeen to Pakenham, March 3, 1845, FO 5/423, 5/118, PRO; Admiralty to Addington, March 6, 1845, and Foreign Office to Hamilton (at Admiralty), March 8, 1845, FO 5/440, PRO.

7. *Times* (London), April 5, 1845; Aberdeen to Pakenham, April 6, 1845, FO 115/88, PRO.

8. Everett to James Buchanan, April 2, 1845, Desp., GB, NA; Everett to Buchanan, April 4, 1845, *DCUSCR*, 3:945–46; Chamberlain, *Lord Aberdeen*, 336; *Parl. Debates*, 79:115–24, 199.

9. Foreign Office to Colonial Office, April 3, 1845, FO 5/440, PRO; Everett to Buchanan, April 4, 1845, *DCUSCR*, 3:946; Simpson to Sir John Pelly, Memoranda in Reference to the Oregon Question, March 29, 1845, FO 5/440, PRO.

10. Aberdeen to Pakenham, April 18, 1845, FO 5/423, PRO.

11. Aberdeen to Pakenham, April 18, 1845, Aberdeen Papers.

12. In February, Peel had pushed for abolition of duties, both export and import, on over four hundred items, including cotton. Elie Halevy, *The Age of Peel and Cobden: A History of the English People, 1841–1852* (New York, 1948), 80–86; Bourne, *Balance of Power*, 136–37; Everett to Buchanan, April 3, 16, 1845, Desp., GB, NA; *DCUSCR*, 3:944, 948–52; Crosby, *Sir Robert Peel's Administration*, 110.

13. Pakenham to Aberdeen, April 28, 1845, FO 5/425, PRO; Everett to Buchanan, April 16, 1845, *DCUSCR*, 3:948–52. There were exceptions among expansionists in New York, Baltimore, and Washington. See Frederick Merk, *Manifest Destiny and Mission in American History: A Reinterpretation*, 3d ed. (New York, 1970), 39; and *Illinois State Register*, May 9, 1845. For a discussion of the sectional attitudes on expansionism reflected in the press see Merk, *Manifest Destiny and Mission*, 37–38; Pletcher, *Diplomacy of Annexation*, 240.

14. Andrew Jackson to James K. Polk, May 2, 1845, in John Spencer Bassett, ed., *The Correspondence of Andrew Jackson*, 8 vols. (Washington, DC, 1933), 6:404–6. As a teenager, Jackson enlisted in the militia and was captured by a British raiding party. Its commander ordered him to clean his boots, but Jackson refused. The furious officer struck him with his sword, leaving the boy with scars and a lifelong dislike for the British.

15. Pletcher, *Diplomacy of Annexation*, 247.

16. Jones, *American Problem*, 41–42; Pakenham to Aberdeen, May 13, 1845, FO 5/426, PRO; Everett to Buchanan, April 28, 1845, Desp., GB, NA.

17. Pakenham to Aberdeen, May 13, 29, 1845, FO 5/426, PRO.

18. Hietala, *Manifest Design*, 79.

19. Merk contends that Polk was not committed to the 54°40' cause but rather took the more moderate southern position. See Merk, *Oregon Question*, 342–44. If this was the case, however, it is doubtful that the president would have halted negotiations so abruptly after only one offer. For details on McLane's previous mission to London see John A. Munroe, *Louis McLane: Federalist and Jacksonian* (New Brunswick, NJ, 1973), 262–92.

20. Pakenham to Aberdeen, July 29, 1845, FO 5/427, PRO.

21. Buchanan to Louis McLane, July 12, 1845, Dip. Instr., GB, NA.

22. Ibid.

23. Pakenham believed that Polk planned to involve McLane in the process. The British minister told Aberdeen on the 13th that McLane was on his way to London and that Buchanan wanted him to meet with Aberdeen before a U.S. proposal was put to Pakenham. See Pakenham to Aberdeen, July 13, 1845, FO 5/427, PRO.

24. Pakenham to Buchanan, July 19, 1845, NFBL, NA; *DCUSCR*, 3:967.

25. Pakenham to Aberdeen, July 29, 1845, FO 5/427, PRO.

26. McLoughlin to Simpson, March 28, 1845, FO 5/443, PRO; Report of July 1845 by McLoughlin in Pelly to Aberdeen, Feb. 13, 1846, FO 5/459, PRO.

27. McLoughlin letter dated Aug. 30, 1845, in Pelly to Aberdeen, Feb. 13, 1846, FO 5/459, PRO. *The Gazette* (St. Joseph, MO) is a good example; see various issues from May 2, 1845, through Aug. 21, 1846.

28. McLane to Polk, Aug. 11, 1845, in Miller, ed., *Treaties*, 5:35–36; Pletcher, *Diplomacy of Annexation*, 252. According to John Munroe, McLane took the Oregon impasse personally, believing that the administration had intentionally disrupted the negotiations to prevent him from garnering any credit for an Oregon settlement. See Munroe, *Louis McLane*, 518.

29. In early August, rumors circulated that Mexico had deployed troops to the Rio Grande and planned an assault across the river. Polk to Buchanan, Aug. 7, 1845, and Bancroft to Buchanan, Aug. 7, 1845, in John Bassett Moore, ed., *The Works of James Buchanan*, 12 vols. (Philadelphia, 1908–1911), 6:223–25; Allan Nevins, ed., *Polk, the Diary of a President* (New York, 1929), 3–4; Calhoun to Buchanan, Aug. 30, 1845, in Moore, ed., *Works of James Buchanan*, 6:230.

30. Pakenham had argued that the Florida treaty weakened rather than substantiated American claims. See Pakenham to Buchanan, July 29, 1845, *DCUSCR*, 3:967–75; and Buchanan to Pakenham, Aug. 30, 1845, ibid., 288–308.

31. Pakenham to Aberdeen, Sept. 13, 1845, FO 5/428, PRO. Pakenham was correct that party considerations played a role. See Nevins, ed., *Polk, Diary of a President,* 29–30. One of the consequences of Pakenham's rejection was the debilitating effect it had on Aberdeen's propaganda campaign. He had made substantial strides toward convincing the British people that compromise was both necessary and honorable. The collaboration of British economist Nassau Senior and Everett had contributed. See Merk, *Oregon Question*, 282–308. For a discussion of the British arbitration proposals see James O. McCabe, "Arbitration and the Oregon Question," *Canadian Historical Review* 41 (Dec. 1960): 308–27; and Merk, *Oregon Question*, 216–33.

32. Rakestraw, *For Honor or Destiny*, 106; Pletcher, *Diplomacy of Annexation*, 248–49; Bergeron, *Presidency of James K. Polk*, 119; Sellers, *James K. Polk: Continentalist*, 251.

33. McLane to Buchanan, Sept. 3, 1845, James Buchanan Papers, Historical Society of Pennsylvania, Philadelphia (hereafter cited as Buchanan Papers); Buchanan to McLane, Sept. 13, 1845, Polk Papers; Reeves, *American Diplomacy under Tyler and Polk*, 254. McLane's frustration is evident in his correspondence with his son Robert. See Munroe, *Louis McLane*, 521.

34. McLane to Buchanan, Oct. 3, 1845, Desp., GB, NA.

35. Aberdeen to Pakenham, Oct. 3, 1845, FO 5/423, PRO.

36. Polk to McLane, Oct. 29, 1845, Polk Papers; Nevins, ed., *Polk, Diary of a President*, 14–16; Pletcher, *Diplomacy of Annexation*, 299; Reeves, *American Diplomacy under Tyler and Polk*, 255–56.

37. Pakenham to Aberdeen, Oct. 29, 1845, FO 5/429, PRO; Pakenham to Buchanan, Oct. 25, 1845, ibid.; Nevins, ed., *Polk, Diary of a President*, 21–22.

38. Pakenham to Aberdeen, Oct. 28, 1845, Aberdeen Papers; Aberdeen to Peel, Nov. 21, 1845, Peel Papers.

39. Barry M. Gough, "HMS *America* on the North Pacific Coast," *Oregon Historical Quarterly* 70 (Dec. 1969): 300–304; William Irving to Aberdeen, July 30, 1845, FO 5/435, PRO.

40. McLane to Robert McLane, Oct. 10, 18, Nov. 2, 1845, McLane Papers; Munroe, *Louis McLane*, 518; Pletcher, *Diplomacy of Annexation*, 293.

41. For a discussion of manifest destiny see Weinberg, *Manifest Destiny*, and Merk's reinterpretation, *Manifest Destiny and Mission*; *Democratic Review* 12 (July 1845): 5–10; Pletcher, *Diplomacy of Annexation*, 302; and *United States Journal*, May 3, 1845.

42. For a thorough examination of the commercial motivation behind manifest destiny see Norman Graebner, *Empire on the Pacific: A Study in American Continental Expansion* (New York, 1955); Cushing's Treaty of Wanghia had essentially secured a most-favored-nation arrangement with China and had Canton, Amoy, Fuchow, Ning-po, and Shanghai declared "open-ports." See Claude M. Fuess, *The Life of Caleb Cushing* (New York, 1923), 438–39. Some Americans preferred that Oregon follow the Texas model, establishing independence first and then moving toward annexation. For examples see the Baltimore *Sun*, Aug. 21, 1845; *Herald* (New York), Oct. 1, 1845; *Morning News* (New York), Dec. 16, 1845.

43. Seymour to Admiralty, Oct. 5, 1845, FO 5/444, PRO; Pletcher, *Diplomacy of Annexation*, 275, 293; Reports of Lieutenant Peel, in Admiralty to Foreign Office, Feb. 10, 1846, FO 5/459, PRO; Gough, "HMS *America* on the North Pacific Coast," 300–304; Leslie M. Scott, ed., "Report of Lieutenant Peel on Oregon in 1845–46," *Oregon Historical Quarterly* 29 (March 1928): 66–71. The substantial attention devoted to France in Peel's Papers supports the argument that a British arms buildup was more likely directed across the Channel. For a representation of this see Charles Stuart Parker, ed., *Sir Robert Peel from his Private Papers*, 3 vols. (London, 1899; reprint ed., New York, 1970), 3:195–219. It should be noted that while Lord Wellington was shoring up Channel defenses, a threatened resignation by Aberdeen restrained some of the Francophobes in the Peel cabinet. See Jones, *American Problem*, 45.

44. Chicago *Democrat*, quoted in *Times* (London), Aug. 29, 1845; Pakenham to Aberdeen, Aug. 8, Sept. 28, 1845, FO 5/428, PRO; Aberdeen to Peel, Aug. 29, 1845, Peel Papers; Simpson to Hudson's Bay Company London, Oct. 28, 1845, FO 5/444, PRO; Pakenham to Aberdeen, Nov. 13, 1845, FO 5/429, PRO.

45. Pakenham to Aberdeen, Nov. 13, 1845, FO 5/429, PRO. Webster supported compromise but believed that Oregon would become an independent state. Webster's speech is reprinted in *National Intelligencer*, Nov. 11, 1845. McLane later complained to Polk that the actions of Webster and other Whigs undercut the American position. McLane to Polk, Dec. 1, 1845, Polk Papers.

46. Nevin, ed., *Polk, Diary of a President*, 29–30.

47. McLane to Buchanan, Dec. 1, 1845, *DCUSCR*, 3:985; Foreign Office to Pakenham, Nov. 28, 1845, FO 5/423, PRO.

48. Pletcher, *Diplomacy of Annexation*, 307; Nevins, ed., *Polk, Diary of a President*, 17–19. The California discussion reflected the apprehension created by Thomas O. Larkin's reports of British intrigue in the province. See Pletcher, *Diplomacy of Annexation*, 282. See also E. D. Adams, "English Interest in the Annexation of California," *American Historical Review* 14 (1909): 744–63.

49. Richardson, ed., *Messages and Papers*, 4:387–89; Charles Campbell, *The United States and Great Britain, 1783–1900* (New York, 1974), 68.

50. *Niles' National Register* 69 (Dec. 6, 1845): 209; Quaife, ed., *Diary of James K. Polk*, 1:109–16. Many of those who called on Polk were preoccupied with the tariff issue.

51. Res. by Cass, Dec. 9, 1845, *Senate Journal*, 29 Cong., 1 sess., 39; Merk, *Oregon Question*, 379; *CG*, 29 Cong., 1 sess., Dec. 15, 16, 1845, 45–51, 55, 58–59, *App.*, 61; Atchison Res., Dec. 18, 1845, *Senate Journal*, 29 Cong., 1 sess., 57.

52. Calhoun to Francis W. Pickens, Sept. 23, 1845, in Wilson, ed., *Papers of Calhoun*, 22:165; Rufus L. King to Calhoun, Dec. 10, 1845, in Boucher and Brooks, eds., "Correspondence Addressed to John C. Calhoun," 310; Nevins, ed., *Polk, Diary of a President*, 33–35. For Adams's commitment to continentalism see Bemis, *Adams and the Union*, 481–500, esp. 488–89.

53. For the conflict in the Peel cabinet and the potato famine see Blanche Cecil Woodham-Smith, *The Great Hunger: Ireland, 1845–49* (New York, 1962), 40–53.

54. Russell had announced his conversion to repeal of the Corn Laws in November with publication of his *Letter to the Electors of the City of London*, Russell Papers; Crosby, *Sir Robert Peel's Administration*, 142; Merk, *Oregon Question*, 271–72. European leaders fretted at the specter of Palmerston's return. Henry Reeves wrote Russell from Paris that the "name of Palmerston sent down the funds more than a franc." Reeves to Russell, Dec. 15, 1845, Russell Papers.

55. Lord Mahon and Edward Cardwell, eds., *Memoirs of Sir Robert Peel* (London, 1856; reprint ed., New York, 1969), 251, 258–59; Jones, *American Problem*, 48; Aberdeen to Peel, Dec. 25, 1845, Aberdeen Papers.

56. *Morning News* (New York), July 7, 1845; Pakenham to Aberdeen, Dec. 13, 1845, FO 5/429, PRO.

57. Quaife, ed., *Diary of James K. Polk*, 1:117–18. Pakenham also expressed satisfaction that the senator had compromised his earlier all-Oregon position. Pakenham to Aberdeen, Dec. 29, 1845, FO 5/430, PRO; Quaife, ed., *Diary of James K. Polk*, 1:118; Klein, *President James Buchanan*, 181.

58. Buchanan to McLane, Dec. 13, 1845, in Moore, ed., *Works of James Buchanan*, 6:342–43.

59. McLane to Buchanan, Dec. 1, 1845, Desp., GB, NA.

60. Nevins, ed., *Polk, Diary of a President*, 36.

61. Quaife, ed., *Diary of James K. Polk*, 1:139–42; Polk to McLane, Dec. 29, 1845, Polk Papers.

62. Interview, Buchanan with Pakenham, Dec. 27, 1845, in Moore, ed., *Works of James Buchanan*, 6:352–53; Buchanan to Pakenham, Jan. 3, 1846, NTFL, GB, NA.

63. Buchanan to Pakenham, Jan. 3, 1846, NTFL, GB, NA.

64. Pakenham to Aberdeen, Jan. 5, 1846, FO 5/446, PRO.

Chapter 10: The Oregon Treaty, 233–63

1. Pakenham to Aberdeen, Jan. 5, 1846, FO 5/446, PRO. Charles Sellers stresses this idea. See Sellers, *James K. Polk: Continentalist*, 377–78; and Merk, *Oregon Question*, 232.

2. Pakenham to Aberdeen, Dec. 29, 1845, FO 5/430, PRO. Pakenham revealed the identity of those making the suggestion in a separate despatch of the same date.

3. Pakenham to Aberdeen, Jan. 2, 1846, FO 5/446, PRO; Hannegan Res., Dec. 29, 1845, *Senate Journal*, 29 Cong., 1 sess., 73; Allen Res., Dec. 18, 1845, ibid., 58, 68.

4. *CG*, 29 Cong., 1 sess., Dec. 30, 1845, 109–11; Sellers, *James K. Polk: Continentalist*, 366–69, 372; Quaife, ed., *Diary of James K. Polk*, 1:153–56, 159–62; Wiltse, *Calhoun, Sectionalist*, 254; Pakenham to Aberdeen, Jan. 13, 1846, FO 5/446, PRO.

5. Miles, " 'Fifty-four Forty or Fight,' " 303; Pletcher, *Diplomacy of Annexation*, 309; Bourne, *Balance of Power*, 162–63.

6. McLane to Buchanan, Dec. 1, 1845, Desp., GB, NA; Pletcher, *Diplomacy of Annexation*, 314; *Illustrated News* (London), Dec. 27, 1845.

7. McLane to Calhoun, Jan. 3, 1846, in Boucher and Brooks, eds., "Correspondence Addressed to John C. Calhoun," 311–15. Charles C. F. Greville thought that the December leak to Delane was intended to promote American conciliation in Oregon with the enticement of free trade. Charles C. F. Greville, *The Greville Memoirs: A Journal of the Reign of Queen Victoria from 1837 to 1852*, ed. Henry Reeve, 2 vols. (New York, 1885), 2:312; Pletcher, *Diplomacy of Annexation*, 316; Merk, *Oregon Question*, 297–98.

8. McLane to Buchanan, Jan. 3, 1846, Desp., GB, NA; McLane to Calhoun, Jan. 3, 1846, in Boucher and Brooks, eds., "Correspondence Addressed to John C. Calhoun," 311–15. It was indiscreet of McLane to confide in Calhoun. The American minister apparently hoped to set up a scenario in which he would receive credit for settling the dispute. Munroe, *Louis McLane*, 525–26.

9. McLane to Buchanan, Feb. 3, 1846, Desp., GB, NA; *DCUSCR*, 3:997–98. See also *Parl. Debates*, 83:28, 52–55.

10. McLane to Buchanan, Feb. 3, 1846, Desp., GB, NA. The pertinent part of the letter appears in Merk, *Oregon Question*, 259–60, quote on 260; Crosby, *Sir Robert Peel's Administration*, 142–43.

11. McLane to Buchanan, Feb. 3, 1846, Desp., GB, NA; Peel to Queen Victoria, Dec. 8, 1845, in Mahon and Cardwell, eds., *Memoirs of Sir Robert Peel*, 225–26; Ellenborough to Peel, Jan. 18, Feb. 7, 1846, Ellenborough Papers. See also Bourne, *Balance of Power*, 156–60. For a discussion of British naval movement associated with the Pacific Northwest see Gough, *Royal Navy and the Northwest Coast of North America*, chap. 3, passim; Buchanan to McLane, Dec. 13, 1845, Dip. Instr., GB, NA; and *DCUSCR*, 3:312–13.

12. Pakenham to Aberdeen, Jan. 5, 1846, FO 5/446, PRO. See also McLane to Calhoun, Jan. 3, 1846, in Boucher and Brooks, eds., "Correspondence Addressed to John C. Calhoun," 311–14.

13. Aberdeen to Pakenham, Feb. 3, 1846, Aberdeen Papers; McLane to Buchanan, Feb. 3, 1846, Desp., GB, NA; McLane to Buchanan, Feb. 3, 1846, Buchanan Papers.

14. Comments by Winthrop, Jan. 3, 1846, *CG*, 29 Cong., 1 sess., 132–34; *CG*, 29 Cong., 1 sess., Jan. 5, 1846, 139–40, *App.*, 72. Not all southern legislators hedged on Oregon's acquisition. Congressman Howell Cobb of Georgia, for instance, was pressed by his constituents to speak out for America's claim to the whole territory. See letter from George Phillips to Cobb, Dec. 30, 1845, in U. B. Phillips, ed., "The Correspondence of Robert Toombs, Alexander H. Stephens, and Howell Cobb," *Annual Report of the American Historical Association for 1911*, 2 vols. (Washington, 1913), 2:70. For a representation of Cobb's advocacy of this position see *CG*, 28 Cong., 1 sess., 164–67; Ingersoll Res., Jan. 5, 1846, *House Journal*, 29 Cong., 1 sess., 195; Bowlin Bill, Jan. 9, 1846, ibid., 215; *CG*, 29 Cong., 1 sess., Jan. 10, 1846, 179–81, *App.*, 212.

15. Merk, *Oregon Question*, 364–94; *CG*, 29 Cong., 1 sess., Jan. 9, 1846, 175. See also Weinberg, *Manifest Destiny*, chap. 5, passim; ibid., 146; C. F. Adams, ed., *Memoirs of John Quincy Adams*, 12:220–21; *CG*, 29 Cong., 1 sess., Jan. 2, 1846, 340–42. A British writer coldly declared Adams's speech "profligate drivel . . . uttered by the Nestor of the commonwealth, an infirm old man, with one foot in the grave." *Blackwood's Edinburgh Review* 59 (London) (April 1846): 443; *CG*, 29 Cong., 1 sess., Feb. 7, 1846, 332, *App.*, 289.

16. Pakenham said that Crittenden's suggestion made the discussion a three-way contest among the ultras, the moderates, and Crittenden's supporters. See Pakenham to Aberdeen, Jan. 15, 29, 1846, FO 5/446, PRO. Peel would come to believe that war was cheaper than preparedness. Bourne, *Balance of Power*, 167.

17. Pakenham to Aberdeen, Jan. 29, 1846, FO 5/446, PRO; quote reprinted in the *Missouri Reporter*, Jan. 5, 1846; ibid., Jan. 9, 1846.

18. Polk to McLane, Dec. 29, 1845, Jan. 28, 1846, Polk Papers; Quaife, ed., *Diary of James K. Polk*, 1:191–92.

19. French Foreign Minister François Guizot was offended by the jab at France in the balance-of-power section of Polk's December message. With Aberdeen working to warm relations with the Quai d'Orsay, Polk must have had little confidence in French support against the British. See John S. Galbraith, "France as a Factor in the Oregon Negotiations," *Pacific Northwest Quarterly* 44 (April 1953): 69–73. See also George V. Blue, "France and the Oregon Question," *Oregon Historical Quarterly* 34 (1933): 39–59, 144–63. For a discussion of the Anglo-French entente see A. B. Cunningham, "Peel, Aberdeen and the Entente Cordiale," *Bulletin of the Institute of Historical Research* 30 (Nov. 1857): 189–206.

20. Buchanan to McLane, Jan. 29, 1846, in Moore, ed., *Works of James Buchanan*, 6:366; Pakenham to Aberdeen, Jan. 29, 1846, FO 5/446, PRO; Moore, ed., *Works of James Buchanan*, 6:368.

21. Buchanan to Pakenham, Feb. 4, 1846, in Moore, ed., *Works of James Buchanan*, 6:372.

22. Pakenham to Aberdeen, Feb. 8, 1846, FO 5/446, PRO; *CG*, 29 Cong., 1 sess., Feb. 7, 1846, 332–35. McLane later expressed surprise at the administration's reaction to his despatch and showed Aberdeen the provocative passage commenting that there was little justification for such an interpretation by Buchanan. McLane to Aberdeen, March 17, 1846, Aberdeen Papers; Quaife, ed., *Diary of James K. Polk*, 1:240–41, 245.

23. Polk had declared when nominated that he would not seek a second term. Polk was thus a little like Peel, who had determined that his government would go out with the repeal of the Corn Laws. Quaife, ed., *Diary of James K. Polk*, 1:240–49; Richard W. Van Alstyne, "Empire in Midpassage, 1845–1867," in William Appleman Williams, ed., *From Colony to Empire: Essays in the History of American Foreign Relations* (New York, 1972), 92.

24. *CG*, *App.*, 29 Cong., 1 sess., Feb. 10–11, 1846, 841–42; Pletcher, *Diplomacy of Annexation*, 345; Quaife, ed., *Diary of James K. Polk*, 1:249–52.

25. Quaife, ed., *Diary of James K. Polk*, 253; Buchanan to McLane, Feb. 26, 1846, in Moore, ed., *Works of James Buchanan*, 6:377–83, 385–87. Coincidentally, both nations confronted a substantial change in government that would probably make settlement of the Oregon dispute more difficult.

26. Pakenham to Aberdeen, Feb. 26, 1846, FO 5/446, PRO; *Morning Post* (London), Feb. 19, 1846; Merk, *Oregon Question*, 391.

27. Quaife, ed., *Diary of James K. Polk*, 1:257–58.

28. *CG*, 29 Cong., 1 sess., March 4–5, 1846, 456, 458–59, *App.*, 369. There was initial concern that the party rift over Oregon would allow the western

extremists to hold tariff policy hostage to the all-Oregon cause. Quaife, ed., *Diary of James K. Polk*, 1:262–64. Polk would add Buchanan to his list of presidential aspirants later in the month. See Polk's diary entry dated March 22, 1846, ibid., 297.

29. *CG*, 29 Cong., 1 sess., March 5, 1846, 458–60; Quaife, ed., *Diary of James K. Polk*, 1:268.

30. Quaife, ed., *Diary of James K. Polk*, 1:272–78.

31. Ibid., 1:278–89.

32. *CG*, 29 Cong., 1 sess., March 16, 1846, 502–6. Calhoun's address is reproduced in Wilson, ed., *Papers of Calhoun*, 22:685–729.

33. *Parl. Debates*, 84:1113, 1115–16.

34. Ibid., 1116–20.

35. McLane to Buchanan, March 3, 1846, *DCUSCR*, 3:1006–11.

36. The reports on which the Peel government based its opinion appear in FO 5/459, PRO. See also Leslie M. Scott, ed., "Report of Lieutenant Peel on Oregon in 1845–46," *Oregon Historical Quarterly* 29 (March 1928): 51–76; Joseph Schafer, ed., "Documents Relative to Warre and Vavasour's Military Reconnoissance in Oregon, 1845–46," *Oregon Historical Quarterly* 10 (March 1909): 1–99; and Merk, *Oregon Question*, 258–61.

37. *CG, App.*, 29 Cong., 1 sess., March 30, 1846, 424; McLane to Robert McLane, May 5, 1846, McLane Papers.

38. *CG*, 29 Cong., 1 sess., April 2, 1846, 589; *Missourian* [n.d.], in the *Missouri Reporter*, April 23, 1846; Pakenham to Aberdeen, March 29, 1846, FO 5/477, PRO.

39. Quaife, ed., *Diary of James K. Polk*, 1:345. For a thorough treatment of the maneuvering among Democrats toward the 1848 election see Merk's essay, "Presidential Fevers," in *Oregon Question*, 364–94. McLane wrote his son that Cass probably thought war unlikely and was thus making cheap political capital by standing firm at little actual risk. McLane to Robert McLane, May 3, 1846, McLane Papers; Quaife, ed., *Diary of James K. Polk*, 1:297; Pakenham to Aberdeen, March 29, 1846, FO 5/447, PRO. For Polk's message conceding the need for military increases see Moore, ed., *Works of James Buchanan*, 6:428–30; and Quaife, ed., *Diary of James K. Polk*, 1:297.

40. McLane to Buchanan, April 3, 1846, Desp., GB, NA; *Blackwood's Edinburgh Review* 59 (April 1846): 441, 449.

41. McLane to Robert McLane, May 3, 1846, McLane Papers; McLane to Buchanan, May 4, 1846, Buchanan Papers.

42. McLane to Buchanan, March 3, 17, April 17, 1846, *DCUSCR*, 3:1006–11, 1013, 1026; Quaife, ed., *Diary of James K. Polk*, 1:325.

43. Peel to Ellenborough, March 17, 1846, Ellenborough Papers. See Webster letters in Evelyn Denison to Aberdeen, March 24, 1846, Aberdeen Papers; and Robert Rhett to Aberdeen, March 27, 1846, ibid. See also Pletcher, *Diplomacy of Annexation*, 404.

44. *CG*, 29 Cong., 1 sess., April 16, 1846, 681; Pakenham to Aberdeen, April 4, 7, 1846, FO 5/448, PRO; Quaife, ed., *Diary of James K. Polk*, 1:335.

45. Van Alstyne, "Empire in Midpassage," 107–10; Quaife, ed., *Diary of James K. Polk*, 1:337.

46. *CG*, 29 Cong., 1 sess., April 16, 1846, 680–81, and April 23, 1846, 717–21.

47. Pakenham noted House action to protect settlers in the entire region and wrote Aberdeen that it was very objectionable. Pakenham to Aberdeen, April 28,

1846, FO 5/448, PRO; Quaife, ed., *Diary of James K. Polk*, 1:448. Rush's recommendation was transmitted in a letter to Vice President George Dallas. Ibid., 372.

48. Buchanan to McLane, April 28, 1846, Dip. Instr., GB, NA; Pakenham to Aberdeen, May 13, 1846, FO 5/449, PRO; Pakenham to Aberdeen, April 28, 1846, FO 5/448, ibid. McLane, by mid-April, believed that the crucial part of negotiations had been effectively relocated to London. McLane to Buchanan, April 18, 1846, Buchanan Papers; New York *Journal of Commerce*, April 29, 1846. For other examples see *Niles' National Register* 70 (May 1846).

49. Quaife, ed., *Diary of James K. Polk*, 1:375–99, passim.

50. Ibid., 395–403; Moore, ed., *Works of James Buchanan*, 6:484–85; Quaife, ed., *Diary of James K. Polk*, 1:422. For details on the initial stages of the war see Justin H. Smith, *The War with Mexico*, 2 vols. (New York, 1919); and John S. D. Eisenhower, *So Far from God: The U.S. War with Mexico, 1846–1848* (New York, 1989).

51. *Morning Chronicle* (London), May 11, 15, 1846. See also *Niles' National Register* 70 (June 6, 1846): 210; Pakenham to Aberdeen, April 28, 1846, FO 5/448, PRO; and McLane to Buchanan, April 28, May 18, 1846, Desp., GB, NA. Reports verifying the limitations of the Columbia River dated back to Broughton in the 1790s. More recent reports had been supplied by missions such as that of Wilkes in the early 1840s. See Wilkes, "Document: Report on the Territory of Oregon," 269–99.

52. McLane to Buchanan, Feb. 3, May 3, 1846, Desp., GB, NA.

53. McLane to Buchanan, May 18, 1846, ibid.

54. Lord Croker to Aberdeen, May 13, 1846, Aberdeen Papers; Aberdeen to Pakenham, May 18, 1846, *BDFA*, 2:213–16.

55. McLane to Buchanan, May 18, 1846, Desp., GB, NA; *DCUSCR*, 3:1037; McLane to Polk, May 18, 28, 1846, Polk Papers; McLane to Robert McLane, May 18, 1846, McLane Papers; McLane to Calhoun, May 18, 1846, in J. Franklin Jameson, ed., "Correspondence of John C. Calhoun," in *Annual Report of the American Historical Association for the Year 1899* (Washington, DC, 1900), 1081–83; McLane to Calhoun, May 18, 1846, Calhoun Papers; Quaife, ed., *Diary of James K. Polk*, 1:376–79; Aberdeen to Pakenham, May 18, 1846, FO 115/91, PRO; Miller, ed., *Treaties*, 5:79–81.

56. McLane counseled haste because the Corn Laws had been repealed by the House of Commons and would soon be repealed by the House of Lords, and a change of ministry was imminent. Pakenham to Palmerston, July 29, 1846, *BDFA*, 2:221.

57. Quaife, ed., *Diary of James K. Polk*, 1:444–45, 447–48, 451–55.

58. Pakenham to Aberdeen, June 7, 1846, Aberdeen Papers; Quaife, ed., *Diary of James K. Polk*, 1:452. McLoughlin also believed that navigation rights would end with the expiration of the company's charter. Oregon *Spectator*, Nov. 17, 1846.

59. A counterproposal was dismissed by the cabinet with hardly a comment. Quaife, ed., *Diary of James K. Polk*, 1:453. Marcy called Buchanan's course a very queer one privately to Polk after the meeting. Ibid., 454. Walker thought that either all should agree, showing unified support for the message, or the proposal should not be submitted. He did not like the prospect of cabinet members lobbying against it. Ibid., 455–56; Klein, *President James Buchanan*, 181–82.

60. Quaife, ed., *Diary of James K. Polk*, 1:460, 461–63; Pakenham to Palmerston, July 29, 1846, *BDFA*, 2: 221–22.

61. Calhoun had already received this information in a letter from McLane. McLane to Calhoun, May 18, 1846, in Jameson, ed., *Correspondence of John C. Calhoun*, 1081–83.

62. Pakenham to Aberdeen, June 13, 1846, FO 5/449, PRO. For a discussion of future controversies surrounding the partition line see Andrew Fish, "The Last Phase of the Oregon Boundary Question: The Struggle for San Juan Island," *Oregon Historical Quarterly* 22 (Sept. 1921): 161–90; James O. McCabe, *The San Juan Water Boundary Question* (Toronto, 1964); David Hunter Miller, *San Juan Archipelago: A Study of the Joint Occupation of San Juan Island* (Bellows Falls, VT, 1943); Malloy et al., eds., *Treaties and Agreements*, 1:656–58.

63. For the Senate action on the treaty see *CG*, 29 Cong., 1 sess., June 1846. See also *Niles' National Register* 70 (Aug. 15, 1846): 374–84; and idem (Aug. 29, 1846): 408–10.

64. McLane to Buchanan, June 3, 1846, *DCUSCR*, 3:1045–46; *Morning Chronicle* (London), May 25, 1846.

65. McLane, having earlier denied that his February 3 despatch was meant to suggest British war preparation, now referred back to it as though it did. See McLane to Buchanan, June 18, 1846, Desp., GB, NA; and Clarendon to Aberdeen, June 12, 1846, Aberdeen Papers.

66. McLane to Buchanan, July 17, 1846, *DCUSCR*, 3:1066.

67. Oregon *Spectator*, Nov. 12, 1846.

Bibliography

Archival and Manuscript Collections

Aberdeen Papers. Additional Manuscripts. British Library, London.
Lord Ashburton Papers. Public Record Office, Kew, England.
Alexander Baring Papers. Public Archives of Canada, Ottawa.
Baring Brothers Papers. Private Documents. Public Record Office, Kew, England.
James Buchanan Papers. Historical Society of Pennsylvania, Philadelphia.
Lewis Cass Papers. Clements Library, University of Michigan, Ann Arbor.
Creole Affair Collection. Amistad Research Center, Tulane University, New Orleans.
John J. Crittenden Papers. Library of Congress, Washington, DC.
John Croker Papers. Clements Library, University of Michigan, Ann Arbor.
Despatches from U.S. Consuls in Nassau. Amistad Research Center, Tulane University, New Orleans.
Lord Ellenborough Papers. Public Record Office, Kew, England.
Edward Everett Papers. Massachusetts Historical Society, Boston.
Albert Gallatin Papers. New York University, New York.
Great Britain. Foreign Office, America, United States. Public Record Office, Kew, England.
———. Department of Archives, Nassau, Bahamas.
Adeline Ellery (Burr) Davis Green Papers. Perkins Library, Duke University, Durham, North Carolina.
Sir Allan MacNab Papers. Albemarle Manuscripts. Public Archives of Canada, Ottawa.
New Brunswick. Dispatches. Public Archives of Canada, Ottawa.
Lord Palmerston's Letter-Books. Additional Manuscripts. British Library, London.
Lord Palmerston Papers. General Correspondence. University of Southampton, Southampton, England.
Sir Robert Peel Papers. British Library, London.
James K. Polk Papers. Library of Congress, Washington, DC.
William Cabell Rives Papers. Library of Congress, Washington, DC.
Lord John Russell Papers. Public Record Office, Kew, England.
John Rutherfoord Papers. Perkins Library, Duke University, Durham, North Carolina.

Jared Sparks Letters. Clements Library, University of Michigan, Ann Arbor.

U.S. Department of State. Diplomatic Instructions, Great Britain. National Archives, Washington, DC.

————. Despatches from U.S. Ministers to France, 1791–1906. National Archives, Washington, DC.

————. Despatches from U.S. Ministers to Great Britain, 1791–1906. National Archives, Washington, DC.

————. Domestic Letters. National Archives, Washington, DC.

————. Miscellaneous Letters, National Archives, Washington, DC.

————. "Miscellaneous on Northeastern Boundary," E98. National Archives, Washington, DC.

————. Folder marked "NE. Bdry. Negot.," E89. National Archives, Washington, DC.

————. Notes from the British Legation in the United States to the Department of State, 1791–1906. National Archives, Washington, DC.

————. Notes to Foreign Legations in the United States from the Department of State, 1834–1906, Great Britain. National Archives, Washington, DC.

U.S. Department of War. *Military Book No. 23, War Office.* No. 210, National Archives, Washington, DC.

U.S. General Land Office. Records: Letters to Surveyors General, 1796–1901. National Archives, Washington, DC.

Martin Van Buren Papers. Library of Congress, Washington, DC.

Thomas Wren Ward Papers. Massachusetts Historical Society, Boston.

Charles M. Wiltse, ed., Daniel Webster Papers, Dartmouth College, Hanover, New Hampshire.

Published Documents

Abel, Annie Heloise, and Klingberg, Frank J., eds. *A Side-Light on Anglo-American Relations, 1839–1858; Furnished by the Correspondence of Lewis Tappan and Others with the British and Foreign Anti-Slavery Society.* New York: Augustus M. Kelley, 1970. Originally published in Lancaster, PA.

Adams, Charles F., ed. *Memoirs of John Quincy Adams, Comprising Portions of His Diary from 1795 to 1848.* 12 vols. Philadelphia: Lippincott, 1874–1877.

Adams, Henry, ed. *Writings of Albert Gallatin.* New York: Antiquarian Press, 1960.

Adams, Herbert B. *The Life and Writings of Jared Sparks: Comprising Selections from His Journal and Correspondence.* 2 vols. Boston: Houghton Mifflin, 1893.

Aroostook War: Historical Sketch and Roster of Commissioned Officers and Enlisted Men Called into Service for the Protection of the North-

eastern Frontier of Maine. From February to May, 1839. Augusta, ME: n.p., 1904.

Baker, George E., ed. *The Works of William H. Seward*. 5 vols. New York: Houghton Mifflin, 1884.

Bassett, John Spencer, ed. *The Correspondence of Andrew Jackson*. 8 vols. Washington, DC: Carnegie Institute, 1933.

Benson, Arthur C., and Esher, Viscount, eds. *The Letters of Queen Victoria: A Selection from Her Majesty's Correspondence Between the Years 1837 and 1861*. 3 vols. London: John Murray, 1908.

Benton, Thomas Hart. *Thirty Years' View; or, A History of the American Government for Thirty Years from 1820 to 1850*. 2 vols. New York: D. Appleton, 1856.

Boucher, Chauncey S., and Brooks, Robert P., eds. "Correspondence Addressed to John C. Calhoun," in *Annual Report of the American Historical Association for the Year 1929*. Washington, DC: Government Printing Office, 1930.

Brosman, Cornelius J., ed. "The Oregon Memorial of 1838," *Oregon Historical Quarterly* (March 1933): 68–77.

Catterall, Helen T., ed. *Judicial Cases Concerning American Slavery and the Negro*. 5 vols. Washington, DC: Carnegie Institute, 1926–1932.

Chapman, Leonard B., ed. "Rev. Caleb Bradley on the Madawaska War," *Collections and Proceedings of the Maine Historical Society*. 2d ser., 9. Portland, ME, 1898: 418–25.

Clark, Robert C., ed. "Letter of Aberdeen to Pakenham, March 4, 1844, Concerning the Oregon Question," *Oregon Historical Quarterly* 39 (1938): 74–76.

Crallé, Richard K., ed. *The Works of John C. Calhoun*. 6 vols. New York: D. Appleton and Co., 1854–1860.

Cutler, Wayne, ed. *Correspondence of James K. Polk*. 8 vols. Knoxville: University of Tennessee Press, 1993.

Dana, Richard Henry, Jr., ed. Wheaton, Henry. *Elements of International Law*. Boston: Little, Brown, 1836.

Davis, Varina (Howell). *Jefferson Davis, Ex-President of the Confederate States of America: A Memoir by His Wife*. 2 vols. New York: Belford Co., 1890.

Dent, John C. *The Story of the Upper Canadian Rebellion; Largely Derived from Original Sources and Documents*. 2 vols. Toronto: C. B. Robinson, 1885.

Elliott, T. C., ed. "The Peter Skene Ogden Journals," *Oregon Historical Quarterly* 10 (December 1909): 331–65.

Ford, Worthington C., ed. *Writings of John Quincy Adams*. 7 vols. New York: Macmillan, 1913–1917.

Gooch, G. P., ed. *The Later Correspondence of Lord John Russell, 1840–1878*. 2 vols. London: Longmans, Green, and Co., 1925.

Gordon, Hugh T. *The Treaty of Washington, Concluded August 9, 1842, by Daniel Webster and Lord Ashburton*. University of California, James

Bryce Historical Prize Essays, 1905–1907. Berkeley: University of California Press, 1908, 173–257.

Gould, Marcus T. C. *Gould's Stenographic Reporter*. 2 vols. Washington, DC: Gould's Stenographic Reporter, 1841 [Law Division, Library of Congress].

Grattan, Thomas C. *Civilized America*. 2 vols. London: Bradbury and Evans, 1859.

Great Britain. *British and Foreign State Papers*. 116 vols. London: James Ridgway and Sons, 1812–1925.

———. Parliament. *British Sessional Papers* (House of Commons and Lords). London: H.M.S.O., 1801–1900.

Green, Alfred S. "Memorandum Relative to the Territorial Rights claimed by Great Britain in the Oregon Territory; and of the Negotiations between Great Britain and the United States which led to the conclusion of the Convention the 15th June, 1846." Kenneth Bourne and D. Cameron Watt, eds. *British Documents on Foreign Affairs: Reports from the Foreign Office Confidential Print*. Part I, Series C. 6 vols. Lanham, MD: University Publications of America, 1986.

Greenhow, Robert. *The History of Oregon and California*. Boston: Charles C. Little and James Brown, 1844; reprint ed., Los Angeles: Sherwin and Freutel, 1970.

Griffin, Joseph, ed. *History of the Press of Maine*. Brunswick, ME: The Press, 1872.

Hansard, Thomas C., ed. *Hansard's Parliamentary Debates*. 3d Series. 356 vols. London: Wyman, 1830–1891.

Hill, Nicholas, Jr. *New York Common Law Reports, Vol. 15* [4 vols. in one]. Newark, NY: Lawyers' Co-operative Publishing Co., 1885.

Jackson, Donald D., ed. *Letters of the Lewis and Clark Expedition, with Related Documents, 1783–1843*. Urbana: University of Illinois Press, 1962.

Jenkins, William S., ed. *Records of the States of the United States, 1836–41. Maine: Legislative Records, Journal of the State of Maine, Appendix* [Joint meeting of House and Senate]. Washington, DC: Library of Congress in association with the University of North Carolina, 1949.

Johnson, Arthur H., ed. *The Letters of Charles Greville and Henry Reeve, 1836–1865*. London: T. F. Unwin, 1924.

Kendrick, John, ed. *The Voyages of Sutil and Mexicana, 1792: The Last Spanish Exploration of the Northwest Coast of America*. Spokane: Arthur H. Clark Co., 1991.

Knaplund, Paul, ed. *Letters from Lord Sydenham, Governor-General of Canada, 1839–1841, to Lord John Russell*. London: G. Allen and Unwin, 1931.

Lamb, W. Kaye, ed. *The Voyages of George Vancouver, 1791–1795*. 4 vols. London: The Hakluyt Society, 1984.

Lincoln, Charles Z., ed. *Messages from the Governors, Comprising Executive Communications to the Legislature and Other Papers Relat-*

ing to Legislation from the Organization of the First Colonial Assembly in 1683 to and Including the Year 1906, with Notes. 11 vols. Albany: n.p., 1909.

Lipscomb, Andrew A., and Bergh, Albert E., eds. *The Writings of Thomas Jefferson.* 20 vols. Washington, DC: Thomas Jefferson Memorial Association, 1903–04.

Mackenzie, Sir Alexander. *Voyages from Montreal to the Frozen and Pacific Ocean.* London: T. Cadell and W. Davis, 1801.

Mahon, Lord, and Carwell, Edward, eds. *Memoirs of Sir Robert Peel.* London: John Murray, 1856; reprint ed., New York: Kraus, 1969.

"Maine Battle Song" in "Documentary History of the North Eastern Boundary Controversy," *Historical Collections of Piscataquis County, Maine.* Dover, ME: Observer Press, 1910, 282–327.

Malloy, William M., et al., eds. *Treaties, Conventions, International Acts, Protocols, and Agreements Between the United States and Other Powers, 1776–1937.* 4 vols. Washington, DC: Government Printing Office, 1910–1938.

Manning, William R., ed. *Diplomatic Correspondence of the United States. Canadian Relations, 1784–1860.* 4 vols. Washington, DC: Carnegie Endowment for International Peace, 1940–1945.

McIntyre, James M., ed. *The Writings and Speeches of Daniel Webster.* 18 vols. Boston: Little, Brown, 1903.

Meares, John. *Voyages Made in the Years 1788 and 1789, from China to the North West Coast of America.* 2 vols. London: Logographic Press, 1790.

Merk, Frederick, ed. *Fur Trade and Empire: George Simpson's Journal.* Cambridge, MA: Harvard University Press, 1931.

Miller, Hunter, ed. *Treaties and Other International Acts of the United States of America, 1776–1863.* 8 vols. Washington, DC: Government Printing Office, 1931–1948.

Moore, John B. *A Digest of International Law.* 8 vols. Washington, DC: Government Printing Office, 1906.

———. *History and Digest of the International Arbitrations to Which the United States Has Been a Party.* 6 vols. Washington, DC: Government Printing Office, 1898.

———, ed. *The Works of James Buchanan.* 12 vols. Philadelphia: J. B. Lippincott, 1908–1911.

Moser, Harold D., ed. *The Papers of Daniel Webster: Correspondence, Volume 5, 1840–1843.* Hanover, NH: University Press of New England, 1982.

Nevins, Allan, ed. *The Diary of Philip Hone, 1828–1851.* New York: Dodd, Mead and Co., 1927.

———, ed. *Polk, the Diary of a President.* New York: Longmans, Green, and Co., 1929.

Ormsby, William G., ed. *The Grey Journals and Letters; Crisis in the Canadas, 1838–1839.* London: Macmillan, 1965.

Parker, Charles S., ed. *Sir Robert Peel, From His Private Papers.* 3 vols. London: John Murray, 1891–1899.

Peters, Richard, ed. *Reports of Cases Argued and Adjudged in the Supreme Court of the United States.* 90 vols. Philadelphia, 1828–1874.

Phillips, U. B., ed. "The Correspondence of Robert Toombs, Alexander H. Stephens, and Howell Cobb," in *Annual Report of the American Historical Association for 1911.* 2 vols. Washington, DC: Government Printing Office, 1913.

Powell, Fred Wilbur. *Narratives of the Trans-Mississippi Frontier: Hall J. Kelley on Oregon, a Collection of Five of his Published Works and a Number of Hitherto Unpublished Letters.* New York: Da Capo Press, 1972.

Quaife, Milo M., ed. *The Diary of James K. Polk during his Presidency, 1845 to 1849.* 4 vols. Chicago: A. G. McClurg, 1910.

Reeve, Henry, ed. Greville, Charles C. F. *The Greville Memoirs: A Journal of the Reign of Queen Victoria from 1837 to 1852.* 2 vols. New York: D. Appleton, 1885.

Rich, E. E., ed. *The Letters of John McLoughlin from Fort Vancouver to the Governor and Committee: Second Series, 1839–44.* Toronto: Champlain Society, 1943.

————, ed. *The Letters of John McLoughlin from Fort Vancouver to the Governor and Committee: Third Series, 1844–46.* Toronto: Champlain Society, 1944.

Richardson, James D., ed. *A Compilation of the Messages and Papers of the Presidents.* 11 vols. New York: Bureau of National Literature, 1896–1910.

Rush, Richard. *Memoranda of a Residence at the Court of London.* Philadelphia: J. B. Lippincott, 1845.

Schafer, Joseph, ed. "Documents Relative to Warre and Vavasour's Military Reconnoissance in Oregon, 1845–46," *Oregon Historical Quarterly* 10 (March 1909): 1–99.

Scott, James B., ed. *Cases on International Law, Selected from Decisions of English and American Courts.* Boston: Boston Book Co., 1902.

Scott, Leslie M., ed. "Report of Lieutenant Peel on Oregon in 1845–46," *Oregon Historical Quarterly* 29 (March 1928): 51–76.

Scott, Winfield. *Memoirs of Lieut.-General Scott, LL.D., Written by Himself.* 2 vols. New York: Sheldon and Co., 1864.

Seward, Frederick W., ed. *William H. Seward: An Autobiography from 1801–1834. With a Memoir of His Life, and Selections from His Letters, 1831–1846.* 3 vols. New York: Derby and Miller, 1891.

Shewmaker, Kenneth E., ed. *The Papers of Daniel Webster: Diplomatic Papers, Volume 1, 1841–1843.* Hanover, NH: University Press of New England, 1983.

Sprague, John F. "The North Eastern Boundary Controversy and the Aroostook War," *Historical Collections of Piscataquis County, Maine.* Dover, ME: Observer Press, 1910, 216–81.

Stacey, C. P., ed. "A Private Report of General Winfield Scott on the Border Situation in 1839," *Canadian Historical Review* 21 (December 1940): 407–14.

Staples, Arthur G., ed. *The Letters of John Fairfield*. Lewiston, ME: Lewiston Journal Co., 1922.

Stapleton, Edward J., ed. *Some Official Correspondence of George Canning*. 2 vols. London: Longmans, Green, and Co., 1887.

Story, William W., ed. *Life and Letters of Joseph Story*. 2 vols. Boston: Little, Brown, 1851.

Tuckerman, Bayard, ed. *The Diary of Philip Hone*. 2 vols. New York: Dodd, Mead and Co., 1910.

Tyler, Lyon Gardiner, ed. *The Letters and Times of the Tylers*. 3 vols. Richmond: Whittet and Shepperson, 1884–1896. Reprint. New York: Da Capo, 1970.

U.S., *American State Papers, Foreign Relations*. 6 vols. Washington, DC: Gales and Seaton, 1832–1859.

U.S. Congress. *Annals of Congress*.

———. *Congressional Globe*.

———. *Congressional Globe, Appendix*.

———. *House Documents*, 1837–1843.

———. *House Executive Documents*.

———. *House Reports*, 1837–1843.

———. *Register of Debates*.

———. *Senate Documents*.

———. *Statutes at Large*. Multivols. Boston: Little, Brown, 1852–.

Vane, Charles W., ed. *Memoirs and Correspondence of Viscount Castlereagh, Second Marquis of Londonderry*. 12 vols. London: H. Coulburn, 1850–1853.

Webster, Fletcher, ed. *The Private Correspondence of Daniel Webster*. 2 vols. Boston: Little, Brown and Co., 1857.

Wellesley, Arthur R., ed. *Despatches, Correspondence and Memoranda of Field Marshal Arthur, Duke of Wellington*. London: Murray, 1867–1880.

Wendell, John L. *Reports of Cases Argued and Determined in the Supreme Court of Judicature and in the Court for the Trial of Impeachments and the Correction of Errors of the State of New York, Vol. 25*. Newark, NY: Lawyers' Co-operative Publishing Co., 1885.

Wharton, Francis, ed. *The Revolutionary Diplomatic Correspondence of the United States*. 6 vols. Washington, DC: Government Printing Office, 1889.

Wilkes, Charles. "Document: Report on the Territory of Oregon," *Oregon Historical Review* 12 (September 1911): 269–99.

Wilson, Clyde N., ed. *The Papers of John C. Calhoun*. 22 vols. Columbia: University of South Carolina Press, 1993.

Young, William T. *Sketch of the Life and Public Services of General Lewis Cass. With the Pamphlet on the Right of Search, and Some of His*

Speeches on the Great Political Questions of the Day. Philadelphia: E. H. Butler and Co., 1853.

Secondary Sources

Alberts, Robert C. *The Golden Voyage: The Life and Times of William Bingham, 1752–1804.* Boston: Houghton Mifflin, 1969.

Allen, H. C. *Conflict and Concord: The Anglo-American Relationship since 1783.* New York: St. Martin's Press, 1959.

Barnes, Gilbert H. *The Antislavery Impulse, 1830–1844.* New York: American Historical Association, 1933.

Bartlett, Irving H. *Daniel Webster.* New York: W. W. Norton, 1978.

Baxter, Maurice G. *One and Inseparable: Daniel Webster and the Union.* Cambridge, MA: Harvard University Press, 1984.

Bell, Herbert C. F. *Lord Palmerston.* 2 vols. London: Longmans, Green, and Co., 1936.

Bell, James Christy, Jr. *Opening a Highway to the Pacific, 1838–1846.* New York: AMS Press, 1921.

Bemis, Samuel F. *The Diplomacy of the American Revolution.* New York: D. Appleton-Century, 1935.

———. *Jay's Treaty: A Study in Commerce and Diplomacy.* New York: Macmillan, 1923.

———. *John Quincy Adams and the Foundations of American Foreign Policy.* New York: Alfred A. Knopf, 1949.

———. *John Quincy Adams and the Union.* New York: Alfred A. Knopf, 1956.

———, ed. *American Secretaries of State and Their Diplomacy.* New York: Alfred A. Knopf, 1928.

Bergeron, Paul H. *The Presidency of James K. Polk.* Lawrence: University Press of Kansas, 1987.

Bourne, Kenneth. *Britain and the Balance of Power in North America, 1815–1908.* Berkeley: University of California Press, 1967.

Brightfield, Myron F. *John Wilson Croker.* Berkeley: University of California Press, 1940.

Burrage, Henry S. *Maine in the Northeastern Boundary Controversy.* Portland, ME: Marks Printing House, 1919.

Burt, Alfred L. *The United States, Great Britain, and British North America from the Revolution to the Establishment of Peace after the War of 1812.* New Haven: Carnegie Endowment for International Peace, 1940.

Campbell, Charles S. *From Revolution to Rapprochement: The United States and Great Britain, 1783–1900.* New York: John Wiley, 1974.

Chamberlain, Murial E. *Lord Aberdeen: A Political Biography.* New York: Longmans, 1983.

Chitwood, Oliver P. *John Tyler: Champion of the Old South.* New York: D. Appleton-Century, 1939.

Clark, R. C. *History of the Willamette Valley, Oregon.* 2 vols. Chicago: S. J. Clarke, 1927.

Cline, Gloria Griffin. *Exploring the Great Basin.* Norman: University of Oklahoma Press, 1963.

Cole, Donald B. *Martin Van Buren and the American Political System.* Princeton, NJ: Princeton University Press, 1984.

Corey, Albert B. *The Crisis of 1830–1842 in Canadian-American Relations.* New Haven: Carnegie Endowment for International Peace, 1941.

Crawford, Martin. *The Anglo-American Crisis of the Mid-Nineteenth Century: The Times and America, 1850–1862.* Athens: University of Georgia Press, 1987.

Crosby, Travis L. *Sir Robert Peel's Administration, 1841–1846.* London: David and Charles, 1976.

Curtin, Philip D. *The Atlantic Slave Trade: A Census.* Madison: University of Wisconsin Press, 1969.

Curtis, George T. *Life of Daniel Webster.* 2 vols. New York: Appleton, 1870.

Curtis, James C. *The Fox at Bay: Martin Van Buren and the Presidency, 1837–1841.* Lexington: University Press of Kentucky, 1970.

Dalzell, Robert F., Jr. *Daniel Webster and the Trial of American Nationalism, 1843–1852.* Boston: Houghton Mifflin, 1973.

Dangerfield, George. *The Era of Good Feelings.* New York: Harcourt, Brace and World, 1952.

DeConde, Alexander. *This Affair of Louisiana.* New York: Charles Scribner's Sons, 1976.

DeVoto, Bernard. *Across the Wide Missouri.* Boston: Houghton Mifflin, 1947.

———. *The Course of Empire.* Boston: Houghton Mifflin, 1952.

———. *The Year of Decision: 1846.* Boston: Little, Brown, 1943.

Du Bois, W. E. B. *The Suppression of the African Slave-Trade to the United States of America, 1638–1870.* New York: Longmans, Green, and Co., 1896.

Duckett, Alvin L. *John Forsyth: Political Tactician.* Athens: University of Georgia Press, 1962.

Duignan, Peter, and Clendenen, Clarence. *The United States and the African Slave Trade, 1619–1862.* Stanford, CA: Stanford University Press, 1962.

Eaton, Clement. *The Freedom-of-Thought Struggle in the Old South.* New York: Harper and Row, 1964.

Edmunds, John B. *Francis W. Pickens and the Politics of Destruction.* Chapel Hill: University of North Carolina Press, 1986.

Eisenhower, John S. D. *So Far from God: The U.S. War with Mexico, 1846–1848.* New York: Random House, 1989.

Elliott, Charles W. *Winfield Scott, The Soldier and the Man.* New York: Macmillan, 1937.

Engelman, Fred L. *The Peace of Christmas Eve.* New York: Harcourt, Brace and World, 1960.

Faris, John T. *The Romance of the Boundaries.* New York: Harper and Bros., 1926.

Ferrell, Robert H. *American Diplomacy: A History.* New York: W. W. Norton, 1959; 3d ed., 1975.

Fladeland, Betty. *James Gillespie Birney: Slaveholder to Abolitionist.* Ithaca, NY: Cornell University Press, 1955.

————. *Men and Brothers: Anglo-American Antislavery Cooperation.* Urbana: University of Illinois Press, 1972.

Freehling, William W. *Prelude to Civil War: The Nullification Controversy in South Carolina, 1816–1836.* New York: Harper and Row, 1965.

Fuess, Claude M. *Daniel Webster.* 2 vols. Boston: Little, Brown, 1930.

————. *The Life of Caleb Cushing.* New York: Harcourt, Brace and Co., 1923.

Gough, Barry M. *The Royal Navy and the Northwest Coast of North America, 1810–1914: A Study of British Maritime Ascendancy.* Vancouver: University of British Columbia Press, 1971.

Graebner, Norman A. *Empire on the Pacific: A Study in American Continental Expansion.* New York: Ronald Press, 1955.

Guillet, Edwin C. *The Lives and Times of the Patriots: An Account of the Rebellion in Upper Canada, 1837–1838, and of the Patriot Agitation in the United States, 1837–1842.* Toronto: University of Toronto, 1968; originally published in 1938.

Haines, Charles G., and Sherwood, Foster H. *The Role of the Supreme Court in American Government and Politics, 1835–1864.* Berkeley: University of California Press, 1957.

Halevy, Elie. *The Age of Peel and Cobden: A History of the English People, 1841–1852.* New York: Peter Smith, 1948.

Hall, Claude H. *Abel Parker Upshur.* Madison: University of Wisconsin Press, 1963.

Handlin, Lilian. *George Bancroft: The Intellectual as Democrat.* New York: Harper and Row, 1984.

Hargreaves, Mary W. M. *The Presidency of John Quincy Adams.* Lawrence: University Press of Kansas, 1985.

Hidy, Ralph W. *The House of Baring in American Trade and Finance.* Cambridge, MA: Harvard University Press, 1949.

Hietala, Thomas R. *Manifest Design: Anxious Aggrandizement in Late Jacksonian America.* Ithaca, NY: Cornell University Press, 1985.

Horsman, Reginald. *Race and Manifest Destiny: The Origins of American Racial Anglo-Saxonism.* Cambridge, MA: Harvard University Press, 1981.

Howard, Warren S. *American Slavers and the Federal Law, 1837–1862.* Berkeley: University of California Press, 1963.

Howay, Frederic W., ed. *The Dixon-Meares Controversy.* Toronto: Ryerson Press, 1929.

Johansen, Dorothy O. *Empire of the Columbia.* 2d ed. New York: Harper and Row, 1957.

Jones, Howard. *Mutiny on the Amistad: The Saga of a Slave Revolt and Its Impact on American Abolition, Law, and Diplomacy.* New York: Oxford University Press, 1987.

———. *Quest for Security: A History of U.S. Foreign Relations.* 2 vols. New York: McGraw-Hill, 1996.

———. *To the Webster-Ashburton Treaty: A Study in Anglo-American Relations, 1783–1843.* Chapel Hill: University of North Carolina Press, 1977.

Jones, Wilbur D. *The American Problem in British Diplomacy, 1841–1861.* Athens: University of Georgia Press, 1974.

———. *Lord Aberdeen and the Americas.* Athens: University of Georgia Press, 1958.

Kilbourn, William. *The Firebrand: William Lyon Mackenzie and the Rebellion in Upper Canada.* Toronto: Clarke, Irwin, 1956.

Kirwan, Albert D. *John J. Crittenden.* Lexington: University Press of Kentucky, 1962.

Klein, Philip S. *President James Buchanan: A Biography.* University Park: Pennsylvania State University Press, 1962.

Kolchin, Peter. *American Slavery, 1619–1877.* New York: Hill and Wang, 1993.

Kuykendall, R. S. *The Hawaiian Kingdom, 1778–1854.* Honolulu: University of Hawaii Press, 1938.

Langer, William L. *Political and Social Upheaval, 1832–1852.* New York: Harper and Row, 1969.

Leckie, Robert. *From Sea to Shining Sea: From the War of 1812 to the Mexican War, The Saga of American Expansion.* New York: Harper Collins, 1993.

Lofts, Norah, and Weiner, Margery. *Eternal France: A History of France, 1789–1944.* Garden City, NY: Doubleday, 1968.

Mahon, John K. *History of the Second Seminole War, 1835–1842.* Gainesville: University of Florida Press, 1967.

Maloney, Linda M. *The Captain from Connecticut: The Life and Naval Times of Isaac Hull.* Boston: Northeastern University Press, 1986.

McCabe, James O. *The San Juan Water Boundary Question.* Toronto: University of Toronto Press, 1964.

McCormac, Eugene Irving. *James K. Polk, A Political Biography.* New York: Russell and Russell, 1965.

McCoy, Charles A. *Polk and the Presidency.* Austin: University of Texas Press, 1960.

McInnis, Edgar W. *The Unguarded Frontier: A History of American-Canadian Relations.* Garden City, NY: Doubleday, Doran, 1942.

Merk, Frederick. *Fruits of Propaganda in the Tyler Administration.* Cambridge, MA: Harvard University Press, 1976.

———. *Manifest Destiny and Mission in American History: A Reinterpretation.* 3d ed. New York: Alfred A. Knopf, 1970.

———. *The Monroe Doctrine and American Expansionism, 1843–1849.* New York: Alfred A. Knopf, 1966.

———. *The Oregon Question: Essays in Anglo-American Diplomacy and Politics.* Cambridge, MA: Harvard University Press, 1967.

Miller, David Hunter. *San Juan Archipelago: A Study of the Joint Occupation of San Juan Island*. Bellows Falls, VT: Wyndham Press, 1943.

Munroe, John A. *Louis McLane: Federalist and Jacksonian*. New Brunswick, NJ: Rutgers University Press, 1974.

Nevins, Allan. *Frémont: Pathmarker of the West*. New York: Ungar, 1939.

New, Chester W. *Lord Durham: A Biography of John George Lambton, First Earl of Durham*. Oxford: Clarendon, 1929.

Niven, John. *Martin Van Buren: The Romantic Age of American Politics*. New York: Oxford University Press, 1983.

Nussbaum, Arthur. *A Concise History of the Law of Nations*. New York: Macmillan, 1947.

Nye, Russell B. *George Bancroft: Brahmin Rebel*. New York: Alfred A. Knopf, 1944.

Parks, Joseph H. *John Bell of Tennessee*. Baton Rouge: Louisiana State University Press, 1950.

Perkins, Bradford. *Castlereagh and Adams: England and the United States, 1812–1823*. Berkeley: University of California Press, 1964.

———. *The First Rapprochement: England and the United States, 1795–1805*. Berkeley: University of California Press, 1955.

———. *Prologue to War: England and the United States, 1805–1812*. Berkeley: University of California Press, 1961.

Peterson, Merrill D. *The Great Triumvirate: Webster, Clay, and Calhoun*. New York: Oxford University Press, 1987.

Peterson, Norma L. *The Presidencies of William Henry Harrison and John Tyler*. Lawrence: University Press of Kansas, 1989.

Pletcher, David M. *The Diplomacy of Annexation: Texas, Oregon, and the Mexican War*. Columbia: University of Missouri Press, 1973.

Powell, J. H. *Richard Rush: Republican Diplomat, 1780–1859*. Philadelphia: University of Pennsylvania Press, 1942.

Rakestraw, Donald A. *For Honor or Destiny: The Anglo-American Crisis Over the Oregon Territory*. New York: Peter Lang, 1995.

Reeves, Jesse S. *American Diplomacy under Tyler and Polk*. Baltimore: Johns Hopkins University Press, 1907; reprint ed., Gloucester, MA: Peter Smith, 1967.

Remini, Robert. *Henry Clay: Statesman for the Union*. New York: W. W. Norton, 1991.

———. *Martin Van Buren and the Making of the Democratic Party*. New York: W. W. Norton, 1970.

Rich, E. E. *History of the Hudson's Bay Company, 1670–1870*. 2 vols. New York: Macmillan, 1960–61.

Scofield, John. *Hail, Columbia!: Robert Gray, John Kendrick, and the Pacific Fur Trade*. Portland: Oregon Historical Society Press, 1993.

Sellers, Charles G. *James K. Polk: Continentalist, 1843–1846*. Princeton, NJ: Princeton University Press, 1966.

Shenton, James P. *Robert John Walker: A Politician from Jackson to Lincoln.* New York: Columbia University Press, 1961.

Smith, Justin H. *The War with Mexico.* 2 vols. New York: Macmillan, 1919.

Soulsby, Hugh G. *The Right of Search and the Slave Trade in Anglo-American Relations, 1814–1862.* Baltimore: Johns Hopkins University Press, 1933.

Spenser, Ivor D. *The Victor and the Spoils: A Life of William L. Marcy.* Providence, RI: Brown University Press, 1959.

Stephanson, Anders. *Manifest Destiny: American Expansionism and the Empire of Right.* New York: Hill and Wang, 1995.

Stevens, Kenneth R. *Border Diplomacy: The Caroline and McLeod Affairs in Anglo-American-Canadian Relations, 1837–1842.* Tuscaloosa: University of Alabama Press, 1989.

Stuart, Reginald C. *United States Expansionism and British North America, 1775–1871.* Chapel Hill: University of North Carolina Press, 1988.

Thistlethwaite, Frank. *America and the Atlantic Community: Anglo-American Aspects, 1790–1850.* New York: Harper and Row, 1963.

Van Deusen, Glyndon G. *The Jacksonian Era, 1828–1848.* New York: Harper and Row, 1959.

———. *William Henry Seward.* New York: Oxford University Press, 1967.

Walters, Raymond, Jr. *Albert Gallatin: Jeffersonian Financier and Diplomat.* New York: Macmillan, 1957.

Wayland, Francis P. *Andrew Stevenson: Democrat and Diplomat, 1785–1857.* Philadelphia: University of Pennsylvania Press, 1949.

Weinberg, Albert K. *Manifest Destiny: A Study of Nationalist Expansionism in American History.* Baltimore: Johns Hopkins University Press, 1935.

White, Leonard D. *The Jacksonians: A Study in Administrative History, 1829–1861.* New York: Macmillan, 1954.

Wilson, Major L. *The Presidency of Martin Van Buren.* Lawrence: University Press of Kansas, 1984.

Wiltse, Charles M. *John C. Calhoun.* 3 vols. Indianapolis: Bobbs-Merrill Co., 1944–1951.

Winther, Oscar Osburn. *The Great Northwest: A History.* 2d ed. New York: Alfred A. Knopf, 1947; reprint, 1966.

Wirth, Fremont P. *The Discovery and Exploitation of the Minnesota Iron Lands.* Cedar Rapids, IA: Torch Press, 1937.

Woodford, Frank B. *Lewis Cass: The Last Jeffersonian.* New Brunswick, NJ: Rutgers University Press, 1950.

Woodham-Smith, Blanche Cecil. *The Great Hunger: Ireland, 1845–49.* New York: Harper and Row, 1962.

Wright, Marcus T. *General Scott.* New York: D. Appleton, 1894.

Articles and Essays

Adams, Ephraim D. "Lord Ashburton and the Treaty of Washington," *American Historical Review* 17 (July 1912): 764–82.

―――. "English Interest in the Annexation of California," *American Historical Review* 14 (1909): 744–63.

Baldwin, J. R. "The Ashburton-Webster Boundary Settlement," *Canadian Historical Association, Report, 1938* (Toronto, 1938).

Blue, George V. "France and the Oregon Question," *Oregon Historical Quarterly* 34 (1933): 39–50, 144–63.

Blue, Verne. "The Oregon Question, 1818–1828: A Study of Dr. John Floyd's Efforts in Congress to Secure the Oregon Country," *Oregon Historical Quarterly* 23 (September 1922): 193–219.

Bonham, Milledge L., Jr. "Alexander McLeod: Bone of Contention," *New York History* 18 (April 1937): 189–217.

Booth, Alan R. "The United States African Squadron, 1843–1861," in Jeffrey Butler, ed., *Boston University Papers in African History* (Boston: African Studies Center of Boston University, 1964), 77–117.

Brooke, George M., Jr. "The Vest Pocket War of Commodore Jones," *Pacific Historical Review* 31 (1962): 217–33.

Corey, Albert B. "Public Opinion and the McLeod Case," *Canadian Historical Association, Report, 1936* (Toronto, 1936), 53–64.

Cramer, Richard S. "British Magazines and the Oregon Question," *Pacific Historical Review* 32 (May 1963): 369–82.

Creighton, D. G. "The Economic Background of the Rebellions of Eighteen Thirty-Seven," *Canadian Journal of Economics and Political Science* 3 (August 1937): 322–34.

Cunningham, A. B. "Peel, Aberdeen and the Entente Cordiale," *Bulletin of the Institute of Historical Research* 30 (November 1957): 189–206.

Current, Richard N. "Webster's Propaganda and the Ashburton Treaty," *Mississippi Valley Historical Review* 31 (October 1947): 187–200.

Eaton, Clement. "The Freedom of the Press in the Upper South," *Mississippi Valley Historical Review* 18 (March 1932): 479–99.

Elliott, T. C. "An Event of One Hundred Years Ago," *Oregon Historical Quarterly* 19 (September 1918): 181–87.

―――. "The Origin of the Name Oregon," *Oregon Historical Quarterly* 22 (June 1921): 91–116.

―――. "The Surrender at Astoria in 1818," *Oregon Historical Quarterly* 19 (December 1918): 271–82.

Fish, Andrew. "The Last Phase of the Oregon Boundary Question: The Struggle for San Juan Island," *Oregon Historical Quarterly* 22 (September 1921): 161–90.

Galbraith, John S. "France as a Factor in the Oregon Negotiations," *Pacific Northwest Quarterly* 44 (April 1953): 69–73.

Gough, Barry M. "HMS *America* on the North Pacific Coast," *Oregon Historical Quarterly* 70 (December 1969): 293–311.

————. "HMS *Modeste* on the Pacific Coast, 1843–1847: Log and Letters," *Oregon Historical Quarterly* 61 (December 1960): 408–36.

Hand, Augustus N. "Local Incidents of the Papineau Rebellion," *New York History* 15 (October 1934): 376–87.

Holman, Frederick. Presidential Address Delivered to the Oregon Historical Society Annual Meeting at Portland, Oregon, December 19, 1908, *Oregon Historical Quarterly* 10 (June 1909): 1–15.

Horsman, Reginald. "American Indian Policy and the Origin of Manifest Destiny," *University of Birmingham Historical Journal* 11 (1968): 128–40.

————. "Scientific Racism and the American Indian in the Midnineteenth Century," *American Quarterly* 27 (May 1975): 152–68.

Jameson, J. Franklin, ed. "Correspondence of John C. Calhoun," in *Annual Report of the American Historical Association for the Year 1899*, 2 vols. (Washington, DC, 1900), 1081–83.

Jervey, Edward D., and Huber, Edward C. "The *Creole* Affair" (unpublished essay).

Johnson, C. T. "Daniel Webster, Lord Ashburton, and Old Oregon," *Washington Historical Quarterly* 1 (1906–07): 208–16.

————. "Daniel Webster and Old Oregon," *Washington Historical Quarterly* 2 (1907–08): 6–11.

Jones, Howard. "Anglophobia and the Aroostook War," *New England Quarterly* 48 (December 1975): 519–39.

————. "The Attempt to Impeach Daniel Webster," *Capitol Studies* 3 (Fall 1975): 31–44.

————. "The *Caroline* Affair," *The Historian* 38 (May 1976): 485–502.

————. "Daniel Webster: The Diplomatist," in Kenneth E. Shewmaker, ed., *Daniel Webster: "The Completest Man"* (Hanover, NH: University Press of New England, 1990).

————. "The Peculiar Institution and National Honor: The Case of the *Creole* Slave Revolt," *Civil War History* 21 (March 1975): 28–50.

Jones, Wilbur D. "The Influence of Slavery on the Webster-Ashburton Negotiations," *Journal of Southern History* 22 (February 1956): 48–58.

————. "Lord Ashburton and the Maine Boundary Negotiations," *Mississippi Valley Historical Review* 40 (December 1953): 477–90.

Judson, Katharine. "The British Side of the Restoration of Astoria," *Oregon Historical Quarterly* 20 (September 1919): 243–60, 305–30.

Kingston, C. S. "The Oregon Convention of 1843," *Washington Historical Quarterly* 22 (July 1931): 163–71.

LeDuc, Thomas. "The Maine Frontier and the Northeastern Boundary Controversy," *American Historical Review* 53 (October 1947): 30–41.

————. "The Webster-Ashburton Treaty and the Minnesota Iron Ranges," *Journal of American History* 51 (December 1964): 476–81.

Lingelbach, Anna Lane. "Huskisson and the Board of Trade," *American Historical Review* 43 (July 1938): 759–74.

Longley, R. S. "Emigration and the Crisis of 1837 in Upper Canada, 1837–1842," *Canadian Historical Review* 17 (March 1936): 29–40.

Lowenthal, David. "The Maine Press and the Aroostook War," *Canadian Historical Review* 32 (December 1951): 315–36.

Mackay, R. A. "The Political Ideals of William Lyon Mackenzie," *Canadian Journal of Economics and Political Science* 3 (February 1937): 1–22.

Manning, William R. "The Nootka Sound Controversy," *Annual Report of the American Historical Association for the Year 1904* (Washington, DC, 1905): 279–478.

Martin, Lawrence, and Bemis, Samuel F. "Franklin's Red-Line Map Was a Mitchell," *New England Quarterly* 10 (March 1937): 105–11.

McCabe, James O. "Arbitration and the Oregon Question," *Canadian Historical Review* 41 (December 1960): 308–27.

Merk, Frederick. "The Oregon Question in the Webster-Ashburton Negotiations," *Mississippi Valley Historical Review* 43 (December 1956): 379–404.

———. "The Snake Country Expedition, 1824–1825: An Episode of Fur Trade and Empire," *Mississippi Valley Historical Review* 21 (June 1934): 49–62.

Miles, Edwin A. "Fifty-four Forty or Fight: An American Political Legend," *Mississippi Valley Historical Review* 44 (September 1957): 291–309.

Mills, Dudley A. "British Diplomacy and Canada. The Ashburton Treaty," *United Empire: The Royal Colonial Institute Journal, New Series* 2 (October 1911): 683–712.

New, Chester W. "The Rebellion of 1837 in Its Larger Setting," *Canadian Historical Association, Report, 1937,* 5–17.

Pike, C. J. "Petitions of Oregon Settlers, 1838–1848," *Oregon Historical Quarterly* 35 (September 1933): 216–35.

Rawley, James A. "Captain Nathaniel Gordon, the Only American Executed for Violating the Slave Trade Laws," paper delivered before the Tenth Naval History Symposium, U.S. Naval Academy, Annapolis, Maryland (September 1991).

Schafer, Joseph. "The British Attitude Toward the Oregon Question, 1815–1846," *American Historical Review* 16 (July 1911): 273–99.

Shewmaker, Kenneth E. "The 'War of Words': The Cass-Webster Debate of 1842–43," *Diplomatic History* 5 (Spring 1981): 151–63.

Shortridge, Wilson P. "The Canadian-American Frontier during the Rebellion of 1837–1838," *Canadian Historical Review* 7 (March 1926): 13–26.

Stacey, C. P. "The Myth of the Unguarded Frontier, 1815–1871," *American Historical Review* 56 (October 1959): 1–18.

Tiffany, Orrin E. "The Relations of the United States to the Canadian Rebellion of 1837–38," *Buffalo Historical Society Publications* 8 (1905): 1–147.

Tyler, Lyon Gardiner. "The Ashburton Treaty, 1842," *Tyler's Quarterly Historical and Genealogical Magazine* 3, no. 4 (April 1922): 255–56.

Van Alstyne, Richard W. "The British Right of Search and the African Slave Trade," *Journal of Modern History* 2 (March 1930): 37–47.

————. "Empire in Midpassage, 1845–1867," in William Appleman Williams, ed., *From Colony to Empire: Essays in the History of American Foreign Relations* (New York: John Wiley and Sons, 1972).

Watt, Alastair. "The Case of Alexander McLeod," *Canadian Historical Review* 12 (June 1931): 145–67.

Winston, James E., and Colomb, R. W. "How the Louisiana Purchase Was Financed," *Louisiana Historical Quarterly* 12 (April 1929): 189–237.

Newspapers and Magazines

Advertiser (Boston)
Advertiser (New Orleans)
Advertiser (Portland)
Age (Augusta)
Albion (New York)
American (Chicago)
American (New York)
Argus (Albany)
Arkansas Times and Advocate (Little Rock)
Blackwood's Edinburgh Magazine (London)
Boston Daily Advertiser
Commercial Advertiser (New York)
Commercial Bulletin (New Orleans)
Compiler (Richmond)
Constitutional Democrat (Detroit)
Courier (Boston)
Courier (Charleston)
Courier (Montreal)
Courier (Northampton, MA)
Democratic Free Press (Detroit)
Democratic Review
Eastern Argus (Portland)
Edinburgh Review (London)
Enquirer (Richmond)
Evening Star (London)
Examiner (London)
Foreign Quarterly Review
Gazette (New York)
The Gazette (St. Louis)
Gleaner (Miramichi, New Brunswick)
Globe (Washington, DC)

Herald (New York)
Herald (St. John)
Illinois State Register (Springfield)
Journal (Augusta)
Journal (Portsmouth)
Journal of Commerce (New York)
Liberator (Boston)
Madisonian [Daily] (Washington, DC)
Mail (Liverpool)
Mercury (Charleston)
Missouri Reporter
Morning Chronicle (London)
Morning Herald (London)
Morning News (New York)
Morning Post (London)
National Intelligencer (Washington, DC)
Niles' [National] Register
North American Review
Novascotian (Halifax)
Observer (St. John)
Patriot (Boston)
Picayune (New Orleans)
Punch (London)
Quarterly Review
Register & Journal (Mobile)
Republican (Rochester)
Republican Banner (Nashville)
Royal Gazette (New Brunswick)
Sentinel (Fredericton)
Southron (Jackson)
Spectator (Oregon)
Spy (Worcester, MA)
Star Extra (Buffalo)
Sun (Baltimore)
Sun (New York)
Sun (Pittsfield, MA)
Telegraph (Alton, IL)
Times (London)
Union (Nashville)
United States Journal
Whig (Bangor)

Index